Mastering
Advanced Scrum

*Advanced Scrum Techniques for Scrum Teams,
Roles, Artifacts, Events, Metrics, Working
Agreements, Advanced Engineering
Practices, and Technical Agility*

Rituraj Patil

www.bpbonline.com

FIRST EDITION 2022

Copyright © BPB Publications, India

ISBN: 978-93-91030-308

LIMITS OF LIABILITY AND DISCLAIMER OF WARRANTY

To View Complete
BPB Publications Catalogue
Scan the QR Code:

Dedicated to

Chhatrapati Shivaji Maharaj,
all my Gurus, Teachers, Mentors,
and to
all those who do the most for others…

About the Author

Rituraj Patil is an experienced Scrum Master/Agile Coach, who for the past 10+ years has been working with various multinational organizations to develop and deliver high-quality working software products, services, and solution offerings. He is a technology, Lean-Agile (Leadership, Culture, and Management) enthusiast, servant leader, and avid learner. In his professional career, he has played many roles while serving various organizations. He holds a Master of Management Studies Degree in Systems Specialization from the University of Mumbai, Maharashtra, India. He also holds a Master of Technology Degree in Software Development and Management from Vellore Institute of Technology, Tamilnadu, India, and a Bachelor of Engineering Degree in Information Technology from Kolhapur Institute of Technology's College of Engineering (Autonomous), Maharashtra, India. He has successfully completed several internationally recognized training and certifications. He is acting as a conference speaker at various industry conferences and meetups and as a guest lecturer at various top-tier Indian educational institutes, including IIMs, Symbiosis, IITs, VIT Vellore, and many more. He has received many awards, recognitions, and appreciations from the organizations he has served so far.

He comes up with extensive experience in managing multiple globally distributed as well as collocated Agile software product development teams developing applications using various Agile frameworks, tools, and technologies. He is also acting as an industry expert for the Board of Studies of the Department of Computer Science Engineering at Sanjay Ghodawat University, Maharashtra, India, and at Kolhapur Institute of Technology's College of Engineering (Autonomous), Maharashtra, India.

Outside work, he spends his spare time for various Corporate Social Responsibility (CSR) specific volunteering activities. He is also an active member of various global communities contributing for the development of various technology, leadership, education, environmental sustainability, and CSR-specific initiatives. He likes to play Tabla (an Indian classical musical instrument), sings with Karaoke, plays soccer, and volunteers his spare time to help and guide budding IT professionals.

About the Reviewer

Amit Mahulikar is an Agile Practitioner and has been working on Agile transformations since 2012. He has helped several banks, financial institutions and retail houses adapt agility and various frameworks such as Scrum, XP and Scaled Agile (SAFe). Playing the role of Agile Change Agent, he has worked closely with client organizations based out of India. Being an MBA Graduate, he is also a SAFe Program Consultant (SPC 5.0) and holds the position of a Senior Manager at an MNC based out of Pune.

Acknowledgement

There are a few people I want to thank for the continued and ongoing support they have always given me while I was writing this book. First and foremost, I would like to thank my beloved mother - Aai and my better half - Shwetambari for putting up with me, while I was super busy and spending many weekends and evenings on this book. I could have never completed it without their support, motivation, and understanding.

This book wouldn't have happened if I hadn't had the support and guidance from some of the key Agile and Scrum practitioners belonging to the agile software product development global community. My gratitude goes to all those practitioners, change agents, servant leaders, my teachers, guides, mentors, leaders, colleagues, friends, relatives, supporters, and all the organizations I have worked with and served so far, for all the wonderful opportunities, help, support, guidance, encouragement, and motivation they have always given to me.

I would like to give a special thanks to Amit Mahulikar and Priyanka Deshpande, for reviewing this book and providing the necessary inputs to improve it. Finally, I would like to thank BPB Publications for giving me this amazing opportunity to write my first ever book with them.

Scrum On!

Preface

Agile Software Product Development and Delivery is an approach which is always expected to be performed under co-operative, collaborative, and complex adaptive systems-based environments. It promises to deliver high-quality Software Products within a variable scope, effective cost, and iteratively time boxed agile way of working to meet the ever-changing requirements of businesses, customers, and stakeholders. Scrum is one the most popular and powerful agile frameworks for the purpose of Agile Software Product Development and Delivery. It is a structured collection of valuable concepts, methods, and practices around which the processes need to be constructed and to be modified to increase the software development teams' responsiveness to change. It also encourages teams to perform iterative, incremental, early, and often Agile Software Product Development and Delivery.

Scrum Guide (crafted by Ken Schwaber and Jeff Sutherland, the originators of Scrum) contains the definition of Scrum Framework. It has an overview of Scrum Roles, Artifacts, Events, and Rules, but there are no sufficient details given in it to utilize the advantages of a fully functional Scrum based Agile Way of Working. The Scrum Practitioners and the Scrum Teams must make use of some additional Add-ons/Techniques which are not getting covered under the Scrum Guide.

These Add-ons are mostly related to the overall Structuring, Collaboration, and Communication within the Scrum Teams, Scrum Roles and Working Agreement within the Scrum Teams, Effective and Efficient Product Backlog Management, Relative Estimation, Scrum Events, Advanced Engineering Practices and Technical Agility, Scrum Metrics, Scaling Scrum, and few other additional aspects of a Scrum Team's Agile Way of Working.

This book tries to emphasize on such additional Add-ons/Techniques which need to be effectively utilized by the Scrum Practitioners and the Scrum Teams to establish and improve a fully functional Scrum based Agile Way of Working. This book not only helps them to encourage their responsibility, accountability, and ownership, but also guides them to become more self-managing, self-organizing, and high-performing.

The key take-aways from this book are to share an overall understanding of Agile Software Development, Delivery, and Way of Working of the software development teams, to share an overall understanding of Scrum Framework (created by Ken Schwaber and Jeff Sutherland) and its association with the Agile Values and Principles (given at **https://agilemanifesto.org/**), to spread the knowledge about Advanced Scrum Add-ons/Techniques within the Scrum Practitioners (using which they and their Scrum Teams can feel empowered and can become more high-performing, self-managing, self-organizing), and to trigger a thought process for the Scrum Practitioners using which they can evaluate on applicable and appropriate Advanced Scrum Add-ons/Techniques, suitable to their Scrum Teams.

Readers of this book will feel more competent to implement a fully functional Scrum Framework based Agile Way of Working within their Scrum Teams. This book will help them to increase the overall productivity and effectiveness of their Scrum Teams leveraging most of the benefits of the Advanced Scrum Add-ons/ Techniques to deliver the potential shippable increments of their high-quality software products.

Over the 15 chapters in this book, you will learn the following:

Chapter 1 introduces Fundamentals of Agile Software Development, Delivery, and Way of Working for the software product development teams.

Chapter 2 provides an overall comparative understanding of agile frameworks such as Scrum, Kanban, Scrumban, Extreme Programming (XP), Dynamic Systems Development Method (DSDM), Feature-Driven Development (FDD), and Crystal and so on.

Chapter 3 gives an overview of Scrum Framework, which is the most popular and most commonly, widely used agile framework by the entire global software development community.

Chapter 4 is one of the key chapters which discusses, in depth, about many improper actions, reactions, behaviors, patterns, and entities in place within the Scrum Teams, because of which their Scrum based agile way of working starts to malfunction.

Chapter 5 introduces the Advanced Scrum Add-ons/Techniques, which are the ultimate solutions to establish and improve Scrum based Agile Way of Working within the Scrum Teams.

Chapter 6 describes the Advanced Scrum Add-ons/Techniques for Scrum Teams, who are struggling with the issues related to their structuring and alignment.

Chapter 7 describes the Advanced Scrum Add-ons/Techniques for the 3 Scrum Roles - Product Owner, Scrum Master, and Developers.

Chapter 8 describes the Advanced Scrum Add-ons/Techniques to help the Scrum Teams to perform effective and efficient Product Backlog Management.

Chapter 9 describes the Advanced Scrum Add-ons/Techniques to help the Scrum Teams to perform effective and efficient Relative Estimation of their work items.

Chapter 10 describes the Advanced Scrum Add-ons/Techniques to help the Scrum Teams to utilize their Scrum Events more effectively and efficiently.

Chapter 11 describes the Advanced Scrum Add-ons/Techniques to help the Scrum Teams with a proper utilization of the Advanced Engineering Practices to improve their Technical Agility.

Chapter 12 describes the Advanced Scrum Add-ons/Techniques to help the Scrum Teams to establish and use some effective and efficient Scrum Metrics.

Chapter 13 describes the Advanced Scrum Add-ons/Techniques to help the Scrum Teams to scale up Scrum.

Chapter 14 describes the additional Advanced Scrum Add-ons/Techniques to help the Scrum Teams to enhance and improve their Scrum based Agile Way of Working.

Chapter 15 gives a quick reflection of the latest updated version of Scrum Guide i.e., Scrum Guide 2020.

Downloading the coloured images:

Please follow the link to download the
Coloured Images of the book:

https://rebrand.ly/26aa7f

Errata

We take immense pride in our work at BPB Publications and follow best practices to ensure the accuracy of our content to provide with an indulging reading experience to our subscribers. Our readers are our mirrors, and we use their inputs to reflect and improve upon human errors, if any, that may have occurred during the publishing processes involved. To let us maintain the quality and help us reach out to any readers who might be having difficulties due to any unforeseen errors, please write to us at :

errata@bpbonline.com

Your support, suggestions and feedbacks are highly appreciated by the BPB Publications' Family.

BPB is searching for authors like you

If you're interested in becoming an author for BPB, please visit **www.bpbonline.com** and apply today. We have worked with thousands of developers and tech professionals, just like you, to help them share their insight with the global tech community. You can make a general application, apply for a specific hot topic that we are recruiting an author for, or submit your own idea.

The code bundle for the book is also hosted on GitHub at **https://github.com/bpbpublications/Mastering-Advanced-Scrum**. In case there's an update to the code, it will be updated on the existing GitHub repository.

We also have other code bundles from our rich catalog of books and videos available at **https://github.com/bpbpublications**. Check them out!

PIRACY

If you come across any illegal copies of our works in any form on the internet, we would be grateful if you would provide us with the location address or website name. Please contact us at **business@bpbonline.com** with a link to the material.

If you are interested in becoming an author

If there is a topic that you have expertise in, and you are interested in either writing or contributing to a book, please visit **www.bpbonline.com**.

REVIEWS

Please leave a review. Once you have read and used this book, why not leave a review on the site that you purchased it from? Potential readers can then see and use your unbiased opinion to make purchase decisions, we at BPB can understand what you think about our products, and our authors can see your feedback on their book. Thank you!

For more information about BPB, please visit **www.bpbonline.com**.

Table of Contents

CHAPTER 1

Fundamentals of Agile Software Development, Delivery, and Way of Working

Introduction

In this chapter, readers will get to know about the fundamentals of agile software development, delivery, and way of working. They will also get an overall understanding of how the software development teams can get familiar with agile values and principles from the *Manifesto for Agile Software Development*, using which they can establish and enhance their Agile Way of Working.

Objective

After studying this chapter, you should be able to:

- Understand the fundamentals of agile software development, delivery, and way of working for the software development teams.

- Understand values and principles from *Manifesto for Agile Software Development*.

- Understand the need of digital and agile transformations in organizations.

- Understand latest interesting trends of global agile adoption and transformation.

- Understand the concept of organizational agility, agile way of working, and stages of group development.

Alex 'The Program Manager' (in a meeting, having discussions with Paul 'The Newbie Scrum Master' and rest of the Scrum Masters):

"Hello All! I would like to welcome you all in today's Scrum of Scrums. This is for the first time we are having this Scrum of Scrums, where we have all the Scrum Masters representing their Scrum Teams under our Program.

To be honest, instead of calling it as a meeting, I would like to call it as a regular weekly conversation to share, discuss, and brainstorm on how the yesterday's weather was, what kind of challenges we are facing, how to overcome those challenges, and how we are progressing as a 'One Program Team'.

I hope you all must be excited to start this new journey to scale up our Agile Way of Working at Program Level. This is just a beginning and we surely have a way to go!"

Paul 'The Newbie Scrum Master' (thinking deep inside and talking with himself):

"Scrum of Scrums? Weekly conversations? Yesterday's weather? One Program Team? Scaling up Agile Way of Working? What are these jargons? Am I the only one here, who is feeling clueless?"

Alex (meanwhile continuing):

"I strongly believe that 'Agile is not an Anarchy!'. We need to have some mechanism in place to make sure that we are giving our best while 'Being Agile and not just Doing Agile'. We need to make sure that, we are failing fast and failing safe to learn, unlearn, and re-learn, while embracing the change and delivering the expected value to our customers, constantly.

Let's get into an agreement that, our Scrum Teams need to be self-organizing, self-managing, cross-functional, and high-performing. Let's reflect on how to become more efficient and effective, so that we all can have a shared understanding and ownership for the purpose of continuous learning and continuous improvement.

Let's make our customers and stakeholders happy! We are here to collaborate and co-operate. So, let's focus on various aspects of improving our overall Agile Way of Working. Let's have the outcome-oriented action items in place for the improvements we would like to see within us."

Paul (again thinking deep inside and talking to himself):

"Oh my god! Sorry, but I am still not getting you Alex!

Agile is not an Anarchy? Being Agile and not just Doing Agile? Failing fast? Failing safe? Learn, unlearn, and re-learn? Self-organizing, self-managing, cross-functional, and high-performing Scrum Teams? Shared understanding and ownership for the purpose of continuous learning and continuous improvement? Outcome-oriented action items?

Why do we even need all of this? I think, I should speak out now! Should I?"

Being someone (who is an agile enthusiast or an Agile Coach or a Scrum Practitioner or a Scrum Master or a Product Owner or a Product/Project/Program/Release/Delivery Manager or simply a Software Development Team Member or anyone else, who is having the basic know-how of the Scrum Framework) as a part of a software development team and making use of the Scrum Framework might have been a part of such conversations.

Such kinds of conversations may vary in terms of the roles and responsibilities of conversation participants and in terms of the overall context and content of discussions happening. They might also vary in terms of organizational levels at which they are happening. They might be happening at the team level or might be few levels up.

> *"Words of the jargon sound as if they said something higher than what they mean."*
> *- Theodor Adorno*

Alex 'The Program Manager' is throwing some jargons and trying to explain the fellow Scrum Masters about 'Being Agile and not just Doing Agile'. However, for Paul 'The Newbie Scrum Master' (or for anyone else who is a part of a software development team and who is also a newbie for Agile and Scrum Framework), it is resulting into a big question mark. It is hence significantly important for all the team members of a software development team to understand the core fundamentals of Agile Software Development, Delivery, and Way of Working first, to further understand what Alex is saying.

> *"Your beliefs become your thoughts, Your thoughts become your words,*
> *Your words become your actions, Your actions become your habits,*
> *Your habits become your values, Your values become your destiny."*
> *- Mahatma Gandhi*

Agile software development, delivery, and way of working is an extraordinary combination of approaches considering a collection of agile frameworks and their associated procedures, which needs to be established using the core values and principles stated in the *Manifesto for Agile Software Development*. These core values and principles are acting as an ultimate guideline for the complete Agile Way of Working of software development teams, considering all the procedures being done by them to perform the development and delivery of the working software. These values and principles help software development teams to discover the applicable and appropriate ways to be analysed, evaluated, and applied based upon their own context and fit.

> *"Obey the principles without being bound by them."*
> *- Bruce Lee*

Manifesto for Agile Software Development (present at **https://agilemanifesto.org/**) throws a light on the 4 basic values and 12 supporting principles. This manifesto helps the agile software development, delivery, and way of working approach, where the highest importance is always given to delivering a high-quality working software.

Back in the past, the following 17 extra-ordinary people in the world of software development had met to discuss on the future of software development. They highlighted various pain points related to various software development practices being followed by them at that point of time. There were discussions and disagreements:

Kent Beck	James Grenning	Robert C. Martin
Mike Beedle	Jim Highsmith	Steve Mellor
Arie van Bennekum	Andrew Hunt	Ken Schwaber
Alistair Cockburn	Ron Jeffries	Jeff Sutherland
Ward Cunningham	Jon Kern	Dave Thomas
Martin Fowler	Brian Marick	

One common problem which was at the crux of their discussions was related to the organizations and associated people, who were giving too much of importance to standardized software development processes, with an upper hand always given to planning and documenting the Software Development Life Cycle (SDLC). Because of this, the ultimate provisioning of value and satisfaction for businesses and customers of organizations was getting treated with the lowest/least priority. Sometimes, this particular aspect was also getting ignored completely.

To address this problem, these 17 folks had come up with a *Manifesto for Agile Software Development*. It is a reference guideline introducing a brand-new approach of Agile Way of Working for software development and delivery. This manifesto entirely changed the world of software development having an anticipation to speed up the process of development and delivery of high-quality working software. They uncovered the better ways of developing the software with an expectation of doing it, helping others to do it, and by focusing on four values and 12 principles mentioned by them in the same manifesto. The following four values are simple to understand.

- Individuals and interactions to be more valued over processes and tools
- Working software to be more valued over comprehensive documentation
- Customer collaboration to be more valued over contract negotiation
- Responding to change to be more valued over following a plan

These four values from *Manifesto for Agile Software Development* always need to be followed by the software development teams having an anticipation from themselves that, the items mentioned on the left always need to be more valued by them over the items mentioned on the right.

The value *'Individuals and interactions over processes and tools'* gives more emphasis on valuing the people who are developing and delivering high-quality working software, rather than valuing the processes or tools which are getting used to develop and deliver the high-quality working software product.

"All human interactions are opportunities either to learn or to teach."
- Stephen Covey

This brings us to the attention about a reality that, even though proper processes and tools are essential to develop a software, a sensible group of software developers is a must have to perform software development and delivery to begin with. Once this group is in place, it acts as a software development team that needs to perform software development and delivery specific activities to establish and improve their suitable Agile Way of Working, as per their needs and desires.

"Technology is nothing. What's important is that you have a faith in people that,
they're basically good and smart, and if you give them tools,
they'll do wonderful things with them."
- Steve Jobs

It is the team, who needs to respond to the needs and requirements of business and customers/end-users to perform the activities related to software development. The team needs to have interactions (both internally within the team itself and externally with the stakeholders) to make sure that they are on the right track, by avoiding and overcoming deviations, if any. If this thought process is executed by giving more importance to the processes and tools, the team becomes less approachable to the ever-changing requirements of business and customers. This causes a big risk of missing customer needs. This also has an adverse impact on the software product outcomes resulting into rework and causing wastage of efforts, time, and cost.

No one can disagree with this fact that the processes and tools are genuinely required while implementing a good quality software. They act as the enablers and one cannot skip their usage path. However, those processes and tools cannot work on their own. People need to make them work. Human beings are social animals and hence they can work collaboratively to do the needful with established processes and available tools. They are more effective for people, when people are working together as a One TEAM following a 'T'ogether 'E'veryone 'A'chives 'M'ore philosophy.

The value *Working software over comprehensive documentation* states about an expectation from the software development teams that, they should create documentation that provides some value. Software development teams should always give more value to working software over comprehensive documentation. Any comprehensive documentation can potentially hamper the team's overall progress by consuming their valuable time and effort, which can be ideally utilized somewhere else bringing in more value for the them.

If the team gets occupied for a long time to produce documentation of requirements, analysis, design, and test cases, there is a possibility that documentation will become obsolete by the time of development. Working software needs to be incorporated with the frequently changing customer needs. Software development team members spending their precious time on comprehensive documentation will introduce a delay in their overall progress, because of which they will fail to adapt and cater ever-changing requirements of their customers.

"We don't need an accurate document. We need a shared understanding."
- Jeff Patton

There is another possibility of a problem getting occurred with the teams is that, they are analysing, designing, and documenting components of the software, which may not be needed at all. This acts as a simple wastage of effort, money, and time, while documenting entities that might not be getting used at all. Teams sometime spend a significant amount of time, while generating documentation before the software is constructed, hence there is a delay while bringing in more value to the customers.

Team needs to follow a philosophy that they are creating a documentation that provides a value without obstructing their progress and avoiding delays or deviations. One way to look at it is, to come up with a variety of tests to test the software. These test cases can be used as documentation, which can be held responsible as a single source of truth to cross-verify the expected behavior of the software.

This is to make sure that whether the software is working, as per the customer/ end-user expectations or not. Functional tests, non-functional tests, manual tests, automated tests to perform unit testing, integration testing, system integration testing, and acceptance testing need to be in place to improve the overall quality of software and to make sure that the software is stable and there are less defects.

"One test is worth a thousand expert opinions."
- Bill Nye

Team gets a helping hand utilizing these different types of tests, which allows them to ensure that they are developing a working software, which is getting integrated, validated, verified, and deployed further, so that its end-users can make use of it. At the same time, they also need to make sure that, they are producing only the most valuable documentation for the software under development. Their focus should be always on constructing the working software and it should be the primary parameter to measure their progress. Customers are more worried about the best way to solve their problems. It is the responsibility of software development team to assist them, by frequently showcasing the working software to them.

The value of '*Customer collaboration over contract negotiation*' highlights an important aspect of the relationship between the software development team developing a software and their customers who are going to make use of it. Customers have their needs that need to be addressed by the working software.

The software development team needs to get into a frequent collaboration with their customers to get to know about their genuine needs and problems. It can be also done as a joint effort between the software development team and the applicable businesspeople, where they can interact, analyse, explore, and evaluate on customer requirements with collaboration. In this case, the contract signed by an organization and its customers should not even matter.

> *"If everyone is moving forward together, then success takes care of itself."*
> *- Henry Ford*

As far as the stakeholders and customers who have signed the contract (to make sure that the customers are getting what they want and need) are happy and satisfied with the overall progress of software development specific activities and they are also able to see the actual progress in terms of the working software, this kind of collaboration will be able to perform its own magic automatically.

> *"No one can whistle a symphony. It takes a whole orchestra to play it."*
> *- H.E. Luccock*

Software development teams can still deliver the software as per the original expectations of customers. The moment the customers change their thoughts, needs, and wants (which also has an impact on the prioritization of functionalities getting developed and delivered), it is always good for the teams to be adaptable. They should embrace such type of changes to strive to address ever-changing customer needs; instead of getting themselves stuck with the initially defined expectations.

The value *Responding to change over following a plan* encourages incorporating change and not just following a fixed plan. All kinds of customer-specific changes have associated costs, efforts, and time, and many more, factors, which are unavoidable. Following certain standardized software development activities along with having a thorough understanding of ever-changing customer requirements, lets the software development teams to have the cost of change to be reduced. Teams need to be self-sufficient to measure the impact of changes and react when changes occur.

> *"Adopt the attitude that continuous planning is a good thing. In every iteration, expect your plans to change (albeit in small ways if your planning is effective). Don't fall into the trap of thinking that the plan is infallible."*
> *- Ian Spence and Kurt Bittner*

Trust and transparency are the two factors helping the teams, using which they can communicate their progress regardless of any change occurring and causing deviations. This is because the change is constant and inevitable. By having the proper expectations set along with the presence of openness and trust in between teams and stakeholders, the teams need to inform their stakeholders about their honest opinions to make sure that the decision making always stays as a consensus-based activity.

The *Manifesto for Agile Software Development* also mentions about 12 principles (to be followed by the software development teams), which are advocating the four values mentioned before. The following 12 principles are simple to understand.

- Our highest priority is to satisfy the customer through early and continuous delivery of valuable software.
- Welcome changing requirements, even late in development. Agile processes harness change for the customer's competitive advantage.
- Deliver working software frequently, from a couple of weeks to a couple of months, with a preference for the shorter timescale.
- Businesspeople and developers must work together daily throughout the project.
- Build projects around motivated individuals. Give them the environment and support they need and trust them to get the job done.
- The most efficient and effective method of conveying information to and within a development team is face-to-face conversation.
- Working software is the primary measure of progress.
- Agile processes promote sustainable development. The sponsors, developers, and users should be able to maintain a constant pace indefinitely.
- Continuous attention to technical excellence and good design enhances agility.
- Simplicity -- the art of maximizing the amount of work not done -- is essential.
- The best architectures, requirements, and designs emerge from self-organizing teams.
- At regular intervals, the team reflects on how to become more effective, then tunes and adjusts its behavior accordingly.

The principle '*Our highest priority is to satisfy the customer through early and continuous delivery of valuable software.*' can be summarized in two words as *Customer Satisfaction*. Software development teams should always keep in mind that their highest priority is to satisfy their customers by making sure that they are always delivering high-quality working software, both early and continuously.

While delivering a valuable software, the definitive path to ensure customer happiness is to deliver the software, early and by following sooner the better approach. It is also to deliver iteratively, that is, repeatedly in a sequence of outcomes and incrementally, that is, continuously adding value for every delivery. The software development teams need to do this by continually listening to their customer requirements. By following this approach, an incremental and iterative delivery of working software gives timely value to the customers in a much rapid manner. It also helps the software development team to find out the actual needs and wants of their customers while embracing the change, if any.

The principle *'Welcome changing requirements, even late in development. Agile processes harness change for the customer's competitive advantage.'* can be summarized in two words as *Embracing Change*. Software development teams should always be ready to accept changing requirements coming from their customers/end-users. They should not resist the change, rather they should embrace the change. Change is neither avoidable nor predictable. Teams should know the importance of planning to address the customer needs but for them, it should always be secondary. They should connect themselves with the changing requirements to harness the ever-changing customer needs, even though they are late in the actual software development phase. Their ability to respond and act towards changing requirements automatically brings the competitive advantages for customers.

An open feedback channel in between software development teams and their customers can create a series of discussions between them. These discussions can further go into multiple rounds/loops while enhancing the overall quality of working software. Using this approach, the customer needs are addressed, by checking all the possibilities.

The principle *'Deliver working software frequently, from a couple of weeks to a couple of months, with a preference to the shorter timescale.'* can be summarized in two words as *Frequent Delivery*. Many software development teams take years of time to develop and deliver their software to the customer. They lack in forming a pace with appropriate quality when it comes to their way of working. It results in the absence of faster time to market and missing early benefits of frequent customer feedbacks. This has a further harmful impact on overall Return on Investment (RoI). To avoid all of this, teams should deliver working software regularly. Software delivery timescale can vary based upon various aspects involved in the process and activities of software development, but the teams should always give preference to the delivery timescale, which always needs to be a shorter one.

The principle *'Business people and developers must work together daily throughout the project.'* can be summarized in two words as *Collaborative Working*. This principle specifically talks about a relationship between the businesspeople (stakeholders, vendors, sponsors, executives, and senior management, and so on) and the developers. In most of the cases, the software development teams do not find it practical to directly work with their customers or end-users, that too on a day-to-day basis. However, businesspeople already know the customer needs based upon which the entire software development activity is supposed to be carried on.

Daily interactions in between the businesspeople and the software development team always need to prevent any kind of misinterpretations and/or communication gaps. It also needs to offer them to cross-check if there are any understanding gaps or any other important aspects are missing. Incapability of software development teams and businesspeople to collaborate with each other increases the chances of delays, deviations, and failures. They should interact and work together, as if they are mirror images of each other, especially when it comes to the shared understanding and being on the same page, that too daily and throughout the process of software development.

The principle '*Build projects around motivated individuals. Give them the environment and support they need and trust them to get the job done.*' can be summarized in two words as *Motivational Support*. This principle can be easily correlated with the first value of Agile Manifesto, which says to give more importance to individuals and interactions over processes and tools. There are many ways by which individuals (who are supposed to be an integral part of a software development team) can be highly motivated. If they believe that the software getting built by them is not worthy of their time and/or if the anticipations from their side are unattainable, it somehow impacts their morale and it gets down. It is a challenging job to keep the individuals motivated. It is hence required for a software development team to share their thoughts on how things are looking to them, if there is anything that needs an attention, and how to resolve their problems. It is crucial to create a healthy working environment, where individuals need to believe that all the means of help and support from management is always available for them. This helps them to keep their intrinsic motivation alive, which further enhances their proactive collaboration and natural satisfaction on the job.

The principle '*The most efficient and effective method of conveying information to and within a development team is face-to-face conversation.*' can be summarized in two words as *Interactive Conversation*. Agile Manifesto suggests that face-to-face interactions within the development team members play an important role to have efficient and effective information sharing. Such communication should be done on every occasion. It has many aspects like facial expressions, voice tone, body language, and so on, using which the participants in a conversation get to know about individual reactions and reflections. Restricting face-to-face interaction lowers down the amount of information exchange in teams. Teams should always encourage face-to-face communication which fosters required co-operation combined with thoughtfulness. Sometimes the teams are not co-located. For such globally distributed teams, face-to-face conversation needs to be done by using a proper support of tools and technology. Interactive face-to-face conversation using such tools improves the overall rapport building in teams.

The principle '*Working software is the primary measure of progress.*' can be summarized in two words as *Working Software*. Measuring the progress of software development teams is bit tricky. One can say that the basic measure of progress can be to measure the software development specific work-items, which are completed when the software is tested and delivered to the customer. However, working software is something that is tested by the end-user. The involvement of end-users to validate, verify, test, and accept software getting delivered to them is a must have for the software development teams.

One more way to measure the progress of the teams is to assess the amount of work that is remaining and to be completed. End-users should be able to assess the progress of a software development team by considering and assessing the value they are getting through an incremental and iterative delivery of working software. It reduces rework and efforts required to perform corrections if the working software is less error prone. Hence, measuring the progress of software development teams while having their acceptance of alignment with the working software always remains vital.

The principle *'Agile processes promote sustainable development. The sponsors, developers, and users should be able to maintain a constant pace indefinitely.'* can be summarized in two words as *Sustainable Pace*. It is the main responsibility of software development teams to develop and deliver the working software iteratively and incrementally, while maintaining a sustainable pace. Teams need to make sure that all the activities of software development are being performed incrementally and iteratively, so that the working software can be delivered to the end-users incrementally and iteratively. A constant pace of interactions and collaborations in between the stakeholders, the developers, and the end-users can help all of them to establish healthy and long-lasting relationships along with an improved optimism.

The principle *'Continuous attention to technical excellence and good design enhances agility'* can be summarized in two words as *Enhanced Agility*. Various aspects of technical excellence and good design techniques enhance technical agility within the software development teams. Agility is the ability to respond, change, and move rapidly with an ease of acceptance. It makes an impact on the overall functioning of the working software.

Software development teams making use of the best designing and programming practices always need to observe and reflect on the adoption of such best practices and standards. Involvement of the subject matter experts in the teams to have a realistic technical excellence and good design architecture to be in place is the best way of enhancing technical agility. Such involvement also acts as a learning experience for the rest of the team members.

The principle *'Simplicity -- the art of maximizing the amount of work not done -- is essential.'* can be summarized in two words as *Simplified Outcomes*. Instead of building a complex software (which can deal with all the possibilities and which takes the development team's significant amount of time), they need to focus on the most essential and simple software functionalities. Simplicity also ensures that teams are reducing unrequired and useless endeavours and activities. This saves their valuable efforts and has a positive impact while eliminating the waste and saving their time and money.

The principle *'The best architectures, requirements, and designs emerge from self-organizing teams.'* can be summarized in two words as *Self-organizing Teams*. To address the ultimate purpose of continuous improvement of efficiency, effectiveness, collaboration, and teamwork in the software development teams, it is important for them to establish, inspect, assess, and enhance their self-organization to perform required actions on their own with less supervision and its associated procedures by management. It initially requires training, coaching, and mentoring, where they need to thoroughly learn and imbibe various human behavioral attributes. Some of the core behavioral attributes are trust, transparency, openness, focus, commitment, empathy, integrity, respect, courage, self-awareness, mindfulness, shared understanding, help, support, guidance, knowledge sharing, responsibility, accountability, shared ownership, collaboration, communication, co-ordination, co-operation, persuasion, growth mindset, and many more. To enable self-management and self-organization within themselves, the software development teams need to inculcate these behavioral attributes.

The principle *'At regular intervals, the team reflects on how to become more effective, then tunes and adjusts its behavior accordingly.'* can be summarized in two words as *Reflective Fine-Tuning*. Software development teams need to continuously observe, analyse, evaluate, describe, discuss, brainstorm, and reflect on themselves to make sure that, they are becoming more and more effective and efficient. They should also investigate on the factors with proper reflections from all the sides, where they think that they need to fine-tune themselves. Reflective fine-tuning can also help them to fix any of the problems occurring in the development and delivery cycle of working software, that too quite early. Adjustment of fine-tuned behavior to become more effective should be done by the teams more regularly.

With the introduction of *Manifesto for Agile Software Development*, the software development community got exposed to the diverging viewpoints. It further opened several perspectives of looking towards these agile values and principles following different interpretations altogether. This also triggered a thought process to look at these values and principles, as per the own individual desires of teams. Software development teams started to look at the Agile Manifesto with a variety of perceptions, where the primary aspect of *embracing change* was acting as a root cause for it.

> *"To change ourselves effectively, we first had to change our perceptions."*
> *- Stephen R. Covey*

In today's world of Digital Transformation and Industry 4.0/5.0, that is, the 4th/5th industrial revolution, which is utilizing the power of Information Technology and which is full of Volatility, Uncertainty, Complexity and Ambiguity (which is also referred as VUCA world), one might think that whether *Manifesto for Agile Software Development* is still valid, applicable, and to be followed by the software development teams or not.

> *"Most misunderstandings in the world could be avoided*
> *if people would simply take the time to ask, What else could this mean?"*
> *- Shannon L. Alder*

Since the inception of the *Manifesto for Agile Software Development*, the values and principles mentioned under it have been adopted by many organizations, teams, and individuals. The *Manifesto for Agile Software Development* always gives an opportunity to the software development teams to focus and to reflect upon themselves, so that they can thrive for the purpose of continuous learning and continuous improvement.

This is the main reason behind organizations, who want to go for agile transformations always aim at the methods helping and supporting their self-managing and self-organizing teams to establish a proper and flexible collaboration, rapport, and relationships building. It always also acts as a primary interest for those teams before they start to do any kind of agile software development. The organizational agile adaptation mindset hence plays an important role to execute their agile transformation initiatives, considering the agile values and principles mentioned in the *Manifesto for Agile Software Development*.

Organizations catering for the ever-changing needs of their customers through a variety of processes of agile software development and delivery need to establish their own suitable way of working, using which they can start, sustain, and grow their organizational agility. Organizational agile transformation starts at the individual level that needs to be further extended to the team level and finally to the organizational level. Organizations tend to create their agile transformation roadmaps, which they want to follow considering various aspects, characteristics, and current trends of the business and IT world.

Even though digital transformation and agile transformation seem to be two separate entities, they still can be applied together in organizations, who want to avail the combined benefits of both. Digital transformation in organizations provides an opportunity for them to go for digitalization of their business, which further helps them to achieve greater customer satisfaction, capable returns on investments, and few other promising benefits through their digitalized IT products and services. On the other hand, agile transformation in organizations brings in a proper attention to business value, customer emphasis, flexibility to adapt and to respond for change, faster time to market, reduction of costs, time, money, and effort, transparency, continuous delivery of value, and continuous improvement while doing the same, and few other capable advantages.

Digital transformation is a transformation considering all the aspects of transforming organizations, using a properly established digitization mechanism, whereas agile transformation is a transformation considering all the aspects of transforming organizations, using a properly established Agile Way of Working.

"It's not about perfect. It's about effort. And when you implement that effort into your life.
Every single day, that's where transformation happens.
That's how change occurs. Keep going. Remember why you started."
- Jillian Michaels

The 14th Annual State of Agile Report (published at **https://stateofagile.com/**) represents the overall state of agile at the global level in which, there are many reflections related to the teams and organizations, who are making use of Agile Way of Working to perform activities related to their overall functioning.

One can clearly see the following interesting and dynamic trends of global agile adoption, using which it can be confirmed that, in today's technology savvy and ever-changing world, agile is one of the buzzwords which is in full demand.

1. More and more organizations are going for the agile adoption. It is not only software development and IT but the other organizational units - Operations, Marketing, HR, Sales, Finance, and so on, in organizations have also started practising agile.

2. Not all the teams and organization units in organizations have adopted the agile practices. This points out that there is still a big scope for expansion of enterprise agile adoption and transformation specific initiatives.

3. The top five reasons for the organizations to start their journey with agile adoption and transformation are:

    o   To accelerate their software delivery

    o   To enhance their ability to manage changing priorities

    o   To increase their productivity

    o   To improve their business and IT alignment

    o   To enhance their software quality

4. The top five advantages of organizational agile adoption and transformation are:

    o   It provides an ability to manage changing priorities

    o   It increases the project visibility

    o   It improves the business and IT alignment

    o   It improves the delivery time and time to market

    o   It improves the team morale

5. The top five measures of success for the organizational journey of agile adoption and transformation are:

    o   Customer and end-user satisfaction

    o   Business value

    o   On-time delivery

    o   Quality

    o   Business objectives achieved

6. When it comes to global agile adoption and transformation, there are around 54% global organizations already making use of agile practices and still maturing.

7. There are around 20% global organizations that are performing experimentation with agile adoption and transformation initiatives.

8. There are around 11% global organizations that consider themselves to have a high level of competency with the agile practices they are already making use of.

9. There are around 5% global organizations that believe that the agile practices are enabling a greater adaptability for them.

10. There are around only 4% global organizations that are not at all making use of the agile practices.

Irrespective of whichever type/variation of digital and agile transformation-based initiatives organizations are interested to implement, they always want that their identity and existence is expanding to grow their business value positioning, every now and then. This mindset asks them to keep reflecting on themselves to improve continually.

The most suitable methodology to achieve and persist a steady growth and success is to incorporate the right mix of digital and agile transformations in the business value proportion of organizations. The digital transformation can anticipate a proper usage of applicable and appropriate technologies like APIs, Web, Mobile, Cloud, IoT, Automation, DevOps, Data Science, AI, and ML, RPA, Information Security, and so on, whereas an agile transformation can expect a proper usage of applicable and proper agile framework-based way of working.

It is essential for the key people (who are a part of the transformation process) to understand the organization's transformational roadmap, business requirements, and its associated pros and cons. This also requires a substantial involvement of subject matter expertise from all the directions considering all the impacts of organizational transformation in both shorter as well as longer runs. They need to continuously evaluate themselves to make sure that they are going in the right direction even though there might be some obstacles and challenges coming in between their unique transformational journey. The establishment of an Agile Way of Working (with business, people, processes, supporting tools, and technologies of an agile organization) is the first step in the process of the organizational agile transformation journey to achieve organizational agility.

Aaron De Smet from McKinsey and Company defines Organizational Agility as, an ability for an organization to renew itself, adapt, change quickly, and succeed in a rapidly changing, ambiguous, turbulent environment. Agility is not incompatible with stability; agility requires stability. Organizational Agility can be represented using the following figure:

Figure 1.1: Organizational Agility

Organizational Agility can be considered as a collaborative collection of Business, Technical, People, and Process Agility. Each level of agility has its own significance. A proper Agile Way of Working corresponding to each level of agility needs to be established in organizations. It also helps the organizations to become more and more agile, employing the advantages of each level of agility. It assists them to have an ease of agile transformation starting from individuals, then to the teams, and finally to the organization. Levels of Agility are explained as follows:

- Business Agility in organizations is their ability to respond to continuously evolving and improving business dimensions and associated factors in a collaboration with their people, culture, leadership, processes, supporting tools, and few other entities.

  If the business systems and associated Agile Way of Working in organizations are more agile in nature, then it helps to enable leadership with quick decision-making capabilities. The Flow of the customer and business value along with a proper prioritization of corresponding value driven work empowers teams to deliver the value frequently. Business Agility engagement helps teams to improve their business value excellence by also enabling teams, leadership, and stakeholders to work together collaboratively, where delivering customer value is their highest priority.

- Technical Agility in organizations is their ability to respond to continuously evolving and improving technical practices using a variety of supporting tools and technologies in a collaboration with their people, culture, leadership, processes, and few other entities. These practices always need to have a technical excellence-driven process excellence to deliver the customer and business value incrementally, iteratively, frequently, and rapidly.

Adaptable and advanced technical practices not only provide opportunities for the teams and organizations to change, but they also have their strong foundations lying with a potential belief in changeability. Such technical practices must be implemented and utilized for the betterment of customer-specific value delivery. In this process of agile software development and value delivery, Technical Agility always needs to act as a primary enabler for the teams to help them to achieve their agile transformation.

Feasibility studies, value proportioning, fitment, adjustments, re-adjustments, and a final decision (by following a consensus-based decision-making approach) to make use of supporting tools and technologies from an implementation point of view should be done based upon cross-checks and evaluation of existing technical practices. This needs to be done, so that any of the understanding and/or implementation gaps can be easily bridged. This also helps the software development teams to enhance their technical excellence which needs to be achieved over a period. Organizations and their software development teams should not stop here. They should continuously look out for their technical excellence-based agility to get it evaluated and improved further, both frequently and carefully.

- People Agility (can be also called as Cultural or Behavioral Agility) in the organizations is their own ability to adapt and respond to the continuously evolving cultural and behavioral relationships among their people. Its existence mainly depends upon the skills and qualities of people who are part of the teams in the organization. Various aspects of people behaviors such as empathy, emotional connect, rapport, trust, commitment, openness, beliefs, ethics, diversity, agreements, disagreements, thought processes, and many more have a significant impact on the organization's overall culture.

> *"Alone we can do so little; together we can do so much."*
> *- Helen Keller*

In case of challenging situations, it is the People Agility in organizations that causes certain behavioral patterns within their people, using which either they try their best, while responding to the change by challenging themselves or they lose their patience which further causes detrimental effects with their Agile Way of Working. It is hence important for the organizations to always make sure that the People Agility factor is not getting ignored; however, it should be properly taken care by using different techniques. Few simple techniques such as analysing personality traits of people to reflect their behaviors identifying scope for improvements, recognizing efforts of people to motivate them, evaluating happiness and satisfaction index of people, and understanding their viewpoints considering previously mentioned various aspects of people behaviors can surely help them to improve People Agility.

- Process Agility (can be also called as Value Driven Agility) in the organizations is their ability to adapt and respond to the continuously evolving customer and business needs based on the values and processes in a collaboration with their people, culture, leadership, processes, supporting tools, and few other entities.

> *"If you can't describe what you are doing as a process,*
> *you don't know what you're doing."*
> *- W. Edwards Deming*

As mentioned in the Agile Manifesto, the value '*Individuals and interactions over processes and tools*' always asks the software development teams to give more emphasis on valuing the people who are responsible to enhance their own Organizational Agility rather than valuing the processes or tools which are getting used to achieve the same purpose. However, the required set of agreed processes cannot be ignored by them. They always need to utilize such processes by having continuous interactions.

> *"The important thing is not your process.*
> *The important thing is your process for improving your process."*
> *- Henrik Kniberg*

Process Agility acts like a mirror for organizations where they need to check on how their existing processes are in place, what are the gaps and bottlenecks with those processes, which areas of those processes can be improved (so that such change enhances customer and business needs-based value proposition), how to eliminate process waste in terms of efforts, money, cost, and time, and many more parameters, how an organization can adopt agile practices and associated processes using agile frameworks to establish and further improve their Agile Way of Working, and many more. Process Agility also opens exclusive opportunities for the teams to review and accelerate upgradation of their processes reflecting impacts of process improvisation.

An Agile Way of Working for agile organizations is basically a simple, nimble, and flexible working agreement to be established, agreed, and to be accepted by individuals, software development teams, and organizations for themselves. It always needs to authorize and encourage all of them to continuously deliver the customer/end-user value-driven outcomes.

It always needs to be achieved by them by keeping their focus on delivering high-quality working software while following all the agile values and principles. An Agile Way of Working should always be simple to understand, simple to implement, and simple to enhance. It should be nimble in nature, which means that it should be quick and light in terms of its overall functioning. It should be flexible, so that individuals, teams, and organizations can customize it as per their own needs. To establish the same, it requires a significant effort, dedication, commitment, and patience. It can be represented using following figure:

Figure 1.2: *Agile Way of Working*

Teamwork and collaboration should be the prime drivers behind the overall establishment of an Agile Way of Working for a software development team. High-performing agile software development teams are always having 'We' mindset instead of 'I' mindset, where the exciting activity of high-quality working software building is something that really matters to them with a complete involvement of all the team members. Agile Way of Working works much better if the teams are co-located; however, it also works fine with distributed teams.

For an agile team (having an appropriate agile mindset and outlook), a continuous support from management and stakeholders always acts as an underlying foundation to become a better agile software development team. Once such a team structure is in place, it looks to be simple for them where they need to remember that, initially agile teams behave like toddlers. They need to grow in stages along with a proper nurturing over the time. The following figure shows the same using the concept of Stages of Group Development, given by Bruce Tuckman:

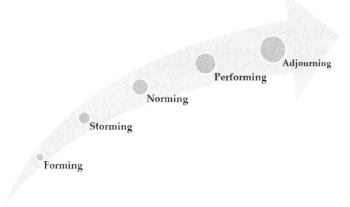

Figure 1.3: *Stages of Group Development concept*

As mentioned in this concept, there are following phases or stages required for an agile team to start, develop, and grow with. Each stage plays an important role while building high-performing agile teams, starting from the time they meet till they dissolve:

- Forming is the first stage where the team members are getting introduced to each other. They get familiar with each other considering their skills, past experiences, roles, and responsibilities, and many more aspects. It is a bit chaotic stage where they also feel that they need some coaching, mentoring, guidance, help, and support from management to define their roles and responsibilities to get aligned with team's vision, purpose, goals, and objectives, and so on. Expectation from teams at this stage is to start with the expected rapport and relationships building.

- Storming is the next stage where the team members know enough about each other, based on their individual personality traits and behavioral patterns. There is a possibility of disagreements and conflicts, and so on, which is because of missing trust along with different viewpoints and difference of opinions present in a team. It is okay to have these kinds of disagreements, but it is the responsibility of management to help them make sure that a valid, logical, and consensus-based decision making is always taking place. All sorts of brainstorming need to happen, so that the team members can recognize disagreements and resolve them at the earliest, to agree with the decisions taken by them.

- Norming is the next and the most important stage where the team members start to focus on formulating a working agreement supported by a shared understanding of roles and responsibilities. Team members having such a shared understanding start to contribute. Their relationships get settled. They start to ask for help and start to provide help to each other. Sometimes storming can still occur but the team members agree to disagree with more collaborative interactions because of the boosted trust and because of a consensus-based valid and logical decision-making process in place. To summarize this stage, they start to work as a one solid unit.

- Performing is the next stage where the team has a steady performance. Understanding and implementation of their shared objectives along with a proper collaboration and communication is well-established. If the team achieves this stage, it is indeed a great accomplishment for them. All the team members are well versed with their roles and responsibilities. Sometimes they can operate with a minimum or without any influence from the management side. They hardly have any disagreements and conflicts. If there are any disagreements, they treat them as worthwhile perceptions. The team is always motivated and shows all the positive reflections of being a high-performing team.

- Adjourning is the next and final stage (which was additionally introduced by Bruce Tuckman along with Mary Ann Jensen later), where the team starts to finish their work items and tasks. The team achieve their goals, so that it finally gets adjourned. It sometimes acts as a challenging stage for some team members because they are familiar with their established routine, which is supposed to be impacted during and after this stage. In this stage, the management needs to help and support the team to plan their next voyage.

Navigating through the stages of development is always a worthwhile experience for the agile teams. Along with a shared understanding of common objectives and goals, it is equally important for them to choose a relevant agile framework which needs to help them to establish their own Agile Way of Working. By making use of an apt agile framework, their Agile Software Development, Delivery, and Way of Working specific processes can be easily established and can be frequently enhanced.

Points to remember

- There are four basic values and 12 supporting principles mentioned in the *'Manifesto for Agile Software Development'*. These values and principles help the software development teams to discover the applicable and appropriate ways to be analysed, evaluated, and applied based upon their own context and fit.

- Digital transformation in organizations provides an opportunity for them to opt for digitalization of their business, which further helps them to achieve greater customer satisfaction, capable returns on investments, and few other promising benefits through their digitalized IT products and services.

- Agile transformation in organizations brings in a proper attention to business value, customer emphasis, flexibility to adapt and to respond for change, faster time to market, reduction of costs, time, money, and effort, transparency, continuous delivery of value, and continuous improvement while delivering continuous delivery of value, and few other capable advantages.

- As per the 14th Annual State of Agile Report, more and more organizations are opting for agile adoption.

- Establishment of an Agile Way of Working is the first step in the process of Organizational Agile Transformation journey to achieve Organizational Agility.

- Organizational Agility is a collaborative collection of Business, Technical, People and Process Agility.

- Teamwork and collaboration should be the prime drivers behind the establishment of an Agile Way of Working for the software development teams.

- Stages of group development concept helps the agile software development teams to develop and deliver a continuous value stream by adapting to the ever-changing customer needs, while being at a sustainable pace.

In the next chapter, readers will get to know about various popular agile frameworks such as Scrum, Kanban, Scrumban, XP, DSDM, FDD, Crystal, and few more.

CHAPTER 2
Agile Frameworks

Introduction

In this chapter, readers will get an overall understanding about various agile frameworks such as Scrum, Kanban, Scrumban, Extreme Programming (XP), Dynamic Systems Development Method (DSDM), Feature-Driven Development (FDD), Crystal, and few more. Readers will also get to know about the Lean Agile Software Development approach.

Objective

After studying this chapter, you should be able to:

- Understand the need of agile frameworks for the agile software product development teams.
- Understand the interesting trends of global Agile adoption and transformation considering various agile frameworks getting used in global organizations.
- Understand various agile frameworks - Scrum, Kanban, Scrumban, XP, DSDM, FDD, and Crystal.
- Understand Lean Agile Software Development approach.
- Understand Scrum, Kanban, Scrumban, and XP agile frameworks comparatively.
- Understand the interesting trends of global Scrum adoption and Agile transformation in global organizations.

- Understand how the agile software product development teams can establish and enhance their own Agile Way of Working using Scrum, Kanban, and Scrumban - The wonderful trio.

Steve 'The Software Developer' (in a discussion with Nancy 'The Scrum Master'):

"Nancy, I have a serious doubt on if we have established a proper Agile Way of Working or not. Yes, we have Scrum based Agile Way of Working in place, but I personally think that we have all the Scrum Events getting enforced upon us. I mean to say, on the entire team. Daily Scrum can be a perfect example of what I am pointing out here. Don't you think that our Agile Way of Working should be more flexible? Why you always have an expectation from all of us that we are not missing the Daily Scrum? Why we should plan for our next set of action items for next 24 hours, while looking at our already agreed Sprint Goal and that too daily?"

Nancy 'The Scrum Master' (smiling and replying):

"You are really good at observing the things around, Steve! Before I try to answer your question, I want to check with you on few things. You are in your current role as a software developer since more than 8 years now, right? When you were a novice programmer, whether you had possessed all the required knowledge related to best programming practices? You acquired it during the last 8 years, right? Now please tell me, to improve your programming skills, what was your approach?"

Steve (taking a pause to think and answering):

"Okay, let me quickly reflect on my journey so far. May be, I will try to summarize it. Yes, I started as a novice programmer almost 8 years back. Initially, I was knowing Object Oriented Programming concepts, but when I started doing complex software development, I got to know about many other best programming practices and standards from the senior developers.

I was also doing some self-learning; however, whenever I had a feeling of getting stuck with any of the advanced programming concepts or practices, I always used to take some help from the senior developers. I still remember, there were many times when they used to ask me several questions about various approaches of programming, later explaining me about the benefits of the best approach to be followed. Initially, they were enforcing things on me, but later I got used to it, as I got to know that it is for the betterment of code quality and to ensure that we always have the best quality code in place."

Nancy:

"So, initially they offered you help and support. Later you got to know about why they wanted you to do what they wanted you to do, correct? Was it about enforcement or was it about you realizing the value behind what you were doing, as per their way of doing it? Certain things in the first go may look like enforcements, but we should see what difference they are going to make with us in a longer run."

Steve (smiling):

"Woah! You got me answered, Nancy! I am waiting for our today's Daily Scrum. See you there later!"

Software development teams initially struggle a lot while establishing their Agile Way of Working by selecting a suitable agile framework. There are various popular agile frameworks (such as Scrum, Kanban, XP, Scrumban, FDD, DSDM, Crystal, and few more) with their associated characteristics and features; however, the reason behind why most of the times agile software development teams struggle to incorporate their Agile Way of Working with any of these agile frameworks is improper understanding, incorrect expectations, lacking sincere commitment, missing collective ownership, and teams completely ignoring few other factors related to their basic needs and wants.

Many times, it is also observed at the organization level that their efforts are getting wasted because they try to have *one size fits all* approach across all the software development teams. Using this approach, they try to establish an Agile Way of Working across all the teams with a common framework following common standards instead of having some customized implementations suitable for the individual software development teams. They should understand that *one size doesn't fit all*. Different teams have different needs. Hence establishing an Agile Way of Working for individual teams to address their needs with an apt agile framework is always a must have for them.

> *"We all need to figure out what's right for us because nothing about life is one size fits all. Even for an Olympian, that's for sure. And such discovery starts with you paying attention to yourself."*
> *- David Agus*

Agile frameworks keep on evolving because they are incomplete and there is always a need to update their structure, design, and alignment. Hence, in the process of selection of an apt agile framework, the selection process itself should be given a lower priority, whereas suitability for requirements, needs, and wants in an accordance with the expected Way of Working of teams should be given the highest priority. Teams should also have an anticipation to bring together whatever they need, so that they can have their Agile Way of Working more agile and it can function much smoother with its natural ease. Teams should also understand that the outcomes-based value delivery to their customers is more important. Agile Way of Working using an agile framework should keep on enhancing the performance of teams to achieve the same.

The Teams always need to assess, evaluate, and apply required customizations to their already established Agile Way of Working by giving more emphasis on values, objectives, vision, mission, and goals while considering the expectations from the organization and their own customers. This practice needs to be frequently evaluated and refined by acknowledging the core values and supporting principles given in the *Manifesto for Agile Software Development*.

"It doesn't matter how good you are today;
if you're not better next month, you're no longer agile."
- Mike Cohn

Even though the selection of an agile framework to establish an agile way of working should be the secondary priority of software development teams, it is still required for teams to know about agile frameworks to establish a proper governance in place. With this understanding, they can do more exploration to further decide on, which of those frameworks can be used to have an ease of agile way of working for them. The most commonly and widely used popular agile frameworks are Scrum, Kanban, Scrumban, XP, Lean, Crystal, DSDM, FDD, and so on. Lean Agile Software Development is also a popular approach used by many organizations.

There are many similarities as well as differences in between these agile frameworks. These differences can and should act as parameters for the selection and customization of suitable framework for teams. Nevertheless, all agile frameworks have their own unique features as well as ambiguities, they still have their roots belonging to values and principles mentioned in the *Manifesto for Agile Software Development*. Establishment of a simple, nimble, and flexible Agile Way of Working using any of these agile frameworks encourages teams to deliver high-quality working software, both incrementally and iteratively. The most common intention behind popular agile frameworks like Scrum, Kanban, Scrumban, and XP is to be able to alter the processes associated with an established Agile Way of Working under the software development teams once they start to address needs of their businesses and customers.

In the 14th Annual State of Agile Report (published at **https://stateofagile.com/**), one can clearly see the following interesting trends of global Agile adoption and transformation considering various agile frameworks getting used in organizations.

1. Scrum is the most widely used agile framework by 58% organizations globally. Scrum and its associated practices are continuing to be the most used agile framework-based methodologies.

2. Kanban is another agile framework used by 7% organizations globally.

3. Scrumban (a combination Scrum and Kanban) is the second most widely used agile framework by 10% organizations globally.

4. Agile Framework XP is used by 1% organizations, whereas agile framework Scrum/XP hybrid is used by 8% organizations globally.

5. 9% organizations are using other/hybrid/multiple agile frameworks globally.

Scrum is the most well-known and the most commonly, widely used agile framework by agile software product development teams globally. Scrum Framework is originally developed by Ken Schwaber and Jeff Sutherland. It is a simple framework that helps to enable collaborative software development environment under which the agile software product development teams can develop complex software.

Scrum Framework always emphasizes on teamwork-based accountability within the software development team which is called as Scrum Team. Scrum anticipates an iterative and incremental software development and delivery process for which the entire Scrum Team needs to remain accountable and responsible.

As per the Scrum Guide (published at **https://www.scrumguides.org/scrum-guide. html**), Scrum is a framework using which teams can tackle complex adaptable problems and deliver software products of the highest possible value, efficiently and innovatively. Scrum is not a process. It is neither a technique nor a perfect method. It is a framework inside which teams can apply, customize, and utilize various processes, methods, procedures, and techniques, as per their customized needs, while ensuring that the values and other associated entities of the framework to be intact. Scrum Framework illustrates the effectiveness and importance of product development and delivery, so that constant enhancements in the working software, the team, and the working environment itself can be made possible. Scrum involves Scrum Teams and few other associated entities which are Scrum Values, Scrum Roles, Scrum Artifacts, Scrum Events, and associated Scrum Rules. Each entity in Scrum Framework serves a specific purpose required for its usage and success. Scrum Rules unite these entities by regulating the relationships and interactions between them.

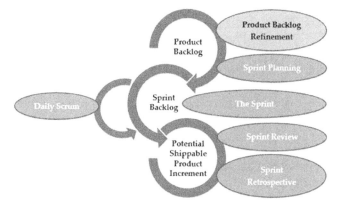

Figure 2.1: Scrum Framework Overview

As per the Scrum Guide, Scrum Framework gives an emphasizes on five values known as Scrum Values. They are commitment, courage, focus, openness, and respect. They must be lived and followed by the Scrum Team. The Scrum Team consists of three roles. They are Product Owner, Developers, and Scrum Master. The Product Owner has a responsibility to maximize the value of high-quality working software to be developed and delivered by the Developers. Developers are the working professionals of the Scrum Team. They need to develop and deliver a fully functional, potentially releasable product Increment of a high-quality working software at the end of each Sprint. Sprint is one of the Scrum Events. Scrum Master has a responsibility to establish and promote the Scrum Framework and to coach the Scrum Team.

There are three Scrum Artifacts - Product Backlog, Sprint Backlog, and Increment, using which the Scrum Teams need to ensure that their overall progress is transparent, visible, and quantifiable. Product Backlog is a prioritized list of all the features, functions, and requirements, and so on, which are required to be done for the working software product. It is frequently refined during the Product Backlog Refinements. Sprint Backlog is the collection of Product Backlog Items (PBIs) selected for a Sprint.

The Sprint is one of the five Scrum Events. It is a time duration of one or two or three weeks or one month during which a completely developed, tested, fully functional, potentially shippable, and releasable working software product Increment is produced. Sprints have steady lengths all over the development effort and a new Sprint starts after the previous Sprint gets over. Increment (can be also referred as a potential shippable product increment or release) is the consolidation of all the PBIs completed during a Sprint and the value of all the increments from all the previous Sprints.

The other four Scrum Events are Sprint Planning, Daily Scrum, Sprint Review, and Sprint Retrospective. Sprint Planning is used to perform the planning for the work to be performed during upcoming Sprint. Daily Scrum is a 15-minute time-boxed Scrum Event that is held on every day of the Sprint for the team, where the team members plan their work for the next 24 hours. It is an opportunity for them to self-reflect on their progress and any issues getting faced under ongoing Sprint. Sprint Review happens at the end of the Sprint to inspect the potential shippable product increment and to adapt the Product Backlog as per the business or customer value prioritization, if required. Sprint Retrospective is a valuable opportunity for the entire Scrum Team to inspect on themselves and to create a plan for improvements as action items to be addressed/worked upon by them in future.

Scrum is based on empirical process control theory, which is also called as Empiricism. Using this Theory of Empiricism, the Scrum Framework engages an iterative and incremental approach of developing and delivering high-quality working software along with an enhanced predictability and a well-managed risk.

There are three pillars supporting the implementation of empirical process control under the Scrum framework. They are transparency, inspection, and adaptation.

Transparency puts a mandate for Scrum Teams to make sure that the significant aspects and characteristics of the process getting used by them are visible to those, who are responsible for the outcome-based delivery of working software. Inspection puts a mandate for Scrum Teams to make sure that they along with their associated people, entities must frequently inspect the Scrum Artifacts (Product Backlog, Sprint Backlog, and Increment) and their overall progress toward the agreed Sprint Goal to find and to tackle unwanted deviations. Adaptation puts a mandate for Scrum Teams to make sure that if anyone concludes that one or more aspects of the process being followed by the Scrum Teams are differing outside acceptable limits and if the subsequent outcome is undesirable, then the process must be adjusted accordingly.

Kanban is a flow-based approach developed by Taiichi Ohno for Toyota. It helps the agile software product development teams to align their prioritized work items. Work items must be managed and worked upon by the teams to enhance their efficiency and manageability by reducing waste, if any. Software development, maintenance, and support using Kanban is simple to start with the present workflow of teams. It allows them to visualize the flow of work and to limit the work in progress (WIP) using *stop starting new work, start finishing existing work* concept, where no major changes are required for the present agile way of working.

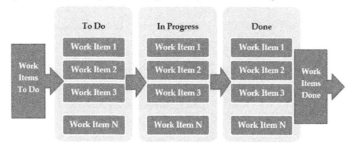

Figure 2.2: *Kanban Simple Flow Approach*

For better visualization of work items to be worked upon by the team, they need to make use of a Kanban Board. Flow of work items is represented on Kanban Board, where all the work items coming from business/customer side (and to be worked upon by the team) need to be organized and prioritized as a To Do list of work items. Once the team starts to work on those work items, they need to move those to In Progress. They further need to move them to Done once those are completed.

The flow of work items needs to be visualized on Kanban Board following a direction from left to right, where left represents team's commitment and right represents team's delivery. Work items can be requirements, ideas, features, enhancements, fixes, or anything else which need to be worked upon by the team to develop and deliver applicable functionalities of a working software product. The Kanban Board helps the team to make their process visible using a *'Pull System'* approach. On a Kanban Board, team needs to pull work items from left to right, so that they keep moving forward and reflect the overall progress of the team.

Team needs to limit their WIP while matching demand with their capacity. Demand is something that is an ask from business and/or customer side to complete those work items, whereas capacity is the ability of the team to address the demand in place. The team hence needs to put certain limits at Kanban Board columns with states as To Do, In Progress, Done, and so on, based on demand and capacity. This helps them to improve on frequent delivery and quality of working software.

Teams can also have few other customized columns on their Kanban Board to reflect on the current specific state of work items. Teams always need to evaluate on the anticipated flow of work items by maximizing the delivery of value and by minimizing the delivery time. In this process, a proper addressal of bottlenecks and issues (causing any deviations) help them to have more simple, clear, well-defined, and changeable policies and processes in place.

Open feedback loops and an appropriate capacity allocation for teams, WIP limits and definition of done for work items, and few other rules for both teams and their work items can result into an ease of functioning for the Kanban-based agile way of working of teams. Kanban emphasizes on few values. They are transparency, balance, collaboration, customer focus, flow, leadership, understanding, agreement, and respect. These core values always need to be lived and followed by the team.

There are no explicit roles defined in Kanban; however, roles can emerge based upon the team's existing structure. They can be filled-in by someone who is having a role of a Service Request Manager and a Service Delivery Manager. The Service Request Manager (who can be a product manager or a product owner or a service manager) recognizes the requirements of customers to enable the organization and prioritization of work items, whereas the Service Delivery Manager (who can be a flow manager or a delivery manager or a flow master) carries a responsibility toward the team, who needs to deliver the work items to the customers.

Kanban makes use of feedback loops. Loops are formulated via quarterly strategy reviews to select the applicable work items, monthly operations review to understand capacity versus demand, monthly risk reviews to understand delivery risks, bi-weekly service delivery reviews to improve processes, weekly replenishment meetings to determine work items, daily Kanban meetings to discuss on daily activities, and delivery planning meetings to plan and monitor the delivery of work items.

Scrumban (Scrum + Kanban) is a hybrid agile framework described by Corey Ladas. It is a combination of Scrum and Kanban. It makes utilization of the flexible nature of Scrum Framework along with the continuous process improvement approach of Kanban, which helps to enhance the overall agility of teams. Scrumban is used by agile software product development teams, which gives them more flexibility by ensuring that they are not getting much overloaded by the means of ever-changing customer needs.

Scrumban provides an association with the structure of Scrum framework along with the flexibility and visualization of the Kanban approach. Scrumban can be extensively used by the teams having an aspiration to perform a transition from Scrum to Kanban. A sudden movement from Scrum to Kanban might result into severe undesirable impacts on the team's agile way of working. Hence, with Scrumban, teams always need to evaluate, establish, and further enhance continuous improvement-based practices from the Kanban approach, by keeping the structure of their Scrum framework-based agile way of working always intact and by following the rules of Scrum:

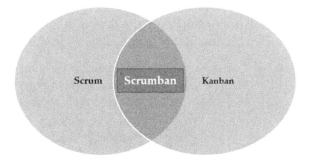

Figure 2.3: Scrumban Approach

Team needs to combine the essentials of both Scrum and Kanban. Applying Kanban principles to their Scrum-based agile way of working employs effective Scrumban. To implement a Scrumban-based agile way of working, the Team needs to use Scrum Artifacts and Scrum Events within a Kanban based Pull System approach. They need to have a visualization of their work items using a Product Backlog, which needs to be a well-organized and prioritized on demand as per their customer/end-user needs. The Sprint Backlog needs to be captured on the Kanban Board reflecting various applicable states for work items.

Team needs to impose WIP limits for each state ensuring that the team is following *stop starting new work, start finishing existing work* concept. The team needs to have more states on Kanban Board to increase their overall transparency to get to know about their own WIP. They need to focus on prioritization of work items rather than estimation, so that they can support on demand planning, as per their customer/end-user needs.

To make Scrumban more hybrid, team also needs to customize existing processes of their Scrumban-based agile way of working, as per their needs. The team needs to utilize the best practices of Scrum approach to perform the Sprint Planning at consistent intervals, also along with the Sprint Reviews and Sprint Retrospectives.

They need to agree on the amount of work they can pull into their Sprints. It is based on the priority and complexity of work items and the Sprint duration. They need to seek and get prioritized work items to work based on demand, where they need to be convinced with the required analysis in place before they start to develop anything. They need to have a placeholder to organize the Backlog of work items.

While implementing a Scrumban-based agile way of working approach, the team also needs to utilize the best practices of Kanban approach. These best practices are related to process improvement, capacity and demand-based allocations, visualization and pull system-based progression of work items, limiting WIP of work items, open feedback loops, value-based delivery, and so on.

Extreme Programming (XP) is an agile framework created by Kent Beck, which helps the software development teams to produce high-quality working software products with better defined quality standards. It is the most certain agile framework seeking and encouraging the use of proper engineering practices during the process of software development. It is effective because it also emphasizes customer satisfaction.

Teams deliver working software products as per exact customer needs rather than delivering everything they could possibly want to deliver. XP-based agile way of working and its associated processes allow teams to address ever-changing customer requirements.

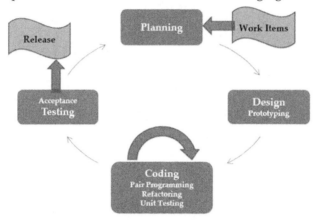

Figure 2.4: Extreme Programming (XP) Approach

XP is more suitable to apply when there are continuously and dynamically changing customer requirements, when there is a small, co-located team, when there might be possibilities of risks getting created because of some new technology with which software development teams are working on, when the customers are unsure about what they want, when there is a need to improve the software quality and responsiveness to the customer requirements, and when the technology getting used by teams is in line with the construction of unit and acceptance tests to validate and verify the working software product functionalities through automation.

Communication, simplicity, feedback, courage, and respect are the five core values of XP that always need to be lived and followed by the whole XP team, where all the contributors of a software development project are the part of a whole XP team. A business representative stakeholder called as Customer is also formed by the team. The customer works with the team having daily interactions with them.

XP teams need to have a simple planning and tracking mechanism in place to determine what they need to perform next. This also helps them to do a forecasting about when the project will be completed. Prototyping-based incremental system design and architecture enables design thinking for the team. The team constructs and delivers the working software product in a series of integrated releases, always considering the customer and business value proposition. The team also needs to make sure that all the customer defined tests for the release of working software product are always passing.

Developers work and code collaboratively in pairs and/or in a group that helps them to keep the working software product always integrated, fully functional, up, and running. They apply the best practices and standards while they are coding, which continuously improves the overall code quality. Advanced software development and testing specific engineering practices like code refactoring, automated unit and acceptance testing, and continuous integration of code, and so on, assist them in enriching the overall quality of working software. These practices also act as handy tools and work as enablers to improve XP team's effective functioning under XP-based agile way of working.

XP team has a shared understanding to work on a common, simple, and proper blueprint of how the working software product will look like. The team works at a sustainable pace. XP-based agile way of working encourages the team to own the responsibility of their code along with the application of consistent coding/programming practices. This provides all kinds of opportunities for the team to work with more co-operation and collaboration. Team members write their own code and review the code written by others. This collective ownership helps them to have the best quality code in place.

XP team needs to sit together in an informative workspace to have a better face to face communication avoiding communication gaps. The team needs to have cross-functional skill sets to accomplish desired outcomes. Using techniques such as pair programming, test first development, and continuous integration, the developers need to develop a quality code while quickly solving the complex problems along with the proper reviews. The team also needs to remain in a focused state to concentrate on their work.

DSDM is an agile framework that gives more emphasis on the complete project lifecycle with the basis of an incremental and iterative delivery of working software. Many software development teams started to make use of DSDM and it got popular based upon a thinking that, the project must be associated to well-defined strategic objectives concentrating on early delivery of genuine benefits to the business and customer value proposition.

DSDM always makes use of this thinking with eight supporting principles. This allows the software development teams to keep their focus alive and to accomplish their goals. These principles are priority of business need, timely delivery, collaboration, quality as non-negotiable, incremental process, iterative development, open communication, and control demonstration.

Using the DSDM approach, the agile software product development teams need to perform a Feasibility Study using which they need to identify and establish necessary business requirements. They also need to work upon constraints to decide on whether the project needs to be worked upon using DSDM is a feasible and viable project or not. Once the Feasibility Study is done and the team decides that they want to work on a project using DSDM approach, they need to perform a Business Study using which all the knowledge-based needs to achieve the business value are studied. This results into application design recognizing the aspect of maintainability of working software.

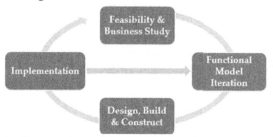

Figure 2.5: *Dynamic Systems Development Method (DSDM) Approach*

Functional Model Iteration is the next step where the team needs to construct a collection of prototypes to demo it to the customers. By revisiting those prototypes, the team needs to take care of altering them using a model-based iteration approach to improve prototyping and designing via enhancements. Implementation is the next phase, where the team needs to develop full-fledged functionalities using code increments. An increment gets completed both incrementally and iteratively. There might be changes requested in the increment while it is getting built by the software development team. Such changes need to be observed, analysed, and addressed using Functional Model Iteration based on the prototypes developed by team.

Feature-Driven Development (FDD) is an agile framework initially devised by Jeff De Luca, which arranges and aligns the process of software development for the software development teams, who are working and making progress on features to be developed in an incremental and iterative manner. Features are nothing but small pieces of functionalities, which are required to be developed and delivered to complete a project to which they are belonging to.

FDD is a model-driven approach, where the agile software product development teams need to perform short iterations to develop and deliver high-quality working software. They need to collaborate with each other to develop a business object model by looking at their customer requirements, problems, needs, and wants.

Figure 2.6: *Feature-Driven Development (FDD) Approach*

There should be a consensus within the whole team while reflecting on the complete software project/product under the object model they need to build. Based on the same model, they further need to identify the features addressing the customer values and needs. A list of features needs to be created as a collective set by them, using which a flexible boundary of the software project/product can be defined. This list of features helps them to establish their own agile way of working. They need to establish and navigate through the processes associated with such FDD based agile way of working.

The team needs to manage these features one by one, so that they can get themselves aligned with the overall implementation approach of features in an incremental and iterative manner. The team's bandwidth, dependencies, and risks need to be addressed, as and when required. Planning, designing, and building small features to deliver a fully functional working software is the end goal of the team.

Crystal is an agile framework that thoroughly supports and stresses on the first principle of the Agile Manifesto that is *Individuals and Interactions over Processes and Tools*. This framework was created for IBM by Alistair Cockburn and has two underlying principles, where the software development teams need to have enough freedom, so that they can find their own ways to enhance and optimize their agile way of working, as per their own needs.

All software development products are unique and ever-changing, which also acts as a reason behind why the software development team is the best choice of group of people to decide on, what and how to establish their own suitable agile way of working.

Hence, the characteristics of Crystal framework are based around the software development team only. Crystal framework based agile way of working should be human powered, which means that the software development processes need to be adaptable and customized as per the needs of the team involved. It should be adaptive in terms of its nature of implementation, which means that no fixed set of tools and technologies the methodology needs to make use of; however, it needs to be modified to meet the specific needs of the team. It also should be ultra-light in terms of its nature, which means that it requires less documentation or reporting.

According to the Crystal framework, teams perform in a different way depending upon their structure, size and priority of work items to be worked upon by them. A team with small size can be better at keeping themselves all aligned with frequent interactions, reducing the need of documentation and status reporting. On the other hand, a team with big size has a higher probability to have communication and understanding gaps, hence having a need of a more organized approach.

As per the varying number of team members in a software development team, different team sizes under a Crystal implementation are categorized by using colours-based naming convention. Teams with less than 8 members are called as Crystal Clear. Teams having 10–20 members are called as Crystal Yellow. Teams having 20–50 members are called as Crystal Orange. Teams having 50–100 members are called as Crystal Red.

Crystal has seven fundamental principles. Frequent delivery of code, continuous reflective improvement in and for teams, and co-located teams having increased communication are the mandatory principles for all Crystal approaches; however, personal safety of the team members, team always focusing on work and having access to subject matter experts and users, and utilization of technical tooling and associated best practices are the other optional principles which need to be adopted by the teams, if required.

Crystal always asks and allows the teams to focus on six major behavioral aspects along with their associated processes. These behavioral aspects are people, interaction, community, communication, skills, and talents.

Lean Agile Software Product Development is a hybrid approach combining benefits of Lean and Agile methodologies to be used by the software development teams. Agile Frameworks such as XP, Scrum, Kanban, and Scrumban always have an anticipation from the software development teams that they are delivering high-quality working software, both incrementally and iteratively while following the values and principles from the *Manifesto for Agile Software Development*. This needs to be united with the principles of Lean to rapidly deliver the working software. Lean is a management philosophy based on practices at Toyota Systems, which is described by a structure of processes. Lean has expectations from teams to reduce risks and wastes enhancing customer value, where this structure needs to be formed.

Software development teams also need to have a Lean Agile Mindset. It is a combination of various behavioral aspects of teams considering their principles, beliefs, feelings, opinions, and actions embracing both *Manifesto for Agile Software Development* and *Lean Agile Thinking*. All the team members need to have a growth mindset based *Lean Agile Thinking* to try out the new things, to challenge themselves to grow, to take failures as opportunities to continuously learn, unlearn, and re-learn, to inspire others and to get inspired from others, to have a positive outlook for out of the box thinking, and to challenge themselves by always seeking continuous improvement.

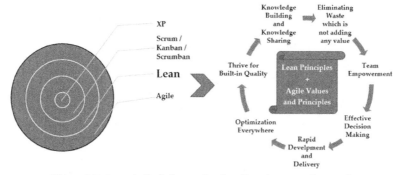

Figure 2.7: *Lean Agile Software Product Development Approach*

The term Lean Software Development was originated by Mary Poppendieck and Tom Poppendieck in 2003. By combining it with the Agile values and principles, the Lean

Agile Software Development approach acknowledges that the software development teams need to have an establishment of an agile way of working using Lean Principles. It can be applied to popular agile frameworks like XP, Scrum, Kanban, Scrumban, and so on. Teams need to make use of XP practices to have a better enablement of technical agility at the crux of their agile way of working. The utilization of Scrum and Kanban fundamentals to enable process agility also plays a key role in the success of Lean Agile Software Development approach for teams. A mixture of Lean and Agile values and principles helps teams to enable overall agility.

The Lean values and principles set a tone to eliminate waste. It is nothing but removing anything which is not adding any value to the team's way of working. They also strengthen, enhance, and promote learning mindset within the team which gives a chance to them to reflect on continuous learning roadmaps. They offer a deferred commitment giving a freedom to teams using which teams always need to establish an agile way of working based on facts and known aspects instead of assumptions and unknown aspects. This is true especially when it comes to customer requirements. Alignment of processes needs to be done on similar lines.

Teams need to develop and deliver as soon as and as fast as possible. This approach ensures that their customers/end-users know about their progress with a presence of open feedback loops. Teams need to get empowered with the presence of more and more collaboration which is the result of knowing and understanding the details of what they are supposed to do. They also need to see the big picture by ensuring built-in quality and excellence. Lean values and principles should be always advocated by an agile organization's agile leadership having a proper capability and knowledge, active and effective communication, growth mindset, complete commitment, and strong discipline.

Scrum, Kanban, XP, and Scrumban agile frameworks-based agile way of working can be seen getting established, worked upon, and further enhanced by the software development teams; however, it is important for them to understand the key differences in between these frameworks before they choose any of them to get started with. Few major parameters based upon which this comparison can be done are given as following. Teams need to understand about which aspect of specific agile frameworks they would like to make use of, as per their needs and suitability.

Parameter	Scrum	Kanban	Scrumban	XP
Agile Way of Working	Highly Expressive	Moderately expressive	Highly expressive	Moderately expressive
Flow of business value prioritization	Needs to be continuously revisited by the Product Owner and the rest of the Scrum Team members during their Product Backlog Refinements	Needs to be revisited by the Team as per their need, where prioritization is optional	Needs to be revisited by the Team as per their need, where prioritization is optional	Needs to be continuously sorted by a collaboration between the business-people and the Team
Usage of explicit processes and policies	To certain extent	To maximum extent	To maximum extent	To certain extent
Team roles	Scrum Master, Product Owner, and Developers	Service Request Manager, Service Delivery Manager, and Specialized Team	Development Team along with the possibility of having Scrum Master and Product Owner	Customer and Development Team
Time boxed development and delivery	Using time boxed Sprints	Using optionally time boxed Cadences and a continuous work-flow	Using time boxed Cadences	Using time boxed Iterations
Parameter	Scrum	Kanban	Scrumban	XP
Work commitment	Mandatory and within Sprints	Optional and within flexible Cadences	Optional and within flexible Cadences	Mandatory and within Iterations
Work decomposition	Mandatory to fit in Sprints	No sizing required	Sizing is optional	Optional to fit in Iterations

Artifacts	Product Backlog, Sprint Backlog, and Increment	Kanban Board	Scrumban Board (like Kanban Board) and Scrum Artifacts	Release, Iteration Plans, Designs, Unit, Acceptance Tests, and so on.
Events/ ceremonies/ review approaches	Sprint, Sprint Planning, Daily Scrum, Sprint Review, and Sprint Retrospective	On demand and optional events to discuss on work items	Events (based on Scrum) to be defined by the team, as per their need	Release Planning, Iteration Planning, Daily Scrum, and other Scrum related events, if needed
Use of advanced engineering practices	To certain extent	To certain extent	To certain extent	To maximum extent using Pair Programming, Test Driven Development, Continuous Integration, and many more
Planning approach	Sprint Planning	Based on delivery and release need	Based on delivery and release need	Simple planning to decide next set of work items
Iterative delivery	Within 1 to 4 weeks Sprints	Based on delivery need	Based on delivery need	Within 1 to 3 weeks Iterations
Parameter	**Scrum**	**Kanban**	**Scrumban**	**XP**
Estimation	Given	Optional	Given	Given
Work in progress limits	Within current Sprint	Limits on the Work in Progress	Limits on the Work in Progress	Within current Iteration

Work visibility	Development inputs and outcomes; Normal visibility of actual work	Development inputs, actual work, and outcomes; High visibility of actual work	Development inputs, actual work, and outcomes; High visibility of actual work	Development inputs and outcomes; Normal visibility of actual work
Team size	Suggested Typical Team Size is 10 or fewer	No specified limitation as such for Team Size	No specified limitation as such for Team Size	Suggested Typical Team Size is in between 5 to 12
Associated rules	Strict	Flexible	Moderate	Strict
Scope of work change	Need to wait for the next Sprint	Added as required	Added as required	Need to wait for the next Iteration
Product owner-ship	Product Owner	Based on the Team defined roles	Based on the Team defined roles	Collective Ownership within Team
Suitability	Development of Products having small work items, where requirements are clear and can be delivered incrementally and iteratively	Support, Enhancements, Bug Fixing, and Maintenance of Operational Products, where changes are required to be done fast	Development, Support, and Maintenance of Products, where requirements are evolving and changes are required to be done fast	Development of Products with constantly changing customer requirements, where changes are required to be done fast, while working with the customer
Management influence	Considerable	Considerably High	Considerable	Considerable

Table 2.1: A comparison between Scrum, Kanban, Scrumban, and XP Agile Frameworks

There are many other parameters using which Scrum, Kanban, XP, and Scrumban agile frameworks can be differentiated by the software development teams. Considering these differences, they should have a stance for why and what they need from a suitable agile framework or a combination of multiple agile frameworks, so that they can satisfy the need of establishment and enhancement of their agile way of working. Such framework-based processes should be a bit customizable keeping the values intact, where teams should give the process of selection a lower priority, as the frameworks keep on developing continuously.

Software development teams need to have a full freedom to explore and use any of the agile frameworks; however, according to the recent State of Scrum Report (published at **https://www.scrumalliance.org/learn-about-scrum/state-of-scrum**) given by Scrum Alliance (**https://www.scrumalliance.org/**), Scrum is the most popular agile framework getting used by the global agile software product development community. We can see the following interesting trends of global Scrum adoption and usage:

1. 94% respondents (of the survey done by Scrum Alliance resulting into the State of Scrum Report) have confirmed that they are making use of Scrum Framework in their agile software development practices.

2. Out of these 94% respondents, 78% respondents have confirmed that they are making use of Scrum along with a combination of other agile frameworks.

3. 16% respondents of the survey have confirmed that they are making use of Scrum exclusively. Only 6% respondents have confirmed that they are not making use of Scrum which looks to be very less.

4. While choosing an agile framework, 71% of executives have agreed that delivering value to the customers using Scrum is remarkable, where as 85% respondents have acknowledged that Scrum helps to improve quality of work life.

5. 97% respondents have approved that they would like to continue to make use of Scrum framework in future.

6. 78% respondents have given an affirmation on they would like to recommend Scrum to their colleagues, friends, and other professionals.

7. 55% of software development projects within the global organizations are Scrum projects, where the average team size is 7.4, the average length of a Sprint is 2.4 weeks, and the average number of Sprints per Project is 5.

8. The overall success rate of Scrum Projects has been calculated as 63% and the average duration of a Project, that is, the average Project length of a Project making use of Scrum framework has been decreased to 11.6 weeks.

9. Globally, 91% of organizations have been offering Scrum training and coaching.

10. Globally, 57% of active senior management of global organizations have been confirmed that they are supporting their Scrum adoption.

This survey is based on inputs given by more than 2000 active Scrum and Agile Practitioners representing 27 industries across 91 countries globally. One can clearly see from the survey trends that, Scrum is gaining more and more popularity over the period. Organizations who are making use of Scrum Framework-based agile way of working are seeing extremely promising results with the success of their software development teams and projects/products with the extent of adoption and utilization of Scrum oriented practices.

Even though Scrum is the most commonly and widely used agile framework by many organizations, many software development teams are making use of a customized agile way of working approach. In this approach, certain specific practices, standards, and rules from Scrum, Kanban, XP, and Scrumban (and sometimes from few other agile frameworks too) are getting selected by them based on their own need. This makes their agile way of working more hybrid and custom-made.

> *"If you tell people where to go, but not how to get there,*
> *you'll be amazed by the results."*
> *- General George S. Patton*

The combination of Scrum and Kanban resulting in a Scrumban-based agile way of working approach is gaining more acceptance having its distinctive relationship with the principles of Lean Agile Software Product Development and Lean Thinking approaches. Teams are thinking and applying a thought process that they can start with Scrum and can optimize their agile way of working later from a certain moment, where the Scrum-based time boxed events are no longer required for them.

> *"If you have a choice of two things and can't decide, take both."*
> *- Gregory Corso*

This thought process has no formal meaning and there should not be any need for the same, as far as it is aligned with and not deviating from the values and principles given under the *Manifesto for Agile Software Development*. Scrum Teams are also making use of some of the required advanced engineering practices from XP Framework which are getting mixed with their Scrum-based agile way of working, as per their need and suitability. These advanced engineering practices help the agile software product development teams to improve their overall Technical Agility.

It is also true that, the amount at which these frameworks are getting mixed up cannot be evaluated and there should not be any need for the same, as far as it is aligned with and not deviating from the values and principles given under the *Manifesto for Agile Software Development*. Each agile framework has its own characteristics, thinking, practices, processes, standards, rules, structure, pros, and cons. It is the team who needs to decide on what kind of agile way of working they would like to have in place, based upon which they can go for a proper agile framework selection.

Scrum, Kanban, and Scrumban altogether can act as a wonderful trio when adopted by the agile software product development teams to establish and enhance their

Scrumban-based agile way of working. Teams need to make use of a combination of best practices belonging to both Scrum as well as Kanban, as per their own desires. Hence, the teams need to have a good grasp and understanding about both Scrum and Kanban in the first go. By combining Scrum and Kanban practices, by following the structure of Scrum, and by allowing the software development teams to get into the flexibility of Kanban (while implementing a Scrumban-based agile way of working) lets the team to expand their capabilities to continuously deliver the anticipated customer value-based outcomes.

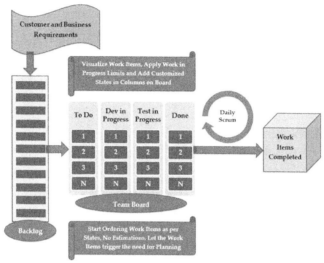

Figure 2.8: Scrum, Kanban, and Scrumban - The wonderful trio

Kanban asks the teams to visualize the workflow, whereas Scrum asks the teams to maintain transparency. Using Scrumban approach, the team needs to simply do the required needful for their work items to be placed on the tasks board to provide a good view of the flow of their work. Team using a board needs to embrace the WIP limits, which is a basic concept from Kanban. The team needs to become self-organizing and pull the work items during the Sprint. This approach discards pre-assignment of the work items. Team's commitment and focus needs to be improved by applying the WIP limits on the columns of the board.

Daily Scrum should give more emphasis on team's positioning, considering the overall progress of WIP work items along with the addressal of issues getting faced by the team. To avoid team members to collect the Tasks that they prefer, WIP limits help a lot. The team needs to have an anticipation from team members to come out of their comfort zone that removes the possibility of team members working in silos. WIP limits also ensure a consistent flow of work which asks team members to pick and start to work on the next set of work items when they are free. This approach encourages team members to do the knowledge sharing by making sure that they are encouraging themselves to learn and work on any of the work items and not on certain specific work items.

Within a Sprint, the team needs to start measuring how many work items they are completing every day and how much time is involved for them to complete the work items from the time at which they have started with them. Team needs to identify patterns, bottlenecks, and few other factors by looking at the columns on the board if work items are staying there for longer duration. This expects team to have knowledge sharing, cross skills training, and improving the overall flow of work on the board by adjusting the WIP limits and the board itself in terms of its structure.

> *"Scrum can be a useful scaffold to hold a team together while you erect*
> *a more optimized solution in place. At some point you can slough off the cocoon*
> *and allow the pull system to spread its wings and take flight."*
> *- Corey Ladas*

The team needs to make the process clear, so that all the team members have a clear idea about when a work item needs to be moved from one column to the next one, by properly representing its current state. The team needs to decide on a Definition of Done for each column of the board, using which the team members can validate the movement of work items from one column to other column on the board.

The team needs to have some explicit agreements to make sure that the work items are moving forward with substantial improvements in quality. The team needs to make use of customized columns with different states to list the work items under them. This approach helps the team members to embrace certain behaviors to build the high-quality working software product with continuously improving processes.

Kanban recognizes the importance of continuous improvement that is its main feature and known as Kaizen. It is a Japanese term with the meaning as *change for the better*. Scrum makes use of Sprint Retrospective Event as an indirect approach to inspect, adapt, and improve on team's overall performance considering various aspects of their own observations, reflections, feedbacks, and insights. Though this is the case, Scrum does not say that continuous improvement should be limited to Retrospectives only. Using a board, team can constantly check at the better ways to improve anything related to the board itself along with a way with which the work items can flow through the board.

Utilizing benefits of Scrum and Kanban resulting in a Scrumban-based agile way of working encourages the team to do experimentation and makes use of results to decide the measures to improve further. An evident difference between Kanban and Scrum is time-boxing. In Scrum, the team creates a balanced logic of urgency having time-boxed Sprints. In Kanban, the team needs to work on a continuous flow of work items represented under the columns on the board. In Scrumban, time-boxed Sprints can help an agile software product development team to set small goals to complete certain work items with the highest priority, as per their agreement with stakeholders. This approach does not need a separate Sprint Planning; hence the team needs to let the work items to trigger the need of planning which needs to be done on a high level and not too deep.

Team needs to make sure that the work items are assigned to the specific column based on their throughput. Throughput is generally based on the actual data to represent the number of work items on the team's board delivered by the team in each period. This metric assists the team to track their performance over time. If the team knows that they can complete XYZ number of work items per Sprint, then they need to make sure that, those XYZ number of work items are in place for the team to start and finish under their every Sprint. This approach maintains a just-in-time Product Backlog of all the prioritized work items.

Daily Scrum helps the team to increase their collaboration, collective ownership, and knowledge sharing. The team can have a Daily Scrum following a standard schedule. Planning always needs to be kept light; however, it should be a part of the entire workflow and not a separate activity. The team should not assign specific work items to specific team members at the time of Planning. They should rather look at ordering the work items under a dedicated column to be created as Ready for Development in between To Do and Development in Progress columns on the team's board. Team always needs to apply the WIP limits to each column on the board, as it acts as a key enabler for the pull-based system. No estimation for the work items is required to be done by the team; however, their focus should be always on prioritization and ordering. This helps the team to have a speedy planning, execution, and delivery.

Team needs to add a mechanism to pull the work items from one column to other column and align their development process accordingly. The work items need to be event-driven, where the team needs to be completely concentrating on adding, developing, testing, and delivering work items belonging to a new software product or an existing software product that has been already released to customers to address any enhancements. The Scrumban-based agile way of working approach always asks the team to cross-check on themselves on how they are responding to the overall structure of their Scrumban-based agile way of the working model in place. One might wonder to understand about in which environment or scenarios, the team can introduce such an agile way of working approach with Scrum, Kanban, and Scrumban - the wonderful trio. It is best suitable when a software development project/product has a possibility of unexpected changes to customer requirements further resulting in changing priorities of work items.

Scrumban works well with self-organizing and self-managing agile software product development teams, where they need to establish trust with their stakeholders and customers. It might take significant amount of time to set the clear expectations. The team needs to evaluate, act, and sometimes rework to achieve and fulfil those agreed expectations gaining trust from their stakeholders and customers. Once the trust is established, it becomes easy for the stakeholders to cherish a trustworthy feeling toward the team. The team needs to be engaged to achieve their agreed objectives and delivery excellence, where they need to continuously improve their agile way of working.

Points to remember

- Agile frameworks keep on evolving because they are incomplete and there is always a need to update their structure, design, and alignment. Hence, in the process of selection of an apt agile framework, selection process itself should be given a lower priority whereas, suitability for requirements, needs, and wants in accordance with the expected agile way of working of teams should be given the highest priority.

- The most commonly and widely used popular agile frameworks are Scrum, Kanban, Scrumban, XP, Lean, Crystal, DSDM, Feature Driven Development (FDD), and so on. Lean Agile Software Development is also a popular approach used by many organizations.

- As per the 14th Annual State of Agile Report, 'Scrum' is the mostly used agile framework by 58% organizations globally.

- Scrum, Kanban, XP, and Scrumban agile frameworks based agile way of working can be seen getting established, worked upon, and further enhanced by the agile software product development teams; however, it is important for them to understand the key differences in between these frameworks before they choose any of them to get started with.

- As per the State of Scrum Report, 94% respondents of the survey (done by Scrum Alliance resulting into the State of Scrum Report) have confirmed that they are making use of Scrum Framework in their agile software development practices. 97% respondents have approved that they would like to continue to make use of Scrum Framework in future. 78% respondents have given an affirmation on they would like to recommend Scrum to their colleagues, friends, and other professionals. The overall success rate of Scrum Projects has been calculated as 63%.

- Combination of Scrum and Kanban resulting in a Scrumban-based agile way of working approach is gaining more acceptance having its distinctive relationship with the principles of Lean Agile Software Product Development approach.

- Scrum, Kanban, and Scrumban altogether can act as a wonderful trio when adopted by the agile software product development teams to establish and enhance their Scrumban-based agile way of working.

In the next chapter, readers will get to know about an overview of Scrum Framework, which is the most popular, most commonly and widely used agile framework globally. Readers will also get an overall understanding about the structure and components of the Scrum Framework, using which an agile software product development team needs to establish a Scrum-based agile way of working. This approach helps them to deliver high-quality working software product, both incrementally and iteratively.

CHAPTER 3
Overview of Scrum Framework

Introduction

In this chapter, readers will get to know about an overview of Scrum Framework, which is the most popular and most commonly, widely used agile framework by the entire global software development community. They will also get to know about how they can establish and make use of a Scrum-based agile way of working to develop and deliver high-quality working software while recognizing the correlation between the Scrum Framework and its association with the values and principles from the Agile Manifesto.

Objective

After studying this chapter, you should be able to:

- Understand how the Scrum Framework has been evolved from its inception until now.
- Understand the Empirical Process Control Theory also known as Empiricism.
- Understand the Scrum Values.
- Understand the structure of the Scrum Team and its associated Scrum Roles.
- Understand the difference between Typical and Servant Leadership Styles.
- Understand the Scrum Artifacts.

- Understand the Scrum Events.
- Understand the Scrum Components along with the Scrum Team's Scrum-based Agile Way of Working.
- Understand some of the interesting facts about the Scrum Framework and its associated entities.

Henry 'The Agile Coach' (in a discussion with Roger 'The Scrum Master'):

"Hey Roger! So, how is your new Scrum Team doing? Hope you are helping them to get settled down. Feel free to get in touch with me in case of any challenges."

Roger 'The Scrum Master' (replying):

"Hi Henry! Yes, we are progressing well. We are coming up with a working agreement to establish our agile way of working soon. I was having some discussions with the team earlier today and it seems that they already know the basics of Agile and Scrum; however, I might need your help soon. I am planning to have a word with Ana. She is getting started with us as a Product Owner. I think, she is getting into this Role for the first time.

I was discussing with her yesterday. She looks to be a bit uncomfortable, when it comes to aligning our Scrum Artifacts using the online tool. She was complaining about the tool, as it looks to be a complicated one for her. I was answering her questions and I think she needs my help to understand the basic concepts of agile software development and delivery, as she is a novice Product Owner. To be honest, I was literally about to lose my patience, while discussing with her yesterday."

Henry (taking a pause to think and asking):

"Sorry, I didn't get you. What was the context of your discussion with her?"

Roger (smiling and answering):

"Ana was asking me about the first value of Agile Manifesto - Individuals and Interactions over Processes and Tools. She had a big concern regarding the usage of the tool. By making use of it, we are supposed to align and track our scrum Artifacts, mainly Product Backlog and Sprint Backlogs. She was having a confusion. She was saying that, if Agile Manifesto reveals that, individuals and interactions are more important than processes and tools, then why am I enforcing her and our team to make use of a tool to have our Scrum Artifacts in it?

She was having a misunderstanding, totally! I told her that Agile Manifesto asks the Scrum Team to give value to processes and tools; however, the expectation is, they should give more value to individuals and interactions. With my further explanation, I think now she got to know that processes and tools are acting as enablers to get the desired outcomes. Individuals and interactions are key drivers, who need to make use of those enablers to solve their problems by developing and delivering working software. I think you need to spend some time with me to share a proper understanding of Agile Manifesto with her. Let's discuss in next week."

Henry:

"Roger that! I will wait for your ask. See you soon!"

In today's scenario, while looking at the significance of digital and agile transformation being adopted by the global organizations, there are many individuals belonging to the global software development community praise agile software development, as they have their strong positive belief and results-oriented past experiences with the overall process of agile software development. The basic concept of agile software development using an agile framework-based way of working looks to be splendidly amazing to them; however, the Scrum Framework looks to be a bit diluted version of Agile Manifesto to them. This thought process might be in place because the Scrum Framework has been getting progressed since 2001 and it is still getting evolved, as per the required changes getting applied to its structure, as and when required.

"What's dangerous is not to evolve."
- Jeff Bezos

Teams doing agile software development following the values and principles from the Agile Manifesto (which was written back in 2001 and no changes were made in it since then) have seen many agile frameworks getting introduced and evolved over the period. They have a thought process that, the Agile Manifesto tries to portray the need of agile frameworks-based way of working for the software development teams, which has caused the formation of many agile frameworks. Be it Scrum, XP, or any other agile framework, there is always a change, modification, and customization getting embraced as a part of the overall structure, processes, practices, standards, and approaches associated with these agile frameworks.

There are many individuals belonging to the global software development community who also have a belief that the Agile Manifesto is now obsolete. Even though there is a disagreement on this belief, altogether with some different thought processes regarding the validity and applicability of Agile Manifesto. One can completely agree with the fact that teams can make use of any agile frameworks; yet the values and principles given in the *Manifesto for Agile Software Development* surely benefit them with an anticipation that, they are always focusing on customer value proposition and performing the delivery of high-quality working software by catering changing customer needs.

"Our maturity will be judged by how well we are able to agree to disagree
and yet continue to love one another, to care for one another,
and cherish one another and seek the greater good of the other."
- Desmond Tutu

The *Manifesto for Agile Software Development* remains intact and unchanged, making sure that the core values and supporting principles are still applicable to the entire world of agile software development and delivery. The *Manifesto for Agile Software Development* is always acting as a benchmark, baseline, guideline, and a standardized way to express agility to the software development teams to deliver working software using any of the agile frameworks, especially the Scrum framework.

Scrum is one of the most popular and most commonly, widely used agile frameworks to develop, deliver, and sustain complex software products. *Figure 3.1* shows the history behind its fascinating inception and overall progression:

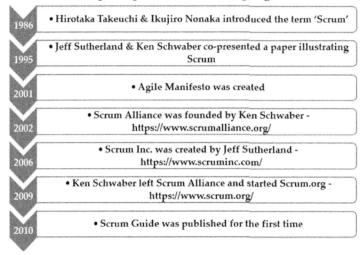

Figure 3.1: *History behind inception and overall progression of Scrum Framework*

In 1986, two Japanese experts - Hirotaka Takeuchi and Ikujiro Nonaka introduced the term 'Scrum' in the context of a different approach to manage a new way of product development. They published an article, *New New Product Development Game* (the word *New* mentioned twice is really a part of the title and more details about the same article can be found at **https://hbr.org/1986/01/the-new-new-product-development-game**) in the Harvard Business Review. They explained a brand-new approach to manage product development having an expectation to increase the speed and overall flexibility of product development process. Their motivation was originated from the case studies of some of the popular manufacturing organizations.

They called this approach as a holistic approach, as the whole process of software development and delivery using a Scrum-based agile way of working needs to be performed by a single cross-functional team across multiple overlapping stages. The team needs to be a team of individuals working toward a common objective and having different functional expertise and skills. This approach can be correlated with a rugby football game in which the teams playing the game try to chase the distance on the playground as a collective unit, while passing the ball back and forth.

Scrum was originated in 1986 by taking a reference of the case studies belonging to the automotive, photocopier, and printer domain-based manufacturing industries. Until that point of time, waterfall-style project management processes were well-established. As an agile framework, Scrum expanded the agile software development community to counter those waterfall-style project management processes. This approach started to promote the iterative and incremental way/thought process of agile software development and delivery under the global software development community.

Scrum Framework was also based on the research done by Ken Schwaber along with Tunde Babatunde at DuPont Research Station and the University of Delaware. Tunde recommended that the attempts to develop complex software products, that were not based on the concept of empiricism, that is, inspection, adaptation, and transparency were destined to have high risks and chances of failure, as the initial circumstances, beliefs, and assumptions about those complex software products might change over the time. Hence, the process of Empiricism by making use of a regular inspection, adaptation, and maintaining a proper transparency is a more suitable approach to develop the complex software products.

In the year 1990, Ken Schwaber used Scrum Framework at his company *Advanced Development Methods*, whereas Jeff Sutherland, John Scumniotales, and Jeff McKenna developed a similar concept at Easel Corporation, referring it as Scrum. Ken Schwaber and Jeff Sutherland worked together to incorporate their ideas into Scrum as a single framework. They validated it and continually improved the same. This approach gave them an opportunity to present it in a paper, published by them in the year 1995, to make their contributions to the *Manifesto for Agile Software Development* in the year 2001. It further caused the worldwide circulation and usage of Scrum as an agile framework to develop, deliver, and sustain the complex software products since the year 2002.

Scrum had an initial prominence on agile software development and delivery, though it has now been used in other domains such as research and development, sales, marketing, operations, human resources, and so on. In 1995, Ken Schwaber and Jeff Sutherland co-presented a paper illustrating the Scrum framework at the OOPSLA conference. Since then, the Scrum Framework is continuously evolving and they both have collaborated to combine their experience to develop and enhance its structure.

In the year 2001, Ken Schwaber worked with Mike Beedle to explain Scrum in the book *Agile Software Development with Scrum*. Scrum's lightweight and easy to understand structure and nature always helps the agile teams to plan and manage their product development specific agreed effort and associated processes. Scrum Framework follows a baseline document called as Scrum Guide which has been first published in the year 2010. It defines the Scrum Framework and has been revised several times by Ken Schwaber and Jeff Sutherland. Its latest version is always getting maintained. The Scrum Guide defines the overall structure of Scrum Framework by explaining Scrum Components - Scrum Values, Scrum Roles, Scrum Events, Scrum Artifacts, and Scrum Rules.

As per the Scrum Guide, Scrum is free, and it is offered in the Scrum Guide. It is a framework within which people can address complex adaptive problems, while productively and creatively delivering the products of the highest possible value. While looking at the Scrum Framework on a high level, it looks to be lightweight in terms of its structure and nature. It is also easy to understand, but when one starts to go deeper into understanding the thorough structure and nature of Scrum, one will surely find it as difficult to master. Scrum is neither a process nor a technique. It is neither a method nor a procedure.

Scrum does not tell software development teams about how to do things, rather it tells them about, what needs to be done by them and allows them to figure out how they want to do it on their own. Scrum is an agile framework within which one can make use of various kinds of processes, methods, and techniques, as per their own needs and suitability. Scrum helps software development teams to enhance the overall efficiency and effectiveness considering their product development, delivery, and management-specific processes.

By making use of the Scrum Framework, a continuous enhancement of the high-quality working software product (to be developed and delivered by the Scrum Team, who needs to make use of Scrum Framework for the same purpose), a continuous enhancement of the team itself, and a continuous enhancement of the working environment in which the team needs to develop and deliver high-quality working software product is done. Scrum can make the team confused sometimes, as it is not strict. This is because the Scrum Team needs to customize what Scrum Framework says to meet their needs and wants with varying contexts.

As per the structure of Scrum Framework, the Scrum Teams need to establish Scrum-specific components. These components are Scrum Roles, Scrum Events, Scrum Artifacts, and the Framework associated Scrum Rules. Every component within the establishment of a Scrum Team's Scrum-based agile way of working provides a certain purpose, which acts as a critical parameter for the use and expected success for the Team's Scrum-based agile way of working. It needs to be followed by them to develop and deliver high-quality working software products, both incrementally and iteratively. Scrum is a well-composed framework. All the components are required to be well-aligned, while establishing and enhancing Scrum-based agile way of working.

> *"Scrum is more about behaviour than it is about process."*
> *- Gunther Verheyen*

The structure of Scrum Framework describes various components using which the software development teams can be facilitated and can get some help in a less rigid manner. This helps them to create a Scrum Framework-based structure to perform frequent inspections and adaptations, also maintaining transparency. Scrum allows the teams to choose a possible set of choices for different approaches to make use of its structure and associated components. These choices need to be accepted by the teams as per their conditions and contexts. Scrum Rules act as an outer boundary within which these possible set of choices need to be explored and applied by the Scrum Teams.

Scrum Framework is established based on a theory called as Empirical Process Control Theory. It is also known as Empiricism. Empiricism emphasizes that the knowledge required to perform the development and delivery of high-quality working software products can be gained by software development teams using their past learnings and experiences to take the required decisions properly, based on what is known to them.

Scrum introduces an iterative and incremental approach using which the expected results can be optimized and risks can be controlled. It needs to be done through a proper applicable mitigation. Every implementation of empirical process control for Scrum Teams is based on three aspects which are inspection, transparency, and adaptation. As it can be seen in *Figure 3.2*, Empiricism encourages Scrum Teams to establish and enhance an agile way of working using Scrum, which always needs to be based on facts, evidence, experiences, and learnings:

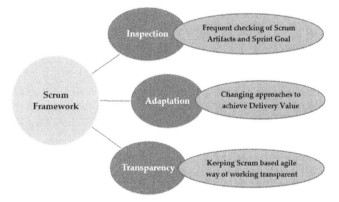

Figure 3.2: *Empirical Process Control (Empiricism) in Scrum*

Inspection has an anticipation from the Scrum Teams that each member of a Scrum Team must often inspect Scrum Artifacts and team's overall progress toward an agreed Sprint Goal to detect unwanted deviations during Sprints. Product Backlog, Sprint Backlog, and Increment are the three Scrum Artifacts. Sprint Goal is a set of objectives agreed by the Scrum Team which needs to be achieved during the Sprint. A Sprint is a time-boxed duration of one month or less than that during which the Scrum Team needs to develop and deliver working software, incrementally and iteratively. The inspection also has an anticipation that the frequent inspection of the Scrum Artifacts and the Scrum Team's overall progress during every Sprint needs to be done by the Scrum Team, but it should not be so frequent that, the process of inspection is acting as an obstacle for their Scrum-based agile way of working.

"Each reaction we have is there to inspect us and reveal our own nature to ourselves and for ourselves; it is never about others."

- *Bryant McGill*

Inspections are most advantageous when they are most of the times conscientiously performed by some experienced assessors such as the Scrum Team members. They need to perform timely checks to make sure that the Scrum Team is always on track and even if there are any deviations, they can do the needful to resolve those to move ahead. Inspections can be done by all the Scrum Team members, being a part of the Scrum Team.

It can be done for the software product under development, for the processes, practices, and techniques getting followed by the Scrum Team, and for the perspectives related to people in the Scrum Team who are contributing to develop and deliver working software product. Inspection is hence done to look, observe, evaluate, and seek for the continuous improvement of people, products, processes, and any other entities associated with the Scrum Team.

Adaptation has an anticipation from the Scrum Team that, if an assessor concludes that one or more aspects of a process under a Scrum Team's way of working is getting deviated out of its acceptable standards and limits causing undesirable outcomes, then the process getting used by Scrum Team needs to be altered and/or adjusted. Such modification must be done at the earliest to minimize any adverse impacts due to further deviation.

"It is not the strongest of the species that survives, nor the most intelligent.
It is the one that is most adaptable to change."
- Charles Darwin

Adaptation is the overall ability of the Scrum Teams to adapt based on their frequent observations, results, and highlights of the inspection (of products, processes, and people associated with the Scrum Teams) being done by them. Adaptation hence actually asks Scrum Teams to reflect and react on the continuous improvement aspect. Scrum Teams need to ask questions to themselves to perform cross-checks on, how they are performing? are they performing better than their yesterday's performance or not? are they seeing any continuous improvements under of their agile way of working or not?

Teams need to understand, analyse, and discuss on the results and observations of frequent inspections, so that they can propose, evaluate, and make use of certain action items, which will help them to decrease the total cost of ownership of delivery using an enhanced software quality, to improvise their faster time to market, to increase their return on investment (ROI) through value-focused delivery, and to improve the overall satisfaction of their customers, businesses, stakeholders, and of themselves too.

Scrum always recommends few formal events for the Scrum Teams, where the Scrum Teams need to perform inspection and adaptation for their product, processes, and people. These events are Sprint, Sprint Planning, Daily Scrum, Sprint Review, and Sprint Retrospective.

Transparency has an anticipation from the Scrum Team that, various important characteristics of the processes followed by the Scrum Team must be visible to all the intended and interested parties, who are involved in the complete process of development and delivery of working software product and to those who are responsible to come up with the outcome-based customer value delivery. Transparency needs those characteristics to be specified by a shared norm, so that the observers can communicate a shared understanding of what is being seen by them. Scrum Team needs to make use of a common language to explain all the applicable and appropriate intended and interested parties about the processes being used by them.

Those Scrum Team members who are executing the actual work during Sprints and those who are checking the subsequent increment (which needs to be an outcome-based customer value delivery) must share a common Definition of Done. This increases the transparency within Scrum Teams. With this approach, it also becomes easy for the team to make sure that they are completing the work and marking the same work as Done, only when the Definition of Done is properly achieved by them.

> *"People with vision master the ability to see through to the heart of issues and investments. They value transparency."*
> *- Robert Kiyosaki*

Transparency implies that the Scrum Teams should present their facts and their overall standing as it is, without any modifications and misrepresentations. All the intended and interested parties involved in the process of development and delivery of working software products should get a transparent view in accordance with each other to get to know about the overall progress. All the Scrum components, especially the Scrum Artifacts and their associated entities should be kept transparent in front of all of them, so that it helps them to establish and build a mutual trust. Transparency also helps them to have their focus, courage, and commitment to help, support, and notify each other in case of any risks, so that they can continuously resolve such risks. Using this approach, they can improve and progress together toward their common goals and objectives.

The whole Scrum Team needs to make every possible effort by taking a collective ownership, while collaborating with each other to achieve their shared goals and objectives. This approach also asks everyone in the team to reflect on no one is working in silos, while eliminating any possibilities and chances of one being a part of the team and having any invisible plans which are differing from the shared goals and objectives of the team. Transparency always needs to be the primary substantial feature in a Scrum Team's Scrum-based agile way of working and its associated processes. It needs to be evident to the entire Scrum Team. It needs to be reflected in their actions, activities, approaches, events, and artifacts, so that they can enact on deviations, if any. The Scrum Team always needs to be transparent about their own progress, processes, approaches, issues, risks, dependencies, failures, concerns, opinions, thought processes, consensus-based decision-making, and about all the entities because of which they think that their way of working is getting affected.

As shown in the following figure, there are five core Scrum Values. They are Commitment, Courage, Focus, Openness, and Respect. Scrum Teams need to live and follow these values to cause the presence of the three key aspects of Empiricism - Inspection, Adaptation, and Transparency. This creates and enhances trust within the Scrum Teams. They learn and discover these values as they get themselves aligned with Scrum Roles, Events, and Artifacts.

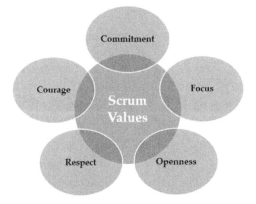

Figure 3.3: Core values of Scrum Framework

The value Commitment talks about perseverance in Scrum Teams. It is applicable to aspects like the behaviors to be displayed and the efforts, actions to be taken by the Scrum Teams. It is also applicable to the ultimate passion to be present in teams, where they need to be always committed to their constructive thoughts and actions.

"Stay committed to your decisions but flexible in your approach."
- Tony Robbins

Commitment has nothing to do with the outcome or result, as most of the times, it involves ambiguity and uncertainty. The expected outcome is also unstable, variable, and unpredictable for complex problems, getting addressed by the Scrum Teams while developing and delivering working software using Scrum in complex environments. Scrum Teams hence need to give their best, while having a complete commitment and dedication to achieve what they are committing during Sprints.

The value Focus talks about responsibility and accountability in Scrum Teams to enable themselves to focus on their expertise, both individually and collectively. Scrum Teams always need to focus on delivering customer/end-user value-based outcomes making their customers/end-users happy. Focus is a key driver to transform commitment into reality.

"I don't focus on what I'm up against. I focus on my goals and try to ignore rest."
- Venus Williams

The Sprint Goal asks teams to focus on the activities to be performed by them within a Sprint, so that they can contribute to make the best possible progress toward Sprint Goal. The Team needs to set the right focus on their work to get the right things done using the right approach. Time-boxed Scrum Events ask the Scrum Teams to focus on what is important now, leaving less important work which may become important in the future. Scrum Teams always need to understand that their focus determines their reality.

The value Openness talks about the transparency of and within the Scrum Teams. All the Scrum Team members need to inspect on what is their current state and position, so that it becomes easy for them to adapt and act accordingly.

"Openness may not completely disarm prejudice, but it's a good place to start."
- Jason Collins

The Scrum Team members need to be open-minded about their learnings, work, issues, problems, concerns, communication, and collaboration. They should be open to collaborate and to enhance their skills and capabilities. Open feedback sharing loops need to be used by them to learn from each other's feedback, which also helps them to continuously improve. Openness causes team members to offer and to seek help and support to and from each other. It opens a platform to discuss on their views, so that they can help each other in the process of decision-making. They can accept their mistakes and change their approach, if required. Openness makes sure that every Scrum Team member is getting heard by others in the team.

The value Respect talks about respecting the overall diversity within Scrum Teams. All the Scrum Team members should have respect for each other. Respect for each other's personal talents, skills, backgrounds, capabilities, strengths, weaknesses, thoughts, experiences, perspectives, and opinions is a must have for all the Scrum Team members.

"If you have some respect for people as they are, you can be
more effective in helping them to become better than they are."
- John W. Gardner

All the Scrum Team members also need to respect the Scrum Framework. They also need to respect their responsibilities while using it. While using a consensus-based decision-making approach, they need to respect the broader ecosystem controlling their individuality. Teams need to respect their customers and stakeholders by considering their ever-changing needs and their sponsors by reducing the features which are never getting used. They need to show respect by spending their valuable time and efforts only on those things that are valuable, required to be done, and to be implemented for their proper usability. They should show respect to their customers and users by fixing their problems, based on the outcome-based values and results of the development and delivery of high-quality working software.

The value Courage talks about showcasing the required courage, as and when it is required to be showcased by the Scrum Team members. It is mandatory for them to show the courage to support all the Scrum Values and all the Scrum Components.

> *"Success is not final; failure is not fatal. It is the courage to continue that counts."*
> *- Winston S. Churchill*

Team needs to understand that they need to have the courage to accept any decision, which has been taken in accordance with the process of frequent inspection and adaptation to be more transparent. Team should have the courage to say no to the things not adding any value. They should build only those features and functionalities under working software product, as per their customer needs. At the same time, they should also have the courage to accept the reality of ever-changing imperfect requirements of customers with an understanding that no plan is perfect to capture them. Team should have the courage to embrace the change while taking it as a basis of invention, creativity, encouragement, and value optimization.

The Scrum Team members need to have a courage to always be transparent by sharing the required information to help and collaborate with each other, to accept imperfections, so that they themselves can bridge the gaps together, to avoid delivering not completed working software products to their customers, to utilize Empiricism to apply time to time change-based approaches as and when required, to share any issues, to analyse any risks, to evaluate paths to succeed together, and to have everyone on the same page in terms of a common, shared understanding. The Scrum Team members need to show the courage to perform consensus-based decision-making, so that they can act and proceed to collaborate further. They also need to have the courage to change the decision if inspection recommends it, so that they can adapt and enact further.

A successful implementation, usage, and a continuous improvement of a Scrum Team's Scrum-based agile way of working completely depends upon the Scrum Team becoming more capable of living these five Scrum Values. Values act as a guiding path playing a significant role in the success of Scrum Teams, while directing them in terms of their plans, work, actions, behaviors, and decisions. Scrum Team members need to have a commitment to achieve the agreed and shared goals, both individually and collectively. They need to focus on the work getting committed by them under the Sprints. They need to give their 100% to achieve their agreed Sprint Goal crafted by themselves only.

The Scrum Team and its associated stakeholders need to have an agreement-based common, shared understanding, so that they can embrace openness by considering the planned and remaining work. They also need to be open about their challenges, risks, problems, and any other issues they come across, while performing the agreed work. They need to have enough courage to do the right thing at right time, while working on complex problems and while solving them. Scrum Team members always need to highly respect each other to establish healthy relationships and harmonized working culture based on an effective communication, collaboration, and teamwork.

As shown in the following figure, the Scrum Team consists of three Roles called as Scrum Roles. They are Product Owner, Developers, and Scrum Master. Roles need to complement each other to showcase collaboration and teamwork. By the definition of the responsibilities associated with these roles, Scrum fosters an agile mindset driven self-organization and self-management within the Scrum Teams. The Scrum Framework also has an anticipation from the Scrum Teams (especially from the Developers) that they need to be cross-functional.

Figure 3.4: *Scrum Team and Scrum Roles*

Self-organization within a Scrum Team implies that, the Scrum Team members need to establish their own Scrum-based agile way of working, using which they need to develop and deliver high-quality working software product without any external interference or command and control. Self-management within a Scrum Team implies that, the Scrum Team members themselves decide on who does what, when, and how, by taking care of all responsibilities to accomplish their goals, without expecting from anyone outside the team to direct them to do the needful while developing and delivering high-quality working software product.

A cross-functional Scrum Team has all the required competencies and skills sets to deliver the working software product without being dependent on others who are not the part of the Scrum Team. The structure of a Scrum Team always needs to be intended to enhance self-organization and self-management. By utilizing this structure, the Scrum Team needs to be more progressive and effective than their previous state to address more and more complex work, while delivering customer value and by taking care of feedbacks from customers using open feedback loops. Such outcome-based customer value delivery needs to ensure that the high-quality working software product is always up and running for its customers.

"Three bloody roles Scrum has, only three.
If you can't get that right, don't call it as Scrum, Okay?"
- Ron Jeffries

The Product Owner is the most important Scrum Role, who needs to work together with the rest of the Scrum Team members, while having continuous interactions with the stakeholders and the product management representatives to understand and recognize the most valuable work thoroughly, which needs to be further worked upon by the Developers. The Developers is another important Scrum Role of Scrum. Product Owner needs to have a trust while relying on the Developers who are solely responsible for the actual delivery of a potentially shippable software increment at the end of every ongoing Sprint.

Product Owner always has the responsibility to maximize the value of working software product getting developed and delivered by the Developers, whereas the stakeholders need to help and support the Scrum Team (all three Scrum Roles - Product Owner, Scrum Master, and Developers) to shape, structure, and formulate the working software product, as per the customer/end-user needs. This may vary a bit across Scrum Teams and across their Scrum-based agile way of working associated formal working agreement.

The Product Owner also has a key responsibility as a Value Optimizer to manage the Product Backlog. The Product Backlog is an ordered list of all the work items to be worked upon by the Developers. There are some activities specific to the Product Backlog Management which are required to be performed by the Product Owner along with the required help of Developers.

The Product Owner clearly needs to capture all the needs and requirements of the stakeholders and customers/end-user under the Product Backlog. Product Owner also needs to order the work items (which are also called as Product Backlog Items (PBIs)) under the Product Backlog to accomplish the goals and objectives of Scrum Teams in line with the customer value proposition. The Product Owner also needs to ensure that the Product Backlog is always visible, clearly defined, well-organized, well-maintained, and transparent to all, by showing what the Scrum Team is going to work on and by ensuring that the Developers have sufficient understanding of the Product Backlog.

The Product Owner is a single person and not a group of people, who needs to take care of the activities mentioned before or can have the Developers to do the needful; however, the accountability for those activities remains with the Product Owner only. The value optimization always needs to be a primary responsibility for the Product Owner.

"The Product Owner is inward facing, drives the sprints, and works with the team.
In these cases, the so-called product owner is little more than a product backlog item writer.
This approach reinforces old barriers, blurs responsibility and authority,
and causes handoffs, delays, and other waste."
- Roman Pichler

The Product Owner needs to capture and represent the needs of customers using PBIs under the Product Backlog. The prioritization of Product Backlog Items (PBIs) also needs to be done by the Product Owner by always giving an emphasis on customer/ end-user value optimization. The Scrum Team and their stakeholders must respect the Product Owner's decisions, to make them visible under the Product Backlog along with their prioritization. Only the Product Owner can ask the Developers to work on different sets of requirements.

The Developers is another important Scrum Role. Developers are nothing but the people or working professionals, who need to be committed to create any aspect of a usable, releasable Done product increment of a high-quality working software product to the customers at the end of every Sprint. They always need to achieve their agreed end-goal of delivering the product increments. Developers need to have interactions with each other, so that they can collaborate better, while choosing prioritized work items from the Product Backlog. With the selection of work items from the Product Backlog, they need to create required activities to be worked upon by them. They also need to have an overall understanding about their prediction to complete those activities, which needs to be reflected in the Sprint Backlog.

As a part of an ongoing time-boxed Sprint, the Developers need to perform re-planning of their work to boost their own outcome-based customer value delivery. This needs to be done by them daily, which needs to support the concept of Empiricism having an anticipation from every Developer to perform frequent inspections and adaptations. They need to contribute to develop and deliver a potentially releasable/ shippable increment of the high-quality working software product at the end of every Sprint.

In this process, if multiple Scrum Teams are getting involved then there might be a possibility that, this potentially releasable/shippable increment from each Scrum Team might have a need to be integrated with the increments of other Scrum Teams. All these Scrum Teams need to communicate, collaborate, and co-ordinate with each other to make sure that everything needed is in place.

"The benefit of allowing a team to self-organize isn't that
the team finds some optimal organization for their work that
a manager may have missed. Rather, it is that by allowing the team
to self-organize, they are encouraged to fully own the problem."
- Mike Cohn

The Developers always need to be self-organizing as well as self-managing, where they need to encourage their self-awareness and self-management by themselves only. They need to navigate their own work by keeping themselves motivated all the time, so that the potentially releasable/shippable "Done" increment of the high-quality working software product can be delivered at the end of every time-boxed Sprint. They also need to keep in mind that the most important aspects of continuous learning, continuous sharing after learning, and continuous improvement are must haves for them.

The Developers are solely responsible to construct the potentially releasable/ shippable Done increment for which they need to be self-managing. They also need to be continuously motivated and empowered by the organization's stakeholders and top management, so that they can plan, maintain, collaborate, communicate, co-operate, coordinate, and handle their work by themselves. Using such a motivation and support, the subsequent collaboration and harmonized teamwork can elevate their overall understanding, performance, productivity, efficiency and effectiveness.

The suggested size of the Scrum Team as per the Scrum Guide is 10 or fewer people. The Scrum Team always needs to be small and sufficient (in terms of its size) to support their Scrum-based simple, nimble, and flexible agile way of working, while establishing a better structure, positioning and alignment. The size of the Scrum Teams also needs to be sufficient to accomplish the substantial work to be taken up by them within their every ongoing Sprint. The Scrum Roles - Product Owner and/ or Scrum Master should be always excluded from the Developers, unless and until the Product Owner and/or Scrum Master are performing the actual work from the Sprint Backlog during their Sprints.

Having less Scrum Team members might reduce collaboration, interaction, and co-ordination impacting team's overall performance and productivity. This structure might also cause capabilities and skills-specific limitations, because of which the Developers might not be able to deliver the potentially releasable/shippable Done increment of working software product by the end of every Sprint.

On the other hand, having more Scrum Team members might create an unnecessary need for them to have an overloaded collaboration, interaction, and co-ordination, which might result into an additional overhead as a waste. Scrum Teams having more than 10 team members might also create bigger complications and chaos, which might have an unfavourable impact on the process of Empiricism.

The Developers always need to be cross-functional, self-organizing, and self-managing. By the means and anticipation of cross-functional Developers, they need to have all the required skill sets, capabilities, values, and behavioral aspects (both individually and collectively as a one team), which are necessary and helpful to develop and deliver the potentially releasable/shippable Done increment of a high-quality working software product by the end of every ongoing Sprint.

No specific titles and/or designations are required to be given to the Developers irrespective of what kind, genre, type, and classification of work is being performed by the individual Developers along with their specific skill sets and capabilities. The Developers always need to transform their well-prioritized, well-ordered, well-balanced, and well-estimated Product Backlog (which needs to be prioritized and ordered by the Product Owner, as per the value optimization of changing customer/end-user needs) into Sprint Backlog and finally into the potentially releasable increments based on the well-negotiated Sprint Goals agreed by the Product Owner for all the Sprints.

The individual Developers should not be a part of any sub-teams, no matter what competency (such as business analysis, design, architecture, development, testing, build, deployment, delivery, and so on) is being addressed by individual Developers or a specific group of Developers. The distinct Developers can have specific skills and competencies; however, all the Developers are entirely accountable for the delivery of product increments.

The Scrum Master is one more important Scrum Role, who is mainly responsible to support and promote the Scrum Framework. Scrum Master needs to help, guide, coach, and support the Product Owner and the Developers to understand the Scrum Framework, its structure, components, rules, values, and other aspects. Scrum Master needs to help the stakeholders and other associated people outside the Scrum Team by letting them know about which of their interactions with Scrum Team are adding value. Scrum Master also needs to eliminate unproductive interactions to maintain and increase the outcome-based value being delivered by Scrum Team. Scrum Master needs to be a Servant Leader. Servant Leadership plays an important role for the Scrum Master to succeed while serving the Scrum Team endlessly.

Servant Leadership is a phrase that was created by Robert K. Greenleaf in his essay that he had published in the year 1970. As per the essay," The *Servant Leader needs to be a servant first. A servant-leader focuses primarily on the growth and well-being of people and the communities to which they belong. While the traditional leadership generally involves the accumulation and exercise of power by one at the top of the pyramid, the servant leadership is different. The Servant Leader shares power by putting needs of others first, by helping people to develop and perform as highly as possible."* Following are the aspects, where the typical and servant leadership differs:

Typical Leadership	Servant Leadership
Leading others with an accumulation and exercise of power by one being at the top of the organizational hierarchical pyramid	Leading with influence by serving others, while mainly focusing on the growth and well-being of others
Focused on organizational objectives	Focused on serving the needs of others

Command and control over others	Lead to serve others with awareness, empathy, persuasion, and foresight
Less listening and more speaking	More listening and less speaking
Seeking Leadership as an opportunity to progress obtaining higher designations in organizational hierarchical pyramid	Seeking Leadership as an opportunity to serve and lift others, so that others can succeed first
Measuring success based on outputs-oriented delivery	Measuring success based on outcomes and customer value-oriented delivery
Promoting individual ownership more and collective ownership less	Promoting both individual ownership as well as collective ownership

Table 3.1: A comparison between Typical Leadership and Servant Leadership

The Scrum Master always needs to make use of the Servant Leadership style extensively, as he/she needs to serve the Product Owner, the Developers, and the Organization as a whole. Being a Servant Leader, the Scrum Master needs to understand that he/she needs to have a deep commitment to serve others. Scrum Master needs to imbibe active listening skills to understand what others are saying by giving a proper and a complete attention to others, by listening to thoughts, beliefs, opinions, intentions, views, emotions, and feelings of others and by reassuring an open feedback culture.

The Scrum Master always needs to take the highest level of accountability and responsibility for the actions, decisions, and overall execution of the Scrum Team and their agile way of working. The Scrum Master always needs to lead by example/ influence by demonstrating the values and behaviors which he/she expects to have/ see in others. He/she also needs to be devoted for the overall development and growth of the Scrum Team by offering them resources, using which they can strive for a relentless learning and improvement.

It is also required for the Scrum Master to be self-aware about his/her own values, beliefs, strengths, weaknesses, emotions, actions, reactions, and various other behavioural aspects, which might have an impact on others. He/she needs to perform a self-inspection to enact on any scope for improvement.

While encouraging others to be self-organizing and self-managing, to take the decisions, and to act on their own, the Scrum Master needs to make use of persuasion/ influence instead of command and control. He/she always needs to ensure that any decision-making is a collective, rationalized, and consensus based. The Scrum Master needs to look forward while being in line with the vision, goals, and objectives of the Scrum Team, while having both short-term and long-term focus on the bigger picture. By coaching the Scrum Teams on self-organization, self-awareness, and self-management, it is the core responsibility of the Scrum Master to act as a driving force for extreme ownership. The Scrum Master or a group of Scrum Masters need to create a sense of community within the organization by creating an Agile Center of Excellence (CoE) or a Community of Practices (CoP), where some socializing events can be organized by them to spread an awareness about Agile and Scrum-based agile way of working across the entire organization.

The Scrum Master always needs to be more empathetic valuing the viewpoints of others to have healthy discussions among them by considering both agreements and disagreements on anything under the team's Scrum-based agile way of working. This needs to be done before coming to any logical conclusion. The Scrum Master also needs to make sure that both Scrum Team and the other intended, interested parties involved in the process of iterative and incremental working software product development and delivery have a proper knowledge, a common, shared understanding, help, support, collaboration, and resources, as and when needed. Everyone within a Scrum Team always needs to be happy, satisfied, and equally involved by safeguarding that the important aspect of psychological safety is not acting as a concern for anyone belonging to the Scrum Team.

By inculcating inside and applying outside - the behaviors of Servant Leadership, the Scrum Master can surely expect to have a more committed and engaged Scrum Team by building a better rapport and a coherent relationship, both internally within the Scrum Team and externally with the stakeholders.

> *"Every great product owner needs a great scrum master."*
> *- Roman Pichler*

The Scrum Master needs to serve the Product Owner by ensuring that the goals, scope, and the domain of the software product to be developed and delivered are understood by the Scrum Team. The Scrum Master also needs to search for the methods to perform effective management of Product Backlog, by ensuring that the Product Owner knows about the effective arrangement and ordering of the Product Backlog with a proper value optimization. He/she needs to help the Scrum Team to understand the necessity of clear-cut, concise, and precise PBIs, with a better planning of the working software product to be developed and delivered by them by using the concept of Empiricism. The Scrum Master always needs to be aware of applying agility along with the better facilitation skills to be showcased during all the Scrum Events, as requested and/or required.

> *"As Scrum Masters, we should all value being great over being good."*
> *- Geoff Watts*

The Scrum Master also needs to serve all the Developers by coaching, teaching, helping, and mentoring them to be more self-organizing, self-managing, and cross-functional. The Scrum Master always needs to facilitate all the Scrum Events, as requested and/or required. He/she needs to assist the Developers to deliver high-value, high-quality working software products by removing any impediments occurring in their overall progress. An impediment can be anything such as an obstacle, issue, problem, dependency, and so on, which possibly slows down the progress of the Developers causing a delay and impacting their productivity. The Scrum Master also needs to act as a Coach for a novice Scrum Team, where there is always a need for them to know, apply, accept, and experiment the Scrum Framework.

> *"Great Scrum Masters are not solely focused on their teams*
> *but are able to build communities across the organization."*
> *- Sochova Zuzana*

The Scrum Master always needs to serve at the organization level by leading and coaching the organization (as an expanded horizon) for the purpose of Scrum Framework's acceptance and adoption. He/she needs to plan the overall Scrum-based execution and delivery of working software products within the organization, so that the entire organization can realize the importance of Scrum and Empiricism process-based delivery. This needs to be done by triggering the change, by increasing the competence of teams, by working with other teams, and by increasing Scrum's efficiency inside the organization in general.

The Scrum Artifacts are used to represent the work to be done and the customer value to be delivered by the end of every Sprint. They need to be aligned by maintaining the concept of Empiricism through transparency, inspection, and adaptation. The three Scrum Artifacts are the Product Backlog, the Sprint Backlog, and the Increment (also called as Potentially Shippable Working Software Product Increment). These artifacts specified by the Scrum Framework are explicitly intended to increase the overall transparency of all the details required to perform an incremental and iterative development and delivery of high-quality working software product, so that all the Scrum Team members and their Stakeholders can have a common, shared understanding of all the Scrum Artifacts.

> *"The beauty of artifacts is in how they reassure us we're not the first to die."*
> *- Simon Van Booy*

By visualizing the overall structure and workflow of the Scrum-based agile way of working of a Scrum Team and by keeping the Scrum Artifacts in mind, the Scrum Team needs to get to know about the tracking and tracing of the potentially shippable working software product increment and its associated implementations, as they get created, prioritized, ordered, planned, developed, and delivered by the end of every Sprint. The Scrum Team needs to have a common, shared understanding of the work to be done by them, which needs to be tracked under Scrum Artifacts. While achieving the agreed Sprint Goal, if any change occurs, the Scrum Team needs to capture all the details under the Scrum Artifacts. The Scrum Team members require such details to work on and to keep moving ahead.

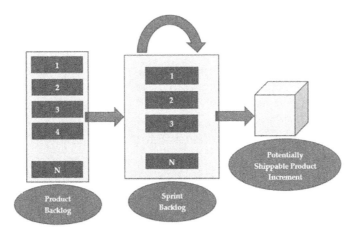

Figure 3.5: Scrum Artifacts

The Artifact Product Backlog tells the Scrum Team about what needs to be worked upon by them in the upcoming Sprints. Product Backlog is an ordered list of everything which needs to be known and to be used for the development and delivery of the high-quality working software product by the Scrum Team. It always needs to act as a single source of all the requirements, enhancements, and any changes required to be done to the working software product. It is the responsibility of the Product Owner and Developers to maintain and manage the Product Backlog by making sure that it is well-organized, well-described, well-prioritized, well-estimated, and well-evolving. The Product Backlog also needs to be available to get it visualized by anyone in the Scrum Team at any given point of time.

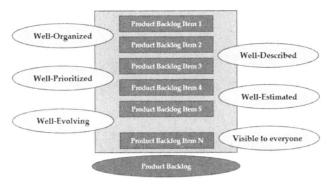

Figure 3.6: Product Backlog

The Product Backlog always needs to record all the requirements, features, functionalities, specifications, use cases, major and minor enhancements, research/ analysis-specific activities, bug fixes, and so on, under the Product Backlog Items (PBIs)/User Stories representing the new functionalities and/or the changes required to be implemented for the working software product, so that all of them can be released to the customers/end-users. The PBIs are the individual elements forming the Product Backlog. It is optional but good to have the PBIs with attributes such as summary, description, goal, business/customer value, estimate, and order, as per the anticipated customer value. PBIs can also include all the details about the tests to be performed, using which the Developers can validate them against the expected behaviors. If they are working fine, they can be marked as Done. The entire Scrum Team needs to be a part of Backlog Refinement to perform creation, organization, refinement, prioritization, and estimation of PBIs. There always needs to be a collaborative effort in between the Product Owner and the Developers during such refinements.

When the customers start to make use of the working software products, they start providing feedbacks. With such feedbacks, the Product Backlog starts to expand resulting into a more comprehensive list. As customer needs are ever-changing, the Product Backlog always needs to act as a live artifact. The changes in terms of customer value optimization considering the customer requirements and technology advancements further affect the Product Backlog making it incomplete. The Scrum Team hence needs to understand this and construct their initial Product Backlog with the best possibly understood requirements. The Product Backlog needs to keep on continuously advancing, as the team delivers the working software product. It also needs to get continuously advanced every release by release. It always needs to be aligned with the constant changes to bridge the gaps in the working software product, making both Product as well as the Product Backlog itself more reasonable, applicable, and valuable.

The PBIs always need to have sufficient details for the Scrum Team to analyse, evaluate, and discuss about them. PBIs having high priority need to be well-organized with better details and their context needs to be well-described. As the Product Backlog keeps on evolving, it becomes easy for the team to create, update, and remove the PBIs once they get to know about any changes in the customer requirements. Progress of such a dynamically evolving Product Backlog should be measured using a Product Goal. The Product Goal always needs to act as a complete commitment to safeguard and to drive the overall vision, transparency, and focus of the Scrum Team by describing a possible future state of the Product being worked upon by them.

While having an anticipation from the Product Owner to organize the Product Backlog, the PBIs with a high value and a high priority always need to be placed at the top of the Product Backlog and those with a lower value and priority always need to be placed at the bottom of the Product Backlog. PBIs should be well-prioritized and well-estimated using at least some rough estimates. The Developers need to give some rough estimates considering the overall effort involved to accomplish every PBI using a consistent measure, which needs to be commonly decided and agreed by them. The PBIs in the Product Backlog always need to be ranked based on their customer/end-user value proposition and the Scrum Team needs to achieve deliberate goals through them. Sometimes, a working software product is being developed by multiple Scrum Teams. In this case, there always needs to be a single Product Backlog to describe the upcoming work to be worked upon those multiple Scrum Teams under their respective upcoming Sprints.

The Product Backlog Refinement is a continuous activity that needs to be conducted by the Scrum Team, where they can add the details, perform estimations, and prioritize/order the PBIs. It needs to be done constantly, where the Product Owner and the Developers need to collaborate and co-ordinate on populating the details after reviewing and revising the PBIs to make the Product Backlog well-organized, well-described, well-prioritized, well-estimated, well-evolving, and completely visible to everyone. The PBIs need to be revised by the Product Owner with the help of Developers, if needed and at any time; however, such a refinement should not consume a lot of the total capacity of the Developers under any of their Sprints.

Refinement needs to be done, so that the PBIs can be considered as ready to be selected by the Developers in the Sprint Planning Event. Once they are selected, there is an anticipation from the Developers that they need to be fully completed and to be marked as Done within the time-boxed Sprints. The Product Owner and the Developers always need to keep the Product Backlog transparent by performing the frequent Product Backlog Refinements. The overall responsibility of estimation of PBIs needs to be taken up and owned by the Developers, where the Product Owner can influence them. Product Owner needs to help them to understand the PBIs by performing trade-offs; however, the Developers (who solely need to perform and deliver the work getting tracked under PBIs within Sprints) need to perform the estimation.

During the Sprint Review, the Product Owner also needs to chase the Developers for the left-over work from the latest Sprint. By comparing the amount of work left over, the Product Owner needs to evaluate the overall progress of Developers to safeguard that they are accomplishing their anticipated work by the required time. Stakeholders need to be all aware about all of this. The Scrum Team can also make use of various practices such as burn downs, burnups, or cumulative flows to forecast their progress, but it is important for them to understand that they are not supposed to substitute the significance of Empiricism while making use of such practices. The overall process of working software product development using Scrum-based agile way of working is a complex process under complex ecosystems, where there is always some uncertainty and risk involved. Hence, by making use of the process of Empiricism and based on what has already happened in the past, the Scrum Team always needs to perform a progressive, rational, justified, consensus-based, and a sense-making oriented decision-making.

The Artifact Sprint Backlog (as a subset of the Product Backlog) always tells the Scrum Team about the work, which needs to be worked upon by the Scrum Team under an ongoing Sprint to which that specific Sprint Backlog belongs to. It is a collection of PBIs selected by the Developers during the Sprint Planning Event of the upcoming Sprint.

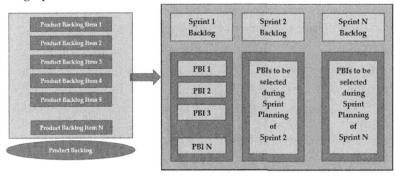

Figure 3.7: Sprint Backlog

The Sprint Backlog always need to contain a blueprint of the potentially releasable working software product increment to be delivered at the end of the Sprint. It needs to be done by recognizing the Sprint Goal. It is a goal or an objective, which needs to be decided by the Developers by having an agreement with the Product Owner at the time of Sprint Planning. It needs to be achieved by them within the Sprint. It is representing a prediction about what all functionalities belonging to the working software product will be delivered by the Developers as a part of their next product increment, along with the actual work which is required to be done by them to convert those functionalities into a Done product increment. Hence the work and the associated activities for the Developers to achieve the Sprint Goal should be visualized in the Sprint Backlog.

The Sprint Backlog needs to act as a plan with sufficient details about the work in progress, which needs to be understood by the team by making use of Daily Scrum Event. The Sprint Backlog can be modified by the Developers during an ongoing Sprint. This makes it more emergent, as the Sprint progresses. The Developers need to keep on working, while exploring and learning more about the work, which is required to accomplish the agreed Sprint Goal. Developers always need to be in line with the Product Owner. This helps them to add, update, and remove the PBIs constituting the Sprint Backlog. They need to update the estimated left-over work while the work is being performed or being completed by them. The complete authority to change the Sprint Backlog during an ongoing Sprint needs to be with the Developers in an alignment with the Product Owner.

> *"If you tell the truth, you don't have to remember anything."*
> *- Mark Twain*

The Sprint Backlog always needs to be extremely evident and transparent. It always needs to act as a single source of truth containing all the work that needs to be done by the Developers, so that they can visualize, evaluate, plan, select, and achieve the same during an ongoing Sprint. Sprint Backlog can also have some improvements to be worked upon by the Scrum Team, which were identified by them only in their previous Sprint Retrospective Event. However, it is not mandatory to have them. Though it is not mandatory, they still can be looked and worked upon by them to address the scope for continuous improvement.

During an ongoing Sprint, the total left-over work under the Sprint Backlog can be consolidated. The Developers need to be responsible to analyse, evaluate, and track the Sprint Backlog at the time of Daily Scrum Event, so that they can understand and anticipate the probability of achieving the Sprint Goal. Developers also need to manage their own progress by performing some frequent follow-ups regarding the left-over work from the Sprint, while it is in progress. The concept of *Start finishing existing work from Sprint Backlog, stop starting any new work from Sprint Backlog* needs to be rigorously followed by the Developers, so that it acts as a Work in Progress limit for them. They also need to have their full focus and commitment to complete their work. Cross-functional Developers clearly help themselves to co-ordinate and convert the Sprint Backlog into a working software product increment.

The Artifact Increment, which is also known as the Product Increment always asks the Scrum Team about what work the Scrum Team has completed by the end of the current Sprint along with how it is done by them. At the end of every Sprint, the potentially shippable/releasable Done increment of a working software product must be released by the Developers after an acceptance from the Product Owner, making sure that they have what they need in place. The potentially shippable/ releasable increment of a working software product is always a collection of all the PBIs completed during a Sprint along with the value of the increments of all the previous Sprints.

The Scrum Team needs to have a Definition of Done which needs to be agreed upon by themselves only. It needs to consider a set of items as a checklist against which every PBI needs to be evaluated and validated. This checklist must be completed by them before any of the PBIs are accepted by the Product Owner and marked as Done. Fulfilling this checklist means that every PBI must be having a fully functional working condition and meeting the Definition of Done defined by the Scrum Team.

Everyone needs to have a clear understanding of what is the agreed Definition of Done, so that a transparency to mark the PBIs as Done can be ensured. The Definition of Done also helps the Developers to get to know about how many PBIs they need to select during the Sprint Planning Scrum Event. If the Definition of Done for a Product Increment is getting followed by the Scrum Teams, it needs to be established as an expectation from all the Scrum Team members, where they must follow it as a minimum. If it is getting followed partially, then they must define the same by considering the working software product, as per its suitable applicability for them.

If the working software product is being worked upon by the multiple Scrum Teams, then all the Developers belonging to all the Scrum Teams must define the

Definition of Done together. This helps them to have a collaborative understanding. They always need to make sure that, each new individual Product Increment along with all the previously delivered Product Increments, altogether are working as per the agreed expectations. Definition of Done always needs to be enhanced with a criterion to address more value-added and higher quality-focused customizations, as the Scrum Teams get mature over the period. The working software product getting developed and delivered by the Developers always needs to be associated with its proper Definition of Done, which needs to serve as a guideline for any work being performed by the Developers.

By following the Definition of Done, the Product Increment always needs to act as a consolidation of an inspectable, completed work and as a collection of completed PBIs toward the end of the Sprint. The Product Increment of a high-quality working software product always needs to be developed and delivered in a fully functional working condition and it should not be dependent on the decision of Product Owner to release it to the customers/end-users or not. It always needs to be a direct action toward the agreed Sprint Goal, which always needs to be collaboratively achieved by the entire Scrum Team.

As transparency is one of the key pillars of Empiricism, it is crucial for the Scrum Team to maintain transparency for the Scrum Artifacts as well. Having the Scrum Artifacts properly established creates an ask for the Scrum Team to retrospect on themselves, where their own choices (to boost the outcomes and customer value-based delivery by controlling possible risks) need to be made by themselves. This needs to be based on the real identified state of the Scrum Artifacts. There is a possibility that, if the Artifacts are not as much transparent as they are expected to be, then the choices being made by the Scrum Team may get wrong. This also has an impact on the customer value getting delivered by the end of every Sprint. It might get devalued and might further increase the potential risk of low/no acceptance.

It is hence a collective responsibility of the Scrum Master, the Product Owner, the Developers, the Stakeholders, and all the other interested parties to understand and address the need of transparency for the Scrum Artifacts. The Scrum Master needs to guide and help everyone to have a complete transparency of all the Artifacts and their contents. By performing a frequent inspection of the Artifacts, by identifying, detecting, and understanding the patterns inside their contents, by listening to what an individual and the team is saying, and by perceiving the gaps in between the expected and actual results, the Scrum Master needs to act proactively, so that a complete transparency under the Scrum Artifacts can be achieved. It always takes a significant amount of time for him/her to communicate, co-ordinate, co-operate, and collaborate with the team to have an expected transparency of Scrum Artifacts.

The Scrum Events are the ultimate opportunities for the Scrum Team, where they can have an open communication and information sharing along with the proper presence of Empiricism to help themselves while working together closely, collaboratively, and efficiently; also improving their knowledge to become more efficient, effective, and mature, as they progress ahead. The five Scrum Events are Sprint, Sprint Planning, Daily Scrum, Sprint Review, and Sprint Retrospective:

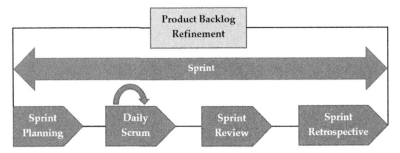

Figure 3.8: Scrum Events (except Product Backlog Refinement)

The Scrum Team always needs to make use of Scrum Events under their Scrum-based agile way of working to have a consistency in their performance. This also helps them to reduce the unnecessary discussions out of the Scrum Framework's Structure. Every Scrum Event is a time-boxed event associated with a maximum time duration and it needs to be followed by the entire Scrum Team. The team always needs to utilize every Scrum Event as an official opportunity given to them to inspect, adapt and enact.

Duration for the Scrum Event Sprint is fixed which cannot be reduced or extended; however, the other Scrum Events may come to an end once the desired objective of those events is accomplished by the Scrum Team. Scrum Team members need to safeguard themselves for the aspect of time spent, which should be proper and eliminating any kind of waste with the associated procedures. Sprint acts as a container entity for all other Scrum Events. All the Scrum Events always help the Scrum Teams to enable and foster inspection and adaptation by making their agile way of working more transparent. If the Scrum Team ignores the presence, inclusion, and importance of the Scrum Events, it always results into an ambiguity, further reducing the overall positive impact of Empiricism.

The Scrum Event Sprint is also called as the crux/heart of the Scrum Framework. It is a time-box of one month or less than that, within which a fully developed, tested, workable, potentially releasable, shippable, done high-quality working software product increment is delivered by the Scrum Team. Sprints need to have a reliable time-boxing, in accordance with the overall development and delivery efforts needed. Sprint always acts as a container entity which includes Sprint Planning, Daily Scrums, Development work (to be performed by the Developers), Sprint Review, and Sprint Retrospective. The following figure shows a high-level comparison in between the Waterfall Model-based Software Development and the Scrum Framework-based Software Development:

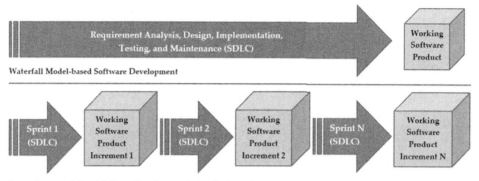

Figure 3.9: *Waterfall Model-based Software Development*
v/s
Scrum Framework-based Software Development (using the Sprints approach)

The traditional Waterfall Model-based software project development and its delivery is a stage-based sequential method, which delivers the working software at the very end of the project. On the other hand, Scrum Framework-based software product development and its delivery has an anticipation from the Scrum Team that, they are delivering a potentially shippable product increment of a high-quality working software in a frequent manner following an iterative and incremental delivery approach. Under this approach, each iteration needs to be treated as a Sprint. The working software product hence keeps on enhancing incrementally after each Sprint, where the Developers need to follow the complete and proper Software Development Life Cycle (SDLC) during every Sprint, as per their customized needs.

The Scrum framework always ensures that the complex software product development work is getting divided into simple fragments for which the organizations need to have dedicated Scrum Teams. This approach has an impact on the success of their software products. By developing and delivering the working software products iteratively and incrementally, organizations can deliver their products as services offerings to their customers faster and effectively. In this process, the customer feedbacks need to be received and incorporated frequently. By giving an emphasis on a fact that the outcome-based customer value delivery to be done by the Scrum Teams always needs to be moulded with the feedbacks received and not based on any false assumptions done by themselves. This also provides a platform for the Stakeholders and the Customers to get closely engaged and collaboratively connected with the Scrum Teams.

The Scrum Team needs to start a new Sprint immediately after the previous Sprint comes to an end. During an ongoing Sprint, the Scrum Team needs to make sure that there should not be any changes being made during an ongoing Sprint that might act as a risk to achieve the Sprint Goal. Even if any changes are being made, they need to be negotiated in between and handled by the Product Owner and the Developers. The Scrum Team also needs to keep an eye on the overall quality and its associated parameters, so that the quality does not get compromised. Also, as the Scrum Team proceeds and gets to know more after doing their analysis, exploration, research, and development about the work to be completed by the end of an ongoing Sprint, the scope of the work can be clarified, refined, compromised, and re-negotiated, where there always needs to be a consensus in between the Product Owner and all the Developers.

Scrum Team always needs to take every Sprint as a project, which can be of one week or two weeks or three weeks, taking less than one month's time duration. By the end of every ongoing Sprint, the Scrum Team needs to achieve their deliverables based on the agreed Sprint Goal. It needs to consist of what needs to be developed and delivered by them along with an adaptable plan. The Definition of Done for the PBIs/User Stories might get changed when the duration of Sprint is a longer one. This results into a probability of things getting developed and delivered with an increased uncertainty, complexity, risks, dependencies, and an overall scope. In this case, Empiricism always needs to guarantee that every Sprint is enabling a certainty of the Scrum Team's progress toward the Sprint Goal.

Every Sprint always needs to have the Sprint Planning Event before it starts, where the work to be performed under the Sprint needs to be planned by all the Scrum Team members. Once the Sprint starts and it progresses, the Daily Scrum Event always needs to be in place, where the Developers need to inspect, adapt, and enact on their daily progress against the PBIs/User Stories getting worked upon by them. The Sprint Review Event always needs to be held toward the end of the Sprint to inspect the potentially shippable working software product increment and to adapt the Product Backlog, if required. The Sprint Retrospective Event also always needs to be held toward the end of the Sprint, which is an opportunity for all the Scrum Team members, where they can inspect on any problems and issues occurring during the ongoing Sprint and adapt, enact with all the possible solutions along with any improvements to be worked upon by themselves in near future. This is how the Scrum Event Sprint always needs to act as a container event entity for all other Scrum Events. There always needs to be consensus on how all the Scrum Team members would like to utilize their planned Sprints.

The Sprint can be terminated before its time-box is over, where the authority of its cancellation always needs to remain with the Product Owner only. This can be done by the Product Owner under an agreed influence of Stakeholders, Developers, and Scrum Master. The Sprint may get cancelled if the Sprint Goal associated with that Sprint becomes outdated or obsolete. This may happen if the organization changes its direction or if there are any drastic changes in the marketplace conditions and/or in terms of the technological advancements for the technology getting used by the Developers. The Sprint needs to be terminated if the work which is being worked upon under an ongoing Sprint is not making any sense based on its associated entities and conditions. The cancellation happens hardly ever, since the Sprint always needs to be of short duration; typically, less than one month's time.

If the Sprint gets terminated, all the completed Done PBIs are required to be reviewed by the Product Owner. The Product Owner needs to accept the work if it can be said as potentially releasable. The Developers need to re-estimate all the incomplete PBIs/ User Stories, so that they can be moved back to the Product Backlog from the ongoing Sprint's Sprint Backlog. They can be re-investigated by the Scrum Team later, at the time of next Product Backlog Refinement. Cancellation of a Sprint is ideally an uncommon/ rare situation, after which the whole Scrum Team needs to re-plan everything under a separate Sprint Planning Event. They need to start another Sprint to address this change, while having a formal agreement with their external Stakeholders.

The Scrum Event Sprint Planning expects from the Scrum Team that, they should plan the work, which needs to be performed by them in an upcoming Sprint for which the Sprint Planning is happening. They need to do such planning by including the collaborative work of the whole Scrum Team. It always needs to be a time-boxed event for a time duration of maximum of eight hours for a typical Sprint of one month. This time duration needs to be shorter for the shorter Sprints. It is the responsibility of the Scrum Master to have it scheduled, to keep it within the said time-box and to make sure that, all the participants are having a proper understanding of its purpose.

During the Sprint Planning Event, all the Scrum Team members need to decide on the work they need to deliver as a part of the Product Increment by the end of the upcoming Sprint. This is specific to which work-specific PBIs from the Product Backlog are required to be delivered by them and how they are going to deliver the Product Increment. They need to have a plan for what needs to be done by them during the upcoming Sprint. The Developers need to anticipate the PBIs from the Product Backlog to be developed during the Sprint, along with an agreement with the Product Owner. Only those PBIs should be considered, where if the Developers can complete them in a Sprint, it can be said that they have achieved the Sprint Goal. Product Owner and Developers need to discuss on the Sprint Goal, which needs to be achieved by the Developers by the end of the Sprint. During the Sprint Planning, all the Scrum Team members need to collaborate to understand and to finalize the work to be done in the upcoming Sprint.

Figure 3.10: Sprint Planning

Sprint Planning needs to make use of the Product Backlog as a primary input. During the Sprint Planning, the Scrum Team also needs to consider and refer to previously completed Product Increment, expected capacity of Developers during the upcoming Sprint, and the earlier performance of Developers.

The Developers need to decide on how many PBIs they are willing to select from the visible, well-ordered, and well-prioritized Product Backlog to the Sprint Backlog under the upcoming sprint, which needs to be evaluated, known, and decided based on an agreement with the Product Owner. They also need to define the Sprint Goal, which is an objective to be achieved by performing the development and delivery of PBIs/User Stories within an ongoing Sprint. The Sprint Goal always needs to be formulated as the first output of Sprint Planning, which needs to help the Developers to understand the purpose behind every working software product increment which they are implementing by the end of every Sprint.

During the Sprint Planning Event, the Developers also need to decide on how they are going to evaluate, select, and perform the actual work in terms of the PBIs/User Stories under their upcoming Sprint. They also need to decide on how they will be converting those PBIs/User Stories into a potentially releasable Done working software product increment, after defining a well-negotiated, agreed Sprint Goal and choosing the required PBIs/User Stories from the Product Backlog into the Sprint Backlog.

The Sprint Backlog always needs to be formulated at the time of Sprint Planning Event. It always needs to contain the PBIs/User Stories which are selected by the Scrum Team to be worked upon by them under their upcoming Sprint, along with the high-level plan to develop and deliver those PBIs/User Stories. The Developers need to follow the agreed Software Development Life Cycle specific activities to perform the work, which is required to convert the selected PBIs into a potentially shippable working software product increment. The amount of work having differing variations, sizes, and effort estimations need to be properly planned by them. The work represented by the PBIs/User Stories and to be taken under the Sprint Backlog during Sprint Planning always needs to be sufficient for the Developers, for which they need to self-organize, collaborate, and carry it out along with any changes required in the upcoming Sprint.

> *"Planning is everything. Plans are nothing."*
> *- Field Marshal Helmuth von Moltke*

For an appropriate selection of prioritized PBIs/User Stories and any required clarification for them, the Product Owner needs to help the Developers by doing some flexible trade-offs. If there is a need of re-negotiation for the Developers because of any overload or inadequate work, they need to discuss with the Product Owner for the same. Any Subject Matter Experts to guide on technical and/or functional aspects of work can be also invited by the Developers for the Sprint Planning Event.

During the Sprint Planning, the Sprint Goal is also required to be created, which needs to be an agreed goal/objective-oriented collection of entities to be achieved by the Developers under the upcoming Sprint by performing the implementation of PBIs/User Stories taken by them under the Sprint Backlog for that Sprint. Developers always need to look at their agreed Sprint Goal by always keeping it in their mind. It always needs to show them a path about why and what they are developing and delivering under the next Product Increment. The PBIs/User Stories selected under the Sprint Backlog should be targeted by the Developers to achieve a single and comprehensible purpose of bringing in delivery of the highest important customer value. By looking at the agreed Sprint Goal, Developers need to understand the same and collaborate with each other by showcasing a collective ownership rather than working in silos.

The Scrum Event Daily Scrum is an exclusive opportunity given to the Developers, where they need to inspect, adapt, and enact on their daily progress for PBIs/User Stories being worked upon by them under an ongoing Sprint. It needs to be a daily event time boxed as 15 minutes under an ongoing Sprint for the Developers. Developers need to plan their work for the next 24 hours, which helps them to boost their communication, collaboration, and performance. The Daily Scrum needs to be conducted every day at the same time and same place to ease the sophistication, where the Developers need to inspect their own work in progress, as compared to the previous Daily Scrum. Developers also need to make use of the Daily Scrum Event to inspect their overall progress toward the Sprint Goal, along with how their progress is happening to accomplish the work taken by them under the Sprint Backlog.

The possibility of Developers accomplishing their agreed Sprint Goal is supported by the Daily Scrum. They need to retrospect daily to understand how their individual and collective ownership is getting utilized by the virtue of themselves, while acting as a self-organizing and self-managing team to achieve their agreed Sprint Goal. They always need to have a proper anticipation of the development and delivery of a potentially shippable high-quality working software product increment by the end of ongoing Sprint.

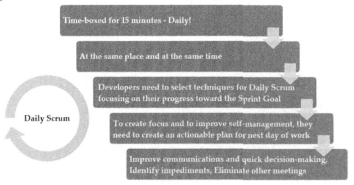

Figure 3.11: *Daily Scrum*

Developers need to understand and formulate the overall composition of Daily Scrum Event, which needs to be organized in such a way that, it should aim at the overall progress of the Developers to accomplish their agreed Sprint Goal. The Scrum Master is always responsible to guarantee that the Developers are having the Daily Scrum Event daily, by teaching them to keep it within a time-box of 15 minutes; however, the Developers are solely responsible for having/conducting the Daily Scrum. They always need to have a discussion under their Daily Scrum by following a time-box of 15 minutes.

During their Daily Scrum, the Developers can select and use an appropriate structure and some effective techniques to focus on their progress toward the agreed Sprint Goal and to produce an actionable plan for the next day of work. This approach always helps them to create a focus, to improve their self-management, communication, quicker decision-making, to identify impediments, and to subsequently reduce the need for other meetings. If the Developers need to have specific discussions about impediments, they need to have them separately after the Daily Scrum Event. The Daily Scrum Event is not the only the time where the Developers need to be allowed to adjust their plans. Instead, they should often meet throughout the day to have more detailed discussions to adapt and/or re-plan the rest of their work during the Sprint.

The Daily Scrum always needs to be conducted as an internal meeting for the Scrum Team. If anyone else other than the team is present, it is the responsibility of the Scrum Master to make certain that others are not interrupting the Daily Scrum.

Daily Scrum is certainly helpful for the Developers. They can improve their interactions, communication, decision-making, and knowledge sharing. They can also reduce/remove the need of other meetings. It helps them to highlight their impediments, issues, and concerns in the process of development and delivery of working software product, so that they can overcome such impediments. Daily Scrum always needs to make use of Empiricism, where the Developers need to perform an inspect and adapt activity, that too daily.

The Scrum Event Sprint Review needs to be held at the end of the Sprint, where the Scrum Team needs to inspect the Product Increment and adapt the Product Backlog, if required. Sprint Review needs to be an informal event and it should not be a formal status meeting. The overall representation of the Product Increment during the Sprint Review needs to have an anticipation from the Scrum Team to have responsibility, accountability, and ownership by stimulating the feedback and by nurturing the collaboration with their stakeholders.

Figure 3.12: *Sprint Review*

At the time of Sprint Review, by establishing and channelising a proper co-ordination and collaboration with the Product Owner and the Scrum Master, the Developers always need to develop and deliver an optimized customer value through the development and delivery of high-quality working software product. They need to showcase it as a potentially shippable product increment to their Stakeholders. Stakeholders also need to interact and collaborate with the Developers to share their valuable feedbacks about the product increment. These feedbacks are required to be captured and to be worked upon by the Developers in the next upcoming Sprints. Such feedbacks can surely help the Scrum Team to improve the existing implementation of functionalities. Scrum Team needs to accept all the feedbacks in a positive way, using which the scope for continuous improvement of product can be addressed.

Sprint Review asks the Scrum Team and their Stakeholders to interact and collaborate with each other, considering what the Scrum Team has achieved toward the end of the Sprint. For a typical one-month Sprint, the Sprint Review needs to be conducted as an event for four hours, whereas for Sprints shorter than one-months' time duration, it needs to be kept shorter. Considering the customer value-oriented outcomes, both Scrum Team and Stakeholders need to further adjust/alter the Product Backlog by accommodating any changes required, so that those can be captured under the Product Backlog. The Scrum Team needs to further work on the prioritized feedbacks and changes captured under the Product Backlog.

> *"Any Scrum without working product at the end of a sprint is a failed Scrum."*
> *- Jeff Sutherland*

It is required for the Scrum Master to make sure that the Sprint Review is getting conducted at the end of every Sprint and all the participants are having a proper understanding behind its intent. It is also the Scrum Master's responsibility to teach, guide, help, and support everyone to have them engaged in the Sprint Review and to have it within the agreed time-boxed duration. The Sprint Review under a Scrum Team's already established Scrum-based agile way of working needs to be constituted by the means of following practices:

- The Scrum Team and its Stakeholders invited by the Product Owner need to be the participants for the Sprint Review to be conducted by the end of every Sprint.

- The Product Owner needs to describe which all PBIs/User Stories have been worked upon by the Developers in the Sprint, which of them are Done, and which are not.

- Developers need to showcase what they did during the latest Sprint, what problems they faced, and how they solved those problems. They need to demonstrate the work under the Done/Completed PBIs/User Stories. Any questions, concerns, and doubts being raised by the Stakeholders are required to be answered by them.

- The Product Owner needs to explain and discuss about the current state of the Product Backlog. If required, the Product Owner also needs to anticipate the expected delivery and the delivery timelines based on the team's progress so far.

- All the participants under the Sprint Review need to interact with each other, so that they can collaborate on what they need to do in the upcoming Sprint. Hence, a useful feedback is expected to be given for the upcoming Sprint Planning.

- They also need to review the roadmap, priorities, timeline, scope, capabilities, dependencies, risks, and so on, with respect to the upcoming product increment.

- They need to review the market conditions and associated usage of product to identify the next most valuable functionalities to be implemented by the Developers.

- The Product Backlog needs to be revised after the Sprint Review which needs to outline the possible set of PBIs/User Stories for the upcoming Sprint. Any feedbacks, changes are required to be captured into the ever-evolving Product Backlog.

The Scrum Event Sprint Retrospective also needs to be conducted toward the end of the latest Sprint. It is an opportunity for all the Scrum Team members, where they can look back and retrospect on how they performed during their latest Sprint along with a plan of action items to be enacted upon by themselves for any improvements to be addressed by them. For a typical one-month Sprint, a Sprint Retrospective needs to be for at max 3 hours and for the shorter Sprints, it needs to be shorter than that. The Sprint Retrospective always needs to be conducted after the Sprint Review of an ongoing Sprint and before the Sprint Planning of the upcoming Sprint.

Figure 3.13: Sprint Retrospective

Before the Sprint Retrospective, the Scrum Team needs to inspect on how things went during the latest Sprint. They need to observe, evaluate, identify, and record their opinions and feedbacks. It is required for the Scrum Master to make sure that the Sprint Retrospective is getting conducted after every Sprint Review and all the participants are having a proper understanding behind its intent. During the Sprint

Retrospective, the Scrum Master always needs to contribute as a peer team member by ensuring his/her overall accountability and responsibility over the Scrum Team's Scrum-based agile way of working, its Empiricism based practices, and associated processes.

At the time of Sprint Retrospective Event, The Scrum Master needs to consolidate and arrange the feedbacks received and the Scrum Team needs to perform voting to decide on which are the highest priority feedback items to be discussed by them. The Scrum Master needs to facilitate the event to have a productive discussion and brainstorming on the highest voted feedbacks, so that a plan of action items for any improvements to be acted upon by the Scrum Team in near future can be populated.

According to the Scrum Team's agreed agile way of working in line with the core values of Scrum framework, the Scrum Master always needs to help, guide, coach, mentor, encourage, and support the Scrum Team to improve their existing processes and practices based on their suggested improvements during the Sprint Retrospective. It helps them to make their way of working more efficient, effective, and agreeable during the upcoming Sprints.

Scrum Master needs to help everyone to have a proper, constructive, and a fruitful Sprint Retrospective. He/she also needs to make sure that it is being done within the agreed time-boxed duration. During every Sprint Retrospective, the Scrum Team needs to look at various options to be worked upon by them to increase the overall quality of every product increment. This needs to improve their agile way working-specific processes by reflecting and enhancing their Definition of Done. Such changes applicable to their Definition of Done associated with the development and delivery-specific processes should be aligned with the people, process, product, and organization-specific agreed benchmarking and standards.

> *"Scrum is like your mother-in-law; it points out ALL your faults."*
> *- Ken Schwaber*

The Sprint Retrospective Event needs to serve the purpose of inspecting how the latest Sprint went for the team. While sharing the feedbacks, the Scrum Team needs to consider various aspects such as team's overall performance, people, relationships, processes, practices, approaches, problems, impediments, tools, and so on. The Scrum Team also needs to recognize and discuss on the things that went well during the Sprint, the things that did not went well during the Sprint, and on any constructive suggestions where they can improve. They need to vote on the feedbacks based on their priority to decide on which of them they need to discuss and work upon. They need to create a plan of action items to adapt, act, and carry out continuous improvements to their Scrum-based agile way of working.

After every Sprint Retrospective, the Scrum Team needs to have improvements identified which they need to implement in near future. This whole process truly needs to reflect an Empiricism based shared understanding, where all the inspections being done by the Scrum Team along with the adaptations for all the improvements being done by them need to be properly derived and shared. Although improvements can be implemented later, the Sprint Retrospective needs to provide a golden opportunity to the Scrum Team, where all the Scrum Team members can focus on the process of inspection and adaptation and to maintain transparency at its highest level. They need to have the required action items defined against the specifically identified/recognized feedbacks, suggestions, and improvements, which they would like to implement in near future.

Sprint Retrospective is a wonderful opportunity for the entire Scrum Team, using which they can appreciate each other on the things that went well during the latest Sprint. Scrum Team members can also come up with unique ideas and suggestions, which they would like to see as a change to be embraced by themselves. Such ideas and suggestions can be shaped and enhanced further after having the required discussions at the time of Sprint Retrospective. They can also come up with the potential risks regarding product roadmap, scope, quality, timeline, budget, and many more other aspects, along with the possible mitigation plans. The Sprint Retrospective Event always needs to be baselined based on the concept of Empiricism, where all the Scrum Team members always need to seek for continuous learnings and associated persistent improvements.

Scrum Teams always need to make a best possible use of all the components associated with the Scrum Framework. Along with the concept of Empirical Process Control (Empiricism), the core components like Scrum Values, Scrum Roles, Scrum Events, Scrum Artifacts and Scrum Rules, and so on, need to be properly established and exhibited by the Scrum Teams.

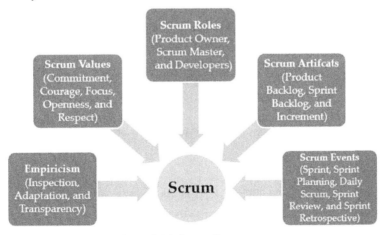

Figure 3.14: Scrum Components

Scrum-based agile way of working always needs to respond and embrace the change with a presence of Empiricism to constantly inspect and adapt. This helps the Scrum Team to enact and enhance with a continuous learning and improvement of their people, product, processes, standards, procedures, methods, approaches, and other required entities.

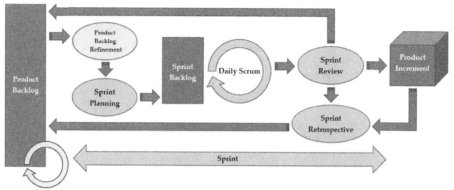

Figure 3.15: *The Scrum Team's Scrum-based Agile Way of Working*

All the Scrum Artifacts always need to be established and used by the Scrum Team, using which they can get the required information that they along with their stakeholders need to be always cognizant about. Scrum Artifacts help them to get to know about the working software product functionalities which are already under development and the activities required to be performed by the Scrum Team. This needs to consider the overall agreed process of development and delivery of working software product increment, which needs to be completed by the Scrum Team during each Sprint. Artifacts need to continuously evolve, as the Scrum Team progresses ahead along with their progressive Sprints.

All the Scrum Events need to be explicitly conducted by the Scrum Team to empower themselves with the required and expected collaboration, trust, and transparency. The expected, ideal implementation and continuous evolution of the Scrum Framework-based agile way of working of a Scrum Team provides many benefits to those who are supposed to own and perform the development and delivery. Such agile way of working helps them to ensure better quality. The Scrum Team needs to accomplish their Product and Sprint specific Goals, where a constant feedback sharing, feedback acceptance, and feedback addressal always needs to be established and to be worked upon by them. This always helps the Scrum Team to build and deliver high-quality product increments.

All the five core Scrum Values need to be always lived by the Scrum Teams to get to know about how they need to plan, collaborate, behave, communicate, take decisions, and work on their activities. In this way, the Scrum framework enhances the communication, collaboration, co-operation, co-ordination, and teamwork within the Scrum Teams.

The Scrum Team members themselves need to take care of all aspects of accountability, responsibility, and ownership, which is essential for the entire process of development and delivery of a potentially shippable working software product increment using Scrum-based agile way of working. It helps them to deliver amazing results/outcomes. The Scrum Teams keep on continuously improving by taking a full ownership of their Scrum-based agile way of working, while leading with the expected quality, efficiency, effectiveness, progress, and overall performance. This needs to be done by them, while being more proactive and having an improved involvement, interactions, and contributions.

The Scrum framework always helps the Scrum Teams to have a higher and boosted Team Morale. By making use of the Scrum-based agile way of working, the Scrum Team members look to be happy and satisfied. They are highly motivated, creative, collaborative, and always ready to learn new things by showcasing a growth mindset. The overall process of software development and delivery using Scrum Framework looks to be fulfilling, worthwhile, and rewarding to them. The cross-functional and self-organizing Scrum Teams allow themselves to develop and enhance their skills and capabilities, to take care of their consensus-based decision-making on their own with less supervision from the management side. This makes them more empowered and agile by enhancing their abilities to strive for excellence and to become high performing.

Scrum framework also helps the Scrum Teams to reduce their overall time to market. It has been demonstrated to provide the customer value optimization-based delivery of high-quality software products to the customers, which is generally around 40% faster than the traditional methods of software development. By making use of its magnificent characteristics, Scrum increases overall ROI of organizations. Significant reduction in the overall time to market is one important reason behind the software development teams making use of the Scrum Framework, who realize a higher ROI. Since Scrum-based software product development and delivery is an iterative and incremental approach, the revenue and other relative pursued benefits for the organizations making use of Scrum can be availed much quicker, better, sooner, and further resulting into higher ROI, as the Team becomes more mature.

Scrum Teams always need to keep in mind about some of the following interesting facts about the Scrum Framework and its associated entities:

- Scrum Teams need not to be co-located always. They can be distributed and can still perform and deliver well, even though it is a bit challenging in real.

- Every Developer need not to have all the skills required to build the product; however, to be a cross-functional Scrum Team, everyone needs to learn and collaborate to continuously improve on their skills over the time.

- The Developers need not to be dedicated, but it is a good to have; however, a Scrum Team member can play multiple roles.

- Along with the PBIs, the User Stories (which are belonging to the XP agile framework and which are the informal, natural language descriptions of one or more features of a software product) can be used by the Scrum Teams to capture the work to be done by them under their Product Backlog.

- Burndown Chart (which is a graphical representation of the Scrum Team's remaining work versus time in an ongoing Sprint) is not mandatory in Scrum.

- The Product Owner needs to write down the PBIs, but it is not a must have for him/her. He/she can have the Developers to do the needful for the same; however, the accountability remains with the Product Owner only.

- Developers do not need to have a separate Product Backlog. A single Product Backlog should capture all the customer needs and requirements using the PBIs or User Stories.

- The Developers do not commit to accomplish the work planned during the Sprint Planning Event. They need to create a forecast of work, which they believe that will be done by them. This forecast has a possibility to change, as they explore more and things become known to them, as the Sprint progresses.

- The ongoing Sprint itself is the place for the Developers to explore, find, and implement solutions and to be more cross-functional and self-managing.

- The Sprint Backlog can evolve with the changes during an ongoing Sprint.

- Release Planning can be done by the Developers but not explicitly. The potentially shippable working software product increment needs to be a collection of Done PBIs at the end of every Sprint. It should sustain Empiricism. It also needs to be an enabler to accomplish the Scrum Team's Goal. It also needs to be fully working irrespective of whether and when the Product Owner decides to release it to the Customers.

- Estimations of efforts for the activities involved in the process of development and delivery of high-quality working software products should not be based on solutions. They should be always based on the complexity, uncertainty, and risks associated with the problems to be addressed by the working software product.

- Sprint Backlog for an upcoming Sprint always needs to have the PBIs to be selected and delivered by the Developers. In this case, planning is important, but plans are not.

- At the time of Sprint Review, along with inspecting the Product Increment and adapting the Product Backlog, the Developers also need to demonstrate the work (which is completed during the Sprint and marked as Done) to the Stakeholders. They also need to answer questions being raised by the Stakeholders and record the feedbacks to be addressed for the Product Increment.

- By utilizing their Scrum-based agile way of working, the Software Products getting delivered by the Scrum Teams need to be functionally and non-functionally intact. They need to be delivered in a proper agile environment, where the Scrum Team needs to have a proper agile mindset to be more agile.

- Daily Scrum is not an event to share the status updates. Developers need to focus and reflect on improving their agreed Sprint Goal based on the concept of inspection and adaptation, so that they can progress by resolving their issues.

- Functionalities getting tracked under the PBIs can be delivered to Customers any time during an ongoing Sprint and need not to wait until the end of the Sprint.

- Daily Scrum always needs to be conducted daily, even in the absence of Scrum Master. Developers always need to be self-organizing and self-managing to minimize their dependency on the Scrum Master to resolve their every problem.

- The Scrum Team needs to appropriately utilize every Scrum Event. All the Events should be properly conducted to utilize their own distinctive intents.

- The entire Scrum Team (and not only the Product Owner) needs to feel free to get in touch with and to interact with the stakeholders and vice-versa.

- Documentation giving value needs to be in place and it cannot be omitted.

- Scrum is not at all messy. Scrum clearly describes its structure, components, values, roles, artifacts, events, rules, and so on. Scrum always encourages self-organization within the Scrum Teams and value optimization for their customers. Therefore, the Scrum Teams always need to be more open, disciplined, focused, and collaborative.

Points to remember

- Scrum is one of the most popular and most commonly and widely used agile frameworks to develop, deliver, and sustain complex software products. It is a framework within which people can address complex adaptive problems, while productively and creatively delivering products of the highest possible value.

- The Scrum Framework is established based on a theory called as Empirical Process Control Theory. It is also known as Empiricism. Every implementation of empirical process control for the Scrum Teams is based on three aspects which are inspection, transparency, and adaptation.

- There are five core Scrum Values of Scrum framework. They are Commitment, Courage, Focus, Openness, and Respect.

- Scrum needs to be used by the Teams called as Scrum Teams. The Scrum Team consists of three Roles called as Scrum Roles. They are Product Owner, Developers, and Scrum Master.

- The Scrum Artifacts are used to represent the work to be done and the customer value to be delivered. The three Scrum Artifacts are the Product Backlog, the Sprint Backlog, and the Increment.

- Scrum Events are the opportunities for the Scrum Team, where they can have an open communication and information sharing along with Empiricism to help themselves while working together closely, collaboratively, and efficiently; also improving their knowledge to become more efficient and mature, as they progress. Scrum Events are Sprint, Sprint Planning, Daily Scrum, Sprint Review, and Sprint Retrospective.

- Scrum Teams need to make a best possible use of the components associated with the Scrum Framework. Along with the Empirical Process Control (Empiricism), the core components like Scrum Values, Scrum Roles, Scrum Events, Scrum Artifacts, Scrum Rules, and so on, need to be properly established and exhibited by the Scrum Teams.

- Scrum enhances communication, collaboration, co-operation, co-ordination, and teamwork within the Scrum Team. It helps to have a higher, boosted Team Morale. It also helps the Scrum Team to reduce their overall time to market. Scrum increases the ROI of organizations by making use of its exclusive characteristics and features.

In the next chapter, readers will get to know about Malfunctioning of Scrum Framework along with the real need of Advanced Scrum Add-ons/Techniques. It will throw a light on many improper behaviors, patterns, and entities in place within the Scrum Teams, because of which their Scrum-based agile way of working starts to malfunction. Readers will also get to know about the basic need and analogy behind why to prevent, protect, remediate, and correct Scrum Teams from such a malfunctioning.

CHAPTER 4
Scrum Malfunctioning and Understanding the need of Advanced Scrum Add-ons

Introduction

In this chapter, readers will get to know about many improper actions, reactions, behaviors, patterns, and entities in place within the Scrum Teams, because of which their Scrum based agile way of working starts to malfunction. Scrum Malfunctioning can be clearly observed both internally (by someone being a part of the Scrum Teams) and/or externally (by someone being outside of the Scrum Teams). This chapter will also throw a light upon a basic analogy behind why to prevent, protect, remediate, and correct Scrum Teams from such a malfunctioning.

Objective

After studying this chapter, you should be able to:

- Understand what Scrum Malfunctioning is.
- Understand the Symptoms of Scrum Malfunctioning.
- Understand the overall impact of Scrum Malfunctioning on the Scrum Teams.
- Understand the need behind preventing, protecting, remediating, and correcting the Scrum Teams from Scrum Malfunctioning.

Naveen 'The Scrum Master' (in a discussion with rest of the Scrum Team members):

"Our Developers know the importance of DevOps, but they don't want to get started with it. We have had discussed about it in our previous retrospectives. Developers have already said that DevOps specific practices are required to be established and we have action items in place to get started with it, but somehow the Team is not making it into reality. I sometimes wonder that, whether they are serious about it or not. On the other hand, I am also unable to convince our Product Owner to allow the Developers to work on such enablers, along with the other prioritized features in hand. I honestly feel like, I am almost on the verge of giving up, John!"

Gitika 'The System Architect' (immediately jumping in the discussion):

"Huh! I second that Naveen! Even I am also stressed and I probably need to step up to give a proper understanding to our Product Owner, so that he knows about, how the DevOps specific practices are helpful in longer run. Performing builds and deployments manually is consuming our time and efforts. He needs to understand that such enablers are required to speed up their overall functioning."

John 'The Agile Coach' (taking a pause to think and asking):

"You both need to start with breathing exercises to reduce your stress. So, why to delay? Please close your eyes and start doing breathe-in and breathe-out for the next 5 minutes. Your time starts now!"

Gitika (after 5 min of a deep breathing exercise):

"Wow John! That was amazing! Thank You! And I regret, why I was not doing this practice before. My mother was asking me to try it out for years. I am feeling Sorry!"

Naveen:

"Even I also liked it Gitika! It feels much better now with a stress-free mind."

John:

"Great! Now, please correct me if I am wrong. Don't you think that Product Owner and Developers are giving you excuses, like what you were doing with your mother Gitika? Don't you think that they are simply delaying what needs to be done at the earliest? I simply asked both of you to do deep breathing and tried to move away your excuses. Please try doing the same with them. Start leading with influence. Let them define a roadmap, using which they can start. I hope, you both are getting me!"

Naveen:

"Thanks a lot, John! Let us take it as a challenge! We'll work on it in our next Sprint."

Most of the times, the growing, self-organizing, self-managing, and cross-functional Scrum Teams and their Scrum Masters tend to make use of the Scrum Guide as it is. They use it as a readymade guideline to establish and enhance their Scrum-based agile way of working. It looks to be simple for them to formulate a strategy, using which they can begin with the formulation of the required set of components and structure of the Scrum Framework, while following the recommendations from the Scrum Guide. However, along with the required set of customizations getting applied as per their own needs, wants, and suitability, their Scrum-based agile way of working always needs to be in line with the values and principles of the *Manifesto for Agile Software Development*.

While establishing a Scrum-based agile way of working from the scratch for a Scrum Team and while continuously enhancing an already established Scrum-based agile way of working of a Scrum Team, things might go wrong. In this case, one can see many malfunctions getting introduced, encouraged, and continued without being questioned. This has both short-term and long-term impacts on a Scrum Team.

> *"Malfunctions are inevitable. It's important to push through them during practice versus stopping to fix and restart so that you're prepared for one mid-competition."*
> *- Amanda Beard*

It is the primary responsibility of the Scrum Master to be more meticulous by always keeping an eye on the team's overall way of working considering people, products/projects, and processes. Scrum Master also needs to find issues, gaps, and concerns irrespective of their nature, type, size, and entities associated with them. It is always better for the Scrum Team to take both preventive as well as corrective actions before the small issues become big. These actions need to be taken care by them sooner and seriously, as such issues may have an adverse impact in the long run and it may also result into a big malfunctioning causing hinderance for their complete agile way of working.

Few parts of a team's overall way of working might not be right when it comes to the value proposition, the ease of functioning, speed and quality of delivery, team's overall happiness, satisfaction index, and many more other parameters/entities. By looking at the team's overall performance by considering the amount of outcome based on-time value delivery getting done by them, one can clearly identify if there are any problems, issues, and malfunctions present in their way of working or not.

The process of Empiricism always asks the Scrum Team to keep looking for any such malfunctioning, which needs to be corrected at the earliest. The Scrum Team may keep on saying that they are agile, where everything seems to be normal to them with their existing well-established Scrum-based agile way of working; however, they need to consider a fact that there is always a scope for improvement and it should not be ignored by the entire team, especially by the Scrum Master. Continuous improvements are required, while applying applicable and appropriate changes to their way of working.

As shown in the following figure, Scrum Malfunctioning is generally caused by a variety of Product/Project, People, and Process specific improper, irrational and nonsense making actions, reactions, behaviors, patterns, and associated entities occurring within the Scrum Teams. Because of such malfunctioning, their Scrum-based agile way of working also starts to malfunction. Scrum Malfunctioning can be specific to any of the core components of the Scrum Framework, where the Scrum Team's Scrum-based agile way of working might not be established properly and there is always some confusion within the Scrum Team about, whether the Scrum Team is doing right things or not and/or doing things right or not.

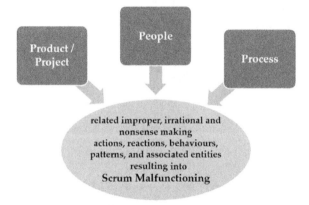

Figure 4.1: Scrum Malfunctioning

While being and acting as a Scrum Coach for the Scrum Team, the Scrum Master needs to play a critical role to make sure that any such malfunctioning along with its impact and resolution is getting properly identified. He/she also needs to ensure that any such malfunctioning is also getting addressed by the applicable Scrum Team members after having a consensus-based decision making in place. If the Scrum Master role and its associated responsibilities are not understood clearly, then the complete endeavour of transforming the teams with the Scrum-based agile way of working might get into a big failure. There are typical symptoms behind Scrum Malfunctioning, which can be seen, observed, and sensed by anyone who is a part of the team or by anyone who is an outsider. It is required for the whole Scrum Team to highlight and enact on such symptoms.

As shown in the following figure, if we consider a boundary around a team's agreed agile way of working then, the symptoms of malfunctioning are generally observed due to some factors, which may be either internal and/or external and/or both to that boundary:

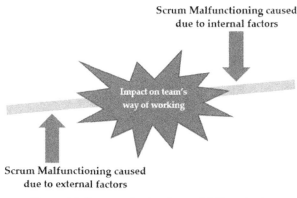

Figure 4.2: Factors affecting Scrum Malfunctioning

There might be factors present within a Scrum Team, because of which Scrum Malfunctioning might be getting caused. Such factors can occur while having a direct trigger point due to a variety of Product/Project, People, and Process specific improper, irrational, and nonsense making actions, reactions, behaviors, patterns, and associated entities occurring within a Team internally. Scrum Malfunctioning within a Scrum Team might also get caused due to some external factors. There might be circumstances, where there is a lack of trust, transparency, openness, focus, courage, commitment, respect, shared understanding, collaboration, communication, co-operation, co-ordination, empathy, integrity, and proper teamwork. There might be communication/understanding gaps, disagreements, destructive conflicts, non-consensus-based decision making, and many other entities causing Scrum Malfunctioning, while the team is having interactions with stakeholders, customers, senior management, other teams, and so on.

The Scrum Malfunctioning can be easily seen as bottlenecks getting created by internal and external factors; however, the willingness of individuals to report and fix them always makes a key difference. It is also required for the team to establish a formal working agreement capturing why, what, who, when, and how things need to be done to establish and enhance their Scrum-based agile way of working. Such working agreement needs to be used as a guideline to follow the processes as expected and as agreed by and for the entire Scrum Team. Such a formal working agreement also needs to be updated by the Scrum Team, when needed.

Malfunction - one size fits all!

The people (especially the Agile Coaches and the Scrum Masters) performing key decision making in an agile organization, who are always engaged with the Scrum Teams and having an ownership of establishing an agile way of working, need to understand the terminology 'One size does not fit all!'.

They try to establish a standardized agile way of working using Scrum Framework across all the Scrum Teams. While using this approach, they tend to forget that each product/project is different. People who are supposed to be the part of those Scrum Teams are also having different skill sets, capabilities, expertise, and experiences. Hence there is always a probability that, the processes and practices to be associated with a standardized agile way of working using Scrum Framework across all the Scrum Teams might cause some improper, irrational, nonsense making actions, reactions, behaviors, patterns, and associated entities. This might result into a Scrum Malfunctioning. It is hence required for them to take this possibility under their consideration when they start to apply any such kind of standardizations. Establishing and enhancing a customized agile way of working by following the baseline belonging to the core structure of the Scrum Framework and supporting the customized needs, wants, and suitability of individual Scrum Teams is always a better approach to go ahead with.

Malfunction - Sprints are not always of same length, causing pace issues in team.

The Scrum Team should not change the Sprint length of their Sprints once the Sprints are getting started. The Sprints always need to be of same length. Team might have a desire to change the completeness of PBIs allowing changes in the original scope of PBIs, if they keep on changing the Sprint length. However, instead of changing the Sprint length, they can add separate PBIs to the Product Backlog. Such PBIs can be always considered as enhancements to be worked on by them.

The Sprint needs to act as a feedback loop, where the Scrum Team needs to take the opinions of their stakeholders into account. With a constant Sprint length, it helps the stakeholders to have a constant check, while performing the reviews of the potentially shippable increment of a working software product. On the other hand, if the Sprint length is varying for any kind of rare, specific, and suitable reasons with which the Scrum Team and the Stakeholders are okay, it should act as an exception.

Malfunction - Sprints are not of optimal length.

To make sure that the Developers are completing the Product Backlog Items (PBIs) taken under the Sprint Backlog of an ongoing Sprint, they need to have enough time in hand during an ongoing Sprint. At the same time, according to the Scrum Guide, the Sprint should not be of longer than one month. Sprint length needs to allow the Developers to self-manage and to get their ongoing Sprint specific work done along with maintaining the built-in quality.

Typically, a PBI or a User Story taken under an ongoing Sprint should not take more than 2 to 3 calendar days. The reasonable Sprint length needs to be of two weeks, as it encourages faster feedbacks and hence the team gets more occasions to improve continuously. Such Sprint length also help the team to develop and deliver a potentially shippable "Done" increment of the working software product at the end of every Sprint. The Sprint length hence needs to be of two weeks, so that a proper understanding of the requirements followed by the actual implementations can be properly done by the Developers. Also, if the Sprint is of two weeks, then the

Team can have an anticipation for the required changes to happen slower and the Stakeholders can get to see the new things developed and delivered by the end of the Sprint.

It might also happen with the Scrum Teams that, the requirements are changing rapidly and it becomes difficult for the teams to balance those fast-changing requirements. In such a scenario, the Stakeholders along with the Product Owner tend to continuously shift their minds to decide the priorities for what needs to be developed and delivered early. The Scrum Teams hence need to shorten the Sprint length to two weeks. Changes keep on happening and hence the team members need to develop their mindset and actions to accept and to work on the fact that requirements may change more frequently. If a Scrum Team is working hard to complete the work they have planned under an ongoing Sprint, it is better to have the Sprint duration shorter; whereas, if the team is doing expected progress on the work they have planned under an ongoing Sprint, it is better to make the Sprint length longer. It totally depends upon the maturity of the Scrum Team and overall agreements within the Scrum Team; however, ideally, the Sprint duration should be of two weeks.

Malfunction - lack of openness/flexibility within the Scrum Team for planning and re-planning.

Even though a Scrum Team's ideal Sprint length is of two weeks, sometimes team members (especially the Developers) work hard and struggle to accomplish their agreed Sprint Goal within two weeks. This might happen because of a variety of reasons such as frequently changing, shaky, and unstable requirements, dependencies found out by the Developers due to their ongoing explorations, their skills are not up to the mark, and few other aspects. If they reduce their Sprint length to make the Sprints shorter, this has an undesirable impact on the Stakeholders, as they cannot cater to frequent Sprint Reviews. It is also true that the Developers need to develop and deliver working software product increment much faster and on time, so that the Stakeholders can get to see the anticipated progress.

In this scenario, the Scrum Team needs to continuously inspect and adapt their overall progress to meet the actualities in terms of their agreed Sprint Goal. The team needs to have Planning and Re-Planning. If the team has a Sprint of two weeks, then the team can plan and/or re-plan in the middle of Sprint. They need to follow *Stop starting new work and start finishing existing work* strategy. If there are Developers who can perform more work, then this strategy can be re-planned.

Malfunction - Less Work in Progress limits for the Developers. Developers work on many tasks at the same time.

Scrum Team making use of a Kanban Board (to visualize their work items, that is, PBIs and associated Tasks, and so on. under every ongoing Sprint) need to limit their overall Work in Progress. If not, then there will be many work items taken up by them at the same time. This approach hampers the strategy *Stop starting new work and start finishing existing work*. Work items get worked upon by them in parallel and by the end of the Sprint, there is a possibility that only few of them are getting completed.

Scrum Team hence needs to aim for reducing and stabilizing their overall Work in Progress by applying some limits. By doing the same, the overall flow of work along with the forecasting of completion of the work items by the end of an ongoing Sprint can get improved. The Team can make use of Scrumban like approach to tweak their Scrum-based agile way of working, where they can pull an additional set of work items from Product Backlog into Sprint Backlog, once the Work in Progress is completed by anyone and who has enough bandwidth to do more within an ongoing Sprint. Work in Progress limits needs to be agreed by everyone in the Scrum Team.

Malfunction - daily Scrum takes more than 15 minutes. Unwanted folks attend the Daily Scrum. Not all the Developers are attending the Daily Scrum.

The purpose of Daily Scrum Event is to reflect on the current progress of every Developer working on the PBIs/User Stories and their associated tasks under an ongoing Sprint. The Daily Scrum should not take more than 15 minutes duration to make sure that the team is staying efficient and focussed. It should not be treated as a status update meeting. All the Developers need to reflect on how they are progressing toward their agreed Sprint Goal and if there are any impediments, blockers, and issues preventing them to do so. However, the issues need to be discussed separately and not during the Daily Scrum.

It is the responsibility of the Scrum Master to make sure that unwanted people are not attending the Daily Scrum. Even if they are attending, the Scrum Master needs to make sure that they are not interfering with the agenda of Daily Scrum. This not only helps to keep the Daily Scrum within 15 minutes time-box, but also allows the Scrum Team to focus and reflect on their agreed Sprint Goal. If anyone from outside the Scrum Team needs to discuss on or share anything with the Scrum Team, it is always better to have separate meetings to have those discussions, as and when required.

All the Developers need to attend the Daily Scrum to reflect, inspect, and adapt. They are responsible to get it right. Scrum Master, Product Owner, or Stakeholders may attend as listeners, but they are required only if it is useful to the Developers. Developers need to drive the Daily Scrum, where it is their accountability to make the use of this ultimate opportunity to reflect on where they are and how they want to proceed in an ongoing Sprint.

Malfunction - Senior Management tempts to interrupt the Scrum Team during their Sprints to convert their Scrum-based agile way of working into Micro-Management oriented approach, which sounds like Waterfallish Scrum.

According to the Scrum Guide, the Scrum Master needs to help those outside the Scrum Team (who can be Senior Management people or businesspeople like stakeholders) to understand which of their interactions with the Scrum Team are helpful and those which are not. The Scrum Master always needs to help everyone to alter these interactions to maximize the value being delivered by the Scrum Team.

If any of such outsiders (having a fixed-minded anticipation from the Scrum Team to run a tight reporting system as a legacy like a Waterfallish Scrum) are unnecessarily interrupting the Scrum Team during their Sprints, the Scrum Master needs to give them an understanding about self-management. Sometimes, such people are not respecting the Scrum Team to make the right decisions. In this case, the Scrum Master needs to discuss with them and have a formal working agreement established to be followed by them, not hindering the overall structure of their agile way of working using Scrum Framework and its associated components, rules, processes, and practices.

Malfunction - Scrum Team is a distributed/not a co-located one. This results into many distractions and issues, where no one has any control to remediate.

Even though Scrum Framework works best with the co-located Scrum Teams, sometimes it might happen that a Scrum Team might be globally distributed one and having time-zone gaps for the team members. Since the team members are not co-located, it may cause limited interactions in between team members and their Stakeholders. It might also get difficult for them to coordinate, collaborate, co-operate, and communicate properly. Yet they can have certain working agreements and a baseline defined by and for themselves to have a proper information sharing, along with the removal of dependencies (if any), so that they can help each other and progress together to achieve their agreed Sprint Goal.

Developers always need to be structured, aligned, and empowered to organize, manage, and complete their own work by themselves only. This encourages self-management and self-organization. By making use of right set of tools and technologies, they can interact and collaborate much better, even though they are not co-located. Though such tools and technologies help them to enhance an overall quality of collaboration, individuals and their interactions should be given the highest importance before the usage of suitable tools and technologies. The distance between the distributed Scrum Team members should not have any kind of impact on their collaboration, commitment, courage, focus, openness, respect, and trust. The Scrum Team and especially the Scrum Master needs to be aware of this fact and they need to behave accordingly. They always need to ensure the highest level of collaboration which helps them to be efficient.

Malfunction - collective responsibility, accountability, and ownership seems to be lacking in the Scrum Team.

There is always a possibility in a Scrum Team that individual Developers have specific skill sets. The working software which needs to be developed and delivered by the Developers has various technical layers or components. The individuals tend to consider themselves to do only a certain piece of work belonging to only certain technical layers. This approach restricts the team to be a cross-functional team.

As per the Scrum Guide, individuals need to personally commit to achieve the goals of the Scrum Team. Developers should have the courage and commitment to do the right thing and to work on the complex problems. The entire team needs to take a collective responsibility, accountability, and ownership to focus on and to execute the work under ongoing Sprints, so that they can achieve their agreed Sprint Goal altogether. By having an alignment with the Stakeholders, they always need to be open about all the work, its associated activities, and the challenges occurring, while performing their Sprint specific work. Developers always need to work collectively and not in silos.

Malfunction - Developers look to be a Component Team and not a Feature Team.

Many times, it is observed that the Developers are functioning as a Component Team and not a Feature Team. A Component-based Dev Team is a Dev Team whose primary area of concern is a component or a collection of components of the working software product being developed and delivered by them. These components can be divided into technical layers such as presentation/user interface/front-end layer, business logic/application programming interface/middleware layer, and database/back-end layer. There might be few more layers involved into technical development/construction/implementation of a software product.

If the individual Developers belonging to such a Component-based Dev Team focus on individual components by giving a secondary priority to the complete software product, they start to work in silos. It reduces the collaboration among them. This also creates dependencies across component-based layers.

However, if it is a Feature based Dev Team (instead of being a Component-based Dev Team), the individual Developers need to work across the technical layers or components. With this approach, they reduce waste created during hand-offs by evaluating their designs, flows, and the complete end-to-end functionality getting implemented, both technically and functionally. A Feature based Dev Team always enhances a collective ownership, accountability, and responsibility with an increased collaboration, where all the Developers need to focus on features/functionalities covering each technical layer or component. This approach also increases the possibility of delivering a potentially shippable increment of a high-quality working software product with its Done features, which are completely Done from their usability point of view.

Malfunction - PBIs/User Stories are not sliced, sized, and mapped well. Also, there is no proper Definition of Done and Acceptance Criteria defined for them.

Scrum Teams sometimes lose their focus while creating the PBIs/User Stories. This results into many dependencies. It also becomes difficult for the Developers to estimate such PBIs and to negotiate on them, while taking them from the Product Backlog to the Sprint Backlog. This happens because the size of the PBIs is too big and they are not mapped well in terms of workflow of the functionalities to be developed using them. Scrum Teams also forget to have the Definition of Done and Acceptance Criteria which needs to be associated with the PBIs, using which the Product Owner can cross-check the quality and completeness of PBIs. Scrum Teams need to learn the techniques such as User Story Mapping, User Story Sizing, and User Story Slicing, and so on. They should also make proper use of the Definition of Done and Acceptance Criteria. It helps them to enhance built-in quality of product increments.

Malfunction - While creating the PBIs/User Stories, they are horizontally sliced into the technical/component-based layers. They are not vertically sliced covering a functionality across all the technical/component-based layers.

Many times, it is also observed that the Component-based Dev Teams are creating the PBIs/User Stories in their Product Backlog, where they are slicing those PBIs/User Stories horizontally into separate technical or component-based layers such as presentation/user interface/front-end layer, business logic/application programming interface/middleware layer, and database/back-end layer. Because of this, PBIs become more technical and less functionality driven. Such structure adds an overhead asking Developers to push their individual PBIs faster, so that they can integrate with the other PBIs under other technical layers, getting worked upon by other Developers. This approach also increases dependencies between PBIs.

Horizontal slicing of PBIs might also drop down the quality of code written, as there will be less integration tests across layers. Also, as mentioned previously, such PBIs are supposed to be worked upon by the individual developers, where they start to work on silos. This reduces collaboration and overall visibility of dependencies and issues occurring across the technical layers. Hence, it is always better to have Feature-based Dev Teams. They need to create vertically sliced PBIs/User Stories across all the technical layers, resolving many problems caused by the horizontally sliced PBIs.

Malfunction - Features, PBIs/User Stories have huge gaps and not well-refined.

The Developers and the Product Owner are sometimes inclined to have an unclean and unprioritized Product Backlog, where the functionalities to be implemented during Sprints and to be tracked under Features, PBIs/User Stories are having huge understanding gaps. Sometimes gaps are technical, sometimes gaps are functional.

Sometimes gaps are both technical as well as functional. It is hence required for the Developers that they are making the best possible utilization of Product Backlog Refinement meetings, where they along with the Product Owner need to discuss on each feature, PBI/User Story under their Product Backlog. They need to fill-in understanding gaps, if any. It is the responsibility of the Product Owner to make sure that he/she is answering concerns, questions, and doubts being asked by the Developers, which do not need to be completely resolved; however, he/she needs to address them fair enough, so that they feel enough convinced about them. PBIs need to be re-discussed by filling in the gaps during upcoming Sprint Planning Event and can be marked as ready to be taken up under upcoming Sprint.

Malfunction - Developers do not want to function as a cross-functional team.

The Developers being a Component-based Dev Team, inculcate a wrong thought process within themselves, where they do not want to be a cross-functional team. They have a fixed mindset and there seems to be a lack of courage and willingness to learn new tools and technologies. Developers also tend to work according to their specialized skill sets, which are most of the times component/technical layer specific. They always want to stick to their specific work area and are not ready to explore other work areas, disregarding the process of learning by doing.

This thought process has a direct impact on team's overall progress and on the speed of delivery, causing increased dependencies and reduced collaboration within the team members. Developers always need to understand that every individual developer may have some specialized skills and work areas of focus, but the accountability and the responsibility of turning the Sprint Backlog into potentially releasable working software product increment always stays with all the developers.

Malfunction - there is a continuous spill over of PBIs/User Stories from the current Sprint to the next Sprint.

It is also observed in many Scrum Teams that, there is always a spill over of PBIs/User Stories from the current Sprint to the next Sprint. Also, the team is not achieving their Sprint Goal. There might be many reasons behind this pattern observed. The expectations, Definition of Done, and Acceptance Criteria for the PBIs are not well-defined and further causing many understanding gaps. Developers may over-commit and estimate work incorrectly. Dependencies may get identified during an ongoing Sprint causing delays. The Product Owner may change the priority of PBIs due to the changing needs of customers. Scenarios may occur where a team member is unavailable due to some unforeseen reasons. In any of such scenarios, the team needs to have a working agreement in place. It can be used by them to prevent as well as fix such problems, which can significantly reduce the spill over of PBIs across Sprints.

Malfunction - Developers sometimes add unnecessary, exaggerated, and fragmented PBIs/User Stories in Sprints, causing scope stretching.

Developers sometimes add unnecessary PBIs/User Stories in their Sprint Backlog, which are not originally present in their Product Backlog. They forget to consult with the Product Owner while doing the same and it causes a scope stretching under Sprints. Scrum Team needs to make sure that the PBIs are always self-sufficient to explain anyone about both technical as well as functional aspects of functionality getting tracked under them. During Sprint Planning, if the Product Owner observes any such kind of scope stretching caused by unnecessary, exaggerated, and fragmented PBIs in Sprint Backlog, he/she needs to cross-check and correct them. This needs to be done to ensure that only the work which is adding value into the product increment is being picked up by the developers.

Malfunction - Developers think that the Daily Scrum is not useful for them.

Many times, Developers do not understand the importance of the Daily Scrum Event. They think that it a status update meeting, which is not true. It is the responsibility of Scrum Master to give them a proper understanding about, why it is important and how it optimizes the probability of Developers to meet their Sprint Goal. During the Daily Scrum, they need to reflect on their progress along with the problems getting faced by them, so that they can inspect, adapt, collaborate, work together, and help each other, as a self-organizing team to deliver the expected product increment by the end of every Sprint.

Malfunction - Scrum Master constantly pushes the developers for their pending action items during ongoing Sprints.

Sometimes, there might be some dependencies occurring during an ongoing Sprint because of which some of the Developers might be getting blocked. In this case, they need to communicate, coordinate, collaborate, and co-operate with other Developers to resolve those dependencies as early and as quick as possible. It should not be always the case that, the Scrum Master always needs to push the developers to act on their pending action items. Developers need to step up to become more self-organized and self-managed.

Malfunction - Scrum Master needs to assign work items to the developers during Sprint Planning.

Many times, Developers in a Scrum Team have an expectation from their Scrum Master that, it is the responsibility of the Scrum Master to assign them work items at the time of Sprint Planning. To have the Developers to be more accountable, self-organizing, and self-managing, under any conditions, he/she should never assign work items from the Sprint Backlog to the individual Developers. He/she should also protect them from anyone else who is doing the same. Only the Developers need to select work items from the Sprint Backlog to work on.

Malfunction - Scrum Master needs to drive and handle the Daily Scrum Event.

Many times, Developers also have an expectation from the Scrum Master that, he/she needs to run the Daily Scrum. However, the Scrum Master only needs to ensure that the Developers have the Daily Scrum. It is the responsibility of Developers to conduct the Daily Scrum. Scrum Master needs to teach the team to keep the Daily Scrum within the 15-minute time-box. Scrum Master can skip the Daily Scrum, if he or she thinks that the team is matured enough in terms of self-organization and they can do the needful in his/her absence; however, if the Scrum Master is one of the Developers, then it is better for him/her to attend the Daily Scrum.

Malfunction - Developers work across multiple Scrum Teams and hence, they seem to have a limited presence for the Scrum Events. Scrum Master always needs to take a follow-up.

It becomes difficult for the Scrum Master as well as for the Developers, when there are Developers working across multiple Scrum Teams. Such Developers remain absent during most of the Scrum Events and hence it becomes difficult to get their proper visibility. Scrum Master also needs to follow-up with them in case if they have any impediments. It is okay to have such arrangements, but such Developers need to be extra aware about the fact that, they need to communicate, collaborate, cooperate, and coordinate by taking an extra bit of care to work together along with the other Developers to achieve their agreed Sprint Goal.

Malfunction - Developers are not reporting impediments properly. This causes deviations and delays for the purpose of completion of their work items.

There is a misconception in Developers about reporting of impediments only at the time of Daily Scrum. Though they can highlight their impediments during Daily Scrum Event, they always need to remember that they should not restrict themselves to wait till the next Daily Scrum to do the same. While being more pro-active, the moment they see anything as an impediment (which is blocking them to proceed with their work items), they need to resolve such impediments on their own. They can also ask Scrum Master to help them by engaging others, if required.

Malfunction - Scrum Team is unable to accomplish Sprint Goal. They are badly impacted due to external hindrances and they are highly vulnerable to those.

Sometimes, Developers struggle a lot due to the external hindrances caused by others outside the team. Because of this, the work items being worked upon by them have deviations causing delays. In such cases, the Product Owner needs to optimize the value of work. He/she needs to discuss with others outside the team to have a balance on both the sides. Developers need to focus on delivering Done product increments and the Scrum Master needs to focus on removing impediments, if any.

Malfunction - Developers are not seriously following *Stop Starting new work and Start Finishing existing work* strategy.

Some Developers keep working on their individual PBIs/User Stories. Such PBIs remain in progress for more than 2–3 days and sometimes end up as potential spill over candidates from the current Sprint to the next Sprint. There might be some dependencies and/or skills, understanding and exploration specific gaps present, which cause further delays. Developers also start with new work items by keeping their already started in progress work items as it is. In such cases, every Developer needs to follow *Stop Starting new work and Start Finishing existing work* strategy (by understanding the consequences of not following it) while achieving the Sprint Goal. PBIs should be completed by the end of an ongoing Sprint and the Developers should follow all the processes, Definition of Done, and Acceptance Criteria, as per their defined Scrum-based agile way of working, ensuring that the PBIs are fully functional.

Malfunction - Scrum Team is not focussing on the Sprint Goal.

Few Scrum Teams get into a trend to lose their focus and attention towards the agreed Sprint Goal. With such a behavior, they forget about many aspects of why they are working together in a Sprint. Sprint Goal hence becomes ineffective causing many problems. Team could not serve to test their assumptions for functionalities getting developed. Their overall progress, flexibility, collaboration, teamwork, prioritization of work, and effective, consensus-based decision making within an ongoing Sprint gets impacted. To avoid all of this, they need to understand the importance of the Sprint Goal. It needs to be crafted considering why they would like to carry out the Sprint, how they need to collaborate to achieve the same, and how they can confirm on its fruitful achievement. Focus on the Sprint Goal is a must.

Malfunction - Scrum Teams are unable to identify the bottlenecks. Even if they find any, they try to ignore. If they report, they do not act seriously to fix them.

In a Scrum Team's already established Scrum-based agile way of working, there are always some bottlenecks present. Scrum Malfunctioning within a Scrum Team starts to happen because of such bottlenecks, where a variety of Product/Project, People, and Process specific improper, irrational, and nonsense making actions, reactions, behavior, patterns, and associated entities keep on occurring within a Scrum Team. Because of them, the Scrum Team's overall agile way of working gets badly impacted. Sometimes the bottlenecks are fully visible. Sometimes they are partially visible. Sometimes they are invisible too. It is the responsibility of each Scrum Team member to be alert about any such bottlenecks seen within the Scrum Team's agile way of working. Daily Scrum, Sprint Review, and Sprint Retrospective Events need to be used by the Team to report such bottlenecks, so that immediate and proper actions can be taken. By making use of Empiricism, it is always expected from all the Scrum Team members that they are identifying any bottlenecks to resolve them at the earliest.

Malfunction - Developers get bored with the required documentation of working software product. They think that it is not at all required.

Developers might keep on complaining about the documentation of software product to be done by them. It seems to be boring for them and hence they lose their interest to create/update the required documentation. They need to consider documentation, which is needed to support their product increments, so that it adds up a value and becomes usable too. As per the *Manifesto for Agile Software Development*, Developers always need to value documentation; however, more value needs to be given to working software. Along with the required documentation, their focus should be on all types of testing, validations, and verifications, so that they can ensure that their product increments are working and fully functional.

Malfunction - Even though the PBIs/User Stories are already completed, as per the Definition of Done and Acceptance Criteria during an ongoing Sprint, Developers tend to mark the PBIs/User Stories as Done at the end of the Sprint.

Many times, Developers complete the PBIs/User Stories in line with the expected Definition of Done and Acceptance Criteria during an ongoing Sprint; however, they tend to mark the PBIs/User Stories as Done only at the end of the Sprint. This way of working restricts them to pull-in some additional PBIs to be worked upon by them once they complete all the PBIs during an ongoing Sprint. They always need to see the possibilities to complete their existing work by showcasing a full commitment, so that they can help other team members to achieve the Sprint Goal collaboratively. In such cases, trust and transparency also plays a crucial role.

Malfunction - Scrum Team thinks that Sprint Reviews are only limited to Demos.

Many Scrum Teams practising Scrum think that the Sprint Review Event is limited to showcase the demo of their working software product increment toward the end of the Sprint. It is true that demos are an integral part of every Sprint Review, but Sprint Reviews are not only limited to demos. Sprint Reviews also need to act as enablers to get feedbacks from the Stakeholders and Customers, where they need to discuss on the market conditions, assess completed Sprint, and review their release timeline. It also expects that the Scrum Team is evaluating the feedbacks received, which helps their Product Backlog to evolve. It also helps the team to focus on what they need to work on next.

Malfunction - entire Scrum Team participates in Product Backlog Refinements.

It is not required to have the entire Scrum Team participating in Product Backlog Refinements. The PBIs require some conversations that the team needs to have in the future. Refinement needs to be an ongoing process to have such conversations. Hence, all the activities related to the product backlog refinement are not required to be done by the entire team. Creating PBIs is a complex process requiring time and PBIs need to evolve over time.

Malfunction - Developers forget to maintain the Sprint Backlog on their own.

Sometimes the Scrum Master and/or the Product Owner of a Scrum Team has an inclination toward maintaining the Sprint Backlog on behalf of Developers. They need to understand that Developers are the exclusive owner of Sprint Backlog containing all the PBIs/User Stories taken by them in an ongoing Sprint. It is their forecast of work to achieve the agreed Sprint Goal. Scrum Master needs to teach them to update and maintain anything related to the Sprint Backlog; however, Developers always need to understand that they need to do the needful on their own displaying self-organization and self-management at its best.

Malfunction - Scrum Team is not sharing feedbacks during Sprint Retrospectives. Also, they are not speaking enough. Opportunity to inspect and adapt gets lost.

Scrum Teams seek for continuous improvements, but many times, they forget to make the best utilization of Sprint Retrospective Event. It is a golden opportunity given to them to discuss on what went well, what did not, and if there are any suggestions to improve their Scrum-based agile way of working. Sometimes they lack with honesty, openness, and willingness to share the feedbacks. They feel like Retrospectives are boring and ineffective. To overcome such feelings, the Scrum Master needs to create a safe environment to enable openness, courage, and trust. The team needs to share their valuable feedbacks and to speak under the presence of such an environment. They should take criticism constructively with a full integrity. It is also beneficial for the Scrum Team to appreciate good things that happened in the Sprint and to discuss and decide action items to improve upon in upcoming Sprints.

Malfunction - Scrum Team keeps on making the same mistakes even though they have lessons learnt from the past Sprints.

Scrum Teams always have lessons learnt from their past Sprints. There might be mistakes done by individuals, which are not getting originally addressed by the team's established Scrum-based agile way of working. Hence, it is required for the team to have a formal working agreement in place capturing required insights of their agile way of working. Such working agreement always needs to be updated and to be used as a guideline to follow processes, as expected and agreed by the entire Scrum Team. It reduces the probability of team members making same mistakes again and again. It also eliminates confusions for why, who, when, what, and how things need to be done.

Malfunction - Developers perform poor analysis causing 11th hours surprises.

Developers sometimes perform poor analysis. Such behavior might cause many 11th hours surprises when they start with the actual development specific activities. It is hence required for the developers to engage with full focus and commitment, while performing analysis by finding all the impacts and dependencies.

Malfunction - Developers over-commit at the time of Sprint Planning and when they come to Sprint Review, they cannot complete what they committed earlier.

Developers sometimes over-commit by taking more work than what they can deliver during an ongoing Sprint. During Backlog Refinements and Sprint Planning, they need to estimate the work items, so that they can understand how much time they are going to spend on each individual work item. However, over-commitment may happen because of many reasons. They might have estimated PBIs/User Stories wrongly or during actual development, they find more dependencies and impact areas that might cause delays. In this case, the Scrum Master needs to coach, teach, and help them to understand relative estimation techniques considering the complexity, uncertainty, and risks involved in the process of development and delivery. Using such techniques, developers need to improve over the time.

Malfunction - Sprint Retrospectives are not productive. Scrum Team discusses on the same issues occurring again and again. Action items are not getting addressed.

During Sprint Retrospectives, Scrum Teams keep on reporting their feedbacks about the issues getting faced by them during Sprints. They also discuss about those issues and come up with set of action items to be worked upon by them in the upcoming Sprint. Sometimes, these action items are not taken seriously and they forget to pay their attention towards them. It is the prime responsibility of each action item owner to execute the expected actions, as decided during the Sprint Retrospectives. Implementing these action items as a part of continuous improvements culture is the adaptation to the inspection of the Scrum Team itself and hence it is a must have for them.

Malfunction - Few Developers discuss within themselves separately. This results into confusion for other Developers having less/no visibility.

Few Developers get into work-related discussions within themselves. It is okay to have those separate discussions not involving all the Developers, whereas the outcomes of those discussions need to be communicated with all of them. Such communication not only keeps everyone aware about what is the impact of any decisions being made in the background, but also increases the visibility for all the Developers. If there are any confusions, individuals can get them clarified.

Malfunction - Scrum Team always wants to rely on external expertise to establish and enhance their own agile way of working and its associated processes.

It is okay to ask external experts to help the Scrum Team to establish and/or enhance their agile way of working; however, there should not be continuous handholding for the same purpose. Scrum Master should teach and coach self-management to them. They need to fail fast and fail safe, so that they can learn, unlearn, and re-learn continuously.

Malfunction - Scrum Team members do not like to have Sprint Retrospectives.

Sometimes, some of the Scrum Team members do not like to have Sprint Retrospectives. This happens because they think that there is nothing that needs to be improved. By keeping such belief, they lose their opportunity to inspect and adapt. Sprint Retrospectives must be there. The complete process of Sprint Retrospectives needs to be followed by the teams to inspect, adapt, and improve.

Malfunction - Developers create Technical Debts, causing a lot of re-work later.

There is always a presence of some form of Technical Debt in the process of software development, which is also called as Design Debt or Code Debt. Technical Debt signifies the implicit cost of extra rework which is caused by any approach taken by the developers. They tend to go ahead implementing easy solutions for time being and not making use of a better and most suitable approach which takes significant amount of time for its implementation. They want to take shortcuts that look okay to them in short term; however, in long term, such things may result into additional overheads, where the team needs to spend their time, effort, and cost to redo things again. Developers need to be transparent about Technical Debts. They need to be properly tracked and worked upon by the team by following a standard procedure, where trade-offs need to happen in between Developers and Product Owner.

Malfunction - Developers lack with the Scrum Values.

Many times, Developers take the agile way of working and its associated practices casually, with a total absence of focus, integrity, seriousness, and commitment. They have no/very low sense of determination. This impacts their overall performance and results into no potentially releasable working software product increment by the end of the Sprints. The team needs to have a right sense of ownership, accountability, and responsibility along with an agreed working agreement emphasizing all the Scrum Values to be seriously followed by them, so that they can convert the PBIs from the Sprint Backlog into product increments.

Malfunction - Scrum Master does not have a willingness to help the Developers.

Few Scrum Masters do not have a willingness to support the Developers who need some help to remove impediments associated with the PBIs being worked upon by them and which they cannot solve on their own. A Scrum Master always needs to keep an eye to track the aging of PBIs during an ongoing Sprint. Ideally, a PBI should not take more than 2 to 3 days to complete. He/she hence always needs to see if any of the Developers are not coping up with such expectation. If a PBI is taking more than 2 to 3 days and its associated tasks are not moving forward, it is the responsibility of Scrum Master to ask the Developers regarding the same. He/she also needs to help and support the Developers to get them back on track.

Malfunction - Scrum Master is unable to restrict the Senior Management and/or the Stakeholders, who are assigning out of the Sprint Backlog work items to Developers.

Many Scrum Masters are unable to restrict the Senior Management and/or the Stakeholders who try to take the Developers away from the team by assigning them some other ad-hoc tasks during an ongoing Sprint. Such behaviors seriously impact the overall accomplishment of Sprint Goal. Scrum Master always needs to educate them by giving them a proper understanding about how team's overall efficiency and collaborative performance gets badly impacted because of such actions. The overall structure, allocation, and collaboration of Developers always make a difference in this case.

Malfunction - Senior and junior Developers do not collaborate well.

It can be seen in many Scrum Teams that, sometimes there are understanding, communication, knowledge related, skills, and capabilities related gaps in between the senior and junior Developers. Knowledge sharing and learning while doing is a must have for them, where they need to have the highest level of collaboration. Senior Developers need to help and support the junior Developers; however, there should not be spoon feeding happening all the time. Both senior and junior Developers need to have thorough zeal and enthusiasm to learn, unlearn, and re-learn, using which continuous learning and relentless improvement can be addressed by them as a one team.

Malfunction - Developers ignore the importance of Technical Agility.

Sometimes, Developers lack with the willingness, strong desire, and ability to work on various aspects of Technical Agility. Technical Agility always needs to be a must have for the Developers. Various aspects of Technical Agility (such as continuous integration, continuous delivery, emergent ways of software product development, automation, optimizing the flow of business value, continuous and built-in quality, and so on) always needs to be the prime focus area for all the Developers of a Scrum Team.

Malfunction - Developers ignore the importance of best, advanced engineering practices to be followed by them while developing and delivering the product increments.

Developers are sometimes unaware of the best, advanced engineering practices which automatically bring in built-in quality. Sometimes they are aware of such practices, but they ignore them. Practices such as pair and mob programming, test and behavior-driven development, code refactoring, micro-services, infrastructure and policy as a code, configuration management, collective code ownership, automated build, deployments, and testing, code reviews, monitoring, logging, and so on, ensure that the team is always releasing the best quality code in production, which is a part of every working software product increment for their customers, as per the release timeline.

Malfunction - Developers ignore the importance of best, advanced practices for testing and quality assurance to be followed by them.

Developers are sometimes also unaware of best, advanced practices for testing and quality assurance. Sometimes they are aware of such practices, but they ignore them. Scrum Framework does not give any direct pointers about the same as it is a framework to develop, deliver, and sustain complex software products; however, it surely encourages the Developers to make use of practices required to improve the overall quality of every software product increment they are releasing by the end of every Sprint. Ideally, to have the Developers to function as a cross-functional team, all the Developers should be able to do both development and testing. These activities need to be factored during an ongoing Sprint. Developers always need to ensure that all the required types of testing such as manual, exploratory, automation, functional, non-functional, smoke, sanity, regression, ad-hoc, continuous, mutation, and so on, are getting performed. They also need to ensure that continuous testing at all the levels such as unit, integration, system integration, acceptance, and so on, is being done, rigorously.

Malfunction - Scrum Teams have separate Sprints to bridge the gaps created by themselves before performing every release.

Few Scrum Teams have an agile way of working consisting of separate Sprints to evaluate on and to bridge the gaps created by them in their previous Sprints, before performing every release. They call these Sprints as Hardening Sprints. Ideally, the Scrum Team always needs to ensure that they are giving their best to accomplish the agreed Sprint Goal and to deliver a fully working potentially shippable working software product increment at the end of every Sprint. While doing the same, they should always align their work items with an agreed Definition of Done and Acceptance Criteria, which always needs to be completely fulfilled by them. If they follow this approach, they should not have a need to create and bridge the gaps under a separate Sprint before the release of product increments. This not only saves time, effort, and cost but also has an anticipation from the team to be more focussed on their Sprint specific work and its associated activities during the normal Sprints only.

Malfunction - Product Owner waits till the end of the Sprint to accept the PBIs.

Few Product Owners have a working style to wait till the end of an ongoing Sprint to accept the PBIs/User Stories, even if the Developers have already completed them from their side earlier in an ongoing Sprint. This behavior causes a significant delay and restricts the Scrum Team from achieving their agreed Sprint Goal, as they proceed ahead with the Sprint specific timeline for an ongoing Sprint. As soon as any of the PBIs are completed by the Developers, the Product Owner needs to accept them or send them back to the Developers after reviewing their completeness, by cross-checking them against their associated Definition of Done and Acceptance Criteria. The Developers need to collaborate with him/her for the same purpose.

Malfunction - Product Owner has availability issues causing unnecessary delays.

It is observed with many Scrum Teams that the Product Owner remains absent for most of the Sprint. Because of this behavior Developers always keep on waiting to get their questions answered from him/her. The value optimization of each product increment is his/her prime responsibility and hence, the Product Owner always needs ensure his/her full availability throughout the Sprint, as and when required.

Malfunction - Product Owner takes too much of control of PBIs in the Sprint Backlog.

Sometimes it is seen that the Product Owner takes too much of control of PBIs under the Sprint Backlog. This might happen due to any kind of changes occurring in the

Sprint Backlog PBIs after the Sprint Planning. Before taking PBIs into the Sprint Backlog, the Product Owner needs to ensure their completeness considering all the aspects of functionality getting tracked under them. After Sprint Planning, once the PBIs have been selected by the Developers inside the Sprint Backlog, it is their responsibility to convert them into potential releasable increment of working software product by the end of the Sprint. If there are any changes occurring under the PBIs in an ongoing Sprint, it is a collaborative ownership and decision making in between the Developers and the Product Owner to cater those changes by doing some re-planning.

Malfunction - Scrum Master lacks to have a collaboration in case of any disruptions.

Many Scrum Masters lack to have a proper collaboration with the Product Owner and the Stakeholders. This happens especially when they are creating disruptions and not ready to do the required trade-offs with the Developers. Scrum Master needs to educate them by giving them a proper understanding about potential harmful impacts on the overall performance of the Developers if there are no trade-offs. Customer value-driven trade-offs are must.

Malfunction - Product Owner tends to remain adamant with the overall way of working.

Sometimes, the Product Owner tends to be adamant with the Definition of Done and Acceptance Criteria of the PBIs. He/she needs to be a bit flexible towards the eagerness from Developers to have customer value-driven trade-offs, instead of sticking with original plans.

Malfunction - Sprint gets forcefully terminated by the Product Owner.

With many Scrum Teams, Sprints might get terminated by some Product Owners, where they enforce their own choice on rest of the Scrum Team members. This should not happen unless and until it is really required. Product Owner has a right to terminate Sprints; however, it should not be done without a genuine reason. There needs to be a consultation with the Developers in any of such cases when the termination of a Sprint is required to be done. The decision always needs to have a proper and logical rationale behind it.

Malfunction - Sprint does not get terminated even though the Sprint Goal has become obsolete.

On the other hand, sometimes many Product Owners do not cancel a Sprint, even though its Sprint Goal has become obsolete and it can no longer be achieved by the Scrum Team. In such scenario, to avoid any kind of wastage specific to any of the development specific activities, the Product Owner should always have a proper consultation with rest of the Scrum Team members to decide on what needs to be done and cancel the Sprint accordingly.

Malfunction - Sprint Backlog gets modified and the Scrum Team (especially the Product Owner and the Developers) is unaware of the changes being done in it.

Without having a proper discussion and consultation with all the Developers, sometimes someone (from the Scrum Team only) creates and/or updates and/or removes PBIs from the Sprint Backlog during an ongoing Sprint. This might result into a confusion and scope change too, which ideally should not happen. In such cases, the Scrum Team needs to have a formal working agreement, using which discussions need to happen to realize the consequences of such actions and to take consensus-based decisions. If any of the new, ad-hoc PBIs are getting added into the Sprint Backlog, then PBIs of similar size from the Sprint Backlog need to be moved back to the Product Backlog.

Malfunction - Developers have less visibility for certain areas of way of working.

In case of some of the Scrum Teams, Developers have very low visibility, when it comes to reviewing the feasibility of Features with the Stakeholders and interactions with the Customers/End-users, if needed. This causes many understanding gaps. The Product Owner should take care of such things; however, to evaluate on technical aspects, he/she should feel free to involve the Developers, as and when it is needed.

Malfunction - Stakeholders and/or Managers assign work to Developers directly.

Sometimes, Stakeholders and/or Managers assign some tasks to the Developers. They call all such tasks as high priority work items that need to be worked by the Developers as soon as possible. Such assignments happen directly without taking a consent of Product Owner. This behavior not only encourages command and control-based leadership style (which is exactly opposite of servant leadership style), but also causes distraction for the Developers to self-organize. It is expected from the Stakeholders that there should be minimum intervention. The Scrum Team also needs to have courage to speak, so that they can avoid such things hampering team's agile way of working and impacting their self-organization. By educating the stakeholders and by following the rules under an agreed working agreement associated with the team's Scrum-based agile way of working, such behaviors need to be discouraged and stopped. The Stakeholders also need to have a willingness to listen and to support.

Apart from all these commonly observed malfunctions, many other malfunctions might be present and can be seen under the Scrum Teams. These malfunctions have many adverse impacts on their Scrum-based agile way of working. Such impacts might cause dysfunctions for short-term or for long-term or for both. The process of identification, discussion, addressal, and remediation for all such kinds of Scrum malfunctions needs to be taken care by the entire Scrum Team, both properly and pro-actively. Along with making their agile way of working simple, nimble, and flexible, they always need to focus on both internal as well as external factors, which cause such Malfunctioning within the Scrum Team. This also has a co-relation with the process of Empiricism, where they should inspect and adapt to eliminate any such kind of malfunctions.

There are many common reasons behind Scrum Malfunctioning. There might be gaps in terms of understanding and applying Scrum Framework, while establishing and enhancing an agile way of working within the Scrum Teams. It is important for them to have a proper knowledge about Scrum Framework, its structure, and its components (Scrum Values, Scrum Roles, Scrum Events, Scrum Artifacts, and Scrum Rules) along with some other helpful concepts such as Empiricism, Structure and Alignment of the Scrum Team, Stakeholder Positioning, Working Agreement, and many more.

There might be few gaps under the overall process of developing people, processes, and the agile way of working itself within the Scrum Teams. It is the primary responsibility of the Scrum Master to teach, coach, help, support, guide, and mentor the Scrum Team to the core of the Scrum Framework. He/she also needs to follow the Servant Leadership style to lead by influence and to build and nurture a self-organizing, self-managing, and cross-functional behavior under Scrum Teams.

There also might be some issues and gaps while managing the products and while having a right sense of agility within both Scrum Teams and Stakeholders. A proper balance with the key aspects like Product Vision, Customer and Product Value Proposition, Business Strategy, Product Backlog Alignment and Management, Management of Stakeholders and Customers, Leadership Buy-in, Communication, Collaboration, Forecasting, Budgeting, Resourcing, and Release Planning can have their own impact on overall agile product development, delivery, and way of working.

All these gaps, issues, factors, bottlenecks, hindrances, and malfunctions always need to be continuously identified, discussed, and bridged by the Scrum Teams. While making a best possible utilization of Scrum Framework based agile way of working, Scrum Teams need to be more agile. They need to perform a continuous inspection for the presence of any of the disrupting factors responsible for Scrum Malfunctioning. To overcome such disrupting entities and factors, Scrum Teams need to adapt every possible set of solutions every now and then. It is equally important for them to understand some advanced techniques along with their need, using which they can explore them further and apply them to resolve malfunctions, if any.

Sometimes, Scrum Teams are not ready to accept this fact that, there are issues and gaps already present with their already established agile way of working. Such gaps causing Scrum Malfunctioning might be getting observed and reported by some of the Scrum Team members, but the other Team members tend to ignore such malfunctions. Even if few of the Scrum Team members are ready to accept this fact, they lack with having a proper interest and enthusiasm to make use of some advanced techniques or add-ons, using which they can reduce and remove such malfunctions.

On the other hand, many Scrum Team members also seem to be a bit stubborn to accept the reality. Sometimes, even though the Scrum Master is having full commitment to tackle this problem using some of the coaching and mentoring-specific techniques, the team is not willing to co-operate. This may also happen the other way around.

Scrum Malfunctioning might result into a big unfavourable impact, if the Scrum Team keeps on ignoring such malfunctions. It might also impact the delivery expectations of product increments causing unnecessary delays. There is also a possibility that the Senior Management might temporarily abandon usage of Scrum Framework, as the delivery of working software product might reach a critical situation. Scrum Teams always need to understand that, it is always better to prevent such malfunctions well in advance by making use of some advanced techniques/add-ons.

"An ounce of prevention is worth a pound of cure.
It's more prudent to head off a disaster beforehand than to deal with it after it occurs."
- Benjamin Franklin

The advanced techniques or add-ons to prevent, protect, remediate, and correct the Scrum Teams from Scrum Malfunctioning can be termed as *Advanced Scrum Add-ons*. They assist them to improve the overall functioning of their Scrum-based agile way of working and to reduce, remove the existing malfunctions present in there.

"The more technique you have, the less you have to worry about it."
- Pablo Picasso

The need for advanced Scrum add-ons, techniques is always being triggered, generated by the means of Scrum Malfunctioning and its harmful impacts on the overall productivity and effectiveness of Scrum Teams. However, it is always essential for the Scrum Teams to understand that making use of an effective and efficient agile way of working consisting of a collection of advanced Scrum add-ons can make a huge difference. It not only ensures that there are less chances of malfunctions getting occurred at a later point of time, but it also enables the process of Empiricism within the Scrum Teams. Advanced Scrum add-ons hence need to be used by the Scrum Teams right from the beginning, while they are starting to establish their Scrum based agile way of working. These add-ons act as handy tools or utilities, using which the Scrum Teams can have an anticipation to become high-performing agile software product development teams.

Points to remember

- It is the primary responsibility of the Scrum Master to be more meticulous by always keeping an eye on the Scrum Team's overall way of working considering people, products/projects, and processes. Scrum Master also needs to find issues, gaps, and concerns irrespective of their nature, type, size, and entities associated with them.

- Scrum Malfunctioning is generally caused by a variety of Product/Project, People, and Process specific improper, irrational, and nonsense making actions, reactions, behavior, patterns, and associated entities occurring within the Scrum Teams. If we consider a boundary around a team's agreed agile way of working then, the symptoms of malfunctioning are generally observed due to some factors, which may be internal and/or external to that boundary. There are factors present within a Scrum Team internally because of which Scrum Malfunctioning might be getting caused. Scrum Malfunctioning within a Scrum Team might also get caused due to some external factors.

- The Scrum Malfunctioning can be easily seen as bottlenecks getting created by internal and external factors; however, the willingness of individuals to report and fix them makes a key difference. These malfunctions have many adverse impacts on their Scrum-based agile way of working. Such impacts might cause dysfunctions for short-term or for long-term or for both. The process of identification, discussion, addressal, and remediation for all kind of Scrum malfunctions needs to be taken care by the entire Scrum Team, both properly and pro-actively.

- Scrum Malfunctioning might result into a big unfavourable impact, if the Scrum Team keeps on ignoring such malfunctions. It also impacts the delivery expectations of product increments causing unnecessary delays. Scrum Teams always need to understand that, it is always better to prevent such malfunctions well in advance by making use of some advanced techniques/ add-ons.

- The advanced techniques or add-ons to prevent, protect, remediate, and correct the Scrum Teams from Scrum Malfunctioning can be termed as *Advanced Scrum Add-ons*. They assist them to improve the overall functioning of their Scrum-based agile way of working and to reduce, remove the existing malfunctions present in there.

In the next chapter, readers will get to know about an introduction to Advanced Scrum add-ons/techniques, which are not only the ultimate solutions to improve Scrum-based agile way of working, but also to reduce and to remove Scrum Malfunctioning within Scrum Teams. They help the Scrum Teams to ensure that they are not falling under the trap of Scrum Malfunctioning. These add-ons are customizable and can be altered, as per the needs and wants of the Scrum Teams.

CHAPTER 5

Introduction to Advanced Scrum Add-ons

Introduction

In this chapter, readers will get introduced to Advanced Scrum add-ons/techniques. They are the ultimate solutions to establish and improve the Scrum-based Agile Way of Working within Scrum Teams. These add-ons not only pro-actively help the Scrum Teams to make sure that they are not falling under the trap of Scrum Malfunctioning, but also act as enablers to reduce and remove present Scrum malfunctions within the Scrum Teams, if any. Many of these Advanced Scrum add-ons are customizable and can be altered, as per the needs, wants, and suitability of the Scrum Teams.

Objective

After studying this chapter, you should be able to:

- Understand what advanced Scrum add-ons for Scrum Teams are.
- Understand the overall need of Scrum add-ons for Scrum Teams.
- Understand how advanced Scrum add-ons can categorically help the Scrum Teams to utilize their powerful characteristics and to achieve a fully functional Scrum-based agile way of working by applying them.

Bob 'The Product Owner' (after completing the product backlog refinement meeting with Raj 'The Scrum Master' and rest of the Developers):

"Folks, one last thing to discuss, before we close this meeting! In our previous Sprint, we were unable to deliver what we had committed during the Sprint Planning. I think, this is happening with us for the second time in a row. I am seriously worried about the quality of our PBIs and I do have a concern there, especially for the Developers. Why our PBIs have too many dependencies? Why they are so big? Why we miss on things under our Definition of Done and Acceptance Criteria? Are we testing our increments properly? I hope you all are getting me!"

Raj 'The Scrum Master':

"Bob, let me ask you couple of quick questions before we go into the quality aspect of our PBIs. I know, you like the game of Soccer! You must have seen the players at Forward position in the game. They need to do the most critical job, right? Do you think that scoring a goal is an easy thing to do? Especially, when there are strong Defenders from the opponent team chasing and tackling the Forwards all the time?"

Bob (thinking for a second and replying):

"Well, that's the beauty of the game of Soccer! Though, scoring a goal is the most critical job for a Center Forward, it's not always his/her individual effort. Rest of the players also need to use some formations, strategies, and techniques; both mentally and physically, to help him/her to target and achieve the end goal. The better they make use of those techniques, better are the chances for them to score goals. Even though there might be strong Defenders tackling them from other side, your team needs to practice and enhance the techniques regularly, to score the goals tactfully."

Raj (smiling and replying):

"I hope you have got the answer for your original concern now. Don't you think, the answer you just gave to my questions answers your concerns about quality of PBIs?"

Bob:

"Spot on Raj! So, this is the reason behind the meeting scheduled by you tomorrow, right? The meeting agenda mentions about some of the advanced techniques you are planning to share with us. I hope to see some action getting started here. Hope you also get a proper co-operation from all the Developers."

Raj:

"Improvements don't happen over a night Bob. However, it's better late than never and when there is a will, there is a way! See you all in tomorrow's meeting! Ciao!"

Many Scrum Practitioners call the Scrum Guide as the Bible of Scrum Framework. Scrum Guide explains about the structure and components of Scrum Framework, which can be referred by the Scrum Teams while establishing their own Scrum-based agile way of working. Scrum Guide emphasizes on which and what all things a Scrum Team needs to put in place as a part of their agile way of working. However, when it comes to how the team needs to do the same (by making use of certain processes and techniques), Scrum Guide does not say anything about it.

"I tend to approach things from a physics framework.
And physics teaches you to reason from first principles rather than by analogy."
- Elon Musk

Generally, a framework is termed as an abstraction or a basic structure or a skeleton or a collection of components underlying a system or a concept, which makes our life easy to simplify and to resolve the complex problems. Scrum is also just a Framework within which one can make use of various processes and techniques, as per their needs, wants, desires, and suitability. Scrum is not at all a process. Scrum is neither a technique nor a conclusive methodology.

After getting a proper understanding of the Scrum Framework, the software product development teams can apply the same to develop and deliver potentially shippable increments of high-quality working software products by the end of every Sprint, both iteratively and incrementally. To have a proper establishment of agile way of working using the Scrum Framework within the Scrum Teams, it is required for them to recognize and apply the Scrum Values along with the concept of Empiricism.

Using the basic structure of the Scrum Framework, the Scrum Teams always need to ensure that they are developing and delivering customer value in every Sprint. They also need to ensure that they are catering the delivery and release of complex software products, where there is always an unavoidable presence of volatility, uncertainty, complexity, ambiguity, and risks involved from the business side. The components of Scrum Framework help the Scrum Teams to determine and establish their agile way of working associated Roles, Events, and Artifacts. Every component within the Scrum Framework is expected to provide a certain objective and it is also required for the Scrum Team's success. The Scrum Rules from Scrum Framework should be rigorously followed by the Scrum Teams, as they need to keep all the Scrum Roles, Scrum Events, and Scrum Artifacts intact, by regulating the correlations and interactions between them.

Scrum Framework gives a full freedom to Scrum Teams. They can decide on the processes and techniques, which they would like to explore, analyse, evaluate, and apply to their own Scrum-based agile way of working. The structure of Scrum Framework can be further extended and can be fully utilized by the Scrum Teams to become more agile. The team members always need to respond to any changes required to be done for the same purpose.

It is significantly important for the Scrum Teams to understand, what is not being said in the Scrum Guide. As shown in the following figure, the Scrum Guide focuses on the basic structure, components, and rules of the Scrum Framework; however, it does not say anything about how the Scrum Teams can make use of Scrum Framework along with various advanced add-ons/techniques to make their agile way of working more simple, nimble, flexible, and systematic. There are no sufficient details in the Scrum Guide to establish and to continuously improve a fully functional agile way of working.

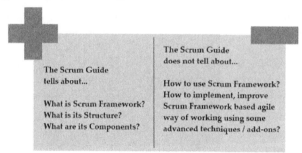

Figure 5.1: Scrum Guide and the need behind Advanced Scrum Add-ons/Techniques

If the Scrum Teams simply follow the Scrum Guide and try to implement their agile way of working, they end up establishing the same, but in a mechanical way of doing it. Hence, this approach is okay for them to just to start with it. However, if the team wants to prevent, protect, remediate, and correct themselves from Scrum Malfunctioning, they need to explore and implement some of the advanced techniques/add-ons under their agile way of working to make it fully functional. Such add-ons, techniques, and practices can be called as *Advanced Scrum Add-ons*.

Using such add-ons, the Scrum Teams always need to challenge their own thought process and agile way of working specific processes without hampering the original structure of Scrum Framework by always considering the Scrum Guide as a baseline. The Scrum Teams need to have an anticipation to apply these advanced scrum add-ons/techniques to utilize their advantages. By following the basic concept of Empiricism, the Scrum Teams need to thoroughly explore various advanced Scrum add-ons. These advanced Scrum add-ons act as key enablers for the Scrum Teams to perform a continuous inspection, adaptation, and to make sure that a proper transparency is also getting persisted within their transparent agile way of working.

To establish a basic Scrum-based agile way of working, Scrum Teams need to learn and understand the values and principles of Agile Manifesto along with the Scrum Framework. As shown in the following figure, knowledge of Scrum is a must have for the Scrum Team. They also need to have the required skill sets and capabilities to perform, as per what is expected from the three Scrum Roles. Skills can be also termed as practiced abilities, which need to be improved by them over the time. The Product Owner needs to take care of value optimization. The Scrum Master needs to take care of coaching, teaching, and mentoring the Developers to bring in the required self-management and cross-functionality. The Developers need to have all the required skills to convert the PBIs from Sprint Backlog to potentially releasable working software product increment by the end of every ongoing Sprint.

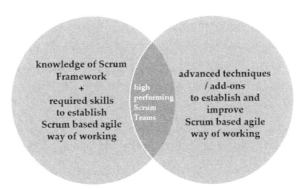

Figure 5.2: *What Scrum Teams need to have to become High-Performing Teams*

Though knowledge and skills are the crucial aspects for Scrum Teams, they also need to learn and understand some advanced Scrum techniques/add-ons, which can guide and assist them using some specific ways to establish and improve their agile way of working. By providing them a structured mechanism, such advanced Scrum techniques/add-ons can always help them to simplify the things around. These techniques can also help them to improve their engagement within themselves to become more efficient and effective. The high-performing Scrum Teams are the Scrum Teams having a collective ownership, accountability, and responsibility to always remain highly focused on their shared goals and to always deliver the anticipated outcome-based results optimizing the overall customer value. They have a unique ability to outperform all the expectations by always giving their 100%.

For a Scrum Team to become a high-performing team, by improving their agile way of working and by reducing, removing any of the malfunctions in their agile way of working, some advanced techniques/add-ons are essential in addition to their knowledge of Scrum Framework and required skill sets.

Scrum Teams need to understand that Scrum is a mindset, which needs to be applied as a systematic approach to solve messy and complex problems using the overall process of development and delivery of high-quality working software products. In this process, they also need to have a formal and a comprehensive understanding of, what and how exactly they need to implement and improve their Scrum-based agile way of working by making use of any of the advanced Scrum add-ons/techniques. They might also need to brainstorm among themselves to set their basic expectations based on the following important aspects.

- How they need to inculcate, demonstrate, and live all the core Scrum Values as a part of their every action?

- How they need to be small, self-organizing, and cross-functional?

- How they need to focus on customer needs and end user's perspective, so that they can collaborate being more creative to deliver the value continuously?

- How they need to make the best possible use of the values and principles of Agile Manifesto (to enhance agility) and of Lean (to eliminate any waste)?

- How they need to make use of Empiricism, to perform frequent inspection and adaptation and to work toward achieving the possible set of outcomes collaboratively?

- How they need to build, nurture, and sustain trust among themselves being transparent all the time and by utilizing their interactions properly?

- Irrespective of any kind of agreements, disagreements, similarities and/or differences of opinions specific to anything, how they can assure a consensus-based decision making, which needs to be an integral part of their agile way of working?

- How they need to share the knowledge having a right sense of collective ownership?

- How they need to have an appropriate alignment on shared vision, goals, and objectives, while being more empowered and having a shared belief, along with a proper understanding of their roles and associated responsibilities?

- How they need to adapt a growth and learning mindset instead of a fixed and stubborn mindset, while being exposed to knowledge sharing, training, on the job learning, and hands-on exposure to anything that they have not tried yet?

- How they need to be disciplined about their own practices and processes?

- How they need to adopt any new practices to improve their overall agility?

- How they need to resolve their impediments, dependencies, risks, and so on?

- How they need to co-ordinate and negotiate with their Stakeholders?

- How they need to establish and endure a happy, healthy, and satisfying working environment by embracing different opinions, conflicts, and failures?

- How they need to encourage themselves to have an agile mindset to learn, unlearn, re-learn, and to support an innovation and experimentation culture?

In the previous chapter, we have seen various malfunctions which are responsible to degrade the overall performance and proficiency of Scrum Teams. A Scrum-based agile way of working within Scrum Teams does not start to malfunction by its own. It is caused only because of the approaches and ways, using which the Scrum Teams keep on trying to establish the same. Advanced Scrum add-ons help them to uncover and resolve those approaches and ways using some handful techniques.

Advanced Scrum add-ons categorically support the Scrum Teams to utilize their powerful characteristics and to achieve a fully functional Scrum-based agile way of working by continuously exploring, evaluating, customizing, applying, reviewing, and re-applying them. By asking the Scrum Teams to continuously retrospect and improve on many aspects, an effective utilization of these add-ons plays a vital role. Using these advanced add-ons, they can expect a variety of positive changes and improvements (which always need to be in line with the values and principles of Agile Manifesto and the basic structure of Scrum Framework) within the Scrum Teams, which can be related to:

- A fruitful establishment along with the continuous review and enhancement of the Scrum-based agile way of working and its associated processes, practices, methods, procedures within the Scrum Teams to make it more valuable, more outcome oriented, and more impactful.

- Helping the Scrum Teams, who are struggling with the structuring, alignment, and collaboration within themselves and with the Stakeholders.

- Making Scrum Roles accountable, responsible, and having a sense of ownership.

- Having the Scrum Artifacts more structured, organized, visible, anticipatory, continuously evolving, and improving.

- Getting the best possible utilization and exemplary advantages out of agreed Working Agreements, Collaboration with Stakeholders, and Scrum Events.

- Helping the Scrum Teams, who are missing the crucial aspect of Scrum Values, Scrum Rules considering various aspects of Effectiveness of Teams.

- Effective refinement of Product Backlog and estimation of PBIs.

- Efficient use of advanced Engineering and DevOps practices for Release Management.

- Value-driven Metrics and constructive Health-Checks to make sure that the Scrum Team is performing, as per valid expectations.

- Competency Building and Knowledge Sharing for the purpose of relentless learning and relentless improvements within Scrum Teams.

- Enhancing the overall communication, co-ordination, collaboration, and co-operation along with the Servant Leadership style within Scrum Teams.

- Many more other aspects to help the Scrum Teams to become high-performing teams, while being more Agile instead of just doing Agile.

Points to remember

- Scrum Guide emphasizes on which and what all things a Scrum Team needs to put in place as a part of their agile way of working. However, when it comes to how the team needs to do the same (by making use of certain processes and techniques), Scrum Guide does not say anything about it.

- The Scrum Rules from the Scrum Framework should be rigorously followed by the Scrum Teams as they keep all the Scrum Roles, Scrum Events, and Scrum Artifacts intact, by regulating all the correlations and interactions between them.

- The Scrum Guide focuses on the basic structure, components, and rules of the Scrum Framework; however, it does not say anything about how the Scrum Teams can make use of Scrum along with various advanced techniques to make their agile way of working more simple, nimble, flexible, and systematic.

- If the Scrum Teams want to prevent, protect, remediate, and correct themselves from Scrum Malfunctioning, they need to explore and implement some of the advanced techniques/add-ons under their agile way of working, to make it fully functional. Such add-ons, techniques, and practices can be called as *Advanced Scrum Add-ons*.

- To establish a basic Scrum-based agile way of working, the Scrum Teams need to learn and understand the values and principles of Agile Manifesto along with the Scrum Framework. Though knowledge and skills are crucial aspects for the Scrum Teams, they also need to learn and understand some advanced techniques/add-ons, which can always guide and assist them using some specific ways to establish and improve their agile way of working.

- Advanced Scrum add-ons categorically support the Scrum Teams to utilize their powerful characteristics and to achieve a fully functional Scrum-based agile way of working by continuously exploring, evaluating, applying, and reviewing them.

In the next chapter, readers will get to know about some of the advanced Scrum add-ons/techniques to help the Scrum Teams, who are struggling with their overall structuring, alignment, collaboration, and communication.

CHAPTER 6

Add-ons for Structuring, Collaboration, and Communication within Scrum Teams

Introduction

In this chapter, readers will get to know about some of the advanced Scrum add-ons/techniques for the Scrum Teams, who are struggling with the issues related to their structuring and alignment. They will also get introduced with various add-ons to enhance their collaboration and communication styles in line with their agreed Scrum-based agile way of working.

Objective

After studying this chapter, you should be able to:

- Understand the advanced Scrum add-ons/techniques for the Scrum Teams to improve their structuring and alignment.

- Understand the advanced Scrum add-ons/techniques for the Scrum Teams to improve their collaboration.

- Understand the advanced Scrum add-ons/techniques for the Scrum Teams to improve their communication.

Mark 'The Agile Coach' (in a discussion with Andrea 'The Product Owner'):

"Hey Andrea, what's up? I was wondering about, how come you wanted to have this one-to-one meeting suddenly. I hope, all's well and your teams are doing fine."

Andrea 'The Product Owner' (replying immediately):

"Yeah Mark! I don't know if I am overthinking on this problem since last 1 week and I am sure, I will go nuts if I keep on thinking more. Our Scrum Teams don't have dedicated Scrum Masters. Two Senior Developers are acting as part time Scrum Masters. They are unable to do a proper justice to the responsibilities of Scrum Master Role. We are missing our Sprint Goals. I think, Teams really need someone, who can teach them Scrum, but not as a part time Scrum Master. How can I ask our Senior Management to get us a dedicated one? There are issues with budget and I am seriously worried now."

Mark:

"Oh, I see! I can understand your pain, but please answer my question first. Without seeing my computer screen, will it be possible for you to guess, to whom I am writing an email right now?"

Andrea (after thinking for a minute):

"Ummm, May be, I can ask someone else to see your screen and tell me, so that I can tell you, right?"

Mark:

"Haha! I am not at all writing an email. I am creating a short presentation, Andrea."

Andrea (laughing and replying):

"Haha! This is not done, Mark! You are not supposed to be here to crack the jokes."

Mark (smiling and replying):

"Yes, you are absolutely right. Things around us are always simple. It's us who we make them complicated. Let's create a requirement proposal to get you a dedicated Scrum Master. At least 1 for 1 of your Scrum Teams! Later, you can go ahead with the proposal and discuss with Management. Don't worry about the budget. I am sure, if this is going to benefit the Scrum Team, they won't deny. By the way, I have already started to create a short presentation for the same purpose. Please feel free to join."

Andrea (replying with a big smile):

"Woah! I am totally speechless, Mark! Let's get started!"

Many Scrum Teams face a variety of issues related to their overall structuring, alignment, collaboration, and communication. The overall structure and positioning of Developers need to be organized carefully and tactfully. They need to be well-aligned and well-empowered to organize and manage their own work, while collaboratively helping each other. In this case, the Developers also need to have all the required knowledge, skill sets, and capabilities to deliver the working software product increments.

The overall system architecture of a software product is always defined based on its technical layers/components along with its features and functionalities. The individual technical layers/components need to be integrated, so that they can interact with each other to provide a reliable user experience behavior comprising the features. The Developers need to build working software products integrating those individual technical layers to provide better user experience, usability, quality, maintainability, performance, scalability, and flexibility, and so on, aspects. Hence, while positioning the Developers, it needs to be optimized for the complete development and delivery process. As it can be seen in the following figure, they need to create PBIs/User Stories across the software product's all the technical layers/components vertically and not across its specific technical layer/component horizontally:

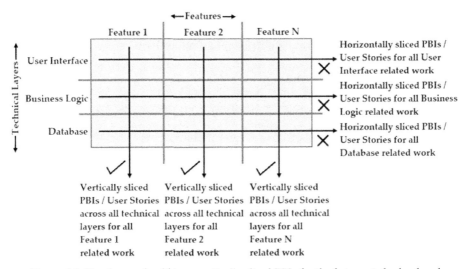

Figure 6.1: Developers should have vertically sliced PBIs for the features to be developed

This approach makes it easy and faster for them to deliver the customer value with fewer dependencies and better alignment within themselves. They also need to have their PBIs as a collection of components, which can be reused and thoroughly tested, so that a fully functional, high-quality working software product can be delivered. Vertically sliced PBIs covering all the technical layers/components always ensure a development and delivery of customer value-based outcomes through working software product increments.

A component-based Dev Team is a team having individual developers with their primary focus on a specific technical layer/component of the software product, which they are supposed to develop and deliver. These components can be divided into technical layers such as presentation/user interface/front-end layer, business logic/application programming interface/middleware layer, and database/back-end layer. There might be a possibility of few more layers involved in a software product's technical implementation. Individual developers in a component-based Dev Team perform development by making use of their technical layer/component-specific skills. As it can be seen in the following figure, this approach causes many issues and problems:

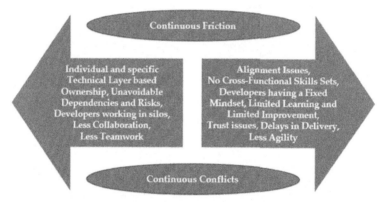

Figure 6.2: Issues with Developers having a structure as a Component-Based Dev Team

If individual Developers belonging to such a component-based Dev Team focus on individual technical layers/components by giving a secondary priority to the complete software product, they start to work in silos. This way of working reduces the overall collaboration and teamwork among them. This structure also creates dependencies across components and it is not at all relevant, valuable from the customer value, outcome-based delivery point of view.

Hence, having the structure of Developers as a component-based Dev Team always minimizes the value proposition. It also slows down the flow of value. Individual Developers working on individual technical layers create many risks. It also requires a lot of additional overhead in terms of communication, co-ordination, cooperation, and collaboration between them to perform all the required activities related to analysis, design, develop, test, build, deploy, and release. If the Developers do not have cross-functional skills, they might waste their precious time to discuss and resolve dependencies, reducing team's overall agility. Developers hence always need to remember that they need to have a collective ownership of work items to be cross-functional.

A component-based Dev Team always tends to look after delivering outputs and not after delivering outcomes. The output can be number of things being done by the individual developers, along with what is being produced because of what they have done. While focusing more on outputs, they miss on the important aspect of outcomes. Outcomes directly relate to the business/customer/end-user value, which is being produced because of an incremental and iterative working software product increment after the completion of every Sprint. While working in silos, individual Developers focus on individual goals instead of a common goal. They have a feeling that they are responsible for only certain pieces of features being worked upon by them.

Dependencies in between technical layers always result in re-planning and re-work, further causing deviations and delays in their Sprint-based delivery. Developers tend to have a fixed mindset, using which they look after only a specific technical layer and not after the entire system. This reduces collective ownership and results in traditional waterfall model-based development and delivery. The code quality also gets impacted, causing issues for customers and causing more re-work.

> *"That which is a feature to a component team is a task to a feature team."*
> *- Ken Rubin*

On the other hand, a feature-based Dev Team is a team structured as a feature-based team, where most of the team members are cross-functional and acting as generalized specialists. They have the required skills to perform end-to-end cross-component development and delivery of the customer-centric features across all the technical layers by applying modern engineering practices. Such kind of structuring approach not only reduces the dependencies across all the technical layers, but also ensures that there is a proper collective ownership along with a suitable presence of communication, co-ordination, cooperation, and collaboration within all the developers.

It is always better to have the structure of the developers as a feature-based Dev Team, emphasizing that, they are having vertically sliced PBIs/User Stories, solving real needs of customers, end-users and accelerating the general customer value-based development and delivery of functionalities getting tracked under those features of a working software product. From the customer's/end-user's perspective, this approach also makes the feedback loop easier, shorter, faster, and better.

Developers having such kind of structuring may have a common misunderstanding-based thinking. They think that all the Developers are expected to know about everything, which is not true. Not an individual Developer but the entire team of Developers needs to have the required knowledge and skill sets to develop and deliver the end-to-end customer-centric features. Continuous learning and sharing of knowledge and skill sets happens within the Developers, when a specialization across technical layers acts as a constraint. To have a generic specialization across technical layers, all the Developers need to help each other, while focusing on high customer value features.

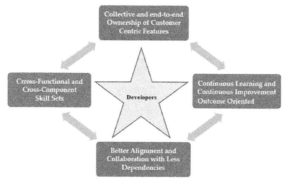

Figure 6.3: *Importance of Developers having a structure as a Feature-Based Dev Team*

By considering the importance of outcome-based value delivery, Developers need to be outcome oriented. They need to have a right focus on the customer value with a complete end-to-end ownership, while being responsible to deliver complete customer-centric features in Sprints. They need to collaborate by minimizing and resolving dependencies between themselves. This is required for them to enhance their shared ownership along with a collaborative accountability and responsibility of all the development and delivery specific agreed activities such as impact analysis, exploration, user experience-driven design, development, code construction, peer reviews, debugging, testing and quality assurance, bug fixing, builds, deployments, releases, and so on. They need to have a courage, openness, commitment, and flexibility for the continuous and comprehensive learning to focus on multiple specializations.

By having some shared responsibilities, the Developers always need to make use of the advanced engineering practices to have an ease of iterative and incremental delivery of working software product increments. Without having specific role-based titles, all the Developers need to encourage themselves, as if they are a multi-competent team performing end-to-end development and delivery of customer-centric features.

A feature-based Dev Team, in its purest form always needs to be ideal, when it comes to aspects such as flexibility-based collaboration and value-based, outcome-based delivery. Developers always need to have a decent sense of understanding and maturity to live all the core values of Scrum Framework. Being a well-balanced cross-functional, cross-component, and multi-disciplinary team, they always need to have an anticipation to be able to accomplish their agreed Sprint Goals.

Feature-based Dev Teams need to work independently by governing the complete ownership and responsibility of all the features. This increases value throughput, as they have their focus on developing and delivering what is the most valuable need for their customers/end-users in terms of the working software product. It also increases their long-term learning ability, as the responsibility is getting broader across all the technical layers/components. By getting an entire feature to work on by the team, the overall planning, organizing, and alignment becomes much easier. It not only ensures that the amount of time and effort getting wasted during handovers in between the individual Developers is getting saved, but also all the Developers are having enough work in hand. Due to fewer handovers, the waiting time and dependencies also get reduced. Delivery of the customer-centric features does not need to wait, as the individual Developers are collaboratively self-organizing.

Developers need to have the best quality code, tests, and other artifacts adhering to the standards and following the best practices. Developers working on shared components create an openness which further helps them to enhance their commitment. It also acts as a source of motivation and job satisfaction, having said that the team needs to have a complete end-to-end responsibility for all their features, PBIs/User Stories, which are customer value driven. This also has a positive impact on the overall happiness and satisfaction index within the teams, while enhancing their productivity and success.

Developers always need to have a proper equilibrium, balance on the diversification of their skill sets, capabilities, assignments, and constructive thoughts. To have a formal alignment and agreement on their Scrum-based agile way of working, there always needs to be a consensus-based decision-making. Since the end-to-end ownership of all the features must be completely collective, Developers need to continuously inspect and adapt, while becoming more self-managing and cross-functional. Individual Developers need to identify ways to enhance their knowledge and skills through the process of knowledge sharing and on-the job learning. While co-ordinating the work with each other, co-operation and communication is also trivial for them, as they have a collective responsibility for the end-to-end delivery of working software product increments.

> *"Getting teams to work well is hard and to work well together is much harder."*
> *- Mary Poppendieck*

Many times, a lack of appropriate structuring and alignment of Scrum Teams might result into many issues impacting a Scrum Team's overall morale. In such scenarios, the Scrum Teams might get into a mode of confusion and frustration, while they might struggle to deliver product increments and to achieve their desired Sprint Goals. There might be challenges related to a lack of collaboration, ambiguous Sprint Goals, limited/less/no collective ownership, a lot of work in progress work-items, disagreements, destructive conflicts, differences of opinions hampering consensus, improper reporting and resolution of impediments, major changes in scope of work during an ongoing Sprint, lack of clarity, lack of prioritization of customer value, and so on.

There also might be few other valid reasons behind why Scrum Teams get into unavoidable deviations and delays impacting their expected delivery at the end of every Sprint. Lack of collaboration is one of the main reasons within Scrum Teams, which disables their ability to work together. Scrum Teams need to know that, collaboration plays a key role to enable them to be the best version of themselves. It allows them to work together to be on the top of their Sprint-based deliverables and to achieve their agreed Sprint Goals. Using collaboration and co-ordination, they need to think, brainstorm, and have healthy discussions to come up with effective solutions to resolve the complex problems under the software product they are delivering to their customers. In the absence of collaboration, if individual team members are working in silos, then there is always a risk of having incomplete, partially completed PBIs at the end of the Sprints. This also has an unavoidable and undesirable impact on the product increments, making them not shippable/releasable.

"The goal is not to write code. If we could ship products and make all this money without writing any code, we would. Your job is to ship products exactly on time.
It doesn't matter whether you're a developer, tester, program manager,
product manager whatever. Everybody's job is the same."
- Chris Peters

Many times, Scrum Teams and especially the Developers do not have a proper understanding about how they need to collaborate and what are the ways for the same. Usually, this happens if individual Developers have job designations-oriented activities to be performed by them. This pattern can be observed if they are working on multiple projects/products in parallel. Such way of allocation of developers has a negative impact on collaboration, as they need to follow different time schedules and the complexity of work acts as a restriction for them, making the overall anticipated collaboration difficult.

To have the Developers taking some training courses to improve their knowledge and skill sets together, helps to increase collaboration. If it is possible to have senior Developers giving trainings to rest of the Developers, it must be done as a collective effort, so that everyone can attend such trainings. Such on the job trainings enhance shared learning experience by allowing, encouraging, and supporting the Developers to build their competencies. Trainings through on the job learning act as a secure environment for them to perform experimentation, where they feel more comfortable to handle risks and try things more innovatively. Even if they fail, they fail safe. They learn from such failures and look forward to the purpose of continuous learning and improvement.

Scrum Team members always need to have a growth mindset. They always need to have a strong belief within themselves to have a constant growth in place and their actions should always correlate to the same belief. It is the responsibility of the Scrum Master to teach them about various ways to reflect and improve on such a mindset. They also need to have a belief that, they can improve on their efforts using their fundamental, valid, and acceptable values, traits, and behaviors along with a mindset to allow them to thrive against challenges.

> *"Anyone who has never made a mistake has never tried anything new."*
> *- Albert Einstein*

While being a part of a self-organizing, cross-functional Scrum Team, everyone needs to understand and enact, considering that they are supposed to move away from an individual ownership to a shared/collective ownership. Hence, by establishing handful of techniques like pairing, Developers can frequently switch their roles as a doer and a reviewer. This approach helps them to perform the work together at the same time and at a common workstation. Such pairing should not be limited to a specific activity like coding/programming. It can be used as a collaboration and on the job learning technique to improve on any of the aspects of the agile software product development and delivery life cycle to improve the built-in quality of all the deliverables.

> *"That absolute alignment of purpose and trust is something that creates greatness."*
> *- Jeff Sutherland*

Many times, Scrum Teams feel that they do not have an anticipated trust within themselves. Lack of team ownership mainly acts as a primary reason behind lack of trust. Collaboration, communication, and ownership within teams are inter-related. To build and nurture trust within the Scrum Teams, they need to make use of a technique like Gamification. Gamification leverages game-oriented analytical and problem-solving thinking by collaboratively engaging the team members. By organizing some team-building activities, they get a chance to get to know each other and have some fun outside of their regular routine. Events such as Hackathons, Lean Coffee, Potlucks, Happy Hours, Interactions-based Team Games can be effectively used by the teams. Using Gamification techniques, they can freely interact with each other. By the means of an effective knowledge sharing and a fun-based learning, they can collaborate in a psychologically safe environment. This helps to improve overall trust among them.

Scrum Guide does not say anything about co-location of Scrum Teams; however, co-location is certainly beneficial to cultivate collaboration and to improve trust and transparency within the Scrum Teams. Co-location ensures fast collaboration, trust, and rapport building. Using dedicated Scrum Boards, teams can plan, inspect, adapt and re-plan their Sprint-based work together. They can also stay focused on their agreed Sprint Goal. Having a visualization of their overall progress promotes collaborative planning and execution, where they can focus on their next set of action items. It also enables interactions and healthy discussions on who needs to do what and when along with how it needs to be done.

If the team is not co-located, they can still make use of some online collaboration tools to bring them together. Using such tools, they can have face-to-face interactions while participating in Scrum Events and for the purpose of any of the pairing-based activities. This approach is useful, especially when the team is trying to establish their Scrum-based agile way of working, its associated processes, and continuous improvements in it.

Many Scrum Team members feel scared and anxious about conflicts. Collaboration within a Scrum Team intrinsically comes with conflicts, which can be of any kind. While embracing the change and navigating toward continuous improvement, teams need to have a desire to be hyper-productive. They might think that conflicts cause disruption in their agile way of working; however, healthy and constructive conflicts, disputes, and disagreements allow them to think more critically. It also brings in the most efficient and effective solutions in the process of complex problem solving, that too collaboratively. It is a mandatory obligation for all the Scrum Team members to see the indications, where anyone seems to be avoiding such constructive conflicts. Team needs to have proper discussions and thoughts sharing during all the Scrum Events. Ideation, creativity, innovation, and an experimentation-based collaboration always needs to be explored by them. It is not always the Scrum Master who needs to push them for all of this. They need to be more proactive and participatory by showcasing an ample amount of courage, willingness, and open-mindedness.

> *"The better capable team members are to engage, speak, listen, hear,*
> *interpret, and respond, constructively, the more likely their teams*
> *are to leverage conflict rather than be levelled by it."*
> *- Craig Runde and Tim Flanagan*

Constructive conflicts are good for the Scrum Teams to grow. It is also important for the teams to understand that they need to have such constructive conflicts to prosper and succeed for excellence. They need to come up with productive ideas with which they can brainstorm and look for better options providing a maximum customer value through their Sprint-based development and delivery of working software product increments. The Scrum Master can identify individuals tending to avoid constructive conflicts. He/she can ask everyone for their opinions, thoughts specific to the topics under discussion. Asking powerful and assertive questions always helps the Scrum Master, where the entire Scrum Team can get into discussions with an active participation from all the sides. In this way, a sharing of valuable thoughts, opinions, suggestions, and better alternatives can happen. Collecting various ideas, alternatives and selecting the best suitable approach after performing such open discussions always helps the Scrum Team to nurture consensus, synergy, trust, and transparency.

Scrum Teams creating their own agreed working agreements including methods to handle conflicts can be one more effective way. Using such working agreement, the Scrum Master can teach, help, and support the team members on how they can navigate through their conflicts. Team members need to focus on the alternatives to improve on their concerns and conflicts. Sprint Reviews and Sprint Retrospectives are the precious opportunities for the Scrum Teams, where after collecting and focusing on facts, they can revisit their Scrum-based agile way of working seeking any modifications for the purpose of continuous improvement. While navigating through constructive conflicts, collaboration is always vital for the self-organizing, cross-functional Scrum Teams to deliver working software at the end of every Sprint. Hence, there needs to be an effective environment fostering effective collaboration.

Most of the Scrum Teams having a strong faith in their own capabilities, skills, and aptitude think about them, as if they are limited. This thought process is a result of their fixed mindset-based thinking. By having such a mindset, they restrict their own progress. Fixed mindset makes it more difficult for them to set their objectives and to make use of an intrinsic power of motivation, which seems to be absent within them. They always try to be in their respective comfort zones by considering growth as impractical. It is required for them to have a growth mindset. By keeping growth mindset as a baseline for a Scrum Team's agile way of working, the following figure highlights on some of the important factors affecting effective collaboration within the Scrum Teams. They always need to be aware of the significance of these factors, as they have a direct impact on the important aspects like team's culture, values, principles, alignments, self-esteem, ambitions, togetherness, bonding, and growth:

Scrum Teams should be	Scrum Teams shouldn't be
Able to respectfully agree / disagree to commit	Too much defensive and / or too much aggressive
Able to listen and respond with full of empathy	Too much of transmitting and / or not at all receiving
Courageous, focused and respectful	Having a feeling of being offended or victimized
Open to receive and enact on any kind of feedback	Playing blame games
Having a positive, growth-based win-win mindset	Indulging into behaviors causing toxicity
Having a focus on productive disputes and disagreements	Self-promoting hero culture hampering collaboration

Figure 6.4: *Factors affecting effective collaboration within Scrum Teams*

Scrum Team members always need to have a confidence on their capabilities, skills, and aptitude. Because of their positive attitude, self-learning habits, optimism, hard / smart work, commitment, truthfulness, perseverance, mindfulness, efforts being made, and a strong determination, it becomes easy for them to reach their genuine potential. Scrum Teams having a growth mindset have more courage and willingness to take all the chances to improve. Using a growth mindset based out of the box thinking, they need to set proper objectives. They need to have a high-level plan to execute and to drive themselves out of their comfort zone. Using Empiricism, they always need to reflect, discuss, decide, and enact on themselves.

The Scrum Master always needs to ensure that the Scrum Team has a collaborative intent along with a right mindset for collaboration. It is crucial for the Scrum Master to have self-awareness about everyone within the Team, using which he/she can boost required behaviors by advocating trust, transparency, partnership, and consistency.

> *"A core premise of agile is that the people doing the work are the people,*
> *who can best figure out how to do it."*
> *- Ken Schwaber*

Considering the feedbacks related to what went well, what went wrong, things to be improved, and so on, Scrum Teams need to reflect on their collaboration and happiness index during their Sprint Retrospectives. This needs to be done using keyword-based direct feedbacks. Each individual Scrum Team member needs to share a keyword or even multiple keywords highlighting their overall impression about what and how they felt, worked, collaborated, and achieved and/or failed during the Sprint. Considering individuals as well as the whole Scrum Team, such keywords can be treated as positive/negative/neutral, representing their honest impression about the Sprint. Using such an approach, they get to know about certain actions, reactions, patterns, anti-patterns, and behaviors causing such kind of impressions. They further need to discuss to take applicable remedial actions and to enact accordingly.

> *"Without self-awareness we are as babies in the cradles."*
> *- Virginia Woolf*

Scrum Teams also need to be self-aware about themselves. Self-awareness is a cognizant knowledge of every individual's personality trait, character, strengths, weaknesses, attitude, behavior, emotions, feelings, and so on. Having a right sense of self-awareness helps Scrum Team members to have a good understanding of their own strengths, weaknesses, beliefs, desires, emotions, fears, and feelings. Realizing these aspects assist them to inspect on how they can improve, while always remaining assertive, receptive, and adaptable. A true self-awareness about the individuals within a Scrum Team and about the entire Scrum Team expands the progressive and productive relationships within a Scrum Team. This assists the Scrum Team to have more successful associations, collaborations, and rapport building with an enhanced presence of mutual trust and affinity.

Scrum Teams need to have an open environment during all the Scrum Events, where all the team members need to have a full involvement. They need to share their inputs showcasing their mindset, perspectives, sweet spots, blind spots, and anything else. This helps the team to realize the possible ways to improve their collaboration. They need to share, discuss, and elaborate on their findings by coming together as a syndicate. They need to be open to receive and enact on any feedback by being respectful to varied perspectives. They need to track such valuable inputs, feedbacks using appropriate collaborative tools. This approach helps them to visualize and to improve on their collaboration mechanisms, practices, and patterns.

Along with the self-awareness, self-accountability is another important aspect that needs to be explored by the Scrum Team members. Self-accountability is all about having a right sense of choices, decisions, actions, and behaviors being made by individuals within a Scrum Team. It needs to be achieved by having a recognition about the decisions to be taken having an impact on team's deliverables. It also has a correlation with their collaboration strategies and relationships as a part of their Scrum-based agile way of working. By making use of the Fundamental Interpersonal Relations Orientation (FIRO) theory, introduced by William Schutz, teams need to obtain deeper intuitions to check their understanding about their own relationships and compatibility levels. As it can be seen in the following figure, Inclusion, Control, and Openness are the three key attributes of FIRO theory. These attributes need to be characterized by team's beliefs, interpretations, desires, choices, decisions, actions, reactions, worries, and so on.

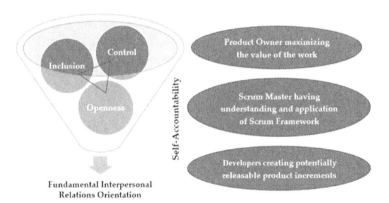

Figure 6.5: *FIRO theory attributes and self-accountability within Scrum Teams*

Scrum Teams have an anticipation to feel respected and admired. They also have a fear of being offended, disgraced, victimized, denied, and or ignored. The intensity and variations of such emotions and feelings have a significant amount of influence on their relationships and they might have a feeling of a low self-esteem. They also might have a fear of openness along with a lack of integrity to accept any mistakes done by them. They might be coming up with excuses, as they are unable to cope up with the expected productivity. This puts up a question on their self-accountability.

> *"Ninety-nine percent of failures come from people,*
> *who are having a habit of making excuses."*
> *- George Washington Carver*

While being a part of a Scrum Team, it is hence required for everyone to inspect on their individual levels of inclusion, control, and openness, which also needs to be correlated with others. Inclusion is all about the action or state of being included within a team under every situation. Control is all about how one can lead with an influence or direct behaviors of others within a team under every situation. Openness is all about being flexible and having a willingness to be accessible within a team under every situation. By establishing a correlation in between these three attributes and by making use of a simple exercise, they can reflect on their self-accountability toward others within the Scrum Team. This time-to-time exercise needs to be done by individuals. It not only underlines the factors affecting them to have a better understanding of their own compatibility with others in the team, but also guarantees that everyone has required action items to improve their self-accountability.

One more crucial aspect to improve the collaboration within Scrum Teams is, having their focus set on shared, common goals and objectives. The Scrum Master always needs to be more focused, when it comes to shielding the team who tends to lose their focus. It is required for the Scrum Master to motivate the team. Having a right mindset and a proper intention of agility, the Scrum Master always needs to keep them aimed at a common, shared purpose. By identifying the team's vision and mission statement, they need to drive their collaborative mindset, conducts, and activities.

> *"Doing half of something is, essentially, doing nothing."*
> *- Jeff Sutherland*

Every Sprint needs to have a well-crafted, well-negotiated, and well-balanced Sprint Goal. To become more and more self-organized and cross-functional, the team needs to have a common purpose and its associated goals and objectives. It helps them to establish shared intentions, so that they can discover the opportunities to advance toward it. During their Sprint Retrospectives, they can create a visualization-based representation by summing up their reflections and intentions. Their working agreement always needs to be up to date with a continuously evolving shared understanding and goals which always need to be agreed upon by them, to achieve their common agreed purpose.

Scrum Teams always need to be truthful and transparent about all their actions. They need to have a realization about themselves that they can achieve their common, shared purpose and its corresponding substantial results when they have a zeal and an enthusiasm to collaborate and work together. To build, sustain, and to grow the unique collaborative relationships, the recognition of their skills and strengths is a must have for them. The Scrum Master always needs to act as a Sensor. By performing a continuous monitoring and by applying an appropriate sense-making, the Scrum Master always needs to sense for the better ways and all the possible set of alternatives to enhance an effective and efficient collaboration within Scrum Teams, so that they can enact on those ways, alternatives. This also helps them to always focus on the crucial aspect of value optimization through an iterative, incremental working software product development and delivery across their every planned Sprint.

Scrum Framework is a team-oriented, people-oriented framework, where the styles of communication getting used by the team members under their Scrum-based agile way of working have a direct influence on their meaningful collaborations. By implementing the effective ways of communication, teams receive faster feedbacks. It helps them to track their overall progress through their interactions.

Various ways of communication help them to bring-in the required agility to embrace the change. It is hence a must have for the Scrum Team members to interact with each other constantly. By giving them enough support and motivation through such interactions, the Scrum Master needs to explain them about, how important it is to have a properly structured and aligned communication to make their delivery expectations (in terms of working software product increments) successful.

For the Scrum Teams to have an impactful communication, they need to define some basic rules under their agile way of working. Rules need to be in line with the basic structure of Scrum Framework and to be agreed by everyone. Rules can be also captured under their working agreement, where the team needs to follow the concept of Empiricism by considering some of the important factors affecting the continuous improvement of impactful communication, as shown in the following figure:

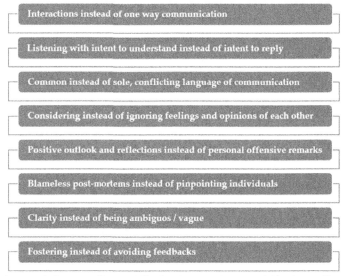

Figure 6.6: Factors affecting Effective Communication within Scrum Teams

Scrum Team members need to have interactions using dialogues and not through one-way communications using monologues. Be it any kind of communication within the team or outside of the team, they always need to consider all the opinions from all the sides. Everyone needs to show active participation while having constructive dialogues. Interactions based on dialogues help to boost openness and respect within Scrum Teams.

> *"In a true dialogue, both sides are willing to change."*
> *- Thich Nhat Hanh*

The Product Owner needs to have a self-introspection about how he/she is communicating with the rest of the Scrum Team members. This needs to be done by him/her, especially at the time of every Backlog Refinement and Sprint Planning, while negotiating with the Developers to decide on the clarity and scope of the work under upcoming Sprints. The Scrum Master always needs to have a self-introspection about how he/she is communicating with the rest of the Scrum Team members, while facilitating every Scrum Event. The Developers also need to have a self- introspection about how they are communicating with the rest of the Scrum Team members, while having any kind of interactions and discussions with them. Such self-introspections considering previously mentioned factors affecting effective communication within Scrum Teams help them to improve their styles and ways of communication.

Many times, it is observed with the Scrum Teams that, the individual Scrum Team members tend to listen to others, having an intent to reply quickly. They do not have an intent to understand, to think, and to reply. Scrum Team members always need to be listening more (than speaking) and having a rational and literal understanding that each one of them has got two ears and just one mouth. They need to make use of active listening, where they always need to try to understand, what is being said and what is not. This needs to be done by them by having a proper intention to understand first.

> *"The most important thing in communication is hearing what isn't said."*
> *- Peter Drucker*

In the process of dialogue-based interactions, when individuals get a feeling that others are actively listening, they tend to become more comfortable by showcasing a much better willingness to speak and share about what understanding is there from their point of view. They also need to be aware of their voice tone as well as their body language to safeguard that it meets the intent of their thoughts and selection of words.

The Scrum Team members always need to learn about upholding an open, acceptable, and appropriate gesture and posture, asking questions, doubts, and concerns openly, reflecting to others by repeating and summarizing with their own words to be on the same page, and so on. The Scrum Master needs to facilitate open discussions to rectify, fix, and resolve the impediments as soon as they are being reported by the Developers. This approach minimizes further delays being caused by such impediments. Dialogue-based interactions not only help to enable a better collaboration, but also to create a better understanding in Scrum Teams.

Every Scrum Team member needs to have an empathy to understand and to consider the opinions, feelings, and emotions of other Scrum Team members. Empathy is the unique ability to get to know, understand, and share the feelings of others. To make sure that there is always a transparency present within and outside of the Scrum Team, team members need to let the truth to be told regarding anything under their established way of working, while always being considerate and empathetic.

> *"Learning to stand in somebody else's shoes, to see through their eyes,*
> *that's how peace begins. And it's up to you to make that happen.*
> *Empathy is a quality of character that can change the world."*
> *- Barack Obama*

Empathetic Scrum Teams always have a higher emotional quotient. They generally do not indulge into any destructive conflicts and pinpointing each other for the mistakes being done. They do not make personal, offensive, and derogatory remarks, comments during any of their interactions. It helps them to have a true collaboration within themselves. All the Scrum Team members need to be accepted for who they are and by the means of their individual personas and associated personality traits. Team always needs to have a positive outlook about their style of communication. It is always better to have face-to-face communication instead of written communication. It not only saves their time, but also ensures that all the participants within any of their dialogues are sharing their viewpoints, perspectives, thoughts, opinions, concerns, and reflections along with their reactions to what is being said by everyone.

> *"Good communication is the bridge between confusion and clarity."*
> *- Nat Turner*

While communicating, any of the topics/subjects/concerns under discussion should not be ambiguous/vague. They should be clear enough to discuss and brainstorm on. Scrum Team always needs to have a common language for better communication. Everyone within the Scrum Team needs to grasp, understand, think, and speak a common language. Using a clear, transparent, and agreed roles and responsibilities, way of working, working agreement, Definition of Done, Acceptance Criteria, and many more entities, they need to have facts and expectations-oriented dialogues in place.

Scrum Team members need to make use of Daily Scrum to have an interaction-based dialogue to inspect and adapt on their overall progress toward the agreed Sprint Goal in last 24 hours. At the time of Sprint Reviews and Retrospectives, instead of playing blame games, team members need to do blameless post-mortems.

"Playing the blame game is stupid and childish.
Even if it is someone else's fault, the blame game is wasted time, effort, and energy
that takes you somewhere that is not going to get you anywhere."
- Loren Weisman

Blameless post-mortem is a process of having dialogue-based interactions within a team to understand about, why a certain entity or a collection of entities are not behaving, as per the original expectations. This needs to be done without blaming anyone. The team members need to participate having the best intentions to act and behave as per the facts, information, and data points they have with them.

Instead of pinpointing and blaming someone (within the team who might be causing such deviations), the team needs to move forward by focusing on rectifying such entities and improving the team's overall performance. There can be lessons learned, which can be used for improvements in the processes, people, product, and way of working, but neither the individuals nor the entire Scrum Team should be blamed. This approach helps the teams to have a healthy, open, and positive team culture by increasing the support for communication to be more trustworthy and transparent. Scrum Teams need to have a proper shared ownership of all their plans, actions, and outcomes. Sprint Retrospectives should not be the place to play blame games. Everyone needs to follow the rules, even if there are any optimistic disagreements. To address the important aspect of continuous improvement, they need to have a consensus to have the action items to work upon during the upcoming Sprints.

"I think it's very important to have a feedback loop, where you're constantly thinking about
what you've done and how you could be doing it better."
- Elon Musk

It can be easily seen that the Scrum Teams ignoring, avoiding, and resisting feedbacks lack with the continuous improvement aspect. They need to understand that the feedback is a gift. Everyone being a part of a Scrum Team needs to keep their senses open to make sure that the feedback loop within and outside of the team is always open, where any kind of productive feedback is being shared and received. The Scrum Master needs to pay an extra bit of attention to cross-check on if anything is blocking the Scrum Team to share their valuable feedbacks. This can be done by the Scrum Master, by asking them about anything which might be holding them back and if they lack to have a reasonable focus and commitment for the same purpose. If anything is blocking them to share their valuable feedbacks, then they need to reflect on such entities at the earliest, so that they can further discuss and enact to improve.

"A candle loses nothing by lighting another candle."
- Father James Keller

Scrum Teams need to continuously share and discuss on knowledge, learnings, feedbacks, innovative and creative ideas, and alternatives to have the ultimate ease of self-organization. They always need to create a communication space and an agreement to fill-in the required knowledge gaps through constant interactions, meetings, formal, informal discussions, in-house trainings, knowledge sharing sessions, and so on. By keeping their communication transparent, by sharing success/failure stories, and by having an open-door communication policy, the Scrum Teams always need to look for their own improvement areas.

> *"The biggest room in the world is the room for improvement."*
> *- Helmut Schmidt*

The following figure stresses upon the primary improvement areas to be explored by the Scrum Teams to have a better communication in place. It also shows the consequences, if there are no improvements seen within the Scrum Teams under those areas.

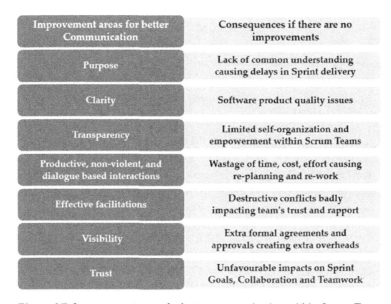

Improvement areas for better Communication	Consequences if there are no improvements
Purpose	Lack of common understanding causing delays in Sprint delivery
Clarity	Software product quality issues
Transparency	Limited self-organization and empowerment within Scrum Teams
Productive, non-violent, and dialogue based interactions	Wastage of time, cost, effort causing re-planning and re-work
Effective facilitations	Destructive conflicts badly impacting team's trust and rapport
Visibility	Extra formal agreements and approvals creating extra overheads
Trust	Unfavourable impacts on Sprint Goals, Collaboration and Teamwork

Figure 6.7: Improvement areas for better communication within Scrum Teams

A Scrum Team always needs to have a common, shared purpose to discuss on, while getting into their every interaction. They need to know about what, when, whom, why, and how they need to communicate with each other to have that common, shared purpose to discuss on with their active participation. Detached and disengaged Scrum Team members tend to remain unresponsive in their interactions. To have an interaction-driven and consensus-based decision-making, the Scrum Master needs to ensure that all the team members are freely interacting within and outside the team. Having a clarity in the interactions is vital. The Scrum Master always needs to make sure that the team members are having a clear idea about the scope of the things to be discussed along with the time-boxing aspect. Sprint Retrospective action items, Sprint Review feedbacks from the customer and stakeholders need to be properly discussed by the Scrum Teams by having a shared ownership to enact on them.

The transparency and clarity of Scrum Artifacts help the Scrum Teams to enhance their interactions. It is the responsibility of all the team members to detect if there is a lack of transparency, so that it can be improved. Such improved transparency helps them to determine and set the overall context for communication. It also facilitates speedy and proper decision-making. Teams having productive, non-violent, and dialogue-based interactions always act good by having constructive interactions.

> *"The Law of Win/Win says, 'Let's not do it your way or my way;*
> *let's do it the best way'."*
> *- Greg Anderson*

Even if there are any disputes, conflicts, and disagreements, the team members need to understand what is causing all of them. They need to avoid disrespectful, competing, and judgemental comments. The Scrum Master needs to preach and teach the Scrum Team to use a non-violent communication style. Such communication style not only improves and intensifies expressive and emotional inter-personal relations, but also helps the Product Owner and the Stakeholders to get what they need often, without looking for any forceful requests. It significantly reduces the tension and friction in between the individuals and improves the overall collaboration, co-ordination, co-operation, proficiency, potential, and determination of Scrum Team members.

While acting as a facilitator, the Scrum Master needs to continuously observe the patterns and entities, which are advocating as well as limiting the interactions. Interactions need to establish mutual respect and trust. By encouraging face-to-face interactions and by pausing the entities restricting effective communication for some time, teams need to have a self-realization to improve the process of communication.

Many times, miscommunication may occur, as what is being told is not what is being understood. Scrum Team members are unable to properly say what they want to say and hence creating understanding gaps. To bridge such gaps, it is hence required to make the communication visual. By making use of sticky notes, physical/virtual whiteboards, flipcharts, and so on, team members need to visualize their thoughts and share the required information. Such visual tools accompanied by relative dialogues support a rapid and consensus-based decision-making by enriching the highest intensity of communication.

> *"Inside the fogs, you think better and thus you see better!"*
> *- Mehmet Murat Ildan*

Using appropriate visual aids and tools, all the conversations related to the artifacts, decisions, processes, feedbacks, and so on, within the Scrum Teams can be enhanced. It promotes face-to-face interactions, eliminating inefficient and redundant conversations. By doing a proper and a regular use of such visual aids, Scrum Teams can easily get into an open, flexible, and active conversation mode, which strengthens the overall quality of their interactions.

As shown in the following figure, to have a clarity, completeness, conciseness, concreteness, courtesy, correctness, and consideration (7 Cs of Communication) within a Scrum Team's every interaction, it is always good to have direct dialogues-based interactions in between all the Scrum Roles. Sometimes, Product Owner tries to get the required inputs from developers through Scrum Master as a mediator. This type of indirect, mediator-oriented communication puts an additional overhead for the Scrum Master to get in touch with the Developers and to get back to the Product Owner. If the Product Owner gets into a direct communication with the developers, it saves a lot of time, effort, information loss, and communication gaps.

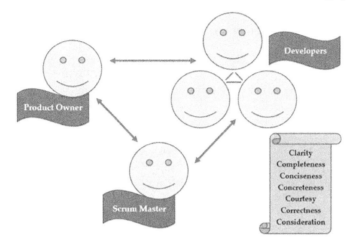

Figure 6.8: Direct dialogues-based interactions within all the Scrum Roles

Creating a highest level of transparency and trust while establishing and enhancing the agile way of working is a must have for the Scrum Teams. The absence of trust among the team members impacts the openness and quality of communication. Scrum Team members need to identify and act on causes if it is not easy for them to speak. By creating and enhancing a flexible and psychologically safe environment, they can share their opinions, ask their queries, and discuss openly without any restrictions.

> *"The ratio of We's to I's is the best indicator of the development of a team."*
> *- Lewis B. Ergen*

By driving an empiricism-based continuous improvement, by encouraging We instead of I mindset, and by facilitating face-to-face interactions using visual aids, the Scrum Master needs to coach the team to be consistent and truthful across their all kind of communication. Scrum Team also needs to perform constant efforts to build and nurture trust among themselves.

Points to remember

- It is always better to have the structure of the Developers as a feature-based Dev Team, emphasizing that, they are having vertically sliced PBIs/User Stories, solving real needs of customers, end-users and accelerating the general customer value-based delivery of functionalities getting tracked under the features of a working software product. Feature-based Dev Teams need to work independently by governing the complete ownership and responsibility of all the features.

- Scrum Teams need to have a growth mindset. It is the responsibility of the Scrum Master to teach them about various ways to reflect and improve on such mindset.

- Gamification leverages a game-oriented analytical and problem-solving thinking by collaboratively engaging the Scrum Team members. The Scrum Master always needs to ensure that the Scrum Team has a collaborative intent along with a right mindset for collaboration.

- Scrum Guide does not say anything about co-location of Scrum Teams; however, co-location is certainly beneficial to cultivate collaboration and to improve trust and transparency within Scrum Teams.

- Constructive conflicts are good for the Scrum Teams to grow. It is also important for the teams to understand that they need to have such constructive conflicts to prosper and succeed for an excellence.

- Scrum Teams need to have an open environment during all the Scrum Events, where all the team members need to have a full involvement. They need to share, discuss, and elaborate on their findings by coming together as a syndicate.

- Self-accountability is an important aspect that needs to be explored by the Scrum Teams. It is all about having a right sense of choices, decisions, and actions being made by the individuals within a Scrum Team.

- Being a part of a Scrum Team, it is required for everyone to inspect on their individual levels of inclusion, control, and openness, which also needs to be correlated with others. Scrum Team members always need to have their focus set on shared, common goals and objectives.

- Scrum Teams always need to be truthful and transparent about all their actions. They need to have a realization about themselves that they can achieve their common purpose and substantial results when they have a zeal and enthusiasm to collaborate and work together.

- Every Scrum Team member needs to have an empathy to understand and to consider opinions, feelings, and emotions of other Scrum Team members. Empathy is the unique ability to get to know, understand, and share the feelings of others.

- Scrum Framework is a team-oriented, people-oriented framework, where the styles of communication getting used by the team members under their Scrum-based agile way of working have a direct influence on their meaningful collaborations.

- By giving the Scrum Team enough support and motivation through their meaningful interactions, the Scrum Master needs to explain them about, how important it is to have properly aligned communication to make their software product successful.

- Blameless post-mortem is a process of having dialogue-based interactions within a Scrum Team to understand about, why a certain entity or a collection of entities are not behaving, as per the original expectations. This needs to be done without blaming anyone. The Scrum Team members need to participate having the best intentions to act and behave as per the facts, information, and data points they have with them.

- Scrum Team members need to have interactions using dialogues and not through one-way communications using monologues. Be it any kind of communication within the team or outside of the team, they always need to consider all the opinions from all the sides.

- Scrum Teams ignoring, avoiding, and resisting feedbacks lack with the continuous improvement aspect. The Scrum Master needs to pay an extra bit of attention to cross-check on anything blocking the team to share their valuable feedbacks. This can be done, by asking them about anything holding them back and if they have a reasonable focus and commitment for the same purpose.

- The transparency and clarity of Scrum Artifacts help the Scrum Teams to enhance their interactions. It is the responsibility of all the Scrum Team members to detect if there is a lack of transparency, so that it can be improved. The Scrum Master always needs to make sure that the team members are having a clear idea about the scope of the things to be discussed along with the time-boxing aspect.

- It is always good to have direct dialogues-based interactions in between all the Scrum Roles. The Scrum Team needs to perform constant efforts to build and nurture trust among themselves.

In the next chapter, readers will get to know about some of the advanced Scrum add-ons/techniques to help the Scrum Teams with their three Scrum Roles and a continuously evolving Working Agreement.

CHAPTER 7
Add-ons for Scrum Roles and Working Agreement within Scrum Teams

Introduction

In this chapter, readers will get to know about some of the advanced Scrum add-ons/techniques to help the Scrum Teams with their three Scrum Roles - Product Owner, Scrum Master, and Developers. They will also get introduced with the useful concept of Working Agreement within a Scrum Team to have a flexible and continuously evolving Scrum-based agile way of working.

Objective

After studying this chapter, you should be able to:

- Understand the characteristics of high-performing teams.
- Understand the advanced Scrum add-ons/techniques for the three Scrum Roles - Product Owner, Scrum Master, and Developers.
- Understand the concept of Working Agreement within a Scrum Team.

Mike 'The Developer' (in a Sprint Retrospective with the Scrum Team):

"Rob, can we discuss on this last feedback? I have raised it on the behalf of all the Developers. We need to know about, where are we going with our code reviews."

Helena 'The Another Developer' (supporting Mike and replying):

"I completely agree with what Mike is saying! We are always busy with our own work during the Sprints. In addition to that, we are also supposed to perform peer reviews of someone else's work. Not fair! To be honest, code reviews are not all required. Each Developer needs to take care of his or her own code and if something goes wrong, they should be held accountable. Our current code review process not only wastes time, but also creates unnecessary delays to promote the code further."

Robert 'The Scrum Master' (smiling and replying):

"Okay! I genuinely consider your opinions. Just tell me one thing. In the morning, before coming to the office, most of you drop your kids to their schools and the same goes with, picking them up in the evening, right? For me, sometimes it's me and sometimes it's my wife, who needs to perform this duty. Now tell me, why it must be always like that? Can't our neighbours take care of our kids?"

Mike (smiling and replying instantly):

"Are you kidding, Rob? Anyway, let me answer. You used the right word, Duty! It's a duty! We do it because, it's our duty to take care of them. Why should our neighbours need to worry about our kids?"

Robert (smiling and replying):

"Bingo! Similarly, you need to do peer reviews because, as Developers, you are the collective owners of your code. It's your duty. Why should someone else need to worry about your code?"

Daniel 'The Another Developer' (replying with a worry):

"But what about less time in hand to perform code reviews along with our own development work?"

Robert:

"I think, you all need to explore techniques like Test Driven Development and Pair Programming. Time to revisit our working agreement to reflect on our Code Review policies! Let's get started! Can we?"

Helena:

"Why not, Rob! Sure! Yes, we can and yes, we will!"

The high-performing agile teams are extremely focused on achieving their purpose, vision, mission, goals, and objectives by always keeping their existing structure intact. They always try to outperform by surpassing all the ideal expectations from them. According to the concept of the high-performance tree from Lyssa Adkins, for a Scrum Team to become such a high-performing agile team, the Scrum Team members always need to have some primary traits and characteristics to be inculcated and lived within themselves. These important traits are shown in the following figure:

Figure 7.1: High-Performance Tree Concept by Lyssa Adkins

High-performing teams always live the five Core Scrum Values to the fullest. They are always self-organizing and empowered to make consensus-based decisions. They always have a strong belief that they can do anything to solve any problem collectively, while always being fully committed to their success. They have a complete collective ownership of their own decisions and commitments. Trust is at its peak within them. They have constructive disagreements. They deliver a proper business value with astonishing results, where they also have a room for their constant collective growth.

To enable a Scrum Team to be such a high-performing team, every individual Scrum Team member needs to imbibe the previously mentioned traits. To meet an expectation of becoming a high-performing team into reality, they need to make use of some of the advanced Scrum add-ons specific to the three Scrum roles. These add-ons need to be embedded in addition to the basic responsibilities of Scrum roles, as they not only help the Scrum Teams to improve their agile way of working, but also have a direct impact on their collective and continuous improvement considering the said traits.

Product Owner is the backbone of a Scrum Team. By always encouraging a product thinking mindset, he/she always needs to support and adopt the product vision agreed with the Stakeholders and the Scrum Team. Such mindset can be achieved by focussing on the product instead of a temporary project. Product is always likely to have a more life than a project. While creating a product vision and its associated product strategy and roadmap, he/she needs to be in line with the stakeholders to represent the real needs of the customer. He/she needs to position himself/herself to consider customer's expectations. It is essential for the product owner to know if the Developers are delivering value-optimized working software product increments or not.

As shown in the following figure, the Product Owner always needs to use Empiricism to have a look into the Product Value aspect, so that the team can remain crystal clear to value proposition and he/she can have regular inspections of the tangible value to adapt accordingly. The entire accountability and responsibility of product value optimization always stays with the Product Owner. By putting a vision in front of the Scrum Team, he/she needs to ensure that, every action the team is performing is for the sole purpose of the complete comprehension, evolution, and optimization of Product Value.

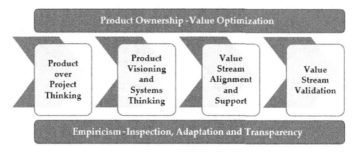

Figure 7.2: Significance of Product Value Optimization

By realizing the ultimate significance of product value optimization aspect, the Product Owner always needs to be a true value optimizer. He/she needs to build and nurture product thinking over project thinking. Product thinking is all about concentrating on generating the most useful and valuable outcomes. As per traditional project thinking, the focus is always on the iron triangle to ensure that the Project Team is delivering specified scope within said budget and on time; however, as per Scrum-based product thinking, the focus needs to be on delivering the highest customer value-based outcomes regularly. Scrum Framework does not ask Scrum Teams to have a faster and cheaper delivery. It supports Scrum Teams to deliver customer value, both incrementally and iteratively.

The Product Owner hence needs to keep an eye on the Developers, who always need to deliver the high-quality working software product, as per the agreed expectations of customer value. This needs to be done by asking, evaluating, and strategizing with the team to validate and work on suggestions, alternatives, pros, and cons having any kind of impacts on the customer value proposition and its optimization through the working software product increments.

The Product Owner needs to set the right expectations with Developers in terms of customer needs and the overall impact of their incremental, iterative Sprint-based delivery on product strategy, roadmap, customers, competitors, and so on. It is the prime responsibility of Product Owner to enhance his/her knowledge related to product thinking, so that the same can be percolated by him/her with the rest of the Scrum Team members.

To support the Scrum Team and to ascertain that the Product Owner and the Developers are always aligned, it is essential for them to have a clear notion about the big picture of why they are doing things which they are doing. The formulation and communication of product vision along with a system thinking approach helps the Product Owner to share the overall big picture of what is his/her desire about the product, in line with the crucial aspect of customer value optimization. Such big picture needs to incorporate value and scope definition in connection with the Features and the associated functionalities to be developed and delivered by the Scrum Team.

To provide the functional, technical reflections and to set the crystal-clear expectations for functionalities having more value, average value, and less value, the Product Owner needs to make use of a technique like MoSCoW prioritization. Such reflections can help the Scrum Team to envision about the product and to define a baseline to evaluate themselves on, whether they have achieved an outcome-based desired value or not.

Such desired value may differ based on various contexts and real-time scenarios of products, customers, end-users, and stakeholders. It can be related to the real-time usage, benefit, and value out of a feature (such as the real-time feedbacks from customers using a feature in terms of its usefulness, customers time spent, and ease of usage while using a feature), business and strategic goals (such as customer expectations), customer growth for revenue generation (such as gaining new customers, retaining existing customers, market conditions and share, and customers upgrades), and cost saving (such as acquisition and running cost per customer), and many other aspects.

Product Owner needs to share value-driven product vision, strategy, and roadmap with the Scrum Team, where they should also have an agreed agreement on measurement of customer value. While focusing on the desired customer value, the Product Owner also needs to be well-aligned with the Developers, so that they can collaboratively analyse and explore various emerging solutions to the complex problems they are trying to solve. There might be changes in market conditions, technology, competition, and so on, where they need to analyse and enable an emergent positioning of real customer value throughout their working software product development and delivery process.

It is required for the Scrum Team to empower the product value emergence during their product backlog refinements. They need to have their product backlog demonstrating prioritized functionalities, which they are supposed to deliver. Product Owner needs to help the Developers to pinpoint the key features, which he/she wants the Developers to deliver with the desired outcomes. Using techniques such as User Story Mapping, User Story Sizing, User Story Slicing, they need to align, break the features into smaller PBIs/User Stories. This approach gives them the flexibility to validate their assumptions and deliver the value faster. They also need to remember that they should not break everything beforehand, as the Product Backlog needs to evolve over time and they need to adapt it depending upon what they are exploring and learning in the process of delivering working software product increments.

> *"Product roadmap should state for each version the projected launch date, the target customers and their needs, and the top three to five features."*
> *- Roman Pichler*

To make sure that the Scrum Team is delivering maximum value, they need to have a shared understanding of the product roadmap and the value stream alignment linked with it. Using a technique like Hypothesis Driven Development, the team needs to focus on the actual value of individual PBIs, which can be also reflected as a key indicator for the PBIs. By frequently inspecting and adapting the product backlog, the Product Owner needs to ensure that the Developers are always in line with prioritized customer value delivery. Product Owner needs to influence, engage, and enable the Developers to cooperate with each other during the product backlog refinements.

It is crucial for the Product Owner to validate the actual value getting delivered by the Scrum Team by the end of each Sprint. Value is a belief until it is validated by the customer, hence they need to release the product increments to get to know about the real customer feedbacks about the value getting delivered. The Product Owner can ask customers to know about the expected value and the actual value. It is important for the team to observe the trends within the customer feedbacks to get to know about how the product increments delivered impacted the customer value proposition. During the Sprint Reviews, the Product Owner also needs to get the inputs from the Stakeholders to keep the actual value stream mapping visible to all.

Scrum always asks the Scrum Teams to evaluate themselves on, how much value they can create through the delivery of fully functional working software product increments and not on how much quantity they have created. Hence, the Product Owner always needs to understand the basic need and importance of continuous learning to bring in outcome-based customer value delivery of product increments. There is always an uncertainty and complexity involved for the Scrum Teams to know about what they need to build and deliver. Hence, the Product Owner needs to support them, so that they can explore, learn, and derive some conclusions. It always needs to be a collaborative and a collective effort in between the Product Owner and the Developers to negotiate, accept, select, develop, and deliver the customer value driven, well-prioritized PBIs/User Stories across every Sprint.

The Product Owner needs to have a full authority to take the decisions specific to the product. He/she needs to feel empowered to take a call for all the important decisions based on the product vision. He/she also needs to ensure that there is always a balanced agreement with Developers. Such approach guarantees that the Scrum Team is engaged with the right focus and commitment for a viable working software product development and delivery. Such powerful, well-balanced, and customer value optimization-based decision-making not only helps the Developers to eliminate any ambiguities and/or gaps, but also improves the in-built quality of the working software product increments getting developed and delivered by them.

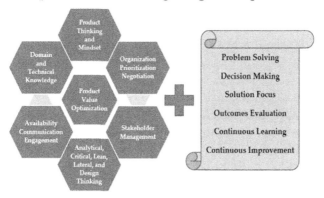

Figure 7.3: Product Owner must-haves

By understanding the customer requirements (to be achieved through the working software product), the Product Owner needs to have a thorough understanding about customer needs, wants, desires, must haves, good to haves, okay to haves, and so on. He/she needs to perform ordering of the Product Backlog, where the value, priority, prospects, risk, and dependencies need to be kept visible and reasonable.

It is always crucial and necessary for the Product Owner to know various techniques such as Kano Model, Value Stream Mapping, Business Model Canvas, Lean Canvas, and Impact Mapping, and so on, using which the agile software development Scrum Teams can perform the impact analysis of Product and Customer/End-User Value Prioritization. While being in line with the Developers, the Product Owner always needs to concentrate on the overall functionality getting developed and delivered by them. He/she needs to have the detailed knowledge about the business domain, market conditions, and overall technical structure of product. It supports the Scrum Team to know the ultimate significance of delivering the right Product built with the right functionalities at the right time.

The Product Owner needs to have a full availability for the rest of the Scrum Team members, stakeholders, and customers. By promoting face-to-face interactions to communicate any kind of information within or outside the Scrum Team, he/she needs to ensure that the information sharing and queries addressal is being done quickly and on time. By providing the product value optimization specific strategic inputs, he/she needs to encourage the team for their smooth functioning, help and support the middle management, and realize how to clarify the overall product strategy with the senior management. By sharing and getting to know about the experiences and lessons learned with the other Product Owners, he/she needs to get involved into the knowledge and best practices sharing related to Product Ownership.

> *"How many trucks does it take to destroy a Scrum Team?*
> *One, if it hits the Product Owner."*
> *- Mike Beedle*

Using the Backlog Prioritization Quadrant, he/she needs to ensure that the product backlog has enough features along with the technical improvement-related enablers, technical debt handlers (if any), and support-related activities. The Product Owner needs to spend enough time to refine the product backlog. By owning the mapping of PBIs/User stories, the Scrum Team needs to have their every Product Backlog Refinement as a conversation from end-user's point of view. The Product Owner needs to influence himself/herself along with the Developers to learn and master techniques like User Story Mapping, User Story Sizing, User Story Slicing, Planning Poker, and so on. These techniques help the Scrum Teams to make their Product Backlog well-organized, well-balanced, and properly visible. There needs to be a continuous support during the interactions with the Developers to elaborate, estimate, and prioritize the product backlog Items, where some of the direct inputs from customers and stakeholders also need to be included. Product Backlog Refinements need to guarantee that there is a shared understanding in the team to improve the quality of Product Backlog.

Along with creating and sharing the product vision, strategy, roadmap, the Product Owner also needs to focus on crafting the Sprint Goals and negotiating on them with the Developers at the time of Sprint Planning. While continuously revisiting the Definition of Ready and Definition of Done with the rest of the Scrum Team members, the Product Owner always needs to be a bit flexible to change the priorities and to allow the Developers to select the PBIs under upcoming Sprints. The PBIs under the Product Backlog always need to be placed as per the defined and agreed customer value proposition and prioritization.

The Product Owner always needs to have a formal working agreement established with the Developers to limit their work in progress, as working on many PBIs/User Stories having high priority at the same time and not delivering most of them by the end of the Sprint has no value for the customer/end-user. This is the reason, it is the sole responsibility of the Product Owner to know about *when and how to say Yes* and *when and how to say No* to the concerned stakeholders/parties around, especially when they want the Scrum Team to deliver many things at the same time. He/she needs to continuously focus on this aspect.

Having a foresight and a proper focus on prospects specific to the growth of Return on Investments and Customer Value through the ultimate approach of incremental and iterative delivery of high-quality working software product increments, the Product Owner needs to be an intrapreneur (an entrepreneur within the Scrum Team) for the software product where he/she is contributing as a Product Owner. Proactive finding and sharing of the dependencies, risks, and threats along with the effective Product Backlog Management from his/her side, helps to ease the implementation and release specific activities for the Developers.

> *"Any Scrum without working product at the end of a Sprint is a failed Scrum."*
> *- Jeff Sutherland*

The Scrum Roles - Product Owner and Scrum Master always need to complement each other. The Product Owner is responsible for the success of the working software product by meeting the customer/end-user needs. The Scrum Master is responsible for the success of the process to help and support the Product Owner and the Developers, while establishing and enhancing their Scrum Team's Scrum-based agile way of working.

Scrum Master is the heart of a Scrum Team. He/she has the responsibility to ensure that Scrum is understood and the Scrum-based agile way of working is followed by the Scrum Team. This needs to be done by him/her by coaching the Scrum Team on Scrum Framework's structure, components, and rules, both theoretically and practically. The role of a Scrum Master is a versatile one, where he/she needs to continuously help and support everyone within the Scrum Team to have valuable interactions for the purpose of value optimization. He/she needs to know about various techniques related to knowledge sharing of Scrum, performing facilitation, coaching, addressing impediments, managing conflicts, and few other aspects. Depending upon the context, the Scrum Master needs to apply those techniques.

> *"A ScrumMaster's role is similar to that of an orchestra conductor. Both must provide real-time guidance and leadership to a talented collection of individuals who come together to create something that no one of them could create alone."*
> *- Mike Cohn*

Scrum Master needs to act as a Scrum Coach to establish and enhance the agile way of working of a Scrum Team and to define the limits within which the Scrum Team needs to decide their formalized working agreement to collaborate with each other. He/she needs to act as a coach for all the Scrum Team members to set their focus on agile values and principles-based mindset and scrum values-based behavior. By continuously identifying and observing the processes, patterns, actions, reactions, and behaviors causing Scrum Malfunctioning and by evaluating the potential impact on less productivity and dysfunctions within the Scrum Team, he/she needs to drive a continuous learning and improvement within the Scrum Team. The Scrum Master needs to work on this by managing conflicts and impediments, by improving the

Scrum Team's agile mindset and agile culture, and by removing all kinds of waste and bottlenecks present within the Scrum Team's agile way of working.

Figure 7.4 shows important characteristics of Servant Leadership (given by Larry C. Spears and Robert Greenleaf), to be lived by the Servant Leaders. Scrum Master needs to inculcate and follow the Servant Leadership style by keeping his/her focus on the needs of the Scrum Team and Customer. This approach asks the Scrum Master to lead with influence, considering the aim of accomplishing the team's and organization's vision, mission, goals, objectives, outcomes, results, and so on.

Figure 7.4: *Servant Leadership Style for the Scrum Master*

The Scrum Master always needs to strive for the Scrum Team's continuous growth and development. By supporting the Scrum Team going through different phases of team development (such as forming, storming, norming, performing, and adjourning), he/she needs to create a balanced team composition/structure. Using Servant Leadership style, he/she always needs to serve the Scrum Team, while leading with influence and by involving them to establish their own agile way of working and its associated processes.

To safeguard that the Scrum Team is following the established, agreed agile way of working during every Scrum Event and during all their interactions within themselves, he/she needs to involve all the Scrum Team members to prepare and plan before coming to Scrum Events. Using this approach, an effective and efficient utilization of all the Scrum Events within time-boxing limits can be achieved. The Scrum Master always needs to give more stress on agile values and principles and on Scrum values. Sharing such belief within the Scrum Teams can significantly increase the probabilities of effective utilization of being agile mindset.

The Scrum Master always needs to have an awareness about self and about his/her Scrum Team members. Such awareness not only helps him/her to understand the personality traits of individuals, but also allows him/her to drive the initiatives to have a synergy within the team. Scrum Master needs to support the continuous improvement of the Scrum Team in a way and till the point that they become self-sufficient to do anything which is required to be done by them. By letting the team to fail safe and learn fast, he/she needs to act on when to and when to not to stop the team from failures, so that the team learns through their mistakes with an anticipation that they are not supposed to do the same mistakes again and again.

While understanding and conveying the meaning of self-organization to the Scrum Team, the Scrum Master needs to reflect the same through his/her own actions, daily. It is the prime responsibility of the Scrum Master to encourage the Scrum Team members and allow them to take their own decisions about their own work. This helps the Scrum Teams to improve their teamwork and collective ownership, to allow them to explore their own better way of interactions, to support them to reduce any dependencies within and outside the team, and to have their highest level of commitment to collaborate and to achieve the common, shared purpose and goals. He/she always needs to teach, coach, and mentor the Scrum Team to take a complete collective ownership of their agile way of working and associated processes.

Scrum Master always needs to be *obsessive* while supporting the Scrum Team, *thoughtful* about neutrality, diplomacy, honesty, and integrity, *open* to endorse an agile mindset and culture, *influential* to build the passion and liveliness within the team, *enabler* to help the team members for their self-organization and growth, *empathetic* to understand others, *truthful* to challenge status-quo, and *motivator* to improve the Scrum Team's agile way of working. To accomplish the Release, Product, Sprint, and any other goals, he/she always needs to develop a healthy and faithful alliance in between the Product Owner and the Developers. Even though the Product Owners always expect from the Developers to deliver more, the Scrum Master always needs to have a rationale to protect the Developers. Therefore, there always needs to be a consistent, shared understanding and a formal agreement in between the Product Owner and the Developers to deliver the expected customer value-based outcomes.

The Scrum Master also needs to make sure that the entire Scrum Team needs to be empowered to prevent and resolve any concerns, open questions, doubts, impediments, issues, problems, bottlenecks, showstoppers, obstacles, hindrances, risks, and dependencies occurring within themselves at any given point of time. This needs to be done by enabling a powerful foresight within them. The Scrum Master (along with the rest of the Scrum Team members) needs to observe, understand, predict, and share the insights about the possible circumstances in near future, so that all the Scrum Team members can enact on any such possibilities, while being more proactive, cognizant, and agile. This also needs to be done through the required, regular collaborative interactions within the applicable individuals or group of individuals within and outside the Scrum Team. The Scrum Master needs to be fully active while resolving any impediments. While being a practical servant leader, he/she also needs to be resourceful and inventive. This approach helps him/ her to remove any impediments, as soon as possible.

Within a Scrum Team's agile way of working, the Scrum Master always needs to understand that his/her active presence is required, only when the Scrum Team needs it. He/she should not disturb the rest of the Scrum Team members unreasonably. By recognizing conflicts and dysfunctions within the team in a primary stage, Scrum Master needs to highlight them. By providing the Scrum Team an open environment to establish and enhance trust, transparency within themselves and through an effective facilitation during all the Scrum Events (especially during Sprint Reviews and Sprint Retrospectives), he/she always needs to look for mechanisms to prevent such conflicts and dysfunctions. If the team is willing to apply any changes to their agile way of working, the Scrum Master needs to help them to evaluate all the pros, cons, short-term, and long-term impacts, considering those changes to be disruptive. The evaluation, application, and re-evaluation process of any such changes always needs to be consensus driven.

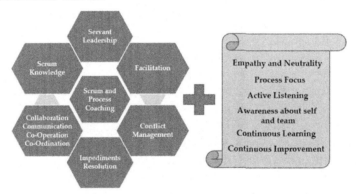

Figure 7.5: Scrum Master must-haves

It is the Scrum Master's prime responsibility to make sure that the entire Scrum Team always has a focus, commitment, consistency, and a steady pace within every aspect of their Scrum based agile way of working. The Scrum Master hence needs to sense, observe, analyse, and reflect on all the actions, reactions, behaviors, and patterns within the Scrum Team, while they are performing their daily activities. Without actively doing nothing, the Scrum Master always needs to continuously observe all the interactions during all the Scrum Events to have an evident and a well-balanced viewpoint for what is happening and to reflect in front of the Scrum Team on scope for improvements, if any. Using different levels of listening, he/she always needs to listen to all the Scrum Team members genuinely and actively, which helps them to have a consensus-based decision-making in place. Such decision-making always needs to be based on, what is being said and what is not.

Effective facilitation for all the Scrum Events is a must have for the Scrum Master. Scrum Events need to have a purpose, usefulness, and a clearly defined outcome.

All the participants should be well-equipped to participate. Using the concept of Liberating Structures (curated by Henri Lipmanowicz and Keith McCandless), the Scrum Master needs to facilitate all the Scrum Events. They help the Scrum Master to rationalize different viewpoints of the team, when they are interacting with each other, while performing various activities such as brainstorming, knowledge sharing, dependencies, risks, and impediments resolution, decision-making, and so on.

Liberating Structures not only embrace a distributed information and thoughts sharing within the Scrum Team to formulate their next set of action items, but also promote purpose, clarity, creativity, and fun exchange, and so on, aspects to ensure that all the Scrum Events are highly participatory and fully productive. During facilitation, the Scrum Master needs to think and apply applicable and appropriate Liberating Structures; however, such usage should not be limited to him/her. Anyone within the Scrum Team can effectively use them by having a proper experimentation mindset and by asking powerful questions to each other.

Scrum Master needs to understand the team's overall composition, using which he/she can plan activities through Gamification. He/she needs to plan and customize the games, while making use of a game-based thinking to involve all the Scrum Team members to enhance their analytical thinking and problem-solving capabilities. By measuring the progress, he/she needs to ask the team members for their individual and collective feedback to inspect and adapt. Rewarding the Scrum Team members to encourage their participation and nurturing their synergy also needs to be taken care by the Scrum Master. By sharing the past experiences, knowledge, and lessons learned, he/she always needs to influence the team, so that they can work in a partnership and take care of their collective ownership which is required for various activities of development and delivery.

> *"The Scrum Master has a responsibility to foster relationships between*
> *the product owner and the development team,*
> *to promote transparency, trust and a sense of one team."*
> *- Geoff Watts*

According to Barry Overeem's various stances of Scrum Master, a Scrum Master always needs to be a *Servant Leader*, whose focus always needs to be on the needs of the Scrum Team members and their customers/end-users. He/she (along with the rest of the Scrum Team members) needs to focus on the goal of achieving results in line with the organization's values, principles, and business objectives. He/she always needs to be a *Teacher* to ensure that Scrum and other relevant methods are understood and enacted. As a *Facilitator*, he/she always needs to set the stage by offering clear boundaries within which the team can collaborate. As a *Coach*, he/she always needs to coach the individuals (on their individual agile mindset), the team (on their collective agile mindset), and the organization (to build and to nurture a complete sense of agility, while being agile and not just doing agile).

Scrum Master always needs to be a *Mentor* to transfer the agile knowledge and experience to the Scrum Team. He/she also needs to be a *Manager* who is always responsible to handle, manage impediments, eliminating waste, managing the process, managing the team's health, managing the boundaries of self-organization, and managing the agile culture. He/she also needs to be an effective *Impediment Remover* to solve the issues blocking the team's overall progress. This needs to be done by considering the self-organizing capabilities of Developers. Scrum Master also needs to act as a *Change Agent* to enable a culture within which the Scrum Team can flourish. The Scrum Master always needs to lead by example and lead by influence to allow, inspire, and motivate the team members to explore their hidden capabilities, so that they can have their unique reflections to achieve their anticipated effectiveness.

Scrum Master needs to be aware of the importance of professional and co-active coaching, using which he/she can bridge the disparities between the Scrum Team's overall thinking about anything which needs to be done by the team and while the team is doing it. By coaching and guiding the team without giving them direct recommendations, the Scrum Master needs to push them to think and improve on their self-organization. The team needs to explore and realize the solutions by themselves while contemplating what is better for them.

> *"Scrum Master, as the promoter of Scrum and self-organization,*
> *should consider how to help a teamwork out their problems themselves*
> *and offer any tools, trainings and insights on how best to do this."*
> *- Gunther Verheyen*

Scrum Master needs to persuade the Scrum Team to use supporting add-ons belonging to the agile frameworks other than Scrum framework. He/she needs to be aware and competent of other agile frameworks such as XP, Kanban, Scrumban, Lean, and so on, by properly understanding their usage benefits, limits, pros, cons, strengths, and weaknesses. He/she needs to support the Developers and the Product Owner to select the required agile product development, delivery, and way of working-specific tools and techniques and to take the agreed decisions by making them truthful, self-sufficient, and empowered. By educating the Stakeholders about the Scrum Team's Scrum-based agile way of working, he/she also needs to explain them about the significance of agile values and principles.

As a collaborative effort with other the Scrum Masters in the organization, he/she always needs to build the sense of community. It can be done through an establishment of an Agile Centre of Excellence (CoE) and/or an Agile Community of Practices (CoP). Through such communities, they need to organize trainings and knowledge sharing sessions about agility, agile frameworks, best and advanced engineering, software development practices, and many other initiatives. Such initiatives help to create a big positive impact on the overall agile mindset and agile culture of the organization. Using the concept of Shu-Ha-Ri levels, they can analyse the agile knowledge maturity of individuals, teams, and organizations to explore and extend a formal structure of knowledge sharing within the entire organization.

Developers are the brains of a Scrum Team. Developers always need to be self-organizing and self-managing. No one is supposed to ask/tell them about, how they need to convert the Product Backlog into the Sprint Backlog and finally into the Product Increments. Developers also need to be cross-functional. There should not be any specific individual roles/titles for them. Rather they should be the individuals having diverse skill sets and capabilities. Their collective skills are required to develop and deliver the potentially releasable increments of a high-quality working software product at the end of every Sprint, where they need to have a collective ownership. Regardless of the type of the work being done by individual Developers, they need to be recognized as a part of the Scrum Team and there should not be any sub-teams within the Developers.

Developers always need to engage themselves in a continuous learning and improvement of their overall technical excellence. Using some of the advanced engineering practices (such as Code Refactoring, Clean Code, Code Coverage, Extreme/Pair/Mob Programming, DevOps, Test/Behavior/Acceptance Test Driven Development, White Box Testing, Automated Functional and Non-Functional Testing, Feature Toggles, Continuous Integration/Continuous Delivery, and so on), they need to improve their software development specific way of working and its associated processes.

These technical excellence-based add-ons not only help them to improve the overall built-in quality of their product increments, but also make sure that the Scrum Team has a more accurate and a rapid product development and delivery life cycle in place. In this process, Developers always need to explore better alternatives through various applicable, appropriate, innovative, analytical, technical, functional, techno-functional, architectural, and experimental approaches.

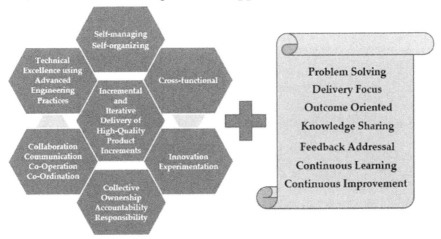

Figure 7.6: Developers must-haves

Developers always need to know and understand their real customers. By co-ordinating with the Product Owner and sometimes, by establishing direct contacts with the customer, they need to realize customer needs, wants, desires, must haves, good to haves, okay to haves, and few other important aspects, so that they can explore and take suitable decisions while implementing things technically. While performing the Product Backlog Refinements, they need to reflect on and capture such aspects as a part of the PBIs getting added and/or updated under their Product Backlog.

Developers always need to believe that such time-to-time refinements always need to happen as a complete collaborative effort in between the Product Owner and themselves, as the scope and quality of the PBIs under the Product Backlog is the basis for a balanced development effort with a solid consistency and swiftness. Sometimes, the Developers might think that it is the responsibility of the Product Owner to make the Product Backlog well-defined and well-refined; however, it always needs to be a collaborative effort in between the Product Owner and all the Developers. During the Product Backlog Refinements, they also need to understand and reflect on the criticality of all the functional, non-functional, and technical activities, by understanding all the sides of product value optimization from the Product Owner and the Stakeholders.

As a cross-functional team, the Developers are required to be highly focused on delivering the product increments by innovatively performing all the activities required to accomplish their agreed Sprint Goal. Using a technique like Swarming, the Developers can choose a PBI having the highest priority from their Sprint Backlog to work upon in the first go. By having all the possible Developers to work collaboratively, by reducing the handovers in between them and by following the concept of *Stop Starting and Start Finishing*, they need to complete the same PBI at the earliest. This needs to be continued for all the other PBIs based upon their associated highest to lowest priorities. Using such an approach, they can deliver the PBIs, where any feedback from the Product Owner always needs to be captured and worked upon by creating a continuous Customer Value Delivery Flow.

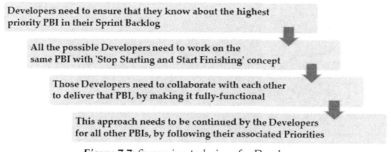

Figure 7.7: *Swarming technique for Developers*

Using an add-on like Skills Matrix, the Developers need to organize knowledge-sharing sessions, where they can share their learnings with each other to bridge the skills-specific gaps present, if any. By organizing some active hands-on workshops/

training sessions, the Developers always need to perform continuous learning and knowledge sharing activities within themselves. Developers having more experience need to teach and mentor the other Developers having less experience. Such interactions are required for the Developers to build a mutual trust and to help, support, and collaborate with each other to achieve a collective knowledge-building-based excellence over the period.

"When to use iterative development?
You should use iterative development only on projects that you want to succeed."
- Martin Fowler

To keep a constant pace with the fast-changing technological ecosystem of complex adaptive software systems, all the Developers need to realize the prominence of continuous technical innovation and experimentation. It helps them to innovate, fail, learn, unlearn, and re-learn fast as well as safe. This always needs to be a part of their incremental and iterative software development and delivery-specific activities within the actual Sprints. It is always better to not to have any other Sprints (such as Sprint 0 before the actual Sprints and / or Hardening Sprints after the actual Sprints) apart from the actual / normal Sprints.

Developers need to participate in all the Scrum Events with the highest level of zeal and enthusiasm, to make use of those events and to have some healthy discussions. Their Scrum-based agile way of working needs to keep them at the crux of all the Scrum Events, where they should not avoid or ignore any meaningful interactions. During these interactions, they need to plan, re-plan, align, re-align, and reflect using appropriate data points, facts, and figures to make sure that they are always doing the required sense-making. The absence of such interactions within and outside of the Scrum Team does not give them a correct perception about their inspection to reflect on where they are, their planning to reflect on what they are supposed to do, their orientation to reflect on where they are supposed to go, their viewpoint to reflect on what they are thinking, and their adaptation to reflect on agreed action items. By practicing a collective ownership, they always need to enact upon their own agreed action items. Having a collective ownership of their Sprint-based deliverables not only helps them to reduce their overall delivery time, but also enables their cross-component-based knowledge building and sharing.

By ensuring that their Sprint Backlog specific PBIs / User Stories are always updated, the Developers always need to keep a truthful manifestation to reflect on their current positioning during their current ongoing Sprint. By showcasing self-management and self-organization, they need to collaborate with the Scrum Master for the same purpose by avoiding a constant push from him / her. They also need to profoundly understand, follow, revisit, and enact on their agreed Definition of Ready as well as Definition of Done. They should be using the same for the purpose of marking their fully functional PBIs with Done state.

To bring-in more discipline and consistency within the agile way of working, a Sequential Development approach can certainly help the Developers. In this approach, Developers need to cluster the PBIs under their Product Backlog to concentrate on a specific Feature, one at a time. By putting the effective and agreed Work in Progress limits, they can limit their context switching in between multiple Features. It also helps them to remain coherent and to focus on fast, prompt, and timely delivery of PBIs. While using this approach, they need to refine the PBIs in Product Backlog in such a way that, prioritization and sizing for the PBIs getting selected by them in the next Sprint Planning should not fluctuate much.

Multiple Developers working on a single product always need to be mindful about any of the outside integrations and dependencies, which need to be managed by them only. They can involve the Scrum Masters, but only when it is really required. They need to handle their own composition and alignment. In case of any missing skill sets or subject matter expertise, they need to seek some help and collaborate with each other. They also need to learn about feedback sharing and addressal, which needs to be there in an open, truthful, and polite manner. They should not wait for the next Sprint Retrospective, to share and address any of their feedbacks seeking for the continuous improvement. By following the *Sooner the Better* approach and by recognizing the timing, context, and impact of their feedback sharing and its addressal, they need to do the needful, as and when it is essential.

Having a growth-based agile mindset and igniting its correlated intrinsic motivation to contribute a tiny bit more every time, Developers always need to incorporate and cultivate a collective commitment and responsibility. They should not wait to complete their PBIs by the end of their ongoing Sprint. Also, an active presence of any subject matter expert or any specialist within the Developers always needs to make sure that such available expertise and knowledge is being shared with all the other Developers and they are properly doing and utilizing the same by removing any kind of wastage of expertise which is already present within the Scrum Team.

There always needs to be some buffer time kept for them during the Sprint, where the Developers can handle any 11th hour issues occurring within the team. Even if there are not any, they can still utilize this time for the purpose of knowledge transfer and/or for the purpose of continuously improving their existing code base using any of the advanced engineering practices. Their teamwork, interactions, and collective collaborations always need to foster a positive energy and a fun learning-based environment, so that they can always stay motivated to be the best version of themselves. It also helps them to always contribute with their 100% by showcasing their active participation as a one team.

By evaluating and supporting various Sprint Retrospective formats, they always need to support the Scrum Master to cherish a fun-based, creative, innovative, and learning-oriented mindset. Such agile way of working helps them to showcase their highest efficiency, which enables and enhances their rapport building by having a positive impact on team's culture. It makes the team's overall environment happy, healthy, and satisfied.

For a continuously and smoothly functioning well-disciplined Scrum-based agile way of working, it is important for the Scrum Teams to have a formal working agreement created by them only. Such working agreement needs to be captured somewhere to make it visible and transparent to the entire Scrum Team. As the Scrum Team gets more matured, team needs to revisit and update their working agreement regularly. Considering the Scrum Master as a caretaker of Scrum and its associated processes, rest of the Scrum Team members should not think that, he/she is trying to forcefully impose the Working Agreement (having some stringent rules and regulations) on them. Instead, they need to understand that the Working Agreement is required to support the entire Scrum Team, where most of the times, the individual Scrum Team members are having different personas, traits, thoughts, choices, opinions, strengths, weaknesses, and past experiences. As shown in *Figure 7.8*, a Working Agreement always needs to focus and highlight on some of the important aspects related to the product, people, and processes for a Scrum Team's specific context:

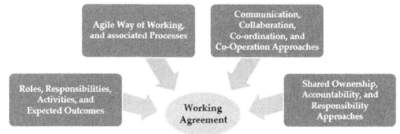

Figure 7.8: Working Agreement for Scrum Teams

A working agreement of a Scrum Team should always include an overview of their roles, responsibilities, activities to be performed, expected outcomes to reflect on who, when, what, and how they need to work on, and their agile way of working (and its associated processes, add-ons, techniques, procedures, and approaches, and so on) to reflect on how they need to work together. It should also include an overview of various approaches to reflect on how they need to interact with each other within and outside the team and how they need to have a right sense of shared ownership, accountability, and responsibility to achieve their common, shared purpose and goals.

The Scrum Team members need to agree with their own working agreement, using which they can efficiently collaborate with each other and work together as a one team. By following the same, the Scrum Team needs to function and to perform all their activities with a full commitment and highest level of integrity. By holding each other accountable and responsible, the Scrum Team members need to collectively tackle their problems, issues, failures, constructive conflicts, and disagreements.

A working agreement facilitates the Scrum Team to represent a unique perspective of their growth mindset and culture, where they need to underline their core values, principles, common vision, mission, goals, and objectives. Using such an agreement, they always need to have a shared understanding to anticipate a consensus-based decision-making and a collective ownership to collaborate for the purpose of entire team's success rather than individual success. It also acts as a baseline which they can refer anytime and treat themselves as more accountable, responsible, and self-organized.

> *"Make fair agreements and stick to them."*
> *- Confucius*

By considering some of the following example aspects and their associated factors, a Scrum Team needs to have open discussions to formulate their formal working agreement:

- What is the vision, mission, and common purpose of the Scrum Team? What are their goals and objectives? How can they have a shared understanding about all of them?

- Who are their stakeholders and customers/end-users? How will they ensure that they are addressing their customer/end-user needs by delivering the potentially shippable working software product increments and following a Sprints approach?

- What are the entities the Scrum Team wants to capture under their formal working agreement? How will they make sure that it is in line with their Scrum-based agile way of working? How will they ensure trust and help, support each other as a one team?

- How will they ensure that they are inculcating all the Scrum Values when it comes to their every action, as an individual as well as as a team? How will they be living and showcasing the Scrum Values through their overall behavior and way of working?

- What are the roles, responsibilities, and boundaries within the Scrum Team?

- How will they capture clear accountabilities for each Scrum Role, when they have given an authority to carry out their individual roles but as a one team?

- What are the expectations and how the team will make sure that they are following their agreed expectations? How the Scrum Team will be holding themselves accountable and responsible for their shared responsibilities?

- What are the approaches the Scrum Team will be using to communicate, collaborate, co-ordinate, and co-operate effectively?

- How will the Scrum Team perform information exchange within and outside the team? What are the ways, protocols, and tools for the same?

- What are the considerations for the Scrum Roles, Artifacts, Events, Rules, and so on, to answer why, what, who, when, where, and how aspects for them?

- What are the approaches the Scrum Team will make use of to have a consensus-based decision-making in place? How will they resolve their constructive conflicts?

- What all techniques the Scrum Team needs to explore to become more self-managing, self-organizing, and cross-functional? How they will be able to determine them?

- What are the ways they want to explore to achieve their agreed Sprint Goals?

- What are the approaches the Scrum Team will make use of to inspect their overall progress and productivity? How will they handle issues related to the frequently occurring bottlenecks, hindrances, and obstacles causing their low productivity?

- How will the Scrum Team enhance, improve their capabilities, skill sets, and knowledge? What approaches will the Scrum Team make use of for the purpose of continuous learning and knowledge sharing?

- What approaches will the Scrum Team make use of to ensure that they are following various aspects/standards of user experience, quality, maintainability, cost efficiency, scalability, high-availability, maintainability, adaptability, correctness, security, and performance, and so on, for their working software product increments? What are the benchmarks, rules, and policies for all these aspects/standards?

- How will the Scrum Team members formulate, update, and agree with a properly defined Definition of Ready, Definition of Done and Acceptance Criteria at Sprint, Feature, and PBI level? How will they limit their Work in Progress? Which techniques will they apply to have efficient Product Backlog Refinements?

- What kind of decisions the Scrum Team can take? Which approaches they need to follow to ask someone outside the team while taking any of the decisions? How will they inform all intended parties/stakeholders about the decisions taken?

- Which all tools and technologies the Scrum Team will make use of for their numerous activities? Which special techniques will the team explore to become cross-functional?

- Which all approaches will the Scrum Team put in place to resolve their issues, challenges, or impediments? How will they enact on any impediments causing delays?

- What will the Scrum Team do to improve on innovation and experimentation culture?

- How will they track and plan their whereabouts, availability, backup plans, risks, dependencies, and emergencies, and so on, factors impacting their Sprint-based delivery?

- How will they make use of feedback loops to share, plan, re-plan, and execute actions on constructive feedbacks for the purpose of continuous improvement?

- Which all processes the Scrum Team needs to have under their Scrum-based agile way of working? How will they continuously improve those processes?

- How will they make use of Empiricism to address misalignments under their agile way of working? How will they work to become high performing?

- How will they make sure that they are regularly updating and maintaining their already established formal Working Agreement?

The working agreement should not be considered as a forceful policing practice to be followed by the Scrum Teams. It needs to act as an agreement-based strategy for them, where they need to capture their agreed expectations and have a better common, shared understanding about their responsibilities. It should uncover the rules, regulations, and disciplines a Scrum Team needs to agree and adhere with, while being more capable.

Figure 7.9: Working Agreement Structure

While formulating, updating, and maintaining a working agreement, there might be some aspects for which the Scrum Team members tend to have a quick agreement within themselves; however, there also might be some other aspects, where the Scrum Team members might be having disagreements/conflicts/differences of opinions. In this case, it is the responsibility of the Scrum Master to facilitate some interactive discussions, where the rest of the Scrum Team members need to negotiate and try to maintain a harmony.

The Scrum Master needs to perform a crucial role to help, support, and influence the Scrum Team members to have a constructive brainstorming. By adhering to the Agile Values and Principles along with the Scrum Values and Empiricism, he/she always needs to coach them to explore and reflect on various aspects to have some effective agreements in place, where there always needs to be a correlation with an inclusive agile way of working.

The Scrum Team can make use of their Sprint Retrospectives at the end of their Sprints to periodically review, update, and maintain their already established and agreed formal working agreement along with their Definition of Ready and Definition of Done. They always need to have a consensus on updation/customization of the same when it is necessary. Documenting the working agreement is always a better approach for the Scrum Team, which helps them to avoid any confusion and to be on the same page of understanding all the time. Formulation of working agreement substantially helps the Scrum Team to have a presence of a well-harmonized working environment, within which they can constantly inspect and adapt, to continuously improve their agile way of working.

Points to remember

- High-performing teams are extremely focused on achieving their goals, objectives by keeping their existing structure intact. They always try to outperform by surpassing the ideal expectations from them.

- Product Owner is the backbone of a Scrum Team. By encouraging product thinking mindset, he/she always needs to support and adopt the product vision agreed with the Stakeholders and the Scrum Team. By realizing the significance of product value optimization, the Product Owner always needs to be a true value optimizer.

- Product Owner needs to build and nurture product thinking over project thinking. He/she needs to share value-driven product vision, strategy, and roadmap with the Scrum Team, where they should also have an agreement on measurement of value. He/she needs to have a full authority to take the decisions specific to the product.

- Scrum Master is the heart of a Scrum Team. He/she has the responsibility to ensure that Scrum is understood and the Scrum-based agile way of working is followed by the Scrum Team. The Scrum Master always needs to strive for the Scrum Team's continuous development. It is his/her responsibility to make sure that the entire team has a focus, commitment, consistency, and a steady pace within every aspect of their agile way of working.

- Developers are the brains of a Scrum Team. Developers always need to be self-organizing, self-managing. Developers also need to be cross-functional. Developers always need to engage themselves into continuous learning and improvement of their overall technical excellence. Developers always need to know and understand their real customers. Developers need to realize the prominence of continuous technical innovation and experimentation.

- It is important for the Scrum Teams to have a formal working agreement created by them only. It should include an overview of their roles and responsibilities, activities to be performed, expected outcomes to reflect on who, when, what, and how they need to work on, and their agile way of working.

- The Scrum Master needs to perform a crucial role to help, support, and influence the Scrum Team to have a constructive brainstorming. The Scrum Team can make use of their Sprint Retrospectives at the end of their Sprints to periodically review, update, and maintain their already established and agreed formal working agreement.

In the next chapter, readers will get to know about some of the advanced Scrum add-ons/techniques to help the Scrum Teams to perform an effective and efficient Product Backlog Management.

CHAPTER 8

Add-ons for Effective and Efficient Product Backlog Management

Introduction

In this chapter, the readers will get to know about some of the advanced Scrum add-ons to help the Scrum Teams to perform an effective and efficient Product Backlog Management.

Objective

After studying this chapter, you should be able to:

- Understand various considerations for the Scrum Teams during their Product Backlog Refinements.

- Understand the Product Backlog Management/Refinement must-haves for the Scrum Teams.

- Understand the Product Backlog Management/Refinement strategy for the Scrum Teams.

- Understand the User Story Mapping technique for the Scrum Teams.

Bill 'The Scrum Master' (in a discussion with Jim 'The Product Owner'):

"I can understand your availability issues, but please find some time to be available for the team, when they need you the most. Please try to understand me, Jim!"

Jim 'The Product Owner' (replying with a confused tone):

"You have already seen the quality of Features we are receiving, where I always need to go back to the Stakeholders to understand and fill-in the gaps, which also delays our Sprint based delivery. I don't know why, but sometimes I feel like, why I am irrationally agreeing to all the demands of our Stakeholders. I can sense that our Developers are having a feeling of inconvenience and most of the times, they are too much overloaded with work, that too with full of chaos and misinterpretations."

Bill:

"Do you remember the SWOT Analysis technique which we had discussed some time back? I think, last time you told me that you are performing it once in a quarter, right? Just tell me one thing. What about keeping those Opportunities which you want to grab, temporarily on hold and work on your Weaknesses to grab those Opportunities later once your Weaknesses turn into your Strengths?"

Jim (smiling and replying):

"Bill, please don't get away from the original topic! Be it any technique you would like me to apply to them, I just want to see both the Team and Stakeholders happy."

Bill (replying quickly):

"Okay, Jim! Let's have meetings with the Stakeholders to get to know about the customer problems, use cases, value proposition, must haves, good to haves, okay to haves, and clear expectations. It's better to have a shared understanding about all these things to be captured under every Feature. Just remember one thing; we will accept only those Features under our Product Backlog for which there is a clear and enough understanding. Features with ambiguities need to be kept on hold, temporarily. Those can be discussed with them in the next meeting to bridge those ambiguities and gaps. We can also involve the Developers in our discussions, if required. How this SWOT approach sounds?"

Jim (replying with a worry):

"But what about their expectation from us to continuously deliver more and more to our customers?"

Bill (smiling and replying):

"Yes, we have to; but we should deliver right things and things right, right?"

The process of Product Backlog Management (through a series of continuous and regular Product Backlog Refinements) is important for the Scrum Team, where they need to create and/or update the required specifics, priorities, and estimates, and so on, for the PBIs/User Stories in the Product Backlog. The Scrum Team needs to strategize about when, where, and how they need to do the refinements, considering that the Product Backlog is well-balanced with the overall capacity of Developers during their ongoing Sprint. The Product Owner and the Developers need to work together to assess, revise, and adjust their PBIs/User Stories, where the PBIs can be revised at any time by the Product Owner. He/she always needs to make sure that the PBIs with the high priority are generally available with more specifics than those with the low priority. During the refinements, it becomes easy for the Developers to have properly estimated PBIs when they have more detailed specifics about them. *Figure 8.1* highlights on the Product Backlog Refinement considerations for the Scrum Team:

Figure 8.1: *Product backlog refinement considerations #1*

During the Product Backlog Refinements, those PBIs/User Stories that can be fully developed and tested by the Developers within their upcoming Sprint need to be considered as ready to be discussed during their upcoming Sprint Planning. The Scrum Team needs to maintain a transparency and a proper visibility for the customer value, priority, knowledge, risks, and dependencies for the PBIs/User Stories.

The Scrum Team also needs to consider an effective and efficient organization of PBIs/User Stories (in the Product Backlog), the customer's/end-user's overall urgency, their own implementation strategy, and feedbacks from all the sides. The Product Owner needs to be responsible for the customer value and priority specific decision-making, whereas both the Product Owner and the Developers need to be responsible for knowledge, risks, and dependencies specific decision-making. The Developers only have a final say on the estimations of PBIs/User Stories; however, the Product Owner can try to influence them by performing required trade-offs with them.

During the Product Backlog Refinements, the Scrum Team always needs to emphasize on the following aspects of optimizing the customer value, which they are supposed to deliver.

- They need to prioritize and order the PBIs/User Stories having more customer value before those having less customer value under the Product Backlog.

- They need to reflect on the overall estimation, effort, dependencies, and risks for every PBI/User Story, which has a direct impact on the prioritization of customer value. Without evaluating on all these parameters, they will not be able to completely measure and track the significance of decisions being taken by them.

- They need to perform a considerable exploration and knowledge gain for every PBI/User Story, to proactively resolve ambiguities and gaps present, if any.

- They need to consider all the feedbacks from stakeholders and customers/end-users.

- They always need to ensure that any of the PBIs/User Stories having dependencies with other PBIs/User Stories need to be placed in such a way that, those dependencies will not cause any unnecessary deviations and delays for their Sprint based delivery.

- They need to align the activities having the highest customer urgency/priority at any given point of time, to resolve any of the recognized and probable risks.

> *"The product backlog is not only a list of requirements.*
> *It is the snapshot of the current understanding of the next steps -*
> *goals, risks or options on the path to a great product."*
> *- Andreas Schliep*

The Product Backlog always needs to be a prioritized list of features, functionalities, and all the capabilities the Developers are supposed to develop and deliver as working software product increments in their Sprints, both incrementally and iteratively. They also need to consider their product backlog as an indication of their existing comprehension about the ambitions, goals, objectives, understandings, alternatives, possibilities, probabilities, risks, and dependencies, and so on. The ordering and prioritization of the PBIs/User Stories under the product backlog needs to be done in such a way that the high-priority PBIs/User Stories should be at the top and low priority ones should be at the bottom.

Most of the success of a Scrum Team's agile way of working always depends upon the Product Owner's ability to convince the stakeholders, especially when it comes to the final decision-making about the product. He/she always needs to be the sole identity to perform any kind of decision-making specific to prioritization of PBIs/User Stories in the product backlog, considering the customer value optimization aspect. It is hence crucial for the Product Owner to have a complete empowerment to perform prioritization under the product backlog. Sometimes, the Stakeholders might be trying to influence the Product Owner in the process of Product Backlog prioritization; however, it is the responsibility of the Product Owner to discourage such influence resulting into a prioritization by proxy.

It is the prime responsibility of the Product Owner along with the Stakeholders to frequently revisit and review the product roadmap, strategy, and release plan, by following an agreed timeline such as once in a quarter/once in a couple of months. If required, they need to revise and modify all of them to make them more realistic. This needs to be done to safeguard the product roadmap, strategy, and release plan to be in line with the customer/end-user needs, customer/end-user value optimization, and overall market conditions.

The Product Owner always needs to ensure that the Product Backlog is truly reflecting the product roadmap and strategy. Such reflection needs to be open and to be shared with the rest of the Scrum Team members with a complete transparency. By considering the Sprint-based deliverables, the product roadmap, strategy, and release plan needs to be visible and available to the entire team at any given point of time, using which they need to know about how they are supposed to progress and achieve their Sprint Goals. The Product Backlog constantly needs to have an enough comprehension about the PBIs/User Stories to be worked upon by the Developers for the upcoming couple of Sprints. Apart from this, the Scrum Team needs to create and/or update the PBIs/User Stories addressing few other capabilities such as enablers, themes, epics, and so on. This is to ensure that they have a sufficient understanding about the complete Product Backlog, which can be further revisited in the process of refining the PBIs/User Stories.

The Scrum Team always needs to remember that the creation and/or modification of any of the PBIs/User Stories under the Product Backlog is a collective exercise for the whole Scrum Team. It is not only the Product Owner, but also the Developers who need to break down the Features (containing the customer requirements) into smaller pieces (that is, into PBIs/User Stories), both collectively and collaboratively. The Product Owner always needs to provide them the why and what aspect, whereas the Developers need to reflect on the how aspect against all the features and associated functionalities which they are supposed to break into PBIs/User Stories. During the Product Backlog Refinements, they always need to discuss and brainstorm with each other to have a consensus on all the functional, non-functional, and technical aspects considering the actual, possible, and feasible scope of the PBIs/User Stories. This helps them to establish a common, shared understanding before they select any PBIs/User Stories in their Sprint Backlog during Sprint Planning.

While keeping an eye to manage the Product Backlog, the Product Owner also needs to have a continuous dialogue with the Stakeholders and the rest of the Scrum Team members. This is required for them to get into a composed agreement, where the Scrum Team can make use of their Product Backlog as a single source of truth to track their innovative ideas, value-adds, technical enhancements, and enablers to enhance the Product. The Product Backlog always needs to be continuously evolving while considering the aspects such as product roadmap, strategy, and customer value optimization. The Scrum Team also needs to have their Product Backlog well-prioritized, well-described, well-estimated, and well-balanced to represent the best possible utilization of Developers under their ongoing Sprint at any time.

The Scrum Team contributing to the Product Backlog Refinements always needs to enact on the fact that, the PBIs/User Stories under their Product Backlog need to comprise of slightly more than just a summary. PBIs/User Stories always need to have enough details about the summary, description, supporting documents, acceptance criteria, estimates, dependencies, and any other important information required to bring in more clarity and transparency. On the other hand, the Scrum Team also needs to remember the fact that, the PBIs/User Stories are not having too much of overload of details resulting into a huge list of acceptance criteria. Normally, acceptance criteria with handful of aspects should be more than sufficient for them. To decide on such acceptance criteria (and its associated specifics) and to have it more detailed, the Product Owner should not spend too much of his/her time while formulating the same. If the Developers have a consensus with the Product Owner about enough refinement of the PBIs/User Stories, they need to agree and stop there. The Product Owner needs to be wise enough to involve the Stakeholders or any other Subject Matter Experts in the process of backlog refinement.

The Product Backlog should not be a huge collection of isolated PBIs/User Stories. It should not contain obsolete, irrelevant, and surplus PBIs/User Stories, especially those PBIs/User Stories which have not been investigated by the Scrum Team for an agreed, prolonged duration. The Product Owner always needs to keep an eye on such existing PBIs/User Stories. The Product Backlog should not be overloaded with the PBIs/User Stories because of which it might become over-sized and unmanageable.

Based on the varying contexts, the Product Owner always needs to remove any such obsolete, irrelevant, and surplus PBIs/User Stories to limit the Product Backlog. It needs to contain only enough number of PBIs/User Stories for upcoming Sprints. The Scrum Team cannot guess anything about the market conditions and the customer needs in a context of a longer duration. This causes an uncertainty about how they can decide on what they need to develop and deliver in the next six months or in the next one year from now. This is the reason they need not to create and/or update the PBIs/User Stories for next six months or one year in advance. Doing the same is a complete wastage of their time and effort.

The PBIs need to be sliced vertically based on the end-to-end functionality across the features, rather than slicing them horizontally based on the individual technical layers/components. This approach helps the Developers to improve on their skill sets and capabilities to become cross-functional and to deliver the Product Increments rapidly. They need to have the PBIs with an agreed and well-formulated Acceptance Criteria, using which they need to set the expectations in terms of selection, completion, and acceptance of PBIs. They need to have an agreed and well-formulated Definition of Ready (DoR) to select the PBIs during Sprint Planning. Those PBIs which can be potentially completed by the Developers within one Sprint need to be considered as ready for selection in Sprint Planning. They also need to have an agreed and well-formulated Definition of Done (DoD), using which the Product Owner can accept or reject the PBIs. Such standards help them to increase the overall built-in quality of the PBIs and their agile way of working too.

The outcome of Product Backlog Refinements needs to ensure that the PBIs at the top of the Product Backlog are ready to be discussed by Developers in next Sprint Planning. The Team needs to validate and confirm on such PBIs using a Definition of Ready (DoR) checklist. Following is an example of such checklist, where each PBI needs to:

- Be evidently formulated based on the customer/end-user value proposition.

- Have a clear and sufficient understanding of specifics.

- Have clearly identified resolvable dependencies and no blocking dependencies.

- Be well-estimated and small enough to be completed during upcoming Sprints.

- Have a clearly defined, agreed, and testable acceptance criteria covering functional, non-functional, and technical aspects of development and delivery.

- Be understood by the Scrum Team, so that they can complete and demo it in review.

It is safer and better for the multiple Scrum Teams working on the same product to follow one-product-one-backlog rule. It allows them to compare all the features with each other. While making use of this approach, there is also an assurance that the features with the highest priority from the whole product's perspective are getting recognized, prioritized, and ordered accordingly. Along with the features and PBIs, the Product Backlog also needs to include Spikes, when the Developers need to perform research/analysis/exploration, based on their limited knowledge. This is extremely useful for them to save their extra efforts and additional time getting spent for the purpose of evaluating any potential assumptions.

The PBIs/User Stories are not required to be too much detailed and estimated upfront. The considerations for the refinements always need to be synchronized with the exploration and evaluation of the seven crucial dimensions of the working software product (given by Ellen Gottesdiener at **https://www.ebgconsulting.com** and at **http://www.discovertodeliver.com/**). As shown in the following figure,

Scrum Team always needs to convert the Product Roadmap (containing the Vision) to the Product Backlog (by optimizing and fulfilling the Value):

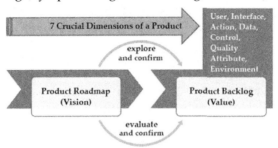

Figure 8.2: Product backlog refinement considerations #2

During the refinements, the Scrum Team always needs to have structured conversations to explore, evaluate, and confirm on the PBIs/User Stories to be refined. Structured conversations improve their overall collaboration. To support the structured conversations using all the seven crucial dimensions of the working software product, it is better to involve the entire Scrum Team in such conversations. However, they also need to ensure that such involvement is getting utilized properly. Developers always need to have an agreement with the Product Owner to challenge him/her for the best possible utilization of their time and efforts to also consider the bug fixes, major and minor enhancements, and technical debt.

The Scrum Team needs to have regular and adequate Product Backlog Refinement sessions, which can help them to have a high-quality Product Backlog in place. At the same time, they should not have too many Product Backlog Refinement sessions, which might result into an unnecessarily detailed Product Backlog. It is hence required for the Scrum Team to have a proper balance on the frequency of Product Backlog Refinement sessions. By having a common, shared understanding that nothing else is more costly than a Feature/PBI/User Story in the Product Backlog, which is not providing any customer value, they must make use of the appropriate advanced add-ons/techniques, as shown in the following figure:

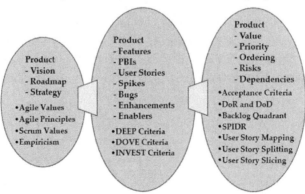

Figure 8.3: Product backlog management/refinement must-haves

By the means of a proper Product Vision, Roadmap, and Strategy, the Scrum Team always needs to know about, where they are supposed to navigate and how can they determine that which direction they need to take to move forward. Before jumping into anything specific to Product Backlog Management/Refinement, it is always important for them to realize the why aspect first.

Considering the Product Vision, Roadmap, and Strategy, the Product Owner needs to continually examine the Product Backlog to guarantee that the Scrum Team is following the right path. While navigating through Product Backlog Refinements, the Scrum Team always needs to validate themselves against the values and principles of the Agile Manifesto. They need to remember that all the values and principles from Agile Manifesto are equally important. However, for the Product Owner, the value *Individuals and Interactions over Processes and Tools* and the principal *Simplicity-the art of maximizing the amount of work not done-is essential* plays a key aspect to have an ease of refinements. Irrespective of whichever tools and technologies the team is making use of, they always need to have some interactions with a proper agenda at the right time and with the right purpose in mind. This mindset helps them to eliminate waste, if any. The Product Owner always needs to ensure his/her availability for both Stakeholders as well as for the rest of the Scrum Team members with a full of desire and a right sense of face-to-face communication. He/she needs to spend time on the most valuable aspects of refinements and to help the team to lessen the risks.

During the Product Backlog Refinements, the fundamental Scrum Values along with the process of Empiricism (Transparency, Inspection, and Adaptation) are also the essential must-haves for the Scrum Teams to adhere to. They need to make sure that:

- Their Product Backlog is always and as much as possible - transparent, where anyone from the team can access it, can discuss about it, and can share ideas to refine it in a much better way. Such transparency always allows them to continuously inspect the Product Backlog.

- Inspections mainly need to happen during all the Scrum Events; however, the Scrum Team should perform inspections all the time. They need to do it during their interactions within themselves and with their Stakeholders, as and when needed. By following such a way of working, they need to offer opportunities to themselves and to their Stakeholders, while helping them to create opportunities to adapt, to enact, and to continuously improve the overall quality of Product Backlog.

- By adapting to continuously improve, they need to keep on moving in the right direction, while keeping their common, shared purpose and goals in their mind.

- Empiricism (Transparency, Inspection, and Adaptation) needs to be properly utilized to have their Product Backlog as an evolving Scrum Artifact, where they need to capture the valid change requests (from the customers/end-users and stakeholders) and the valid changes in accordance with the technological advancements and the changing market conditions. The process of backlog refinement needs to support them to have proper interactions within and outside of the Scrum Team.

By understanding that the Product Backlog can have other work items (such as Bugs, Spikes, Enhancements, Enablers, and many more), the Scrum Team should not place everything as a User Story in it. Though User Stories need to have a specific outline, it is not required for the other non-User Story kind of work items to follow the same outline.

It is not compulsory for the Scrum Team to have every work item/Product Backlog Item under their Product Backlog to be written as a User Story. The team needs to start contemplating in terms of Product Backlog Items (PBIs), by having an understanding that not every Product Backlog Item is a User Story; however, every User Story is surely a Product Backlog Item. The Product Backlog can contain some exploration/analysis/research-oriented work items called as Spikes, issues/defects/errors/failures in the working software product called as Bugs, customizations/improvements/modifications in the working software product called as Major/Minor Enhancements, some other capabilities/functionalities to improve the working software product called as Enablers, and so on.

By making use of add-ons/techniques such as Detailed, Estimated, Emergent, and Prioritized (DEEP) Criteria, Description, Order, Value, and Estimate (DOVE) Criteria, and Independent, Negotiable, Valuable, Estimable, Small, and Testable (INVEST) Criteria, the Product Backlog and its associated contents can be effectively and efficiently handled by the Scrum Team during their Product Backlog Refinements.

The Scrum Team always needs to ensure that their Product Backlog is properly detailed, estimated, emergent, and prioritized by making use of the DEEP Criteria. The DEEP Criteria always helps the Scrum Team to have a well-specified, well-ordered, and a continuously evolving Product Backlog.

The Scrum Team also needs to ensure that every PBI/User Story under their Product Backlog needs to have a basic information in terms of its description, order, value, and estimate by making use of the DOVE Criteria which needs to be associated with the Product Backlog. The description needs to explain what the PBI/User Story is all about. The order needs to specify the priority of the PBI/User Story under the Product Backlog. The value needs to indicate the potential value of a PBI/User Story to be delivered to their customers/end-users. An estimate needs to reflect on what relative estimate the PBI/User Story needs to consume for its complete development and delivery, to make it fully functional within a Sprint. The Scrum Team also needs to confirm that, the DOVE Criteria are being operated upon by all the activities being performed by them and every PBI is being thoroughly formulated by applying the same.

While creating and refining the PBIs under the Product Backlog, the team also needs to follow and apply the INVEST Criteria. They need to ensure that every PBI/

User Story is INVEST Criteria compliant. Here, Independent signifies that every PBI is a potentially releasable unit of work. Negotiable signifies that the Product Owner needs to be open to negotiate on the scope and contents of the PBIs with Developers. Valuable signifies that every PBI is providing business value on its own. Estimable signifies that the PBIs are tangible enough that the Developers can give an approximate relative estimate to reflect on how the size of PBI looks to be. Small signifies that every PBI can be completed in a short amount of time, so that the team can receive a quick feedback, based on customer value getting delivered. Testable signifies that every PBI can be tested using various types of tests; before the code written for that PBI gets released into production, where its actual usage is to be done by the customers.

To order the PBIs under the Product Backlog, the Developers need to discuss with the Product Owner on value, priority, risks, and dependencies. Such discussions during the process of Product Backlog Refinement help them to determine which PBIs are most valuable and which are less valuable. For the Product Owner to confirm on such decisions, he/she needs to pause, think, and reflect on the PBIs having the highest customer value and the PBIs having potential risks, complexities, and dependencies. The Product Owner also needs to use these primary considerations to maximize the value proposition present inside the Product Backlog. Such a *Sooner the Better* approach helps the Developers to deliver reasonable customer value through Product Increments by anticipating potential risks and dependencies, if any.

While prioritizing the work items under their Product Backlog, the team needs to explore all the possibilities. Using an add-on such as Product Backlog Prioritization Quadrant, the Product Owner needs to consider various aspects related to business and technical needs, past and future needs, and various activities like new features development, support related activities, technical debt handling, architectural innovation, and so on. It is important for him/her to understand all the functional, non-functional, and technical aspects to optimize the Product Value. These aspects need to be considered in accordance with the customer needs, wants, desires, must haves, good to haves, okay to haves, and not okay to haves, and so on, viewpoints. It helps him/her to have the required trade-offs with the Developers. It is the key responsibility of the Product Owner to balance on all these aspects and viewpoints.

> *"If we have a fully defined backlog, we no longer have a true*
> *Agile Product Development situation. Instead, we have a project."*
> *- Ron Jeffries*

There is always a possibility that the Product Backlog may turn out to have huge number of work items in it, which are mainly the PBIs and/or User Stories. To maintain such a Product Backlog, the Scrum Team needs to have potential work (of no more than the next couple of months) reflecting the Product Roadmap. The Scrum Team always needs to keep it adaptable to address any other associated work items coming up later once a further required exploration is done by them. By having the Product Backlog containing enough amount of work items, Developers always need to be more focused and responsive to their Sprint-based deliverables. The overall success of Sprints-based development and delivery of working software product completely depends upon the quality of PBIs getting selected by the Developers in the Sprint Backlog from the Product Backlog. Hence, it is essential and vital for the Developers to have a proper understanding of PBIs in place at the time of Sprint Planning.

Many times, the Scrum Team members face problems related to sizing of PBIs/User Stories, especially with big-sized PBIs/User Stories. In case of such PBIs/User Stories, the scope of the functionality getting covered under them seems to be huge. This restricts the Developers to split them into small sized PBIs. This also makes it difficult for them to complete such PBIs within a single Sprint. In such a scenario, they need to apply Mike Cohn's Spikes, Paths, Interfaces, Data, and Rules (SPIDR) approach.

SPIDR approach helps the Scrum Team to split the work items into SPIDR. Spikes ask them to perform technical exploration/analysis/research to better understand the work items. Paths ask them to split the work items based on the overall workflow through the working software product functionalities. Interfaces ask them to develop and deliver a simple version of the working software product. Once it is delivered, they can implement rest of the required and additional set of functionalities during the next Sprints. Data asks them to think about the usage of the data and the type of data to be used under the functionalities to be implemented. Rules ask them to reflect on the continuous optimization of functional, non-functional, and technical rules to be considered under the functionalities to be implemented. Using the SPIDR approach, the Scrum Team always needs to consider various aspects such as value, priority, ordering, sizing, feedback, correlation, risks, dependencies, and so on. They also need to remember that they are not splitting the work items only for the sake of splitting them.

The following figure emphasizes on a unique distinctive strategy, which can be effectively and efficiently used by the Scrum Team members during their Product Backlog Refinement sessions:

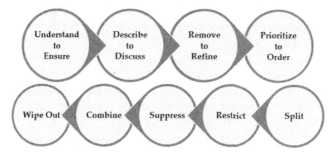

Figure 8.4: Product backlog management/refinement strategy

By applying an add-on such as Kano Model, the Scrum Team (especially the Product Owner) always needs to know the actual need of the Product, its associated features, and the specific benefits the customers/end-users are going to get out of those features. The Scrum Team should also describe the actual benefits to the stakeholders, so that they can discuss on the expected outcomes out of the Features and PBIs/User Stories, which the Scrum Team is supposed to have under their Product Backlog. The Scrum Team should remove any of the existing PBIs/User Stories from their Product Backlog which is not helping them to achieve their anticipated outcomes. Once it is done, they need to prioritize the remaining PBIs, so that they can order them and continue with the creation of new PBIs.

Such ordered and well-prioritized Product Backlog then needs to be split based on the value, priority of new and existing PBIs. Any new decoupled Features, PBIs/User Stories can be also placed in the Product Backlog for the purpose of new product development and delivery, so that the Scrum Team can concentrate upon existing as well as new work items. By evaluating and restricting the scope of the PBIs, the Scrum Team needs to adapt an obvious, precise, and quantifiable common purpose for the next couple of months, based on which they need to formulate their Product Backlog.

By eliminating the PBIs that are not supporting them to achieve their agreed common purpose, they always need to create some abstract PBIs under their Product Backlog to have a crisp, clear, and a streamlined Backlog. This tactic not only requires them to have a look into and to investigate those PBIs for the near future, but also helps them to convert their Product Backlog into a continuously progressing repository of work items.

> *"A good product backlog is shaped like an iceberg; small items at the top,*
> *bigger items below there, and who knows what under the waterline."*
> *- Mike Cohn*

It is always good for the Scrum Team to have an outcome-based Product Backlog, where they always need to align with the reflection of next expected outcome from the product roadmap and strategy. Using such an outcome-based perspective, the Scrum Team needs to address the probability of complexities, changes, uncertainties, and ambiguities, if any. They need to suppress any irrelevant, unnecessary details present in the PBIs/User Stories by keeping the PBIs/User Stories self-sufficient and to be understood by themselves. They also need to consider the overall composition of the Product Backlog to be kept as more adaptable. By consolidating the features into User Journey steps and by considering the workflow under the functionalities to be developed, they need to assess the contents under the PBIs/User Stories to be kept enough detailed.

By combining the specific and required details under the PBIs/User Stories, the overall size of the Product Backlog can be significantly reduced by making it manageable. The Scrum Team needs to do the same by replacing the PBIs having low priority with the high priority ones and by anticipating them with the required updates. Sometimes, the Stakeholders and/or Product Owner tend to ask Developers to create some PBIs, even though such PBIs seem to have low value and low priority. In the future, because of any of the valid reasons, those PBIs appear to be outdated ones and hence get placed at the bottom of the Product Backlog.

In this case, it is always required for the team to evaluate the actual need of such PBIs under the Product Backlog. It should always contain work items to deliver customer value in upcoming couple of Sprints. Before creating such low value and priority based PBIs, the team needs to double-check with the Product Owner and reject any of such PBIs in accordance with the value proposition. They also need to wipe out all the obsolete and irrelevant PBIs present in the Product Backlog to ensure that the Product Backlog is not becoming messy and bulky.

By establishing and sharing the customer value proposition aspect, the Product Owner always needs to emphasize on the customer value by asking questions to the Stakeholders and to the Developers, to determine the actual value. Using their knowledge, intuitions, and opinions, it becomes easy for the Product Owner to have a proper value estimation. Based on such value estimation (getting reflected into the Product Backlog) and by knowing which all PBIs they are supposed to select for the upcoming Sprint, the team needs to have those PBIs as ready to be discussed before their Sprint Planning. They need to address this expectation by ensuring that they need to do everything, which is needed to accomplish their agreed Product Goal. It is hence required for the Scrum Team to have regular Product Backlog Refinement sessions.

> "Handing off all the details about the story to someone else
> to build doesn't work. Don't do that."
> - Jeff Patton

Using a technique like User Story Mapping, the Scrum Team needs to refine all the User Stories by making them granular and by gaining more insights, details under them. Instead of considering the Product Backlog to be just an ordered list of work items, they need to create a big picture by making use of a practice called as User Story Mapping. A Story Map permits them to place the PBIs, especially the User Stories in a better progressive order by using some better picturing options to have a better visualization.

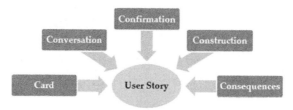

Figure 8.5: The 5C Concept under User Story Mapping by Ron Jeffries and Jeff Patton

The Scrum Team needs to write down, create, and formulate the User Stories to capture the product functionalities on the Cards. Each Card needs to include one User Story added with the sufficient information on it, so that the Scrum Team can find out rest of the required details on it. All the Cards need to be placed under the Product Backlog and need to be organized, prioritized, ordered, and estimated based on the important aspect of customer value optimization. Cards always need to have a short title to read them and to refer them at the time of Scrum Events, especially at the time of Daily Scrum Event. Cards also need to have a proper description to reflect on who, what, when, why, how, and few other important aspects along with some metadata to underline the customer/end-user value, priority, relative estimates, dependencies, risks, status, and any other required details.

During the Product Backlog Refinement sessions, the Scrum Team needs to have interactive conversations against the User Stories. They need to discuss with each other on the functionalities getting tracked under those User Stories. They need to work together to address all the questions, concerns, doubts, opinions, thoughts, perspectives, alternatives, and ideal solutions, where they need to build a common, shared understanding to be on the same page. Team needs to anticipate their discussions and viewpoints around the User Stories to have a consensus in the process of formulation of User Stories. By coming up with the use cases, user personas, workflows, and UI and UX specific aspects through a proper usage of online/offline tools, they need to explain their expectations and understanding to the Product Owner to be on the same page. While having such conversations, they also need to be ready to apply required modifications to the User Stories, if any.

By recognizing and by acknowledging the possible alternatives, the Scrum Team needs to have a confirmation on what they are supposed to capture and to keep under their User Stories. They also need to come up with an agreed acceptance criteria to support the validation of completeness of the User Stories. Acceptance criteria need to help them to commit on the PBIs during the Sprint Planning, where they need to consider all the things they will be developing, validating, verifying, testing, and delivering to confirm that every User Story is fully functional. To have a proper construction of all the User Stories, the Developers always need to be well-prepared, knowing most of the required and relevant functional, non-functional, and technical details to be captured under the User Stories. This needs to happen through their interactive conversations, so that they can establish a shared understanding within themselves. They also need to continuously inspect, learn, adapt, and enact on all the consequences which are getting shared as acknowledgments and feedbacks against the working software product to be delivered by them. By accepting all the valid feedbacks received from the stakeholders and customers/end-users, they need to capture them under the new User Stories to fill-in the implementation specific gaps, if any. To carry out an effective feedback addressal, their focus always needs to be on continuous learning and continuous improvement. For this purpose, they need to do the required needful by executing a learning outlook and by applying an ideation, experimentation-based approach.

A User Story Map is a simple map to visualize the User Stories created by the Developers. It expresses the type of a user performing an action by doing something to reach an objective. The Scrum Team making use of a User Story Map always needs to describe the users by including some of the required details about the user actions along with a lightweight persona sketch of the user. They also need to capture the user's activities and behaviors using some short verb phrases, which should act as a basic building block of the Story Map.

A User Story Map also needs to include all the user specific goals to be achieved out of the User Stories, where a user actions specific summary needs to emphasize on the tasks and activities to be done by the Developers. It also needs to capture all the required aspects of all the user actions and activities, using which the Developers need to complete the smaller tasks supporting the bigger tasks.

By capturing the user specific actions and activities to organize the tasks to be done by the Developers to reach a common goal, the Story Map needs to formulate its structure. It needs to be organized to follow the specific order of the User Stories considering the user persona and the workflow of user actions. The Scrum Team also needs to remember that some specific users might have different actions to perform different things by following a different order. The Story Map hence needs to follow a conversational flow to clarify such alterations with a conversational purpose under their User Stories.

The Story Map also needs to contain the specifics of the User Stories, which can be populated by further splitting and slicing them down into activities, tasks, sub tasks, alternative tasks, and exceptions. This needs to be done to track the work at the lowest level of effort. The team also needs to split and slice the activities and tasks, which they anticipate that users might be using to achieve their objectives. By following a Release Slicing approach under the Story Map, they need to map the Activities, Tasks, and User Stories to their planned Releases, so that they can perform some hypothesis-driven experiments to deliver a Minimum Viable Product (MVP). Such a Minimum Viable Product (with some basic features implemented in it) can be released to some of its pilot customers/end-users to grab their attention.

The Scrum Team also needs to operate with the Story Maps to understand about the user personas, user actions, and user behaviors, so that they can imagine about all of it soon. They need to capture the present user needs, wants, desires, pain points, specifics, observations, and alternatives under the Story Map. The Story Map needs to emerge with the analysis, exploration, and discovery of user personas, actions, and behaviors. While mapping all the user actions and user behaviors under the Story Map workflows, the Scrum Team needs to map the entire process by looking at the big picture. The following figure emphasizes on the overall process of User Story Mapping:

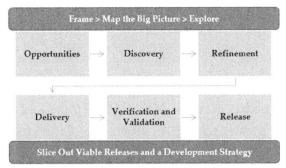

Figure 8.6: User Story Mapping process

The Story Map always needs to evolve with the Scrum Team's overall understanding of user personas and the product features getting delivered for them. It is hence required for the team to perform opportunity assessments as a first step in the User Story Mapping process, using which they need to create an opportunity backlog to capture and record all the user needs, wants, and requests. They need to spend a significant amount of time and effort to understand all the details about who, what, and how aspects of user personas. They need to prioritize the opportunity backlog using the outcomes of their discussions. Before mapping the User Stories inside the Story Map, they need to frame the user specific Features. They need to evaluate on, what the features are all about and what problem is getting addressed by the delivery of those features. They also need to evaluate on, who all are the different types of users who will be using those features, how they will be using them, and what is the ultimate value and benefit they will be getting out of those features.

Detailing and confirming the Product Features using Discovery is the next step in User Story Mapping process, where the team needs to identify the Minimum Viable Product and its associated features. While acting as an enabler for the creation of the Product Backlog, the Discovery step needs to determine what the team is supposed to implement during their upcoming Sprints. The Scrum Team needs to explore and reflect on the problems and the corresponding possible, feasible, and useful solutions by considering the Feature Value Optimization. By mapping a big picture of user personas, user actions, and user behaviors, they need to focus on building up and overall understanding of the entire solutioning to be implemented by them. This is required for them to identify all the user activities with their corresponding workflows. During the discovery phase, such mapping of a big picture of user activities always needs to shape the backbone of the Story Map.

The Scrum Team then needs to break the features into multiple PBIs/User Stories. They also need to start defining, describing, and refining the User Stories/PBIs during the next steps of User Story Mapping process known as refinement and delivery. By utilizing the product team planning and story workshop sessions, the Scrum Team needs to discuss with the Stakeholders on the overall progress of

Sprints and Release. It eases the refinement and selection of the work items for the upcoming Sprints.

The Scrum Team also need to plan and re-plan for their anticipated work to make their User Stories/PBIs ready for the upcoming Sprints. In this process, a Definition of Ready (DoR) needs to be formulated, refined, and followed by them. Refinements need to happen regularly to capture and record the details under the Product Backlog, where they also need to define and agree on a proper Acceptance Criteria and an agreed Definition of Done (DoD) for the PBIs/User Stories. The Scrum Team also needs to explore on compiling the Story Map contents by converting large User Stories into small tasks/activities along with all the required details captured under them. They need to think on all the better ideas, business rules, technical integrations, risks, dependencies, pre-requisites, variations, exceptions, alternatives, and ideal solutions, which they need to add to the Cards in Story Map. They need to discuss and agree on modifying and rearranging the Cards to perform User Story Splitting and Slicing.

It is required for the Scrum Team to slice and split the Cards under the Story Map to formulate their potential Product Backlog to be converted into Product Releases later. It helps them to bind and limit the development and delivery limits across Sprints and Releases. The team needs to make the Story Map as an incremental Product Release Roadmap to highlight the expected outcomes. To identify the overall success of refinements against the actual delivery of Product Releases in the future, the outcomes need to elaborate on, how the Product Releases are lined up (to deliver the anticipated customer value) with the agreed Objectives and the corresponding Key Results (OKRs) based metrics. OKRs is a simple goal-setting framework, which needs to be used by the Scrum Teams to define, track, and evaluate their objectives against the corresponding outcomes.

A distinctive Story Mapping of the value and all the priorities of the Features and PBIs/User Stories (across the release-based delivery phases) allows the Scrum Team to explore all the possible set of dependencies and risks. It also helps them to learn rapidly. In this case, the Scrum Team needs to follow a development strategy consisting of three phases to deliver the features by following a timeline. They are Opening, Mid, and End Game. *Figure 8.7* shows an example User Story Map with some of its basic elements:

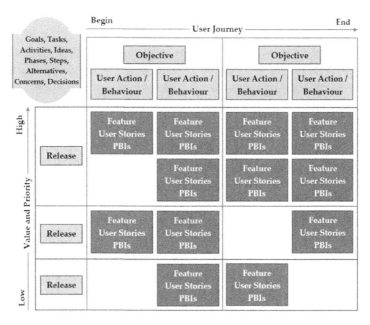

Figure 8.7: *An example of a sample User Story Map*

The first phase of development strategy needs to be treated as an Opening Game, where the Developers need to implement the basic operational Features (broken into PBIs/User Stories) from the Story Map. The Product Owner, the Stakeholders, and the actual End-Users from the Customer side need to evaluate the Features created by the team, where they need to review and examine the overall functioning and implementation approach. To make up the existing functionalities more useful and intact, the Mid Game phase needs to be the next phase. In this phase, the Developers need to implement all the major functionalities on the top of basic operational functionalities delivered earlier.

"It's not a testing problem,
it's a design problem manifesting as a testing problem, usually."
- Kent Beck

By applying some proper verification, validation, and review specific processes, the Scrum Team needs to perform all kinds of required testing by considering the different viewpoints of previously mentioned intended parties. The Scrum Team also needs to enact upon all the improvements, enhancements, and feedbacks. They always need to guarantee that there is enough amount of testing getting performed against all the PBIs/User Stories being completed and delivered by them in their every ongoing Sprint.

By utilizing the final phase called as End Game, the Scrum Team needs to revisit and refine the Product Features and PBIs/User Stories across their Sprints, where they need to mark those Features as ready for release. They need to ensure that all the Features, PBIs, User Stories, and their associated Tasks/Activities are fully functional and ready to be deployed as a part of a planned release. This is required to be done to evaluate the overall release readiness, based on the overall completeness of work items from the Story Map to the Sprint Backlogs for all the Sprints associated with a particular release.

There might be a possibility that some unexpected and/or remaining work might be occurring during the phase of development, testing, build, deployment, and release for which the Scrum Team might need to re-plan. Considering the fulfilment and acceptance of work items (after the verification and validation of functionalities getting tracked under them), the Scrum Team needs to perform the build and deployment-specific activities to release the working software product to the customers/end-users.

Once a planned release is done, it is the primary responsibility of all the Scrum Team members to start with measuring the released product's overall performance by comparing the same with the expected outcomes in a stipulated amount of time and by using OKRs framework. This approach helps them to collect sufficient data points to validate the key results/outcomes to decide the actual value and usefulness of the released software product. To embrace a proper customer value optimization, the Product Backlog, the User Story Map, and the Sprint Backlog always need to correlate with each other. It is required for a Scrum Team to have regular Product Backlog Refinements, where they need to cross-check on this correlation.

While executing the process of User Story Mapping technique, the Scrum Team also needs to apply the following aspects of User Story Splitting and Slicing techniques.

- Team needs to have the Features asserting the views of customers/end-users, also capturing the details about users, value, usage, and frequency of usage.
- Team needs to have all the User Stories to describe unique functionalities of Features to be developed and delivered by them. They need to have an anticipation that once they have delivered a User Story, they should be able to learn something out of it. User Stories getting split from features need have a combined value to the end-users, when delivered under iterative and incremental Product Increments.
- Considering the overall User Journey, the Value and Priority of Features (and their corresponding User Stories getting formulated on Cards) needs to be placed on the Story Map in a sequential order. By addressing the dependencies, the placement of Features needs to follow an expected User usage sequence.
- Team needs to have an agreement on grouping the User Story Cards based on the frequency of usage, that is, how critical a User Story is for an end-user.

- By focussing on the logical breaks in the overall workflow of functionalities (getting tracked under the User Stories) and by applying the INVEST Criteria, the team needs to have Independent, Negotiable, Valuable, Estimable, Small, and Testable User Stories. The User Stories also need to define some valuable functionalities, which the team can deliver, review, and assess on their own.

- By identifying the smallest set of Features and their associated User Stories which are required to be useful to the end-users considering the customer perspective, the team needs to decide a Minimum Viable Product release.

- After splitting a Feature into enough required PBIs with a vertical slicing across components, the team needs to split them into development-specific Tasks.

- Team needs to ensure that the Tasks are describing all the required aspects of the actual development work and the completion of Tasks is resulting into a fully functional, demonstrable, and testable high-quality Software Product.

- Considering all the development-specific Tasks under their PBIs/User Stories, the Developers need to have all the User Stories to be filled-in with some relative estimates. It helps them to have a forecast in place to make the User Stories fully functional and to deliver them under the upcoming Product Increment.

- By arranging the User Stories in a sequential order based on the end-user's criticality perspective, the Story Map always needs to give a clarity about all the dependencies in between the User Stories. The most important User Stories always need to be placed at the top of the Story Map. In this way, the Developers can get a complete visibility of their priorities, which can provide them an ease of implementation thought process, once they start to work on the User Stories.

Points to remember

- The process of Product Backlog Management (through a series of continuous and regular Product Backlog Refinements) is important for the Scrum Team, where they need to create and/or update the required specifics, priorities, and estimates, and so on, for the PBIs/User Stories in the Product Backlog.

- The Product Backlog needs to be a prioritized list of Features, Functionalities, and all the Capabilities the Developers are supposed to deliver as Working Software Product Increments within their Sprints, both incrementally and iteratively.

- It is a prime responsibility of the Product Owner along with the Stakeholders to frequently revisit and review the Product Roadmap, Strategy, and Release

Plan. It is always good for the Scrum Team to have an outcome-based Product Backlog.

- The Scrum Team always needs to remember that the creation and/or modification of the PBIs/User Stories under the Product Backlog is a collective exercise for the whole Scrum Team. During refinements, the team needs to have the structured conversations to explore, evaluate, and confirm on the PBIs to be refined. To order the PBIs under the Product Backlog, the Developers need to discuss with the Product Owner.

- The Product Backlog should not be a huge collection of isolated PBIs. It should not contain obsolete, irrelevant, and surplus PBIs. The PBIs need to be sliced vertically based on the end-to-end functionality across the Features, rather than slicing them horizontally based on the individual technical layers/components. The Team needs to validate and confirm the PBIs using a Definition of Ready Checklist.

- It is safer for the multiple Scrum Teams working on the same Product to follow one-product-one-backlog rule. It allows them to compare the Features with each other. There is also an assurance that the Features with the highest priority from the whole Product's perspective are recognized, prioritized, and ordered.

- By establishing and sharing the customer value proposition aspect, the Product Owner always needs to emphasize on customer value by asking questions to the Stakeholders and to the Developers, to determine the actual value.

- Using the User Story Mapping technique, the Scrum Team needs to refine all the User Stories by making them granular and by gaining more insights, details under them. A User Story Map is a simple map to visualize the User Stories created by the Developers. While executing the process of User Story Mapping, the Scrum Team also needs to apply User Story Splitting and Slicing techniques.

In the next chapter, readers will get to know about some of the advanced Scrum add-ons/techniques to help the Scrum Teams to perform an effective and efficient Relative Estimation.

CHAPTER 9

Add-ons for Effective and Efficient Relative Estimation

Introduction

In this chapter, readers will get to know about some of the advanced Scrum add-ons to help the Scrum Teams to perform an effective and efficient relative estimation of their work items. Readers will also get to know about various relative estimation techniques, which can help the Scrum Teams to identify, analyse, and reflect on the complexity, uncertainty, ambiguity, risks, and dependencies of the work items to be worked upon by them. They will also get an overview of the concept of relative estimation, using which the Scrum Teams can have an understanding about the relative effort required to complete their work during the Sprints.

Objective

After studying this chapter, you should be able to:

- Understand various considerations for the Scrum Teams regarding the sizing and timeline mapping of Product Backlog work items.
- Understand the correlation of communication, complexity, and consistency specific to estimation.
- Understand the need of estimation for a Scrum Team.
- Understand absolute and relative estimation comparatively.

- Understand the process of relative estimation for the work items in Product Backlog.

- Understand various relative estimation techniques for the Scrum Teams.

Jennie 'The Scrum Master' (in a serious discussion with Mary 'The Agile Coach'):

"Hey Mary, have you heard anything about things happening around me and my Scrum Team? I am not happy with this sudden change. I don't know why the Senior Management wants me to go away from my team now. Not at all a fair decision!"

Mary 'The Agile Coach' (smiling and replying):

"C'mon Jennie! We have other teams waiting for you. Feel free to do miracles with them. Let me take this opportunity to call out my favourite quote - 'Life is a Sprint and you have got to be Agile', right?"

Jennie (replying with a complaining tone):

"Huh! Since last 1 year, I am closely associated with my team. Teaching, mentoring, coaching, and helping them to enhance their agile way of working. Preaching Agile and Scrum values always. We have done so many things for the purpose of product, process, and people improvement. Team still looks to be struggling a bit with things like relative estimation. Suddenly, our Product Owner tells me that, the team doesn't need me anymore. How come they decide on this? What do you think? Should I talk to our Delivery Director? I am surprised, confused, and frustrated, totally!"

Mary:

"Jennie, please stop overthinking! Let me ask you something. Why is your son not staying with you? Why he got himself relocated to the other State? He spent almost 20 years of his life with you, right? You were completely accountable for his upbringing, to support him for his education and to fulfil all his needs and wants, right? If this is the case, then how come you allowed him to move away from you?"

Jennie (taking a pause and replying):

"Honestly speaking, I wanted him to be more responsible for his own decisions. He went to the other state for the purpose of higher education. Instead of becoming an obstacle for his career aspirations and instead of stopping him, I was all okay with his choice and decision to move away from me. I actually wanted to give him his required space, so that he could try and learn things on his own."

Mary:

"Exactly! Your team is not asking you to move away. Let's give them their choice and space to see, how they learn things on their own in your absence. You have already done a fantastic job with them so far."

Jennie (smiling and replying):

"Oh, Thanks Mary! Thanks for your quick eye-opening advice. Let's hope for the best."

The Scrum Team needs to recall that all the work items under their Product Backlog need not be and will not be of the same size. They are also not required to be present at the same level of specifics. The work items can be of different sizes such as large, medium, small, and so on. The larger work items correspond to larger pieces of functionality, whereas the smaller work items correspond to the smaller pieces of functionality getting tracked under them. As shown in the following figure, the work items need to be considered as epics, features, PBIs/User Stories, and Tasks, and so on based on their individual sizing:

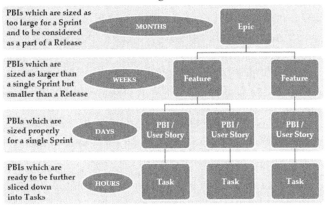

Figure 9.1: *Sizing and Timeline mapping of Product Backlog work items*

It is important for the Scrum Team to understand various types of sizing of work items in their Product Backlog. The Product Backlog can contain epics, which are the PBIs sized as too large for a Sprint. As the order of significance for them is in months to make them releasable and fully functional, the Scrum Team always needs to consider them as a part of a release/multiple releases. Scrum Team can have epics broken into multiple features/themes to describe the large-sized functionalities getting tracked under them. They need to remember that there is no standardized agreement for large size and it can differ from a Scrum Team to another Scrum Team. The Product Backlog can also contain features as a collection of PBIs/User Stories, which are sized as larger than a single Sprint. Delivery of valuable functionalities through such customer-facing features can take weeks to make them fully functional and releasable. The Scrum Team can have features to be further broken into the PBIs/User Stories. They can consider them as medium sized, where there is no standardized agreement for medium size and it can differ from a Scrum Team to another Scrum Team.

The Product Backlog hence can also have the PBIs/User Stories, which are sized properly for a single sprint. To make them releasable and fully functional, the Scrum Team, especially the Developers need to have them aligned with their agreed Definition of Ready. This needs to be done by the Developers before they select them for their upcoming Sprints. Developers also need to have the PBIs/User Stories to be further sliced down into tasks/activities, which they need to complete and deliver by the end of the upcoming Sprints. It is always better to have single Sprint-sized PBIs/ User Stories to mark and differentiate them as Sprint Ready PBIs/User Stories. By following such a sizing and timeline mapping approach (for epics, features/themes, PBIs/User Stories, and for tasks/activities), the Scrum Team can get an ultimate benefit before they start estimating the work items at the time of Product Backlog Refinements and/or at the time of Sprint Planning.

Apart from value, summary, description, and order, an estimate also needs to be one of the recommended attributes for the PBIs, while the Scrum Team is performing Product Backlog Refinements and Sprint Planning. The work to be done by them might be of varying size and estimated effort; however, it often needs to be defined during the Sprint Planning itself. It does not explain while referring to the exact interpretation of the estimates for the PBIs, as the Developers need to start by designing the system and continue to develop the associated work which is required to convert the Product Backlog into Working Software Product Increments. The Scrum Team hence needs to consider the definition of value and complexity of PBIs while performing the estimations. The Product Owner needs to define the value and scope of PBIs, so that the Developers can confirm on the complexity and effort of PBIs.

> *"Any intelligent fool can make things bigger and more complex.*
> *It takes a touch of genius and a lot of courage to move in the opposite direction."*
>
> *- Albert Einstein*

The complexity along with its associated predictability for any of the risks always acts as a primary concern for the Scrum Team. Consideration of such complexity is required for the Scrum Team to address the complex adaptive problems under complex environments to be collaboratively solved by them. By utilizing the built-in power of Empiricism through a proper enablement of transparency, inspection, and adaptation, the Scrum Team needs to improve their overall predictability, so that they can regulate any of the potential dependencies and risks. Estimates for all the PBIs/ User Stories need to be considered as a part of a teamwork-based exercise to improve the overall transparency. The Product Owner should not struggle to order the Product Backlog without the presence of transparency, where the exercise of estimating the PBIs needs to be given more value than the subsequent estimates. There always needs to be a collective estimation in place to have a common shared understanding of all the knowns and unknowns by considering the value, complexity, and risks involved. If the Developers do not have a consensus about collective estimation, they need to face the consequences of lack of collaboration and co-operation. It also might have a bad impact on the process of actual implementation of PBIs during the Sprints.

The overall complexity to estimate and implement the PBIs can have a probable variation in case of any of the dependencies occurring for the PBIs. When such dependencies are present and not recognized by the Developers, the process of estimation of PBIs can result into a confusion. When such dependencies are recognized by Developers, they get exposed to the complications. To have a better decision-making, they need to focus and have a better clarity over all kinds of dependencies. This approach always asks them to have their estimation as a collective, collaborative exercise. As the Developers need to be self-managing, self-organizing, and cross-functional, they need to follow a mechanism to uncover the ways with which they might need to approach their estimations. They need to refer to what has already happened in the past for a better consensus-based decision-making in the future.

By keeping this as a small condition, it has a significant impact on how the Scrum Team needs to deal with estimation along with forecasting. They need to inspect on what has been done in the past to disclose the complexity, so that they can give a try to lessen the same. The Scrum Team always needs to have a proper and well-balanced composition and involvement of a sufficient number of Developers. This way the actual process of Backlog Refinement along with the estimation of PBIs needs to be kept simple and straight forward. The complexity of the PBIs can also be determined with the level of consistency. A higher consistency helps them to reduce complexity and enhance predictability. As shown in the following figure, the process of communication within a Scrum Team with a lesser number of team members creates less complexity. It always helps the process of Empiricism to remain useful.

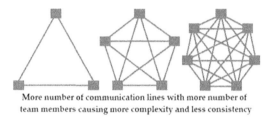

More number of communication lines with more number of
team members causing more complexity and less consistency

Figure 9.2: *Communication, Complexity, and Consistency based on Metcalfe's Law*

The Scrum Framework always helps the Developers to become better at estimates by asking them to expand their consistency under the complex environments to solve the complex problems. The Scrum Team needs to have estimates for the PBIs/User Stories in place. Estimates always need to act as a part of their non-stop decision-making process, where they need to have more transparency. Estimates given by them should not create a false sense of commitment and assurance for the Stakeholders. The Scrum Team needs to ensure that they are improving on their own predictability by remaining truthful to their original forecasting and by responding to the change and to value the same.

Instead of treating the estimates to enact as timeboxes or deadlines, the Developers need to incorporate new complexities as soon as they come to know about them. By performing a continuous inspection, they need to learn to forecast on what and how much they are not likely to be able to forecast. By having a complete ownership of the product functionalities being developed and delivered by the Scrum Team, it is always required for the Product Owner to act as a Value Optimizer rather than only performing the analysis of customer requirements to come up with the PBIs. This is required, so that the Developers can properly estimate the PBIs by considering their value rather than getting frustrated to achieve the original estimates once they start to implement the PBIs.

> *"Estimates are never wrong. They are an assessment on that point in time with what was known at the time. That reality proved to be different is another story. That doesn't invalidate the estimates."*
> *- Willem-Jan Ageling*

By considering unexpected, changing priorities and by continuously reflecting on the decision-making aspect, the Scrum Team needs to keep a track of how much amount of time they are spending on the work and its associated activities, which they might not have foreseen originally. By asking themselves to assert upon their actual capabilities and findings, such intuitions will help them to improve on generating more value by reducing complexity and by empowering them to become more certain.

Developers always need to think on developing and delivering resourceful solutions to solve complex problems in complex environments. Such complex environments have uncertainty, causing an increased risk. In this process, they might create something that might not have been done by them using the same approach in the past. It is required for the Scrum Team to recognize that they will hardly be able to create forecasts, which will be realized the same way as it was realized by them earlier. Also, if the team is more certain about it, then they will be lacking with a willingness to act in response to new comprehensions. Team needs to have a basic realization about uncertainty, which allows them to become better to handle it. Once the team starts to explore and learn more, they can discover the things on their own.

> *"If we don't take our time, while designing and developing, to do something properly, productivity will go down drastically and kill the project."*
> *- Robert C. Martin*

The Scrum Team always needs to assess and maintain a suitable reference for uncertainty and complexity, so that they can inspect on and agree with what and how much they will be able to achieve during their Sprints. By keeping their estimates based on their own inspections, the Scrum Team always needs to keep a high-level track and trace of all the work items and the corresponding customer value which they are supposed to deliver to their customers. During the product backlog refinements, the Developers always need to have a sole responsibility to establish and agree on the estimates.

The Scrum Team needs to believe that an estimate is basically a guesstimate. It is their best possible guess-based estimate to reflect on by when they will be able to complete a work item, which they are estimating. The following figure shows some of the key aspects about the basic need of estimation for the Scrum Teams and the value it gives to them:

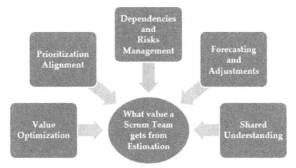

Figure 9.3: *The basic need of Estimation for a Scrum Team*

Estimates always play a crucial role to manage the dependencies and risks, where the Scrum Team gets to know about when they can do what to collectively overcome those dependencies and risks. Estimates also help the Scrum Team to get themselves aligned with their priorities, so that they can take some critical decisions to select the most valuable alternatives out of all the available alternatives. Based on the past empirical data points and facts, estimates always assist the Scrum Team to perform a basic forecasting and projection to adjust and to be ready for the future. In case of any disagreements, estimates ask the Scrum Team to validate their common, shared understanding by always optimizing the customer value.

The Scrum Framework does not enforce the Scrum Teams to make use of a specific estimation technique. It rather acts as a collection of rules and guidelines to enable the process of Empiricism, where the Scrum Teams need to explore on their own and choose an estimation technique, which fits their needs to have an ease of estimation of work items. While doing the same, the Scrum Teams always need to emphasize on the core structure of Scrum Framework, Scrum Values, and the overall process of Empiricism.

By having a collective reflection on the lead time, cycle time, and few other parameters, by limiting the overall Work in Progress, and by making use of a Continuous Integration and Continuous Delivery approach, the matured Scrum Teams can also come up with the Sprint Backlog having PBIs/User Stories in it, but with no estimates. Such an approach helps them to become cognizant about continuous customer value delivery without using any estimates.

The process of estimation always needs to be considered as a mechanism to find out an estimate or an approximation for the work and its associated activities to be performed by the Scrum Team. Estimation also needs to act as a useful value for them to forecast the amount of time the work is going to consume for them, even if the input data is complex, inadequate, uncertain, or uneven and the value is getting derived from the best possible and available information for what they need to do.

"Estimating isn't about estimating at all. Estimating is about creating a shared understanding of the requirements, and a shared understanding of the solution. When teams have problems estimating, it's almost never an estimating problem, it's a shared understanding problem."
- Mike Cottmeyer

It is required for the Developers to collaborate with each other during the Sprint Planning Event, where they need to collectively focus on the PBIs/User Stories (from the Product Backlog) based on their value, order, and priority to populate an individual estimate for them. Ideally, the size of PBIs/User Stories needs to be anticipated in terms of a relative estimation such as User Story Points.

An individual estimate needs to be a relative unit of measure to express an estimate required for the complete effort needed to make a PBI/User Story fully functional and potentially releasable under its applicable working software product increment. Estimates are required for the Developers to plan their work items considering an anticipated timeline, where the Scrum Team needs to measure their own progress. Estimation is required to be done during Sprint Planning, using which they need to get accountable for the work items, which they are supposed to work on. By easing out the measurement of the Scrum Team's overall progress, estimates not only help the Scrum Team to occupy the Sprint with the work items, but they also get a benefit to forecast their last stop destination within a specific Sprint.

As a novice Scrum Team is pretty much unaware about the requirements getting tracked under their work items, performing the activity of estimation of work items may seem to be a bit confusing activity for them. They need to spend enough time to get themselves acquainted with the type of work items and associated projections over the time.

As the Developers get more and more exposure about the product and its associated features, they need to continue by having a particular sense of how they are going to consider the work items and their corresponding efforts/estimates, which they need to anticipate to complete them. The Scrum Team members always need to understand the overall importance of relative estimation. Relative estimation is one of the numerous distinct types of estimation to be used by them to estimate their PBIs/User Stories, together by performing a comparison or by grouping the work items of equivalent difficulty and not using the absolute units of time (such as minutes/hours/days). It eliminates the drawbacks of absolute estimation of work items by avoiding any unnecessary precisions and confusions.

Developers need to use the process of estimation to foresee the most reasonable volume of effort expected by them to develop and deliver the potentially shippable working software product increments. While performing estimations, they need to consider various functional, non-functional, and technical attributes along with the potential time required for them to carry out the essential activities. This approach helps them to estimate the cost linked with the overall effort, time, and value involved in the activities. Research has already proven that, while being positive or negative rather than being realistic, the Developers are not always capable of delivering the product increments based on absolute estimations. The ever-changing customer needs, requirements, and corresponding changes in the scope of product features and functionalities may result into some potential unknowns, which always makes the absolute estimation unreliable.

Instead of speculating on the absolute effort required to complete the work items and instead of performing absolute estimation based on the size of work items as a guess, it is much simpler for the Developers to connect and correlate similar work items by establishing a sense of relatively comparing them. Relative estimation is a procedure to estimate the work items by comparing their similarities and differences in terms of complexity and not estimating them in terms of units of time such as minutes/hours/days. By using the relative estimation approach, the overall comparison of work items can be done in an easier, simple, and quick manner, as compared to the absolute estimation approach.

Most of the times, the Developers making use of absolute estimation (to reflect on how much time they will take to complete their work items and associated tasks) do not feel comfortable about their own estimates. While performing such estimation, they may not have all the required details about all the unknowns, complexities, dependencies, and scenarios, and so on. This affects them by making them uncomfortable and unconvinced. Many times, the Product Owner and/or the Stakeholders consider the estimates given by the Developers as time-based guaranteed commitments. This might trigger as a wrong interpretation of estimates to them. They should rather use the estimates given by the Developers as a feedback-based input, so that they can take their required decisions.

On the other hand, the relative estimates are not measured in time and they cannot be considered as time-based commitments at all. While making use of relative estimation, the Developers cannot have time-based estimates. They need to consider and have some slack anticipating various unknowns, complexities, dependencies, scenarios, and few other details.

By having an intrinsic motivation and a common sense to determine the relative sizing of work items, Developers can perform a relative comparison of work items, so that a categorization of either relatively greater or relatively smaller-sized work items can be established. This is the reason behind why the Developers belonging to many Scrum Teams are less hesitant to make a proper use of relative estimation instead of absolute estimation. They feel much more comfortable to confirm on, whether a work item is bigger or smaller than the other work items by simply doing a comparison.

A common observation specific to the mindset of Scrum Teams during the Sprint Planning illustrates that they perform better by making use of relative estimation. Relative estimation usually takes less amount of time to reflect and decide on the Scope, Uncertainty, Complexity, and their existing Knowledge. While being team centric than time centric, it also looks to be simple and easy for the Scrum Teams to review and refine their relative estimates. Relative estimates are easy to describe and simple to rationalize their expectations. As shown in the following figure, during the Product Backlog Refinements and/or during the Sprint Planning, the Scrum Team needs to apply relative estimation techniques to the prioritized work items under their Product Backlog. There are variety of relative estimation techniques/add-ons, which can be explored by the Scrum Teams to select the most suitable one.

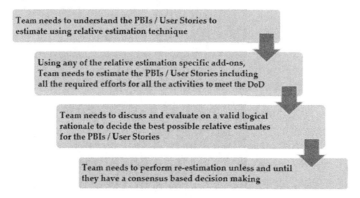

Figure 9.4: *Process of Relative Estimation for work items in Product Backlog*

As per the Scrum Guide, the estimates for the work items under the Product Backlog/ Sprint Backlog should be always provided by the Developers who are supposed to perform the actual development and delivery of those work items; however, the decision to make use of a more suitable relative estimation technique always remains with the entire Scrum Team.

The Scrum Team can make use of a relative estimate like User Story Points, which is also called as Story Points. It is a relative unit-based sizing technique to be used by the Scrum Teams for the purpose of relative estimation. They can specify their relative estimates in terms of a collectively agreed sizing of work items. Story Points always need to be aimed to make the process of relative estimation simpler. Instead of estimating the PBIs/User Stories using absolute estimation in hours/days, the Developers need to have a consensus on, how much relative sizing-based effort (relative to the other PBIs/User Stories) they will need, to make their every PBI/ User Story fully functional and to get it released to the customers/end-users.

The Developers making use of absolute estimation to estimate their work items in hours/days may come up with a different understanding and reflections about estimates. This can be based on many factors such as gaps in their overall understanding, knowledge, skill levels, and experiences. This is the reason; the individual Developers may say that it will take a varied amount of time to complete the same work items. They also may not have a consensus on agreed efforts required to complete them.

> *"The real reason for using Story Points is that they are accurate.*
> *Story points are therefore faster, better, and cheaper than hours and*
> *the highest performing teams completely abandon any hourly estimation*
> *as they view it as waste that just slows them down."*
> *- Jeff Sutherland*

Instead of performing absolute estimation to estimate their work items in hours/ days, if the Developers apply relative estimation based on Story Points, they have a shared understanding to reflect on the complete relative sizing to complete the work items. In this case, they should not try to match Story Points with hours/days. They need to continuously inspect on how many Story Points they can collectively achieve during an ongoing Sprint.

With this approach, it becomes easy for them to predict on how many ideal, associated Story Points are likely to be good for them to select the work items and to work on them during the upcoming Sprint. Story Points always need to correspond to the expected sizing required to complete the PBI/User Story and to make it available for the customers/end-users to use. The Scrum Team needs to make use of some reference PBIs/User Stories, relative to which they need to estimate sizing and have a rough sign of how much time the work items will consume to make them fully functional and potentially releasable. It is not at all required for the Scrum Team to know how much time the PBI/User Story is exactly going to take.

To have quick estimations in place, the relative estimation of already completed PBIs/User Stories can be referred by the Developers. Using this approach, they can estimate much more rapidly. As they cannot predict on how many hours, they are exactly going to take to complete their work, they can estimate without giving a particular time commitment by preventing the need of a precise commitment, while performing relative estimation using Story Points.

As the relative estimation process using Story Points stipulates an unspecified time range, selecting a particular Story Point from a sequence of Story Points (such as Fibonacci Series) lets the Developers to capture and incorporate the inclusive scope, uncertainty, complexity, knowledge, dependencies, and risks associated with the work items. Developers can get better at coping with the timeline-specific expectations from the Product Owner, Stakeholders, and Customers. They can also plan their future work under their upcoming Sprints more efficiently and effectively. Usage of Story Points is simple to understand, but tough to operate on. This is because, the Developers need to find a work item with a smallest effort required to complete it and correlate the same with other work items to come up with relative estimates.

Relative estimation using Story Points always needs to be a subjective measurement of efforts required for the Developers to make the PBIs/User Stories fully functional. Story Points need to be unit-less numbers to estimate the PBIs/User Stories as per their sizing and to categorize the requirements based on a comparable complexity. Developers need to make use of relative estimation as an estimation approach to size their work items to be relative to each other, where a Story Point (which needs to be decided by the Developers and to be associated with every PBI/User Story) needs to be a number highlighting various aspects such as scope, uncertainty, complexity, knowns, unknowns, risks, and dependencies associated with the PBIs/User Stories. As Story Points are relative, they should not be correlated with days/hours.

During Product Backlog Refinements and/or during Sprint Planning, it is required to involve all the required Developers to share their different viewpoints and opinions about the work items to be estimated using the relative estimation approach. Instead of giving absolute estimates in a time format of hours/days, they need to reflect on to rate the relative effort of work using a sequence of Story Points such as Fibonacci Series. This helps them to take the required harder and quicker decisions about the complexity of work. Not only Story Points, but the Developers can also make use of any other relative estimation technique to have their own agreed scale of relative estimation, using which they can get the PBIs/User Stories assigned having less disagreements. Relative estimation always asks the Developers to resolve their complex problems based on scope, uncertainty, complexity, and their existing knowledge. It is not at all based on the actual time to be spent to complete the PBIs/User Stories. Hence, relative estimation is an effective and efficient approach to sustain their continuous focus to deliver the customer value, instead of wasting their precious time to complete the process of estimation of PBIs/User Stories using absolute estimation.

During the Sprint Planning, a Scrum Team can make use of a relative estimation and planning technique such as Planning Poker. This technique asks the Developers to establish a formal agreement while associating the Story Points to individual PBIs/User Stories, where all the Developers need to share their individual opinions to reflect on the relative Story Points. As shown in the following figure, the Developers need to have a set of cards associated with a number sequence as Fibonacci Series (1, 2, 3, 5, 8, 13, and so on...) placed on them, using which they need to decide on how many Story Points a PBI/User Story needs to be associated with:

Figure 9.5: Planning Poker Cards

The Product Owner needs to read the customer value prioritized PBIs/User Stories from the Product Backlog. Developers need to use the Planning Poker cards to reflect on the level of effort that they believe the individual PBI/User Story holds in terms of a Story Point sizing-based relative estimate. In case of any disagreements, the individual Developers with the lowest and highest Story Point estimates need to justify on, why they want to have those many Story Points to be associated with those individual PBIs/User Stories. By providing valid justifications, they need to vote again till they reach a consensus. Once they have a consensus-based agreement, they need to associate the agreed Story Points to every PBI/User Story.

The Scrum Teams need to slice/split the PBIs/User Stories into more granular pieces and re-estimate, if they have Story Point-based estimation associated with the PBI/User Story as more than 8 or 13 points. This is required for them because they need to have their PBIs/User Stories with a highest degree of confidence to complete them within a single Sprint. There is always a possibility that, by the time the Developers start with the actual implementation of PBIs/User Stories , the customer/end-user requirements might get changed.

Hence instead of wasting time to estimate the work items accurately, they should reflect and confirm on a ballpark figure of Story Points. By utilizing the Sprint Retrospectives, the Scrum Team needs to introspect on relative estimation specific insights from previous Sprints. It can surely help them to revise the baseline of Story Points. By discussing about some of the already developed and delivered PBIs associated with specific Story Points, they can evaluate on their relative estimation approach in the upcoming Sprints.

While making use of Story Points based relative estimation, it is always important for a Scrum Team to avoid the most seen mistakes. They always need to have a common, shared understanding about how they will be making use of Story Points based relative estimates. They should not try to equate Story Points to any absolute measure of time. Some of the PBIs/User Stories can be complex and require a lot of time to make them fully functional. If the Developers have already performed similar kind of work in the past, it is easy for them to do the relative estimation based on their prior experience, whereas sometimes they might take much more time even if a PBI/User Story is a simple one, as they might be performing something like that for the first time.

The uncertainty and complexity of implementation of PBIs/User Stories getting reflected under the process of relative estimation needs to be captured in Story Points using the Fibonacci Series sequence, where the association of a specific Story Point from the same sequence is supposed to indicate the extent of uncertainty and risks involved. Story Points always need to reflect on a rough estimate which might assist the Scrum Team to find out the overall effort to deliver the functionality getting tracked under the PBIs/User Stories along with the value getting delivered. During the process of relative estimation, Story Points need to be decided by all the Developers by considering the complexity, uncertainty, risk, dependency, and other factors influencing the effort. As each factor is not enough to decide its impact on the relative effort separately, the team needs to consider all the factors together.

Though the Story Points getting associated with every PBI/User Story under the Product Backlog are not supposed to be perfect, they always need to reflect on the considerations required for the future planning. Also, in case if the Story Points for any of the work items being already worked upon by the Developers during an ongoing Sprint seem to be wrong to the Developers, they should not adjust them. If they try to correlate and convert the Story Points into hours/days, they will not get the actual benefits and value in terms of the swiftness and usefulness of relative estimation. Developers establishing such correlation by increasing or decreasing a single-Story Point with a specific type of time range might create a false sense of understanding and commitment to the Product Owner and the Stakeholders. While using the Planning Poker technique based relative estimation, the Developers should not average out the Story Points, as it might create some more confusion.

The Scrum Team should not assign Story Points based upon an understanding of a specific Developer working on a specific PBI. Assignment of Story Points relative to the reference PBI/User Story always needs to be a collective decision of all the Developers. Based on varying skills, capabilities, and experience, PBIs may vary with the range of Story Points for Senior and Junior Developers. All the Developers should have an agreement on Story Points getting associated with valid justifications. The Developers should not adjust their reference PBIs, especially when their structure is not fixed and it might also have a bad impact on the baseline of Story Points.

> *"Because the estimate for each feature is made relative to the estimates for other features,*
> *it does not matter if our estimates are correct, a little incorrect, or a lot incorrect.*
> *What matters is that they are consistent."*
> *- Mike Cohn*

It is always better for the Scrum Team to make use of a range of recently delivered PBIs/User Stories as a quick reference for relative estimation, so that they can frequently inspect their understanding to adjust their own definition of Story Points. When the Developers know that any of the small tasks and/or spikes will take only few hours to make any of the associated work items fully functional, they should not apply Story Points. They should not hold back on spending a fixed percentage of time to fix any of the Bugs and hence they should not apply Story Points against bugs too.

Any development activity specific bugs always need to be considered as a part of the original estimation of work items against which there is always a possibility of occurrence of bugs. Considering a value-driven outcome of Product Backlog Refinement and/or Sprint Planning, all the Developers need to understand and come up with all the required associated tasks and activities under their PBIs/User Stories. Estimation of tasks can be kept in hours; however, the Developers always need to keep their focus on completing the Tasks, giving less importance to hours-based estimates. Also, while pushing any of the unfinished PBIs/User Stories from the current ongoing Sprint to the next upcoming Sprint, it is not needed for them to perform estimation one more time.

In the process of relative estimation using Planning Poker, Developers might tend to agree with the opinions of Senior Developers, suppressing their own individual opinions. To have a consideration for all the reflections and opinions from all the Developers, it is always better to have the Senior Developers to explain their thoughts and then to have the rest all the Developers to perform Story Points based relative estimation. To arrive with an agreed conclusion, it is crucial for all of them to discuss on disagreements, so that they can learn and have better relative estimates in the future.

Like Planning Poker Cards, Bucket System is another effective relative estimation technique. Using this technique, Developers can speed up their overall process of estimation, especially when they want to estimate the large number of PBIs/User Stories under their Product Backlog. As shown in the following figure, Developers can think of this technique (like Planning Poker Cards), where they need to use Story Points or any other relative measurement of effort to be mapped with each bucket:

Figure 9.6: *Bucket system*

Sizing of the buckets needs to follow a sequential order of Story Points such as a Fibonacci Sequence (1, 2, 3, 5, 8, 13, and so on…), where the Developers need to discuss and map the work items to a suitable bucket size. This technique can be efficiently used when the Developers are supposed to instantly estimate many work items under their Product Backlog. The buckets always need to represent relative sizing of estimates by using a sequential order of Story Points against which the Developers need to place the PBIs/User Stories. They need to restrict their discussions and decision making for already mapped PBIs/User Stories.

Associating a single point-based estimate to the PBIs/User Stories always implies that the Developers need to have a formal agreement within themselves to keep their agreed relative estimation occasionally precise. In this case, a single point-based estimation might cause a false understanding to the Product Owner. Hence, a three-point-based estimation can also be used by the Developers, which can ensure and guarantee that there is more consistency. The Developers need to use this technique with a most optimistic estimate (O), a most likely estimate (M), and a pessimistic estimate called as a least likely estimate (L) for the PBIs/User Stories under their Product Backlog. The Developers can easily discuss and reflect on their understanding about the overall effort, especially for the tasks which are being performed by them for the first time (to make them fully functional) and/or if they have got less/limited experience/exposure to work on those Tasks.

T-Shirt Sizing is another effective relative estimation technique. It is more suitable to estimate relatively large-sized PBIs/User Stories under the Product Backlog. Developers need to classify and associate their PBIs/User Stories in Product Backlog using an appropriate and applicable T-Shirt Sizing with the labels such as Extra Small (XS), Small (S), Medium (M), Large (L), Extra Large (XL), and so on. Based on the concept of elimination, this relative estimation technique can be used by the Developers to throw away the PBIs/User Stories based on their individual sizing, so that the PBIs/User Stories having almost identical individual sizing can be grouped together. To have a consensus-based agreement to decide the T-shirt sizing of PBIs/User Stories, all the Developers need to share their open, honest, and reasonable opinions. The following figure shows an overview of T-shirt Sizing based relative estimation concept to be utilized by the Scrum Teams, especially by the Developers:

Figure 9.7: T-shirt sizing

Dot Voting is a simple, fast, and an effective relative estimation technique for the Developers. It is more suitable, when they have a small collection of PBIs/User Stories in the Product Backlog. By limiting the total number of PBIs/User Stories, this technique can help them to estimate small-sized PBIs/User Stories along with an ease of consensus-based estimations. Every Developer needs to select the PBIs/User Stories, which he/she wants to put a dot vote for. In this process, greater number of dots means more effort is needed. The number of dots on work items always need to represent the efforts involved to make them fully functional. The following figure shows an overview of the Dot Voting relative estimation concept:

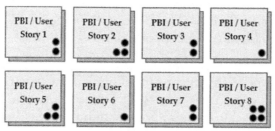

Figure 9.8: Dot voting

A relative estimation technique such as Large/Uncertain/Small can also be used by the Developers to perform a rough estimation, where they need to classify the PBIs / User Stories based on their high-level sizing such as Large/Uncertain/Small.

Such categorization needs to be followed by them to discuss on various aspects of functionalities and dependencies associated with the complex PBIs/User Stories. This approach can be efficiently utilized by the Developers to compare the PBIs/User Stories varying with the relative sizes to act as a simplification for the Bucket System technique.

Another relative estimation technique for a small number of PBIs/User Stories under the Product Backlog is Affinity Estimation, using which the Developers need to look out for the resemblances, connections, and similarities of the PBIs/User Stories to relatively estimate them. By visualizing the association of PBIs/User Stories and by sequencing the workflows under those PBIs/User Stories, the Developers need to find the similarities and cluster the applicable and comparable PBIs/User Stories. The Developers also need to group the similarities found in between the PBIs/User Stories to assign different relative estimates to different groups of PBIs/User Stories.

It is valuable for the Scrum Teams, especially for the Developers to explore and to have a consensus on any of these relative estimation techniques to estimate their PBIs/User Stories under the Product Backlog. Performing such relative estimation process during the Product Backlog Refinements and not only during Sprint Planning Event certainly adds some extra value to safeguard the overall understanding and functioning between Developers, as they get more time to clarify and bridge their understanding gaps, if any.

The Sprint Planning always needs to have a flexible time-boxing allocated for the Developers to associate relative estimates to PBIs/User Stories using any of the relative estimation techniques, where they first need to relatively evaluate and compare the work items, based on their complexity, uncertainty, dependency, risks, and many other aspects. By involving all the Developers in the process of relative estimation of PBIs/User Stories ensures that opinions from everyone are being considered and valued; however, it is always better for the Scrum Team to evaluate on, if such involvement is not acting as an additional overhead causing any kind of delays for their Sprint-based deliveries.

All the relative estimation techniques have their own pros/benefits. They can be essentially customized as per the team's own expectations, utilization approaches, and suitability along with their overall way of working to have an agreed consensus. Instead of using a particular technique, they can also try to combine multiple techniques by customizing them, as per their own need. It is always required for the Scum Master to comprehend that relative estimation takes some time to establish a baseline and it should not be applied forcefully. By comparing the relative size, complexity, uncertainty, risks, and dependencies of the PBIs/User Stories, the Developers need to experiment around relative estimation techniques to select and decide on which approach/technique is more suitable for them to become better at forecasting and to deliver the Product Increments in line with their agreed Sprint Goal.

Even if it might look like a duplication of effort, still it may indeed benefit the Scrum Teams, especially the Developers when they estimate their Product Backlog as well as their Sprint Backlog. Estimating the Product Backlog lets the Scrum Team to evaluate on their forecasts about how much and by when they can develop and deliver the work items as a part of their upcoming Sprints. However, the Scrum Team can also evaluate on their anticipated release scope and timelines along with their delivery capacity and frequency, which can help the Product Owner to take some valuable decisions to order and prioritize the Product Backlog based on the expected benefits and the associated cost of work items. Estimating work items under the Product Backlog helps the team to develop their knowledge by bridging the gaps in the work items (to avoid any sudden surprises, when the Developers start with the actual implementation of work items) and by evaluating the relative scope, uncertainty, complexity, knowns, unknowns, risks, dependencies, and so on.

Estimating the Sprint Backlog always helps the Scrum Team to evaluate on how much amount of work and its associated effort they need to select in their upcoming Sprint. It also assists them to increase an inclusive probability to complete their Sprint level commitment, to evaluate a possibility to achieve their agreed Sprint Goal, and to measure their anticipated workload by mapping, slicing, and splitting the PBIs/User Stories into a smaller sizing.

The PBIs/User Stories need to be roughly estimated by the Developers during the Sprint Planning. By recognizing the required development and delivery specific tasks/activities and by estimating them during the Sprint Planning helps the Scrum Team, especially the Developers to coordinate with each other, both effectively and efficiently. If the PBIs/User Stories selected by the Developers under their Sprint Backlog are not properly estimated, then it becomes difficult for them to fulfil their Sprint commitment. It might also have an adverse impact on the achievement of their agreed Sprint Goal.

The PBIs/User Stories in the Sprint Backlog need be estimated by the Developers at the time of Sprint Planning, while they are formulating their Sprint Backlog as a subset of their Product Backlog. The PBIs/User Stories in the Product Backlog can be estimated after performing the Story Mapping, Sizing, and Slicing process as a part of Product Backlog Refinement Sessions, where all the Developers are already present. During this process, they need to agree with the relative estimation of PBIs/User Stories under their Product Backlog required to reach a limit to consume their next couple of Sprints. To make sure that their anticipated relative estimates are getting reflected correctly against all the available PBIs/User Stories under the Product Backlog, they need to revisit those PBIs/User Stories once per upcoming Sprint, especially when there are any new work items to be added since their prior Sprint.

As relative estimation always helps the Product Owner to prioritize the PBIs/User Stories under the Product Backlog, the Developers might have an opinion that it is all okay for them to estimate those work items during Sprint Planning only, but there might be a significant delay for the Product Owner for the purpose of prioritization, where he/she needs to contemplate on the relative estimation which is to be done by the Developers only.

The Product Owner always needs to be provided with the relative estimates of work items under the Product Backlog until the Scrum Team starts with the Sprint Planning without assuming that, he/she will consider those estimates while prioritizing those work items. Relative estimation at the time of Sprint Planning Event also utilizes much more time to be spent by the Developers causing it to be a detailed one. It is always better if they can do the same process utilizing the time of Product Backlog Refinements.

Developers always need to remember that the relative estimation such as Story Points for the PBIs/User Stories needs to be owned by them, where they also need to consider and correlate with the actual time available for the Sprint while selecting the PBIs/User Stories to work on. This actual time available for the Sprint needs to include normal business days, training days, holidays, vacation days, and so on, where an assumption that the size of the Scrum Team is according to their overall efficiency and is enough to ask the team to commit to the said work. Committing to the work automatically implies committing to all work items within the time box of the upcoming Sprint without necessarily making time-wise break downs.

> *"An estimate is simply a prediction based on known information*
> *and an input at a given point in time."*
> *- Ilan Goldstein*

As per the Scrum Guide, the work that needs to be done by the Developers might be of variable size and of variable estimated effort. Hence the Scrum Team always needs to apply relative estimation using Story Points or T-Shirt Sizing or Bucket System or any other relative estimation unit by concerning and considering the overall complexity of Working Software Product Development and by emphasizing the worth of process of Empiricism.

The main motive behind the relative estimation of PBIs/User Stories should always offer the Developers a basic impression of the overall amount of work to be worked upon by them in their upcoming Sprint. The Developers always need to anticipate the same by showcasing a highest level of commitment to complete it and to achieve their agreed Sprint Goal. To align with this purpose, Developers need to think, reflect, share, and discuss on what all functional, non-functional, and technical things they need to consider along with what all approaches they need to follow to convert their Sprint Backlog into a high-quality working software product increment at the end of every Sprint.

Even if the Developers are supposed to relatively estimate the PBIs/User Stories by always committing to the agreed Sprint Goal, it is not mandatory for them to complete all the PBIs/User Stories taken by them under an ongoing Sprint. There might be some unanticipated issues, dependencies, risks, problems, and comprehensions rising, which may emphasize the responsibility of estimates in a different way than the original way they might be expecting. To be better at estimates, the Scrum Team hence needs to embrace the change by capitalizing it rather than controlling it. By using the process of Empiricism, the Scrum Team always needs to have progressive decision-making-based estimates based on the lessons learned in past.

The Product Owner needs to educate the Stakeholders to make them aware about the relative estimation, its related forecasts, and its impact on the Sprint-based incremental and iterative development and delivery of working software product increments. It always needs to be collectively owned by the Scrum Team.

A perfect accuracy of the estimation process and resulting outcomes is almost impossible. It is not possible for the Scrum Team to ensure that any of the relative estimation techniques getting used by them (to capture and to cover every potential and possible scenario based on complexity, uncertainty, dependencies, risks, and any other possible intuitions) are ensuring complete delivery of their Sprint-based deliverables. As their understanding might get reformed in the process of their own exploration once they start to implement the work items, the estimation of those work items already done by them can intensely change. It is hence required for the Developers to have the estimates as an outcome of essential interactions and a shared understanding within themselves.

> *"Estimating is often helpful; estimates are often not."*
> *- Esther Derby*

The Scrum Team members should always keep this in their mind that rather than wasting much time and effort on the process of estimation, they need to use the same to endlessly learn, implement, and deliver customer value-based outcomes on time. The foremost difficulty of absolute estimation using hours/days may create a misapprehension, misconception, and misinterpretation of obviousness and correctness for the Product Owner and for the Stakeholders. It may further question the Developers to discuss on the unknowns to decide their estimates more comprehensively.

On the other hand, utilizing the advantages of relative estimation can get them a high-level impression of the amount of work to be completed during an upcoming Sprint. By setting up their required focus on their primary responsibility to create high quality, fully functional, and potentially releasable working software product increments, the process of relative estimation always helps the Scrum Team to boost their confidence and determination and to develop and deliver incremental pieces of functionalities iteratively, rapidly, and without wasting never-ending effort to foresee what is approaching next. By means of exploration of relative estimation techniques and their associated alternatives, it is required for all the Developers to relatively estimate their discrete work items.

To have a consensus within all the Developers for the purpose of relative estimation and selection of an achievable amount of work in terms of PBIs/User Stories, Spikes, and associated Tasks/Activities under a Sprint, they should take a reference of already delivered work items in previous Sprints as a leading indicator. Relative estimation always needs to underline the constructive thoughts, discussions, and negotiations in between all the Developers. The Developers having such better productive interactions (both within and outside the Scrum Team) can easily establish a common, shared understanding within themselves as well as with their stakeholders and customers/end-users.

Points to remember

- The Product Backlog work items need to be considered as Epics, Features, PBIs/User Stories, Tasks, and many more, based on their individual sizing. Apart from value, description, and order, an estimate also needs to be one of the recommended attributes for the PBIs/User Stories.

- Scrum Framework helps the Developers to become better at estimations by asking them to expand their consistency under the complex environments. Instead of treating the estimates to enact as timeboxes or deadlines, the Developers need to incorporate new complexities as soon as they come to know about them. The Scrum Team needs to maintain a suitable reference for uncertainty and complexity, so that they can inspect on what and how much they will be able to achieve.

- Scrum does not enforce the Scrum Teams to make use of a specific estimation technique. It rather acts as a collection of rules and guidelines to enable the process of Empiricism, where the Scrum Teams need to explore on their own and choose an estimation technique, which fits their needs to have an ease of estimation.

- Instead of performing absolute estimation (to estimate the work items in hours/days), if the Developers apply relative estimation based on Story Points, they have a shared understanding to reflect on the relative sizing to complete the work items.

- To have quick estimations in place, the relative estimation of already completed PBIs/User Stories needs to be referred by the Developers. Developers need to make use of relative estimation as an estimation approach to size their work items to be relative to each other. It is valuable for the Scrum Teams, especially for the Developers to explore and to have a quick consensus on any of the relative estimation techniques.

- Estimating the Sprint Backlog always helps the Scrum Team to evaluate on how much amount of work and its associated effort they need to select in their upcoming Sprints. It assists them to increase an inclusive probability to complete their Sprint level commitment and to measure their anticipated workload.

- The Product Owner needs to be provided with relative estimates of work items in the Product Backlog until the Scrum Team starts with Sprint Planning without assuming that, he/she will consider the given estimates while prioritizing the work items.

- The Scrum Team members should always keep this in their mind that rather than wasting much time and effort on the process of estimation, they need to use the same to endlessly learn, implement, and deliver customer value-based outcomes on time.

In the next chapter, readers will get to know about some of the advanced Scrum add-ons/techniques to help the Scrum Teams to utilize their Scrum Events more effectively and efficiently.

CHAPTER 10
Add-ons for Scrum Events

Introduction

In this chapter, readers will get to know about some of the advanced Scrum add-ons/ techniques to help the Scrum Teams to utilize their Scrum Events more effectively and efficiently. They will get an overview of a real worth of all the Scrum Events for the Scrum Teams. They will also get to know about the importance of the establishment and continuous improvement of the best practices for the Scrum Teams, using which they can fully leverage the employment of all the Scrum Events making their Scrum-based agile way of working much more productive.

Objective

After studying this chapter, you should be able to:

- Understand various considerations for the Scrum Teams to make them aware of the ultimate significance of all the Scrum Events.
- Understand various techniques for the Scrum Teams to conduct and utilize their Sprint Planning more effectively and efficiently.
- Understand various techniques for the Scrum Teams to conduct and utilize their Daily Scrum more effectively and efficiently.
- Understand various techniques for the Scrum Teams to conduct and utilize their Sprint Reviews more effectively and efficiently.

- Understand the various techniques for the Scrum Teams to conduct and utilize their Sprint Retrospectives more effectively and efficiently.
- Understand the ultimate significance for the Scrum Teams to utilize their Sprints more effectively and efficiently.

Ramesh 'The Agile Coach' (in a discussion with Suresh 'The Scrum Master'):

"Thanks for inviting me in today's Sprint Review, Suresh! I can surely say that your Scrum Team is progressing very well. Impressive collaboration and teamwork so far!"

Suresh 'The Scrum Master':

"Well, the team has improved a lot and the credit goes to you as well! Keep visiting us and keep helping us to find out the bottlenecks and to improve our way of working. By the way, I would like to tell you about a new pattern which I have recently observed in the team. I think it is causing a learned helplessness for the Developers. Why I always need to remind them to take care of their own activities?"

Ramesh:

"I think, you told me some time back that you don't like cooking, right? What happens when your wife insists you to cook and you simply can't say no to her?"

Suresh (smiling and replying):

"Before I go to the Kitchen, I ask her many questions about ingredients, quantity, cooking temperature, and all. She doesn't like to respond and asks me to step out. Easy trick it is, which works sometimes!"

Ramesh:

"Don't you think that your easy trick is an example of a learned helplessness? I think, you always want her to fill-in the void and wait for her to cook the food, so that she can fulfil your expectations, right?"

Suresh:

"Don't compare my trick with learned helplessness. I already said that it works sometimes, not always!"

Ramesh (smiling and replying):

"Ha-ha! Well, you know your tricks better than me. On a serious note, let me give you an input which you can try with your team. Whenever you feel that you need to push the Developers and they want you to fill-in the void, start applying some easy tricks to give them a real sense of self-organization. Using those easy tricks, they need to understand that they need to be accountable and self-sufficient to take care of their own actions without waiting for someone else like you to remind and push them."

Suresh:

"I am already good at applying tricks, but please be there to cook in case if they don't work!"

It is the core responsibility of the Scrum Team, especially the Scrum Master to boost the overall worth, value, and effectiveness of their Scrum-based agile way of working. Scrum Master always needs to make sure that the concepts of Scrum Framework are being understood by everyone within the Scrum Team to make their Scrum-based agile ways of working more effective and successful. In this process of maximizing the possibility of overall success of Scrum, it is essential for the Scrum Teams to understand and ensure that all the valuable Scrum Events are being organized and followed appropriately, effectively, and efficiently.

> *"If you follow 80% of the process, you get 20% of the results."*
> *- Kent Beck*

The Scrum Teams always need to focus on their purpose and align their Scrum-based agile way of working accordingly. Many times, Scrum Teams establish a way of working, where they are not continuously inspecting and adapting for the purpose of continuous learning and improvement. This does not make their Scrum-based agile way of working fully functional. This happens because they do not have Scrum Events with a clear sense of purpose and a proper understanding.

The Scrum Teams not having the Sprint Retrospectives for every Sprint and not having the Daily Scrum daily are some of the typical scenarios, which can be seen with many Scrum Teams. This happens because they do not recognize the real purpose of Scrum Events. They might also find it difficult to recognize the same. If this way of working gets continued for a long time, it results into Scrum Malfunctioning and it has many adverse impacts on the important aspects such as teamwork, team dynamics, team culture, and so on. To avoid all of this, the Scrum Master should always focus on the real purpose of all the Scrum Events. He/she always needs to teach the Scrum Team about the logical reasoning behind all the Scrum Events. The Scrum Team always needs to understand the prominence of all the Scrum Events to maximize the overall worth, value, and effectiveness of their Scrum-based agile way of working.

The Scrum Teams should not forget that they need to regularly develop and deliver small pieces of working software product increments to their customers/end-users. This always needs to be done by them early and often, by using the iterative and incremental delivery approach. With this approach, they need to maintain a consistent pace for all their activities, actions, and behaviors. While considering the continuous delivery of working software product increments, such a consistent and reliable pace always helps them to enhance their overall certainty by lowering down the overall complexity. It is hence a must have for the Scrum Master to understand the expectation of having a consistent pace within the Scrum Team, which is always beneficial for them to develop and deliver complex software products in complex environments. Instead of having longer Sprints, shorter Sprints of two weeks can definitely play an important role to emphasize on the fulfilment of the same expectation of maintaining a consistent and reliable development and delivery pace.

The Scrum Teams hence need to carefully address this expectation of constantly maintaining such pace.

The Scrum Master always needs to be accountable for the overall success of establishment and continuous improvement of a Scrum Team's Scrum-based agile way of working. At the same time, he/she also needs to be a partially visible Servant Leader/Change Agent, who needs to lead by influence, to ensure that his/her presence is there, only when it is required. All the Scrum Events need to have a clear-cut purpose and reasoning behind them. While facilitating and hosting the Scrum Events, the Scrum Master needs to communicate and emphasize on the same purpose, so that he/she can teach the Scrum Team about the real expectations from the Scrum Team and the expected functioning of Scrum Events.

The Scrum Master leading the Daily Scrum is not what he/she should be ideally doing. Daily Scrum is for the Developers to reflect on where they are and where they would like to go next. To enhance the overall self-organization within Developers, the Scrum Master should not be asking them to perform the required actions. An impediment needs to be investigated by him/her, only when the Developers are unable to resolve it. Scrum Master always needs to keep his interests toward the betterment of Scrum Team's way of working, where he/she can examine, feel, sense, and share about the behaviors, patterns, and actions about what is happening within the Scrum Team. This way, he/she can help, support, guide, coach, train, mentor, and facilitate the Scrum Team to continuously learn and improve their Daily Scrum.

He/she needs to teach the Scrum Team about how they can organize and have their Daily Scrum daily, effectively, and efficiently; that too within the standard 15-minute time-box. The Scrum Team needs to have all their Scrum Events strictly time boxed. Time boxing does not ask them to take at least that amount of time. Rather it helps the team members to concentrate. This helps them to achieve one of the core Scrum Values which is Focus. Considering the importance of time boxing, the Scrum Team always needs to conduct all their Scrum Events by following an agreed time boxing. Since there is a limited amount of time, this approach of time-boxing helps the Scrum Teams to keep their focus to discuss and review the most important matters first. Following time-boxing under all the Scrum Events always helps them to have an amplified value of their agile way of working.

"Scrum is a mirror."
- Alistair Cockburn

By rigorously following the concept of Empiricism, the Scrum Teams need to consider the Scrum Framework as a mirror. Scrum Teams always need to preserve their Sprints at the crux of their way of working. During every ongoing Sprint, it is imperative for them to ensure that they are not allowing any modifications which can jeopardize their agreed Sprint Goal. To ensure that the overall quality of their every anticipated product increment is not degrading, they need to perform frequent refinements of their Product Backlog, as and when required. In this process, the overall scope of all the activities of software product development and delivery needs to be comprehensively worked upon by all the Developers. During every ongoing Sprint, they need to perform constant exploration, so that they can learn and try to make the scope more simplified and refined after consulting with the Product Owner.

The Scrum Event Sprint Planning needs to be utilized by the Scrum Team, where they need to determine the work items they would like to select and work on, in their next upcoming Sprint. They also need to have a discussion to establish an agreed Sprint Goal and to come up with an initial anticipated plan to complete the work items. Sprint Planning needs to start with the creation of the Sprint Goal, which needs to be the single common objective to be targeted by the whole Scrum Team. The following figure shows various attributes of the Sprint Goal:

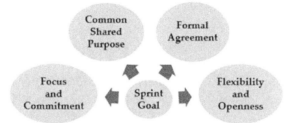

Figure 10.1: Attributes of the Sprint Goal

The Sprint Goal needs to reflect on a formal agreement in between the Developers and the Product Owner to signify an adequate focus and a formal commitment from the Developers, using which they can develop and deliver a fully functional high quality potentially releasable product increment containing the highest customer value. The Sprint Goal always needs to denote and share a common shared purpose, so that the Scrum Team can have an insight about the worth of activities they are supposed to engage themselves with. This always needs to be done by them genuinely, firmly, and by pro-actively carrying a collective ownership, accountability, and responsibility.

The Sprint Goal for a Sprint always needs to be intact. It needs to signify an adequate flexibility and openness, so that the Scrum Team can anticipate any changes and can familiarize with an agreed plan, which is getting formulated under the Sprint Backlog, as they start to explore and learn more.

While always being aligned with the Product Owner, the Developers should always ensure that their agreed Sprint Goal is simple, clear, and a specific one. It also needs to be measurable, so that by the end of an ongoing Sprint, the Scrum Team can confirm on whether they have achieved it or not. By expecting the potential risks, it also needs to be derived, negotiated with its primary focus on the highest customer value getting delivered by the Scrum Team. To make certain that the Developers are always fully committed to their agreed Sprint Goal and even if they finish all the work items (such as PBIs/User Stories/any other work items) from the Sprint Backlog, they can still decide on what else they can contribute to. In this case, the Sprint Goal need not to consist of all the work items from the Sprint Backlog.

The ultimate purpose of Sprint Planning is to reflect on the aspect of optimizing the value of anticipated product increment by selecting the customer value driven PBIs/User Stories in the Sprint Backlog. It is important for the Developers to understand that they need to keep this thought process alive during the Sprint Planning, so that they can always put an emphasis on customer value-based delivery outcomes. While having a formal agreement with the Product Owner, the Developers always need to have a full commitment to achieve as much customer value-based delivery outcomes possible for them to achieve. Sprint Planning also expects the Scrum Team to formulate an actionable plan with a proper clarity and a clear transparency for the upcoming Sprint.

It is always better for the Developers to have smaller tasks/activities consuming their overall effort and time not more than one day. They also need to ensure that they can complete multiple tasks in a single day. This can be considered as a part of a significant progress to make the associated PBIs/User Stories/any other work items fully functional and potentially releasable as a part of the next product increment.

The Scrum Team needs to reflect, confirm, and align on the agreed Definition of Done (DoD) to formulate an improved plan. The DoD always needs to represent the Scrum Team's formal meaning of quality for all the work items with which they need to adhere with. The Scrum Team also needs to guarantee that everyone being a part of the Scrum Team knows what exactly they need to do, as per their commitment for the next product increment to be delivered toward the end of the next upcoming Sprint.

"The first thing to realize when formulating your first Definition of Done is that it isn't cast in stone. You don't need to spend an eternity deliberating what it should be, because it can evolve over time."
- Ilan Goldstein

Considering all the required activities specific to the overall process of development and delivery of high-quality working software product increments, the Scrum Team needs to have open discussions to emerge with an agreed DoD. They need to consider numerous aspects such as, which all advanced and best practices and standards the Developers need to follow while developing and delivering the work items, which all policies they need to stick to, how they will ensure that the functionalities getting developed are fulfilling the end-user expectations and enhancing the end-user experience, how they will ensure that they are reducing the possibility of technical debts, how they will verify, validate, and test the functionalities getting tracked under the work items and being developed by them, how they will ensure that the defects found will be solved by them, how they will achieve all the technical, functional and non-functional aspects specific to the features and functionalities getting developed and delivered by them, which all procedures they will use to achieve the overall technical and quality excellence, how they will confirm on the correctness of all the best practices and standards being followed by them, how they will ensure that they are following all kinds of compliance-specific standards, and few more.

The Definition of Done (DoD) also needs to ensure that all the crucial aspects of completeness, quality, and transparency specific to all the work items are required to be worked upon by the Developers, where they need to have a formal agreement for them. To have a proper planning on these aspects, the Scrum Team always needs to make use of the DoD during their Sprint Planning, openly and carefully.

On the other hand, by following the Definition of Ready (DoR), the Scrum Team always needs to discuss and confirm on the readiness of work items to be taken into the Sprint Backlog, so that they can select the Ready for Sprint work items into their upcoming Sprint. To create an actionable plan for the Sprint and to have a better teamwork, communication, and shared understanding about the designated work, the Scrum Team needs to make sure that every PBI/User Story/any other work item being selected by the Developers under the Sprint Backlog of next upcoming Sprint is evidently understood by all of them.

Sprint Planning asks the Scrum Team members to aim at why, what, and how they need to deliver something which will help them to make their Sprint valuable. To address this expectation, the Scrum Team members always need to look at the work items under the Product Backlog, at their previous product increments, and at their earlier performance. By guaranteeing that the Definition of Ready (DoR) is achieved for all the work items, there always needs to be a shared understanding of the work items getting selected by them into the upcoming Sprint. By predicting their own capacity and by filtering out the scenarios, assumptions, and dependencies, they need to define some precision and prerequisites to confirm on the relative estimates of work items in the Sprint Backlog.

The Scrum Team members also need to ensure that all the work items are having a required and agreed acceptance criteria associated with them, which needs to comprise of all the functional, non-functional, and technical aspects. By having an anticipation to eliminate the overall vagueness from the functionalities getting tracked under work items, the acceptance criteria not only helps the Developers to think, discuss, and enact on how a particular piece of functionality needs to be implemented by them by considering the end-user's viewpoints and expectations, but it also makes it easy for them to decide on which all validations, verifications, and tests they need to do, using which they or the Product Owner can confirm and approve that the work items are complete (as expected), fully functional, and potentially releasable.

During the Sprint Planning, only the Developers need to have a potential right to move the prioritized work items from Product Backlog to Sprint Backlog. The Scrum Master and/or the Product Owner should not assign the Sprint Backlog work items to individual developers. Individual Developers should choose the prioritized work items they want to work on in Sprint. This approach not only helps the Developers to take the opportunities collectively, but also brings in the right sense of ownership within them. At the end of the Sprint Planning, all the Developers need to be able to reflect on the anticipated outcomes along with the important aspect of how they are planning to achieve them in the upcoming Sprint. They also need to convey those expected outcomes to the Product Owner.

The Scrum Event Daily Scrum always needs to be utilized by the Scrum Team, where they need to inspect their overall progress toward the achievement of agreed Sprint Goal. The main objective of the Daily Scrum is always to inspect on where the Developers are standing and to reflect on whether the Developers are going to accomplish the Sprint Goal or not. The Scrum Master needs to allow the Developers to take a collective ownership during the Daily Scrum. By observing what is going on in the Daily Scrum, the Scrum Master needs to coach them by asking some powerful questions when the Event is done.

The Developers need to understand that the objective of the Daily Scrum is not to discuss and resolve their issues and impediments during the Daily Scrum itself. Hence, instead of getting into broad, in-depth, and time-consuming conversations during the Event, they should rather focus and reflect on their overall progress toward the Sprint Goal and re-planning, if required. All the issues and impediments can be highlighted by the Developers, but the possible resolution needs to be done separately after the Event.

Daily Scrum always needs to be kept short following a time-box of 15 minutes. It is intended to enhance the overall communication and transparency within the Scrum Team. The Developers need to come equipped, on time, and having an eagerness to look for anything that is preventing their current effort to achieve the Sprint Goal. They need to talk about where they are standing, which work items are completed, which are in progress, and what are the next actions they need to take. They need to showcase their self-organization and collaboration to get the things done. After sharing their impediments, it is also essential for them to formulate a plan of action items to resolve those impediments. They need to update the Sprint Backlog to ascertain the impact of any impediments. They also need to perform some adjustments and turn up with a devised plan to achieve the agreed Sprint Goal.

By making use of various Daily Scrum formats, the Scrum Master always needs to coach the Developers to have their Daily Scrum more exciting, interactive, and a fun-oriented one. To avoid a monotonously sounding Daily Scrum and to have some meaningful and focused conversations during the Daily Scrum, the Developers need to speak and discuss either person by person or work item by work item. Sometimes, the current speaker can call the next speaker to speak. It is always better to have the Developers discussing and collaborating about the work (belonging to the current Sprint) being performed by them along with a glimpse of preparation for the upcoming Sprint.

The Developers always need to make use of some indications in case if someone is unnecessarily sounding wordy, which is causing lengthy conversations. Developers need to highlight on what they are currently working on, so that the Sprint Backlog can be updated to reflect the actual status of their progress within an ongoing Sprint. Developers can also speak about the work which is ad-hoc and might not be aiming toward the achievement of Sprint Goal. This pattern needs to be observed by the Scrum Master to see, if there are any Developers who are frequently doing the same, so that he/she can take the necessary action to avoid its harmful impacts on the overall achievement of Sprint Goal.

An impediment is an issue which can be anything specific to the product, technology, process, or people, which might slow down the progress of Scrum Team during their ongoing Sprint. This might also prevent an early and often delivery of working software product increments. Resolution and removal of impediments ease out the Scrum Team's agile way of working by causing easier collaborations and better quality within the actual process of development and delivery of work items from Sprint Backlog in an ongoing Sprint. The Scrum Master always needs to help the self-organizing Scrum Team to resolve only those issues which they are unable to resolve by themselves. Only such issues are supposed to be called as impediments.

"A good Scrum Master removes disruptive influences from the Daily Scrum, so it is used for the team's benefit. A great Scrum Master will create an environment where others (particularly the Product Owner) can attend and not affect the behaviour of the team."
- Geoff Watts

Developers always need to feel empowered to take their own decisions about how they will perform their own software development and delivery-specific activities. By making the accountability of Developers clear and obvious, their overall ability to continuously improve on adapting to challenges and to take the benefits out of opportunities given to them can be preserved as limitless.

The Developers always need to self-manage and self-organize by themselves, so that they can self-improve and can get better at their agile way of working-specific standards, processes, practices, tools, methods, and collaborations to become more efficient and effective. By continuously inspecting on how they are performing during their ongoing Sprint and by asking them some courageous, powerful, and appropriate questions, the Scrum Master always needs to coach them on, how they can create an overall environment of liberation and enablement for themselves. While exercising such empowerment, he/she always needs to be able to shield them from any of the external interferences. This needs to be done instead of asking them for consent and not asking them for forgiveness. By questioning their own recommendations, processes, standards, and practices, the Developers always need to have an open mindset to follow all of them. By considering them as limitations, they can have an optimization of their needs related to self-management and self-organization.

It is equally important for the Scrum Team to understand the types, patterns, and frequency of occurrences of impediments by considering their impacts on the customer value getting delivered. Scrum Master needs to have a foresight to sense the next probable impediments, so that he/she can inform the team in advance. Impediments (which are not allowing the Developers to proceed, decelerating their pace, and blocking them to deliver the value) need to be quantified considering their impact on implicated time, cost, effort, and overall co-ordination within Developers. Any impediments along with their harmful impact on quality, cost, and team's happiness index should be reported at the earliest. They should be transparent and the team should make certain that they are getting resolved at the earliest.

The Developers and the Product Owner need to see the impediments during Sprint Planning, so that they can discuss on them. Developers always need to recognize that it is not only the duty of the Scrum Master to resolve and remove impediments. To improve self-organization, it also needs to be a part of their daily activities. It is required for the Scrum Master to assist the Developers to eliminate their impediments, which they cannot do by themselves. At the same time, the Scrum Master should not think that the Developers always need to do this on their own. By keeping an enough involvement, help, and support, he/she needs to be closely associated with them, so that they can work together and get rid of the impediments occurring during the Sprints. While taking their own time, the Developers need to be aware of which impediments they need to resolve, by when and how they can do that, and by when and how they can seek for the support from the Scrum Master to resolve them. The proper resolution and/or removal of impediments always improves the Scrum Team's overall effectiveness.

> *"A good plan violently executed now is better than*
> *a perfect plan executed next week."*
> *- General George S. Patton*

By planning too much during an ongoing Sprint, if the Developers plan all their working hours, they might fail to reach their agreed Sprint Goal. They might also feel that there is no enough time for them to explore and learn new things. It is hence required for the Scrum Master to set some expectations with the Developers, where they always need to prevent themselves from establishing any random goals. Developers should not wait for the Sprint to come to an end to deliver any specific functionality only toward the end of the Sprint.

While tackling the impediments, the Scrum Master always needs to align the rest of the Scrum Team members, so that the pressure created by the impact of impediments can be handled. During the Sprint Review, the Product Owner needs to have a courage to talk about the major impediments that occurred during the Sprint, so that they can be properly highlighted to the Stakeholders. As shown in the following figure, the Scrum Team can make use of the concept of Reinforcement Learning to learn continuously. This learning approach can help them to resolve their impediments more effectively:

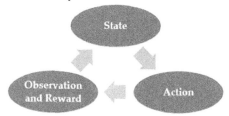

Figure 10.2: *Reinforcement Learning for Scrum Teams*

By using the concept of Reinforcement Learning (given by Richard Sutton and Andrew Barto), the eventual objective of synchronizing the Scrum Team during the Daily Scrum can be easily achieved. The team needs to have a self-realization about their state, behavior, and actions through observations. While performing the activities specific to the incremental and iterative software product development and delivery, every Scrum Team member needs to have his/her own state of self-realization. It further needs to encourage them to generate some action. The power of their habits needs to be conveyed through the actions being done by them, which finally needs to cause an observation and a reward. This needs to be a permanent cycle until they achieve their agreed Sprint Goal during an ongoing Sprint.

While utilizing this flow of Reinforcement Learning, the Scrum Team members always need to have a continuous dialogue to reflect on various aspects such as where they are, what is next for them, is there anything acting as an impediment, which is blocking them to move forward, how can they resolve such impediments, how can they move forward to accomplish their Sprint Goal by getting into a mode of collective ownership, and few more.

This learning approach always helps them to build transparency and a better sense of trust. All the Scrum Team members need to have an outlook through continuous observations to create some good habits. This approach always needs to be applied and utilized by the Scrum Team members by creating a continuous loop of Reinforcement Learning. Such utilization can help them to understand their anticipated habits and functioning patterns. A continuous inspection around the overall progress of the Scrum Team (considering their agreed Sprint Goal) by making use of some of the advanced Scrum Metrics (which will be covered in one of the next chapters) can surely act as a reward for them if everything goes well as per their agreed expectations. Instead of keeping this technique limited to Daily Scrum, it can be also used for the other Scrum Events. While using this technique, the Scrum Master always needs to lead by influencing the behaviors and actions of Scrum Team members. The Scrum Teams creating and nurturing some good habits followed by suitable actions always tend to become high-performing teams.

To ensure that a Scrum Team is always implanting a culture of continuous improvement, the Scrum Team members can also explore the Lean 8 Wastes Snake Continuous Improvement technique. This technique always acts as an enabler for the Scrum Teams who are willing for a betterment of their way of working associated entities. Using this technique, the Scrum Team members can try to eliminate any of the potential waste during their Scrum Events (especially during the Sprint Planning, the Daily Scrum and the Sprint Retrospectives), where they need to utilize the inspect, reflect, and adapt cycle. By aligning the team members and their processes, by reflecting on alternatives to eliminate potential wastes, by limiting excessive processes, by making some cognizant and consensus-based decisions, by performing only what is required, by avoiding rework and unnecessary overheads, and by utilizing the capabilities and skill sets of all the Scrum Team members, all the Scrum Events need to be observed and evaluated by the Scrum Master and other Scrum Team members to seek for continuous process improvement under their established agile way of working.

The Scrum Event Sprint Review needs to be utilized by the Scrum Team, where they need to focus on the customer value optimization from the point of view of their Stakeholders. The presence of key Stakeholders hence needs to act as a must have during every Sprint Review. The Stakeholders are always interested in the customer value optimization aspect being delivered by the Scrum Teams through their incremental and iterative working software product increments. The Sprint Review Event hence always needs to keep its focus on the customer value being delivered, where instead of making use of a purely technical language (containing technical buzzwords and/or jargons), the Scrum Team needs to speak a customer-driven functional language, which can be easily understood by the Stakeholders during their Sprint Review specific interactions with the Scrum Team.

It is also equally important for the Scrum Team that their efforts are getting evaluated based on their Sprint Goal. The Scrum Team needs to demonstrate what all work items and their associated functionalities they have completed, which should be focused on customer value-based outcomes and not on the outputs. The Scrum Team also needs to collect all the valuable feedbacks, opinions, intuitions from the Stakeholders about the product increment being showcased to them. This decides an overall impact made by the product increment on the expectations of Stakeholders. It also helps the Scrum Team to confirm their further decision-making to focus on the upcoming Sprints. Though Developers can showcase a general demo of product increment during the Sprint Review, the Event needs to be much more than a demo.

The participants of Sprint Review need to remember that the Sprint Review is not only about observing what has happened during the Sprint and presenting the next potentially shippable working software product increment. The Sprint Review also needs to be about inspecting the Product Backlog considering innovative opportunities for the purpose of customer value optimization and the next steps to be investigated by the Scrum Team, as per the customer needs, market conditions, and technology advancements.

During the Sprint Reviews, the Developers always need to take the best possible opportunity to demonstrate the work which they have completed during the latest Sprint for which the Sprint Review is being done. The Product Owner needs to review and accept the delivered product increment by providing his/her valuable feedbacks. It is also important for the Stakeholders to understand that they need to share their honest opinions and feedbacks about what is being showcased to them. The feedbacks need to be absorbed under the work items of Product Backlog, so that the Scrum Team has a revised Product Backlog to prioritize their activities for their next Sprint.

Assessing opinions, suggestions, and feedbacks of Stakeholders, measuring their happiness index, and seeking their approval based on their unique level of satisfaction (by considering the whole outcome of Sprint-based deliverables) always plays a key role to decide the overall success of a Sprint Review. Through an effective facilitation and some required dialogues-based interactions, the Scrum Master always needs to keep the Stakeholders and rest of the Scrum Team members engaged in their Sprint Review specific conversations, so that the Sprint Review can be made more exciting.

Sprint Review always asks the Scrum Team members to assess the lessons learned by them during the latest Sprint. By considering the concept of Empiricism at a supreme level, the Scrum Team members always need to inspect and adapt by looking at the outcomes at the end of every Sprint. While having a formal agreement with the Product Owner, they also need to think about what all things they need to add to their upcoming product increments to make them more valuable. By making use of a technique such as Happiness Index Meter and by correlating the outcomes of the Sprint during the Sprint Review, the Scrum Team can easily determine the overall satisfaction level of their Stakeholders. Using this technique, they can ask their Stakeholders to rate the Sprint based outcomes, based on the various functional and non-functional considerations.

> *"A sprint review is a chance for the team and stakeholders*
> *to discuss priorities and plans for the product."*
> *- Mike Cohn*

To guarantee that the Sprint Reviews are turning out to be more valuable, the Scrum Team needs to ask the following example questions to themselves and to their Stakeholders. The thoughts and suggestions through their answers to these questions can help them to point out various aspects, where their Sprint Reviews might have a scope for improvement.

- The Sprint Review Event needs to follow Empiricism to inspect the Product Increment and to adapt the Product Backlog; hence, how can the Scrum Team conduct it for the Stakeholders and Businesspeople to collect their valuable feedbacks and to make the right decisions to deliver a fruitful product?

- How can the Product Owner and the Scrum Master ensure that they have a clarity about who all should attend the Sprint Reviews? How can they ensure that the Sprint Reviews are having an involvement of right people, so that the Product Backlog can be improved and adapted with the required consents?

- How the Sprint Reviews need to be planned and executed? How do the relevant feedbacks, opinions, ideas, suggestions, and thoughts need to be gathered?

- How can it be always guaranteed that all the applicable and appropriate participants joining the Sprint Reviews have a proper understanding about the real purpose of Sprint Reviews and about why the Scrum Team is developing and delivering the product increments?

- To encourage the participants and to frame up their expectations, how can the Scrum Team give them a complete clarity about what they did in the latest Sprint and what exactly they are likely to showcase under their demos?

- How can all the Scrum Team members always make sure that they are having a proper alignment and a common, shared understanding about, where currently they are and where they need to navigate further by considering what has already happened during the latest Sprint?

- How can the Developers make use of *Show and Don't Just Tell* approach during the Sprint Reviews? Also, how can they make it even more improved by allowing the Stakeholders to drive the breakthrough through their findings?

- How can the Developers safeguard that they are not showcasing demos for work items which are not fully functional? How do they want to get themselves aligned in front of their Stakeholders for any of the tasks performed by them, which seem to be either partially complete or outside the Sprint Goal?

- While observing, cross-checking, and validating that whether the Developers have developed and delivered required, fully functional, useful, and potentially releasable product increment, how can the Product Owner allow the Developers to present their accomplishments during the Sprint Reviews? When the product increment is not meeting the Acceptance Criteria and/or DoD, how can he/she communicate such understanding and implementation gaps with the Developers to bridge them?

- How can the Product Owner remain always approachable at the time of every Sprint Review? How can he/she accept and gather feedbacks from the Stakeholders and the Developers to address those feedbacks in the upcoming Sprints?

- For the purpose of knowledge sharing, how can the Scrum Master ensure that all the Developers are participating in the Sprint Review discussions, without enforcing their participation and at the same time, making the Sprint Reviews fascinating enough, so that all the participants will be keen to take their part in? To make sure that the interest and level of participation of the Stakeholders are not dropping and to keep their engagement level high, how can he/she facilitate the Sprint Reviews using some of the effective Liberating Structures?

- To ensure a proper transparency, how can the Scrum Team guarantee that the Sprint Reviews are not getting skipped, even if they have not met their Sprint Goal or there is no active participation and/or continuity in participation of Stakeholders and Customers? What they need to do when the Stakeholders seem to be more passive and disengaged? In such cases, how can the Scrum Team sell the Sprint Review Event by sharing its real purpose with the Stakeholders or can ask them to drive the Sprint Reviews as per their needs, wants, desires, and suitability?

- How can the Scrum Master make use of open-ended, powerful questions to encourage all the participants of Sprint Review to communicate and collaborate through their active participation and sharing of their valuable views, ideas, suggestions, opinions, thoughts, feedbacks, agreements, disagreements, issues, problems, questions, doubts, concerns, and many more aspects? Using some of the effective Liberating Structures, how can he/she always ensure that all the participants are being heard, so that the imagination, knowledge, and insights shared by the Stakeholders can help the Scrum Team to make the right product decisions considering customer value optimization aspect to deliver the finest product increments?

- How can the Product Owner also make sure that he/she can restrict the Stakeholders to make their own demands without any valid customer value proposition-specific justifications, by keeping in mind that he/she always has a complete ownership and a final say about the product? How can the Product Owner employ the Product Roadmap and Strategy together to say no to the Stakeholders requests, which are unrealistic and/or not adding any value?

- Which all product validation techniques can the Developers refer and make use of during the Sprint Reviews? Can they make use of simple product increment demos and ask some open questions to listen to the feedbacks of Stakeholders? Can they have some usability tests to be performed by end-users in advance, to see how they make use of product functionalities using a simulation-based approach? Can they make use of product increment release to a limited number of end-users to collect some insights and later to a bigger number of end-users to collect more insights? Can they make use of some simple observations of end-users, who are making use of the product functionalities to understand how useful they are? Can they make use of Spikes as simple prototypes to validate the feasibility and suitability aspects such as system architecture and technology selection?

- Considering customer value optimization, how can the Scrum Team get to know about the overall impression of their Stakeholders toward the product increment functionalities getting showcased to them during the Sprint Review? How can the Scrum Team get to know about, how likely it is that their Stakeholders would like to recommend their product to someone else? How perfect/imperfect they think their product is? What are their honest feelings and review comments about it? Which existing product functionalities they would like to change and why? Are there any new functionalities to be added and why? Are there any existing functionalities to be completely removed and why? Which existing functionalities they would like to keep as it is and why? Which competitive products in the market they can make use of to do a comparative learning, so that they can bridge the product gaps, if any?

- How can the Scrum Team make sure that the feedbacks getting shared by the Stakeholders are available and getting tracked under their Product Backlog work items to discuss on them during the upcoming Product Backlog Refinements? How they would like to spend their time to analyse those feedbacks and to take some required decisions, if they have a big influence on changes to be done in the Product Backlog and to determine which all changes are required to be done?

- During the Sprint Review, how can the Product Owner share a quick and effective overview of the overall progress of the Scrum Team to their Stakeholders considering the upcoming product releases? How can he/she make use of a Scrum Metric such as Release Burndown Chart to track, trace, and share their progress by foreseeing what is the next thing for the Scrum Team to focus on?

The Scrum Event Sprint Retrospective needs to be utilized by the Scrum Teams, where they need to retrospect and emphasize on the aspect of continuous learning and improvement. Sprint Retrospectives cannot be made optional and it is a must have for the Scrum Master to make it happen at the end of every Sprint. He/she should never cancel and/or stop organizing the Sprint Retrospectives.

Many Scrum Teams have a meh feeling about Sprint Retrospectives. The Scrum Team members have a thought process that there is nothing for them to improve and/or they do not have time to address any scope for improvement. Not conducting the Sprint Retrospectives will retain all these kinds of excuses alive and it will also have a harmful impact on the process of Empiricism and hence, also on the Scrum Team's agile way of working. Team will not get a chance to improve in a long run. Sprint Retrospectives always help the Scrum Teams to inspect on what went well in the latest Sprint, what went wrong in the latest Sprint and if there are any better ideas, suggestions, and alternatives for the Scrum Team to adapt on any improvement aspects soon.

The Scrum Team needs to collect their own honest opinions, observations, feedbacks, and suggestions about the latest Sprint for which the Sprint Retrospective is being performed. This helps them to set some expectations by formulating a proper plan, structure, and exploration of techniques during their Sprint Retrospectives. While being a facilitator, the Scrum Master always needs to coach, teach, train, help, support, guide, and mentor the Scrum Team by providing them a clear and a true purpose behind the Sprint Retrospectives. While conducting the retrospectives, he/she always needs to ensure that the Sprint Retrospectives are always exciting, interesting, and fun-oriented. By expecting a thorough participation of all the Scrum Team members, this needs to be done by him/her by exploring and applying various approaches, practices, tools, techniques, formats, and alternatives. The Scrum Team can create their own Sprint Retrospective tools or they can also explore and select any of the online tools such as such as Retrium, Parabol, GoReflect, EasyRetro, FunRetro, Retromat, FunRetrospectives, TastyCupcakes, and so on. Such tools can assist them to have structured Sprint Retrospectives; however, an active participation and interaction of all the Scrum Team members is the most crucial thing to have the Sprint Retrospectives more effective.

The Scrum Master needs to set the stage by establishing and nurturing a healthy and a safe environment to have an active involvement of the whole Scrum Team. He/she needs to facilitate the Sprint Retrospective Event in such a way that everyone is getting an opportunity to speak and share their thoughts about what was their actual overall impression about the latest Sprint. The ultimate purpose of Sprint Retrospectives is to cultivate an agility-based team culture with a continuous improvement of agility and a better way of working, which needs to be reached by discussing on better approaches and formulation of applicable actionable items. To ensure that continuous improvement is happening, the Scrum Team always needs to have an agreement within themselves based on a plan constituting of some actionable improvements to be further investigated and to be enacted upon by them with a decent clarity and complete transparency.

The outcomes of Sprint Retrospectives always need to comprise of what all issues and problems have been occurred in a Scrum Team's latest Sprint, what is an agreed action plan for the Scrum Team to fix those issues and problems, what are the most optimistic methods, alternatives, and best possible solutions to avoid such issues and problems in future. The Scrum Team needs to have Sprint Retrospectives to reflect on how they can turn out to be more efficient and effective by tweaking and changing their agile way of working, its associated processes, and behaviors to be further enacted upon by them.

> *"The goal of retrospectives is to help teams to continuously improve their*
> *way of working. They need to uncover better ways to improve*
> *and retrospectives can provide them the solution."*
> *- Ben Linders*

To guarantee that the Sprint Retrospectives are turning out to be more valuable, the Scrum Team members need to ask the following example questions to themselves. The thoughts and suggestions through their answers to these questions can help them to point out various aspects, where their Sprint Retrospectives might have a scope for improvement.

- The Sprint Retrospective Event of a Scrum Team always needs to follow the process of Empiricism to inspect the latest Sprint for the purpose of continuous improvement; hence, how can the Scrum Team will conduct it for themselves to collect their valuable feedbacks and make the right decisions to improve their agile way of working?

- How can the Product Owner and the Scrum Master always ensure that the Sprint Retrospectives have an involvement of all the Scrum Team members? How can the Scrum Team ensure that they are asking and replying to the right questions to not only to get to know about a truthful picture of how things are happening, but also to ascertain if there is any confusion?

- How the Sprint Retrospectives need to be planned and executed? How the relevant feedbacks, opinions, ideas, suggestions, and concerns need to be gathered, organized, processed, and discussed to come up with the corresponding action items?

- How it can be guaranteed that all the Scrum Team members joining the Sprint Retrospectives have a proper understanding about the real purpose of Sprint Retrospectives and why they need to share their feedbacks, insights, and opinions by considering their overall impression with respect to the latest Sprint?

- To encourage their participation by framing up their expectations, how can the Scrum Team members get a complete picture of what they did in their latest Sprint, so that they can confirm on what they need to start, stop, and continue doing with?

- How can the Scrum Team members ensure that they are having a proper alignment and a shared understanding about what has worked and what has not worked for them by considering their latest Sprint? How can they make use of inspection and adaptation through Empiricism to improve their overall agility?

- How can the Product Owner always remain approachable at the time of every Sprint Retrospective to discuss on the feedbacks given by the Scrum Team members?

- For the interactive discussions, how can the Scrum Master ensure that all the Scrum Team members are participating in the Sprint Retrospectives, without enforcing their participation and at the same time, making the Sprint Retrospectives fascinating enough, so that all the participants will be keen to take their part in? To make sure that their interest and level of participation is not dropping and to keep their engagement level high, how can he/she facilitate the Sprint Retrospectives using some of the effective Liberating Structures?

- To ensure the commitment, how can the Scrum Team members guarantee that the Sprint Retrospectives are not getting skipped, even if they think that there is nothing for them to improve and/or they do not have enough time to address the scope for improvements and/or if there is no active participation and/or continuity in participation of Scrum Team members and/or even if they are more passive and disengaged? In such cases, how can the Scrum Master motivate the Scrum Team members using the concept of Intrinsic Motivation?

- How can the Scrum Master make use of some open-ended, powerful questions to encourage all the participants to communicate and collaborate through their active participation and sharing of valuable views, ideas, insights, suggestions, opinions, feedbacks, agreements, disagreements, questions, doubts, concerns, and so on? Using some of the effective Liberating Structures, how can he/she ensure that the participants are being heard, so that the imagination, knowledge, and feedbacks shared by them can help them to improve their decision-making capabilities and their agile way of working by always considering the customer value optimization aspect to deliver the finest quality working software product increments, both early and often?

- How can the Scrum Master make sure that the feedbacks received from the Scrum Team members are visible to all of them who are attending the Sprint Retrospectives? How effectively and efficiently can the participants spend their time to analyse the feedbacks, to take the required decisions, and to come up with some improvement action items to be worked upon by them in near future?

- How can the Developers evaluate their engineering and testing-specific software development methods and approaches to work on their Sprint-specific deliverables, to handle any of the technical debts present and to work with the Product Owner to enhance their agreed agile way of working?

- How can the Scrum Teams make their Sprint Retrospectives more interesting, exciting, engaging, interactive, and fun oriented? Which all visualization techniques they would like to apply? How can they realize the real value of their engagement along with gaining a common, shared understanding across their agile way of working processes, which needs to be continuously improved?

- How can the Scrum Team collect and visualize the feedbacks from all the Scrum Team members, to set the stage and expectations during the Sprint Retrospectives using any of the visualization techniques such as Prime Directive, One Word, Draw the Sprint, Explorer-Shopper-Vacationer-Prisoner (ESVP), Sprint Weather, Feeling-Emotion-Satisfaction Index, Teamwork Rating, Looking Back, Improvement Cards, Your Superpower, Sprint Seasons, Diamonds or Charcoal, and so on?

- How can they organize their collected feedbacks to initiate the required interactions and dialogues-based conversations during the Sprint Retrospectives using any of the visualization techniques such as Celebration Grid, Glad-Mad-Sad-Kudos, Emoticons, Health Checks, Visualization Radar, Lean Coffee, Liked-Learned-Lacked-Longer For, What Went Well, What Went Wrong, Ideas and Suggestions for Improvements, Roles-Responsibilities-Meetings Satisfaction Index, Start-Stop-Do-Value, Wow-Wondering-Worried, Dysfunctions Analysis Radar, Superhero, and so on?

- How can the Scrum Team search for and reflect on the patterns, behaviors, causes, and insights to generate a common, shared understanding about their own impressions and to take some consensus-based decisions to decide some applicable action items during the Sprint Retrospectives using any of the visualization techniques such as Lego Feedbacks, Next Actions, Who-What-When, SMART Actions, and so on?

- How can the Scrum Team appreciate all the efforts of all the Scrum Team members and review their Sprint Retrospective itself by having a short Retrospective of Retrospective at the end of every Retrospective and by using any of the visualization techniques such as Energy Level for Next Sprint, Value Evaluation, Kudos Cards Wall, One Final Word, Retro Dart, Return Of Time Invested (ROTI), Team Super Powers, Wow-Happy-Sad, Twitter Wall, Simple Questions, and so on?

- During the Sprint Retrospectives, how can the Scrum Team members reflect to improve on their inspections and adaptations under all the processes by also ensuring a proper transparency? How can they ensure that using such reflections, they are always making use of the best practices and procedures for the overall activity of incremental and iterative development and delivery of a fully functional and potentially releasable product increment at the end of every Sprint?

- During the Sprint Retrospectives, how can the Scrum Team start and continue to challenge any status-quo, when it comes to their already established agile way of working? How can they observe, check, and reflect on their own feelings about their own collaboration, communication, co-operation, co-ordination, engagement, and teamwork considering Product, People, and Process, and many other aspects?

- How can the Scrum Team become more self-organized, self-managed, connected, and committed to drive an agile culture of continuous improvement? How can the Scrum Team members increase their overall trust, effectiveness, efficiency, and productivity by showcasing a highest level of collaboration, self-sufficiency, and self-organization?

- How can the Scrum Team members improve on their skill sets, capabilities, and knowledge? How can the Developers ensure that their development and delivery specific practices, processes, guidelines, and standards are up to the mark, considering their selection and usage of tools, technologies, architectures, and automation? How can they construct a better code based on an appropriate architecture having a proper, formal, and agreed definition of quality? How can they get better day by day?

- How can the Scrum Team ensure that their agreed DoD is not too much flexible and at the same time, not too much stringent? How frequently they need to revisit their DoD? How can they properly refine their Product and Sprint Backlogs? How can they improve their relative estimation to make sure that they are estimating correctly? How can they deal with bad estimates causing unrealistic expectations for the Stakeholders?

- How can they inspect on frequently occurring, similar type of impediments along with any of the poor practices causing any delays and deviations, so that they can improve on any preventive and corrective measures to be taken by them?

- How can they ensure that they are living all the five core Scrum Values (focus, commitment, courage, openness, and respect) to the fullest? How can they improve on their own behavior considering the importance of Scrum Values? At the same time, how can they make their agile way of working more and more learning and fun oriented? How can they promote fun-based experimentation and innovation under every Sprint? How can they eliminate anything, which is preventing them to think that work is fun and which is also destroying their engagements and interactions?

- To safeguard that everyone is getting along with each other, how can the Scrum Team members appreciate each other for all the good work they are doing? How can they identify, what is reducing their speed of delivery, so that they can overcome such entities by helping and supporting each other?

- Considering the aspect of relationships and rapport building within the Scrum Team, how can the Scrum Team members work together collaboratively to certify that they are a 'One Team'? How can they have the happy and healthy relationships within themselves and with others outside the Scrum Team? By taking all the chances to work together with a collective ownership, how can they ensure that they are happy and satisfied with the job they are performing?

- How can they form and enhance their agile way of working by fostering Agile and Scrum values and principles, by encouraging everyone to contribute alike, by giving everyone substantial recognitions, by strengthening the opinions and voices of everyone, by making consensus-based decisions, by encouraging growth mindset, by always sharing positive and actionable feedbacks and inputs, by discouraging destructive conflicts, disagreements, and criticism, by cherishing the diversity, inclusiveness, fairness, trust, and transparency, and by holding everyone accountable and responsible for their anticipated actions?

The Scrum Event Sprint (which is a time-boxed container event restricted to one month or less than that) always needs to be utilized by the Scrum Team, where they need to consider it as a place holder for all the work and activities to be performed by them to create a potentially shippable product increment of a high-quality working software product. It needs to start with the Sprint Planning Event and needs to end with the Sprint Retrospective Event. The next Sprint always needs to start immediately, once the current ongoing Sprint comes to an end. The following figure shows the significance of Sprint by looking at the basic expectations from the Scrum Team:

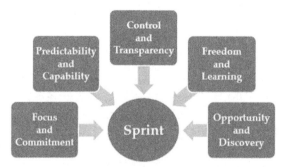

Figure 10.3: Significance of Scrum Event - Sprint

The definitive purpose of the Scrum Event Sprint is always to develop and deliver a potentially shippable product increment containing the most optimized customer value-based outcomes. The value to be delivered always needs to reflect under the Scrum Team's agreed Sprint Goal and it needs to be kept intact during the ongoing Sprint. It is imperative for the Scrum Team to focus on any new ideas, customer needs, market conditions, and technological advancements. This approach increases the overall complexity of work, asking the Scrum Team to remain more focused and to have their full commitment to establish a continuous flow of exploration, learning, and improvement. By having a common, shared understanding along with a well-understood purpose to deliver working software product increment at the end of every Sprint and by rejecting all the interruptions which are not linked with this purpose, the Scrum Team members always need to get into the desired focus and a simple, straightforward commitment to give with their best.

The Scrum Team members need to observe, understand, explore, analyse, uncover, evaluate, and share any new information, which they come to know about, so that they can adapt their plan without dropping their focus and commitment. This approach helps them to bring in an improvised predictability and an enhanced capability during the Sprints.

Even though the Scrum Team cannot assure the exact scope of every product increment, they need to have a predictability and a full commitment to deliver a potentially shippable product increment at the end of every Sprint. It is hence required for the Scrum Team members to work within the Sprints by maintaining a stable pace, where they need to evaluate on what their individual and collective capabilities are to deliver, early and often.

By pondering the complexity, uncertainty, risks, and dependencies, and so on, aspects, once the Scrum Team members realize this predictability - capability correlation and once they collectively start to work together, they can predict the product increment release expectations in a fair way. Their predictions may not be entirely correct but by utilizing a cadence-based Sprints approach, they can improve on optimizing their predictability equations in a long run. To have the cadence-based Sprints, they should not always change the length of Sprints. They need to support their commitment for the incremental and iterative delivery of working software product, as per the customer value proposition. For this purpose, they always need to learn to maintain a suitable cadence.

To have a flexible control and a complete transparency, the Scrum Team needs to keep the length of Sprint, based on how often the customer needs to change their direction. As the Sprint Goal always needs to be intact during an ongoing Sprint, the Developers can have a consistent control to develop and deliver something which has a significant amount of customer value associated with it.

To inspect the product increment and to adapt the required suitable path based on their exploration, the length of the Sprints needs to be decided based upon the frequency of changes in the customer/end-user needs. This tactic provides a flexible control to the Product Owner and to the Stakeholders by avoiding an insecure situation specific to the scope and definition of the overall work to be taken up by the Developers. The cadence-based and time-boxed Sprints not only provide them much more transparency to keep their focus and commitment always high, but also help them to take some conversant and cognizant decisions by having a collective ownership in every ongoing Sprint. With this approach, the potential risks in complex environments can be somehow controlled.

Sprints always need to provide an ultimate sense of freedom to all the Scrum Team members, where they can learn, relearn, and unlearn by the means of innovation, exploration, and experimentation. While setting up a proper focus and commitment for their agreed Sprint Goal, they can utilize all the learning opportunities by inculcating effective self-organization and self-management habits. While performing, inspecting, and adapting collaboratively, they need to learn and validate their right product increments in a right way. The Scrum Teams need to take their every Sprint as a mechanism for opportunistic discovery, where the impacts of any of the failures also need to be a part of their continuous learning. By gaining a competitive advantage, the Scrum-based agile way of working under their Sprints helps the Scrum Teams to embrace the change. Scrum Teams running successful Sprints can enable the benefits of business agility by discovering all the possible opportunities around them.

Points to remember

- The Scrum Master always needs to be accountable for the overall success of an establishment and a continuous improvement of a Scrum Team's Scrum-based agile way of working. The Scrum Team needs to have all their Scrum Events strictly time boxed.

- The Scrum Event Sprint Planning needs to be utilized by the Scrum Team, where they need to determine the work items they would like to select and work on in their upcoming Sprint. The ultimate purpose of Sprint Planning is to reflect on optimizing the value of anticipated product increment by selecting the value driven PBIs in the Sprint Backlog. Sprint Planning asks the Scrum Team to aim at why, what, and how they need to deliver something which will help them to make their Sprint valuable.

- The Scrum Event Daily Scrum needs to be utilized by the Scrum Team, where they need to inspect their overall progress toward the achievement of agreed Sprint Goal. By making use of various Daily Scrum formats, the Scrum Master needs to coach the Developers to have their Daily Scrum more exciting, interactive, and fun-oriented one. It is equally important for the Scrum Team to understand the types, patterns, and frequency of occurrences of impediments by considering their impacts on the customer value getting delivered.

- The Scrum Event Sprint Review needs to be utilized by the Scrum Team, where they need to focus on the customer value optimization from the point of view of their Stakeholders. During the Sprint Reviews, the Developers need to take the best possible opportunity to demonstrate the work they have completed during the latest Sprint for which the Sprint Review is being done. Sprint Review asks the Scrum Team to assess the lessons learned by them during the latest Sprint.

- The Scrum Event Sprint Retrospective needs to be utilized by the Scrum Team, where they need to retrospect and emphasize on the aspect of continuous learning and continuous improvement. Sprint Retrospectives help the Scrum Teams to inspect on what went well, what went wrong in the latest Sprint and if there are any ideas and suggestions to adapt on any improvement aspects in near future.

- The Scrum Event Sprint needs to be utilized by the Scrum Team, where they need to consider it as a place holder for all the work and activities to be performed by them to create a potentially shippable product increment of a high-quality working software product. Scrum Teams running successful Sprints can enable the benefits of business agility by discovering all the possible opportunities around them.

In the next chapter, readers will get to know about some of the advanced Scrum add-ons/techniques to help the Scrum Teams with a proper utilization of Advanced Engineering Practices and Technical Agility.

CHAPTER 11

Add-ons for Advanced Engineering Practices and Technical Agility

Introduction

In this chapter, readers will get to know about some of the advanced Scrum add-ons/techniques to help the Scrum Teams with a proper utilization of the advanced engineering practices to improve their technical agility. They will get to know about a real need behind the advanced engineering practices to develop and deliver the working software product functionalities, early and often. They will also get an overview of some of the best and advanced software engineering practices, which can help the Scrum Teams to develop and deliver their high-quality working software products by making them technologically more intact, compliant and resourceful.

Objective

After studying this chapter, you should be able to:

- Understand why software products have a risk of failure in a variety of ways.

- Understand why a proper utilization of advanced engineering practices is important for the developers of a Scrum Team.

- Understand various advanced engineering practices to improve the overall technical agility of Scrum Teams.

Adam 'The Senior Developer' (in a Sprint Retrospective with the Scrum Team):

"If we continue to have such Technical Debt persisting in our code base, then I am sure that we need to face a huge amount of rework in future. To be honest, this is making me worried. Why can't we take an extra bit of care before checking in our code to the version control?"

Frederik 'The Another Developer' (replying with a confused tone):

"C'mon Adam, we are already doing so many things. What else we need to do?"

Adam:

"I think we need to define some more policies to align our usage of best practices for the Code Reviews, Code Refactoring, Code Coverage, and few other stuffs. We need to think and discuss on, what and how can we make a best possible use of the best of the best practices. I believe that it is a big topic to discuss on. Can we have a separate meeting to discuss more on this, Manish?"

Frederik:

"But we are already making use some of the best practices since last one year. Why we need to discuss again? I think it's better if we stick to the existing practices and continue with them!"

Manish 'The Scrum Master' (taking a pause and replying):

"I still remember those days when I was learning Yoga as a novice practitioner. On the first day of the training, I had asked my Yoga instructor, if I can do difficult Yoga Asanas in next couple of months. He told me to try simple Yoga Asanas first. After a year, my body got a bit flexible to do the difficult Yoga Asanas. You know what matters the most? It's all about continuous experimentation, Frederik!

Can you think of an improved performance of your Sedan by replacing all its parts except its engine? No, right? Even though we adopt best practices, the anticipated outcome can be still a long way. We might not get the value while implementing a new best practice, unless we change our experimentation approach. We need to go for best practices, so that we can apply them and see how effectively we can get better with them. A continuous journey of experimentation it is and it's never too late to be there, where we might not have been before! Remember the phrase? The only bad workout is the one you didn't do!"

Adam:

"Exactly! And I think, it's not too late for us, Manish. It's just that we need to start soon!"

Frederik (smiling and replying):

"Sooner the Better! That's another phrase! Let's discuss on this topic soon, Manish."

Software products always have a risk of failure in a variety of ways. Many of them fail, where it is possible to recognize several familiar and common indicators that can be depicted under the products and their associated processes. The Scrum Team members working on such products might have an incompetence to handle and manage the ever-changing customer requirements. There might be a mistaken perception of customer needs, wants, and desires. There might be some understanding/implementation gaps because of which a super late detection of serious shortcomings is in place. Such shortcomings and flaws might be getting caused because of some bigger glitches and hidden discrepancies in the customer requirements, designs, and implementations. There might be architectural issues in design, where the individual components and modules might not be getting tailored properly.

> *"If everything seems under control, you're not going fast enough."*
> *- Mario Andretti*

There might be some functional, non-functional, and technical issues related to quality, maintainability, extendibility, acceptability, usability, and few other aspects of the working software product. There also might be some deviations happening because of the Developers who are causing some problems due to their lack of knowledge, skills, and co-ordination. It is almost impossible and complicated for them to redesign, redevelop, and redeliver the existing product modules and associated functionalities. This might be happening because it is difficult to track and trace the changes made by them within the working software product considering what, when, where, and why, and so on, aspects. There also might be a presence of some unreliable build, deployment, and release-specific processes. It is crucial for the Scrum Team to understand, identify, and enact upon the fact that they need to have a continuously evolving process to be defined to prevent and fix such problems. They need to continuously inspect on the possible causes behind such problems and focus on the root causes behind them to fix them.

> *"The sky is filled with stars, invisible by day."*
>
> *- Henry Wadsworth Longfellow*

There might be an unorganized/impromptu management of customer requirements, needs, and wants along with a vague and inaccurate communication from the Stakeholders and the Product Owner. The architecture and designing might be delicate and having an irresistible complexity. There might be invisible irregularities and gaps in the requirements, designs, and implementations. There might be an inadequate testing and quality assurance. There might be a deficient usage of automation causing less change propagation. There might be many other causes causing deviations and delays against the anticipated development and delivery of working software product increments. If the Scrum Team members, especially the Developers apply some advanced engineering practices, they will not only be able to get rid of the impacts of such causes, but they will be also in a much-improved position to ensure and maintain a high-quality built-in working software product in an obvious way. This always helps them to keep their overall technical agility flourishing.

Advanced engineering best practices can help the Scrum Teams to develop their software products with a well-established technical agility in place. By using the component-based architectures, they can manage the customer requirements and can model their software product increments effectively. They can effectively verify, validate, and test their software product increments and can also control the changes.

Advanced engineering practices always operate as an authentic support for the Developers to develop and deliver the high-quality working software product. Such practices always help the Developers to enhance their technical agility. Even though the Scrum Framework does not recommend any specific engineering practices, it is always better for the Scrum Teams to explore and apply some of the best engineering practices over the time. An active usage of Extreme Programming (XP) framework and Feature Driven Development (FDD) framework specific practices can always help them to develop an accelerated evaluation of the concepts, methods, and reasoning while building and releasing a working software product. This can empower them to try few innovative things, while performing their Sprint-based activities.

When the Developers can make changes to their working software product modules in a simple, rapid, and adaptable way, agility can be effortlessly achieved. This is the reason that Technical Agility is always at the crux of Organizational Agility. When the Developers are sluggish, lethargic, and having a reluctance to perform some exploratory changes to their working software product, processes, and technologies getting used, their overall positioning and agile way of working does not make any positive difference. In fact, such changes can cause more bugs, errors, and issues.

> *"Right and wrong cease to be useful concepts*
> *when you're talking about software development."*
> *- Kent Beck*

Applying some of the best, advanced software engineering practices can help the Scrum Teams, especially the Developers to deliver a high-quality working software product by making it technologically more intact and compliant. Ideally, such practices should not be only limited to implementing the software product. Rather they should include the entire course of actions, considering all the processes and techniques under their Scrum-based agile way of working. Scrum Teams need to have an anticipation that they cannot have all the practices in place within a single Sprint, but they should surely start somewhere.

The management also needs to understand the fact that they need to have a consistent outlook to support and invest in the recommended software engineering practices. This needs to be done through a constant support for training and onboarding of new tools and technologies and by having a positive anticipation that the Scrum Teams, especially the Developers are enough capable of making use of them. This helps the Scrum Teams to fulfil and advance their Technical Agility specific initiatives to be able to deliver, as expected. The overall suitability, feasibility, and evaluation of outcomes from these practices always plays an important role to make sure that the Scrum Teams are on a right track.

The following advanced engineering practices need to be explored and utilized by the Developers. These are required for them (as per their own suitability), while performing development and delivery of working software product increments during the Sprints.

- Simple Design, Shared Metaphor
- Design by Contract, Design by Interface, Design by Feature
- Component Based System Architecture, Service Oriented Architecture
- SOLID Principles, Language Principles, Design Patterns, Domain Object Modelling
- Separation of Concerns, Design and Code Modularity, Abstraction
- Clean Code, Static Code Analysis, Code Coverage, Code Refactoring
- Collective Code Ownership, Coding Standards, and Coding best practices
- Extreme Programming and Feature Driven Development specific best practices
- Pair Programming, Mob Programming
- Object-Oriented Programming, Functional Programming
- Defensive Programming, Reflective/Responsive Programming
- Chaos Engineering, Micro Services, Serverless-Functions as a Service
- Application Programming Interface (API) Driven Models and Technologies
- Feature Flagging/Feature Toggling, Dependency Injection, Low Code Development
- Outcome Driven Development, Test Driven Development
- Behavior Driven Development, Acceptance Test Driven Development
- Technical Debt Management, Configuration Management, Version Control
- Debugging, Inspections, Formal Verification, Code Peer Reviews
- Continuous Integration/Continuous Delivery and Site Reliability Engineering
- Continuous Deployment, Small Releases, Canary Releases, Ring Deployments
- Continuous Testing, Test Automation, Different types of Software Testing such as Functional, Non-Functional, Unit, Integration, System Integration, Regression, White Box, Black Box, Grey Box, Smoke, Sanity, Ad-hoc, Exploratory, Mutation, Compatibility, Accessibility, and many more

- Automation, Automation of Automation, Large Scale Automation

- Automated Builds, Automated Deployments, and Automated Releases

- Automated Cloud Services (IaaS, PaaS, and SaaS), Containerization (CaaS)

- Infrastructure as Code, Policy as Code

- Automated Provisioning of required Services using Orchestration, Automated Maintenance of Infrastructure, and Automated Monitoring and Logging

The Developers always need to have a pro-active approach to explore and apply the advanced engineering practices. In this process, the Scrum Master and the Product Owner need to give them sufficient freedom, so that they can feel empowered to do the needful on their own. A self-managing and self-organizing nature of exploration needs to be challenged by the Developers to make the best possible use of their own capabilities. This also helps them to enhance their capabilities through a continuous learning process. The following figure shows various aspects of an engineering practice/mindset called as Clean Code, where the Developers always need to ensure that they are addressing all the attributes associated with the Collective Code Ownership and Clean Code mindset:

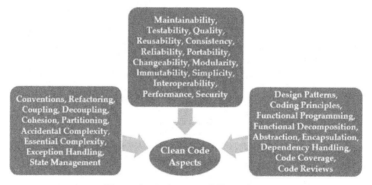

Figure 11.1: Aspects of Clean Code

To guarantee that the variety of aspects of Clean Code are turning out to be more valuable, the Developers always need to ask the following example questions to themselves. The thoughts and suggestions through their answers to these questions can help them to point out if any of these aspects have a scope for improvement, which need to be addressed and to be regularly worked upon by the Developers.

- Which all aspects of the Clean Code mindset are already getting explored and applied by the Developers? Which all aspects are yet to be explored and applied?

- Which all aspects have a positive impact on their Clean Code mindset-based way of working to evaluate and to see if there are any better alternatives?

- How can they ensure that there is a consensus-based decision making in this process? How can the Developers evaluate and measure the effectiveness of various Clean Code aspects, so that they can reflect on customer value optimization aspect? How can they ensure that all the Developers are strictly, rigorously, and collectively following the Clean Code aspects? How can they reduce any understanding gaps?

- How can the Developers gain, absorb, and share their functional, domain-based, and customer specific knowledge? How can they comprehend the complex problems and functionalities getting tracked under their PBIs/User Stories? How can they break those problems into smaller pieces to solve them through their code? Once done, how can they integrate their code constructs?

- How can the Developers plan their code away from the computer, so that they can shape a clear mental model before they start to code? How can they have a shared understanding of their working software product/system and its associated execution environments such as Dev, Test, Staging, Prod, and so on? How can they continuously gain, share, and enhance their knowledge across all the components, technical layers, and modules across the system architecture by not limiting themselves to a specific component, technical layer, and module?

- How can they evaluate and select the types of tools and technologies to be used for the purpose of software development and delivery? How can they choose among open-source or proprietary tools and technologies considering various aspects associated with them? How can they ensure that they are continuously learning various tools, technologies, and programming paradigms such as pair programming, mob programming, object-oriented programming, functional/procedural programming, reflective/responsive programming, and so on?

- Instead of reinventing the wheel, how can they explore, apply, and learn the suitable and already available in-built libraries and utilities, so that they can effectively use them while implementing their use cases through the code? Also, in case of an unavailability of such libraries and utilities, how can they quickly create their own applicable libraries, utilities, and APIs?

- To ensure that the code written by them is fail-safe from the run-time errors and exceptions, how can they use the applicable programming language constructs with some of the valuable features such as sophisticated parsing, looping, branching, mark-up, control, access to internal system variables, binary/text file input/output operations, database support, access to files over the internet, list processing, strong typing, static typing, memory management, immutable data, and so on?

- How can they implement the common APIs on their own? How can they develop an admiration for their code, so that they can practice programming through regular hands-on and train themselves to have a better code with less bad code smells in place?

- How can they make use of some of the object-oriented programming concepts such as composition and interfaces, to enhance the testability and reusability of their code in a long run? How can they implement their code constructs by differentiating shallow code and deep-nested code hierarchies, considering that deep-nested code hierarchy is always difficult to maintain, difficult to reuse, and causing a possibility of errors by making the software product more error-prone?

- How can they ensure that they are making use of effective, best coding/ programming practices, basic standards, and naming conventions? How can they structure and decompose their code to have a well-refactored, well-partitioned, and well-integrated structure across all the modules, technical layers, components, and subsystems? How can they ensure that the code being written by them is always reusable?

- How can they have an objective disclosure-based code construction to make their code more simple, modular, understandable, maintainable, testable, reusable, consistent, reliable, portable, changeable, scalable, immutable, interoperable, performance optimized, compliant, flexible, and so on? How can they apply the data structures and associated code constructs to solve the complex problems more easily and effectively?

- How can they apply the SOLID principles along with the functional, logical, imperative, and object-oriented thinking in practice? How can they manage mutable and immutable states of entities within their code constructs?

- How can they always explore and use the most suitable features of the Integrated Development Environment (IDE) and any other tooling they are making use of to enhance their productivity and to ease off the process of code construction?

- How can they develop their code constructs to allow their IDE to take care of any heavy lifting of test data in case of mocking and stubbing of the automated tests?

- How can they perform white box, black box, grey box testing, and create an automated test-driven code workflow, using which they can ensure that their code is intact?

- How can they detect, classify, and fix any of the existing code smells by properly applying the concept of code refactoring? How can they write much improved code constructs and the corresponding automated unit, integration tests using the Domain-Specific Languages (DSLs)?

- To address the essential and accidental complexities through their code, how can they implement the design patterns and other coding practices such as single responsibility principle, objective disclosing code structure, abstraction, encapsulation, functional decomposition, exception handling, coupling, decoupling, cohesion, information hiding, state management, and so on?

- How can they differentiate loose coupling versus tight coupling in their code? How can they divide their creational logic from business logic inside their code constructs by using approaches such as dependency injection, design by contract, design by interface, defensive programming, assertions, and so on?

- To accelerate and streamline the process of code reviews, how can they have effective, conscious, and systematic code peer reviews? Which all code peer review techniques and policies they need to explore and apply?

- How can they avoid any possible bugs and defects while constructing the code for their PBIs/User Stories, while fulfilling the acceptance criteria and definition of done?

- How can they limit their WIP by ensuring that they are not starting with the code construction of multiple PBIs/User Stories in parallel causing partially done work?

- How can they focus on problem solving and analytical thinking? How can they always select an easier and properly maintainable programming language for their code construction, as complex programming languages cause more mental load?

- How can they read and review the code of each other? How can they ensure that the code has applicable comments in it? How can they also ensure that they are not seeking for any permission from anyone else to maintain their own code, to remove the code smells, to refactor the code, to perform unit, integration tests, documentation, and so on, as all of this is an integral part of the development, which is their primary job?

- How can they fix anything which is not yet broken? How can they master the art of debugging using some proper, handy debugging techniques?

- Instead of using impulsively optimum algorithms, how can they ensure that they are using some of the easiest, naive, and unsophisticated algorithms, which can be applied as per their need, so that they can better understand the utilization of more efficient algorithms while performing coding/programming?

- How can they make their code more understandable and enough self-documented using some naming conventions-based programming standards?

- How can they make the best use of helper functions within their code? How can they keep their API designing simple and add additional options for more flexible use cases later, if required? How can they carefully design and construct their APIs, which are external facing and to be consumed by someone else outside of their reach?

- How can they fail fast and fail safe by implementing the innovative use cases under their code? While checking for the input validation during code construction, how can they think about what can go wrong with all the types of possible inputs to the code they are constructing, so that they can find the possible bugs before they start to occur?

- How can they maintain their coding/programming logic simple and stateless, so that the unit testing can be done more easily? Instead of mixing the logic into stateful methods, how can they break their code logic into separate methods, so that it becomes simpler for them to construct the unit tests in a better, faster and an easier way?

- How can they make use of functions rather than complex data structures? How can they avoid working with the object constructors, which are always difficult to test?

- How can they enhance their code readability, modularity, and maintainability by using an approach such as functional/dynamic programming?

- How can they select and use the appropriate tools and technologies to improve their overall code coverage? Using such tools and technologies, how can they make their code more relevant, extremely flexible, easy to understand, and easy to change?

The Developers always need to understand the importance of architectural design for their software product. Before they start with their code construction, they should not only review the overall architectural design, but should also review and validate their proposed code structure as per the agreed architectural design. This always needs to be done by them to ensure that the code is adaptable, extendable, maintainable, and reusable. By following a high degree of cohesion and a less degree of coupling, they always need to keep all the related code constructs in one module. They also need to take care of having a small number of parameters getting passed from one module to another to reduce the potential design/code smells. By making sure that the system architecture is not rigid, the software product/system can be made more flexible to any changes and/or any major/minor enhancements.

> *"Just because architecture is supposed to be stable,*
> *it does not mean that it should never change."*
> *- Gerson Hermkes*

Ideally, the software product's system architecture and the corresponding architectural design should not be fragile, where any modifications in the code can break the entire software product. It should not be permanent also, where it becomes difficult to order it into the reusable modules and components. It should not be unnecessarily complex, where the design has no explicit advantages. There also should not be any duplication of modules, data, and controls, which are vague, complex, and inaccessible. The overall system architecture should not be unclear/ambiguous, where the Developers are finding it to be tough to comprehend the same. The Developers need to move ahead of Object-Oriented Programming concepts by embracing the SOLID principles and by following the Service-Oriented Architecture (SOA). The following figure shows the SOLID principles, using which the Developers can get rid of their system architecture-specific design smells, while constructing the system design:

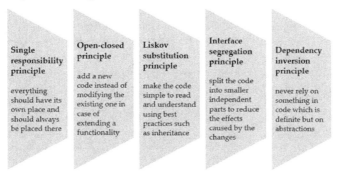

Figure 11.2: SOLID Principles to be used by the Developers

Along with the SOLID principles, there are some language-related principles, which can be also explored and utilized by the Developers. The following figure shows some of them:

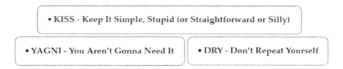

Figure 11.3: Language-related Principles to be used by the Developers

The KISS - Keep It Simple, Stupid (or Straightforward or Silly) principle asks the Developers to keep their code as simple as possible. Code always needs to be divided into fewer parts or modules to not to make it complicated. Avoiding any unnecessary code is also equally important for them. Developers need to keep their code simple, meaningful, and maintainable in such a way that they can always refer to it and debug through it in case of any issues. Developers also need to read, review, and refactor the code written by other Developers.

The YAGNI - You Aren't Gonna Need It principle helps the Developers to navigate through their code and clear out the needless code. Developers need to make use of this principle to carefully plan everything, which they are putting under the code constructs being written by them. Developers need to change their thought process to get rid of the code which is not getting used. They need to have a step-by-step implementation of their code constructs.

The DRY - Don't Repeat Yourself principle asks the Developers to prevent and to minimize the repetitions, duplications, and redundancy in the code constructs by replacing them with proper abstractions, code refactoring, inversion of control, applying pseudocode, data normalization, and few other best practices. The Developers always need to prevent themselves from repeating unnecessary things in their code constructs.

By making use of various code smell detection tools, the Developers always need to identify certain patterns in their own code constructs. Such patterns might be causing some runtime bugs/defects/errors/exceptions/failures and are prominent to cause some more issues for the future development and/or maintenance of working software product in a long run. Code smells occur when the code is not constructed using the best coding/programming practices and standards. Even though the code smells are not actual bugs, they act as possible surface indicators for some deeper problems, which might cause some systemic failures in the future. It is hence required for the Developers to analyse them properly against the expected behavior of working software product features/functionalities. Once the Developers set a proper, required expectation in terms of the expected behavior out of a code construct (in line with the coding/programming best practices, processes, and standards), they might need to refactor their code to have the same expected behavior in place.

The code getting constructed by the Developers always needs to be consistently maintained by the Developers only. It needs to be well-suited, comprehensible, and consistent in terms of its implementation. Having a uniformly consistent code helps the Developers to see through it and anticipate its behavior in its runtime. By having a collective code ownership, the Developers can equally participate to contribute with some innovative suggestions and ideas to improve all the divisions of the code to be written by them. Developers can modify their code to perform the Create, Remove, Update, and Delete (CRUD) operations or any other operations for any of the functionalities getting developed by them.

The Developers can also enhance their existing code for the purpose of refactoring, bug fixing, and addressing new customer/end-user requirements. Collective ownership of code always ensures that all the Developers can perform all the activities related to coding/programming by co-ordinating with each other and no one acts as an obstacle for those activities. This approach becomes simpler when they have all the code implemented with enough code coverage through a proper implementation of required automated unit, integration, system integration, and acceptance tests.

The Developers always need to understand that the coding/programming standards and best practices can always assist them to create a common, shared understanding, control, and discipline within themselves. This approach also asks them to formulate a common language and associated thought process to code along with a better legibility and maintainability of the code to be written by them. By creating the required documentation and by always adhering to the coding/programming standards and best practices, the Developers always need to ensure that they are not an unintentionally constructing a worthless code, which may get converted into a Technical Debt in near future.

Developers also need to make use of some of the code quality tools. The code written by them is not always bug free. Bugs, defects, issues, and errors are likely to happen as no working software product, system is 100% bug free. Hence, it is always crucial for the Developers to use the code quality tools to be on a safer side. By automatically examining the code and by showing the inconsistencies and other possible errors in it, these tools can certainly help the Developers to improve the overall quality of their code. Usage of code quality tools can always help them to detect and define the parts of flaws such as logical errors, implementation errors, security vulnerabilities, concurrency violations, boundary conditions, and so on, in their code.

Refactoring the code always helps the Developers to solve the recognized issues in their code. Continuous refactoring of code always guarantees that the code base is always aligned with the current needs of their customer requirements in a most useful way of maintaining them through the code. It is required for them to ensure that they are not writing functions/methods in code with long lines. Ideally, a method should not have more than 20 lines. Developers also need to assure that the changes getting applied as a part of the refactoring process are not going to break any of the existing functionalities. In this case, the required unit, integration, system integration, regression, and acceptance tests are mandatory.

It is always required for the Developers to apply code refactoring when they feel a genuine need for the same. They should be doing it within their all the code constructs. They need to understand that the development of a working software product functionality by the means of coding/programming is mostly about abstractions. When they apply such abstraction, it becomes easy for them to understand and maintain their own code. Once the software product nurtures, they need to alter the overall structure of their code construction to address new enhancements and associated use cases. If they do not take care of changing code structure using abstractions, it might result into a huge Technical Debt in future, where they need to perform a continuous rework as a work around. This can also make the software product development and delivery slower and buggier during their Sprints. The cost and effort of dealing with the Technical Debt also has an undesirable impact on future deliveries.

"Discipline is the bridge between goals and accomplishments."

- Jim Rohn

The Developers need to follow code refactoring as a strict discipline while modifying any of the internal code structure by ensuring that they are not going to impact the external behavior of the code, which is getting exposed to the customers/end-users. Code refactoring helps the Developers to enhance the built-in quality of the code by making it much more simple, clean, reasonable, and viable. The Developers hence need to exercise code refactoring as a regular practice and the Scrum Master needs to encourage them to perform the same.

> *"TDD makes you write decoupled code (decoupled code = = testable code)*
> *which can make the design of the system better."*
> *- Uncle Bob Martin*

By applying techniques such as Test-Driven Development (TDD) and Behavior-Driven Development (BDD) as a part of their standard development, the Developers can drive their system design through the tests written by them in advance. The Developers need to write unit tests and enough code to make them pass. While continuously refining and refactoring the associated code, they need to keep their code clean and having a proper code coverage.

By using a design technique such as Test First, the Developers can eliminate any waste and can add a more optimized value to their code. By side-stepping any additional generic code construction, they always need to construct a modular code to deliver the basic functionality through it. Using various approaches such as TDD and BDD, the Developers need to write the code to be good enough to pass all the test cases. The Developers always need to understand that the ultimate purpose of unit and integration testing is not to uncover the defects/bugs. It needs to act as a measurement for the anticipated behaviors out of the code, which is acting as an implementation of those anticipated behaviors only. Such tests and the code under such tests always need to be looked together to cross-check the acceptability and correctness of each other. If a Developer modifies any code under their tests causing changes in the behaviors expected by the code, the associated tests should fail.

If the code has an enough coverage with the reasonable amount of unit and integration tests, then the Developers can maintain their code without flouting the ideal behaviors expected from the existing functionalities getting addressed by their code. Instead of writing the code first, writing the tests first helps the Developers to think about the expected behaviors of their code. It also asks the Developers to think about how they will be testing their code before writing the same. The Developers also need to remember that their code refactoring efforts will be more if they are not having enough code coverage getting achieved through the unit tests constructed by them. Unit tests need to test the unit behavior of the code and its associated functionalities being tested and not the actual unit of code implementation. By modifying the code implementation and keeping the behavior as it is, there is no meaning of unit testing. The Developers need to consider their unit test objects as black boxes, which need to thoroughly test the entire code structure in terms of the expected behaviors.

> *"Code without tests is bad code. It doesn't matter how well written it is;*
> *it doesn't matter how pretty or object-oriented or well encapsulated it is.*
> *With tests, we can change the behaviour of our code quickly and verifiably.*
> *Without them, we really don't know if our code is getting better or worse."*
> *- Michael Feathers*

Occasionally failing unit and integration tests reduce the value of code coverage. Developers tend to ignore such tests because they are unsure about the exact root cause behind them. It is crucial for the Developers to fix or remove such failing tests by spending some meaningful effort. While performing white box testing through unit and integration tests against the code, Developers can make their tests fail at least once by purposefully introducing a bug. They can apply rest all positive, negative, and edge-case scenarios to ensure that they are testing almost each code construct. The code should have less mocking of objects. Developers should always look for having enough integration tests, system integration tests, and functional tests to test that the individual units of modules are integrated properly.

> *"You'll learn how to design and code better, reduce time-to-market, produce always*
> *up-to-date documentation, obtain high code coverage through quality tests, and*
> *write a clean code that works. Every journey has a start and this one has no exception."*
>
> *- Viktor Farcic*

To ensure that there is always a 100% code coverage, they need to test all the code paths under unit tests. They should cover most of the possible combinations of test scenarios, unless there is a valid justification for any of the code paths which cannot be tested. They need to remember and follow a philosophy that any code written by them which is not having a proper code coverage along with a proper implementation of unit and integration tests is their sole responsibility. The Developers need to quantify the code coverage by having some policies defined. While performing the code reviews, they need to reject any code which is minimizing the overall code coverage. This is required to ensure that there is a sufficient code coverage.

Along with TDD and BDD, an implementation approach such as Acceptance Test-Driven Development (ATDD) can be also explored by the Developers, using which they can have a collaborative verification and validation approach against the customer requirements. They need to make use of the tests which can be automated to stipulate the customer requirements and to formulate workable conditions for the code to be implemented by them. The Product Owner and the Stakeholders need to collaborate with the Developers, where they need to analyse and learn about how much testing is required for the Developers to test their code and the functionalities being developed by them. Developers need to correct their code in case of any implementation gaps, as per the inputs received. They need to safeguard that they are executing the required unit, integration, system integration, functional, non-functional, smoke, sanity, regression, exploratory, and acceptance tests to ensure that they always have the best quality code in place. They always need to sync their codebase across different environments provisioned for the purpose of development, testing, user acceptance testing, staging, and production, and so on. There can be few other customized environments in place.

Using the concept of microservices, the Developers need to think of a system architecture, which can run with a collection of small services within a single application. Making such services autonomous and having a communication mechanism among them through some well-constructed interfaces can make them lightweight. Every service needs to act as a single method which needs to be mapped as an individual microservice for a single functionality. Developers need to explore different frameworks and programming languages, using which they can create such microservices. Implementation of microservices makes the process of deployments separated, easier, fast, and more flexible for the Developers.

"Indeed, the woes of Software Engineering are not due to lack of tools,
or proper management, but largely due to lack of sufficient technical competence."

- Niklaus Wirth

While using the concepts of Infrastructure as Code and Policy as Code, the Developers can challenge their technical competence to implement an interaction with the infrastructure through some code constructs, where there is a least possible need of manual setups and configurations. Using some Cloud-based service offerings along with some suitable API-driven models, tools, and technologies, the System Administrators and Developers need to consider the infrastructure and its automated provisioning by creating some new APIs or using some existing APIs. Using such APIs, they need to treat their infrastructure as an application code, which makes it possible for them to deploy their infrastructure and servers quickly. They also need to ensure that the configuration of infrastructure along with the infrastructure itself is getting captured under the applicable Cloud services and their associated APIs. This approach helps them to monitor, evaluate, and improve their infrastructure and policy specific need addressal by administering the security compliance. This approach makes the overall process a simple one with an automated provisioning and maintenance of required infrastructure by establishing a proper authentication mechanism.

The engineering practice Configuration Management always helps the Developers to have a standardized configuration of all the kinds of operational tasks, which they need to perform by building their code constructs. Through their available code constructs, most of the configuration-specific changes always need to be regulated. The Developers can make use of Configuration Management to establish and to preserve the overall consistency of a software product throughout its life, where they need to consider the functional, non-functional, and tangible attributes with the corresponding requirements, architectural design, and operational details associated with the software product. The Developers need to make use of various tools to track and control any customizations/modifications in the software product.

Using the concept of Chaos Engineering, the Developers can have better predictable outcomes when the interactions between the individual services of a distributed system-based software product are having chances of unpredictable outcomes. Such unpredictable outcomes may also affect the production environment, where the customers/end-users are accessing them and seeing them as intrinsically messy. The Developers need to detect the system flaws, which make the services unavailable and which might end up into system crashes and failures. Developers need to manage such chaos by focusing on their own procedures related to the development and any environment-specific deployment. Chaos Engineering can help them to take care of such chaos within their distributed system software products and to improve their overall capability to survive any failures/crashes under reasonable circumstances.

> *"The key to following the continuous delivery path is*
> *to continually question your own assumptions about what's possible."*
> *- Jeff Sussna*

DevOps is mindset which also needs to be explored by the Developers as a consolidation of set of practices to integrate the software product development and IT operations. A proper utilization DevOps specific practices can shorten the overall development and delivery life cycle through a Continuous Integration/Continuous Delivery (CI/CD) approach. Techniques such as Version Control need to be used by the Developers for the CI and maintenance of all the code-specific artifacts. CI practice needs to be effectively used by the Developers to integrate their code regularly. They need to do it daily and if possible, it needs to be done as a part of several integrations every day. Each integration needs to be validated and certified by an automated build, making sure that all the automated tests are getting passed.

There always needs to be a detection in case if any of the automated tests are failing and resolution of any such issues occurring in the process of CI/CD. While using CI/CD approach, the Developers always need to expect a substantial reduction in the code integration specific issues or any other issues. It also supports them to have a swift development and delivery of working software product increments. Continuous Integration always asks the Developers to implement test automation, which also forms a baseline for the Continuous Deployment and Continuous Testing techniques. Continuous Development along with the CI/CD approach always needs to utilize the primary value of automation.

CI/CD needs to be regulated for the complete Software Development Life Cycle. It needs to allow the Developers to push and maintain their code, which further needs to be automatically deployed across agreed environments using the power of automation. It makes merging and deployment of code easy; however, the Developers need to take care of all the best practices of CI/CD implementation along with the required collaboration and policy formation. As shown in the following figure, the Developers need to establish a formal and automated way to plan, code, build, test, release, deploy, operate, and monitor the working software product across various environments. This needs to be done by making use of a proper governance structure and usage of CI/CD with version control, automated builds, deployments, and releases, automated tests, infrastructure provisioning, and monitoring, and so on, entities in place.

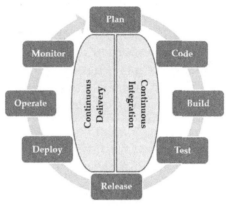

Figure 11.4: *Continuous Integration/Continuous Delivery (CI/CD) Approach*

A Continuous Deployment always needs to take care of a Continuous Delivery of the code by considering every change being done to it. It needs to be a rapid and fail-safe deployment to deploy and promote the code binaries across applicable environments. By performing a meticulous test automation, the Developers always need to ensure that the software product functionalities are functioning as expected. By using the concept of one click/single click Deployment, the Developers always need to have a belief that their code can be easily and rapidly deployed to any environment. Continuous Deployment always needs to be the next step of Continuous Delivery, where any of the code changes with their corresponding successful test automation run need to be automatically deployed and promoted across all the applicable environments. This also helps the Scrum Team, especially the Developers to have shorter release cycles.

"The purpose of Software Engineering is to control complexity, not to create it."

- Pamela Zave

By expecting the highest level of collaboration within the Developers, they always need to have an implementation of small chunks of code with a proper code coverage, so that it can be quickly peer reviewed and can be further merged after addressing code review comments. This also helps them to frequently release the code by reducing the risk of deviations and delays. This frequent delivery approach asks the Developers to formulate and enhance better engineering practices to fulfil the expectations from the Product Owner and the Stakeholders by developing and delivering a high-quality working software product for their Customers. In this process, all the Developers need to take a complete collective ownership of code design, code construction, testing, and deployment to make the working software available for the Customer by integrating the required services offered by a CI/CD solutioning.

It is also important for the Developers to make use of some monitoring and logging specific standards to understand the impact of overall performance of the software product already delivered to its Customers/End-Users. When the Developers think that they have some impact of code changes, they need to make use of suitable tools and technologies to capture, collect, classify, and monitor the required runtime data, specifics, metrics, and logs of their already released software product. Monitoring helps them to detect the causes of unpredicted issues and problems. When the CI/CD services include continuous monitoring and logging, it can surely guarantee the customers, a high availability of services specific to the software product.

By making use of the concept of Feature Flagging/Feature Toggling, soft releases of code can be enabled. The Developers need to apply a Feature Flag/Toggle, which needs to act as a decision-making point inside their code. It can modify the behavior and flow of functionalities getting implemented under the code. Instead of deploying the complete Features, Developers can make use of Feature Flags to deploy only certain required pieces of code across environments. By putting some conditions to enable/disable the Feature Flags, they get a freedom to deploy only those functionalities under the code, which are working fine. This approach also helps them to minimize the risk for any of the deployment-specific issues, where only the fully functional software product functionalities can be deployed. Using this approach, the Developers can decouple any of their deployments from the planned product releases. Feature Flags also provide an ultimate freedom to the Developers, where they can have the ability to decide on which code needs to be deployed and which is not.

The Developers should always anticipate the testing of product functionalities with some real and live users, especially in the production environment. This not only helps them to bring in a better and actual representation and understanding of customer usage, but also gives an overall understanding about how the code is behaving. To perform such testing, Developers need to make use of Feature Flags to control, enable, and disable new features without rolling back the code or without any redeployment. The Developers can also make use of Canary Releases and Ring Deployments to have fail-safe deployments and testing in production.

By utilizing the ultimate benefits of the concept of Functional Programming, the Developers can establish a foundation for higher quality code, resulting into some properly designed and constructed user empathetic working software product outcomes with customer/end-user value optimization. Functional Programming languages offer some extensive features such as high-quality offerings and low cognitive operating costs, using which the Developers can maintain a consistent code base with less bugs and high quality.

The process of Formal Verification and Validation helps the Developers to check and reflect on the overall acceptability of algorithms getting used by them. It needs to be believed and followed as a standardized process to evaluate, assess, and to measure the specification of actual implementation of algorithms. Techniques such as Static Code Analysis need to be explored by the Developers to assess the workflow implementation accuracy of algorithms. Once they have a properly defined agreement on PBI/User Story-specific functional, non-functional, and technical specifications, they can start applying the same to the applicable algorithms which they would like to explore and implement through their code constructs.

They can also make use of some reproductive tools to write their code constructs in line with both algorithms and specifications. They need to focus on Outcome-Driven Development (ODD), using which they can form an appropriate workflow process to promote a speedy development and delivery. Using ODD approach, Developers need to outline some goals. Ownership and assignment of such goals make them more accountable and responsible to accomplish those agreed goals. ODD also benefits them to have a shared understanding of their common purpose, goals, and objectives.

> *"Scrum without automation is like driving a sports car on a dirt track.*
> *You won't experience the full potential, you will get frustrated,*
> *and you will probably end up blaming the car."*
> *- Ilan Goldstein*

Containerization is an evolving technological practice/technique, which can be also explored and employed by the Developers. It automates the capabilities of hosting and deployments under a CI/CD implementation. Containerization helps the Developers to automate their infrastructure provisioning. It ensures that the code behaves properly on different platforms and infrastructures without any differences. Developers can utilize the power of automation through Containers, using which they can deploy across numerous cloud service providers or with any other infrastructure/hosting service providers. They can also bundle all the required system-level dependencies and external references within a container, which can be deployed across its suitable infrastructure.

Using the concept of Serverless-Functions as a Service, the Developers need to make use of cloud-hosted services. It eases the deployment of code on server infrastructure. By performing immediate deployments and executions of code binaries, the Developers can always utilize the functioning of the code. A serverless platform can expose this code functioning, which can be safely and securely accessed through internet.

The process of effective Code Reviews needs to be agreed, established, and continuously enhanced by all the Developers. They always need to think of Code Reviews as the direct opportunities given to them, where they can read, comprehend, review, and evaluate the code written by each other. They need to share and enact upon their valuable perspectives, opinions, and views to enhance the overall quality of their code.

Various forms of Code Reviews via the techniques such as Pair and/or Mob Programming can be always worked upon by the Developers, where they need to collaboratively discuss and validate their code quality. Through such techniques, any code design, construction, quality, performance, and security specific issues can be detected, easily and early. Code Reviews hence ask the Developers to circumvent most of the Technical Debts, which might get unintentionally acquired by them over the time.

> *"Good programmers know what to write,*
> *but great ones know what to rewrite (and reuse)."*
> *- Eric S. Raymond*

The Developers always need to be aware of the Technical Debt getting introduced by them within their own code constructs. Technical Debt is a term used to characterize the cost of rework caused by the Developers when they select certain approaches of design and implementation as easy solutions in current conditions, instead of using some improved approaches that would take them more time to implement. If it is not affiliated with the needs of a growing software product, it might have some adverse impacts on the overall quality of the software product. Technical Debt may also have some harmful impacts on the overall productivity of Developers in a long run.

When the Developers keep the Technical Debt unattended, it further increases across the other code constructs. It is hence required for them to understand that Technical Debt attracts more Technical Debt and any change within the code constructs to eliminate the same always needs to be applied earlier. It becomes difficult for the Developers to handle any such Technical Debt, as the code might get bulky and out of sync over the time, especially when there are some new product functionalities getting introduced during every Sprint. When the software product grows big, it becomes difficult for them to understand and maintain the code. This also impacts the overall development and delivery capabilities of Developers. To guarantee that the Developers are always seeing and addressing the Technical Debt, they need to ask the following example questions to themselves. The thoughts and suggestions through their answers to these questions can help them to point out if any of these aspects have a scope for improvement.

- While working with the PBIs/User Stories/Spikes, as the Developers explore and learn more, their understanding also evolves over the period. In this process, how can they have an ability to learn through a process of experimentation and feedbacks? How can they nullify their assumptions about their code constructs with such understanding? In this case, how can they avoid and address any Technical Debt?

- How can the Developers ensure that they have identified existing Technical Debt in terms of system architecture, design, code, infrastructure, build, tests, test automation, documentation, other applicable engineering artifacts/ processes/aspects, and so on?

- How can they ensure that they have the dedicated work items in their Product Backlog, using which they can make their Technical Debt visible and transparent to each other and to track, trace, and fix the same in a better way?

- How can they agree on a due date to get rid of any existing Technical Debt by also ensuring that they are not creating any new Technical Debt?

- How can they assign a dedicated capacity to address the Technical Debt in every Sprint? To maintain the product quality, how can they form an agreed limit for Technical Debt and make certain that it is not exceeding the same?

- How can they frequently utilize their Sprint Reviews to reflect on the existing Technical Debt, so that the Stakeholders are also aware of it? By considering Technical Debt, how can they inspect their Definition of Done during every Sprint Retrospective? How can they introduce required improvements in it?

- How can they make use of code specific metrics/measures such as Code Coverage, Cyclomatic Complexity, and Rule Violations to evaluate the Technical Debt?

- How can they modify their agreed Definition of Done to be aligned with the proper expectations of code quality? Also, which all policies and processes they need to define and follow to handle and/or prevent any existing and/ or any new Technical Debt?

- To follow the coding-related best practices and guidelines and to avoid later rework resulting into delays, how can they follow an agreed and standardized process to handle the Technical Debt right from the first Sprint? How can they have enough technical PBIs/User Stories to perform technical analysis during the Sprints?

- In case of Technical Debt, how can they have the required trade-offs with the Product Owner to ensure that they are capturing it under the relevant work items to be worked upon by them under an upcoming Sprint? While having continuous discussions with the Product Owner, how can they get to know about when they need to start to take care of existing Technical Debt, so that it will not get more complex further?

- Which all engineering, automation, and testing specific advanced practices they would like to explore and apply to manage/eliminate any existing Technical Debt and to proactively avoid/prevent any new Technical Debt?

- How can they proactively explore their own implementation of code design and constructs for the purpose of features which are getting modified frequently? How can they maintain their focused positioning, so that they can complete their features and functionalities in upcoming Sprints, while cleaning up their existing Technical Debt? How can they manage the same without impacting the incremental and iterative development and delivery of their working software product?

It is a collaborative responsibility of the Product Owner as well as the Developers to contemplate the trade-offs when they are supposed to introduce any new functionality having an impact on existing functionality causing dependencies across the software product modules. The Developers need to have a shared code ownership avoiding a siloed knowledge building and an isolated way of working. Instead of always waiting for the time when they are supposed to perform Code Reviews, they need to discuss, decide, and document their design and implementation-specific approaches well in advance. Generators and Static Code Analysis can help them to understand their programming approach by implementing the small and simple code constructs and increasing the overall code coverage.

> *"The difference between a tolerable programmer and a great programmer is not how many programming languages they know, and it's not whether they prefer Python or Java. It's whether they can communicate their ideas. By persuading other people, they get leverage."*
> *- Joel Spolsky*

Both communication and collaboration always need to act as a basic vital element for all the Developers of a Scrum Team. As the Developers come together to work together and to support and share their responsibilities, their individual and collective morale along with a solid sense of teamwork gets established as well as enhanced. By making use of some online/offline tools and some utilities for the purpose of communication, collaboration, and tracking, the Developers can enable an effective co-ordination and co-operation to inspect, adapt, and enact on a realization of common, shared purpose, goals, and objectives.

By acting as Software Engineers, the Developers need to get themselves emotionally detached from the code and not from the actual process of coding. By considering the code as transient, they need to design, develop, deliver, and maintain a high-quality, fully functional, properly implemented, outcome-based, and evolving software product. By ensuring that they have a clean system architectural design, they need to avoid over-engineering. Applying the most suitable design patterns, they also need to ideate and experiment on faster problem solving. The Developers should not feel embarrassed to accept the fact if they do not know something. They should not feel anxious to share their incomplete work with others. They need to encourage each other to gain the required knowledge through a continuous on-the-job learning, unlearning, and re-learning. This approach also helps them to continuously enhance their skills and capabilities. By reassuring a growth mindset-based agile way of working, they need to learn something new, which they have not performed earlier, so that they can do research and development for the finest possible solutions to the complex problems.

A clear communication along with a constant help, support, and motivation from the Scrum Master, the Product Owner, the Stakeholders, and the Management always acts as an important factor for the Developers to contribute and to achieve their common, shared goals and objectives. It also helps the Scrum Teams having self-managing, self-organizing, and cross-functional Developers to become high-performing and hyper-productive.

Points to remember

- Software products always have a risk of failure in a variety of ways. Many of them fail, where it is possible to recognize several familiar and common indicators that can be depicted under the products and their associated processes. It is crucial for the Scrum Teams to understand and enact upon the fact that they need to have a continuously evolving process to be defined to prevent and fix such failures/problems. They need to continuously inspect on the possible causes behind such problems and focus on the root causes behind them.

- Advanced engineering best practices can help the Scrum Teams to develop their software products with technical agility in place.

- When the Scrum Teams can make changes to their working software product in a simple, rapid, and adaptable way, agility can be effortlessly achieved. This is the reason that Technical Agility is always at the crux of Organizational Agility.

- When the Developers are sluggish, lethargic, and having a reluctance to perform some exploratory changes to their working software product, processes, and technologies getting used, their overall positioning and agile way of working does not make any positive difference.

- Applying some of the advanced software engineering best practices can help the Scrum Teams to deliver a high-quality working software product by making it more compliant.

- Scrum Teams always need to have an anticipation that they cannot have all the advanced engineering practices in place within a single Sprint, but they should surely start somewhere.

- The management needs to understand the fact that they need to have a consistent outlook to support and invest in the recommended software engineering practices. This needs to be done through a constant support for training and onboarding of new tools and technologies and by having a positive anticipation that the Scrum Teams are enough capable of making use of them.

- By evaluating the suitability of advanced engineering practices and techniques, they need to be explored and utilized by the Developers for the development and delivery of the working software product increments during their Sprints.

In the next chapter, readers will get to know about some of the advanced Scrum add-ons/techniques to help the Scrum Teams to establish and use effective and efficient Scrum Metrics.

CHAPTER 12

Add-ons for Effective and Efficient Scrum Metrics

Introduction

In this chapter, readers will get to know about some of the advanced Scrum add-ons/ techniques to help the Scrum Teams to establish and use the effective and efficient Scrum Metrics. They will get to know about various metrics to be sensibly explored, agreed, applied, and assessed by the Scrum Teams. They will also get an overview about how the Scrum Teams can make use of such metrics by considering various aspects such as value, productivity, predictability, stability, quality, collaboration, competence, and so on, how they can continuously measure, track, trace, evaluate, assess, enhance, and improve their overall performance by making their existing people, product, and process-specific entities better.

Objective

After studying this chapter, you should be able to:

- Understand various considerations for the Scrum Teams while defining and establishing their required Scrum Metrics.
- Understand the overall process of formulation and continuous evaluation of Scrum Metrics.
- Understand the concept of EBM framework along with its Key Value Areas (KVAs) and associated sample measurements as metrics.

- Understand various technical and non-technical measurements, which can be thoroughly explored, evaluated, and applied by the Scrum Teams as metrics.

Sam 'The Product Owner' (in a discussion with Ron 'The Scrum Master'):

"Let's add more Developers to our Scrum Team, Ron! Don't you think that this will make our delivery faster and on time? More Developers means more hands to contribute. We'll become more Agile!"

Ron 'The Scrum Master' (smiling and replying):

"Who told you that adding more Developers will solve the current issues in our team? A big team always makes decision making slower. Sorry, but I don't agree with you at all, Sam!

I think, I really need to ask you one question now. You are a big fan of game of Tennis, right? Please tell me, how many players can play a single match of Tennis?"

Sam (replying immediately):

"Oh my god! You are asking me this question as if you don't know anything about Tennis. The answer to your question is either two or four. Not less than two and not more than four. It depends upon, whether it is a singles match or a doubles match."

Ron:

"Exactly! And what if there are more than four players playing the same match?"

Sam (smiling and replying):

"There will be a total chaos and disruption. They won't be able to co-ordinate with themselves and it will be a complete mess. It will become difficult for them to have a control on manoeuvring the ball. There will be less valid returns too. Honestly speaking, I can't even imagine what will happen if we have more than four players on both the sides of the net. But why one will ever change the basic rules of game, if one already knows that the game has its own limits? Sorry, I didn't get you!"

Ron (smiling and replying):

"Can a Tennis match become more Agile having more players playing it? No, right? Scrum Guide recommends 10 or fewer Developers in the Scrum Team. If we add more Developers in our Scrum Team, there are chances that it might create understanding gaps, loss of communication, lack of co-ordination and few other issues. If you still want to do that, then let's have two separate Scrum Teams to see how it goes further, okay?"

Sam:

"Done! What a perfect serve it was, Ron! Advantage to our Scrum Team. Haha!"

By making use of some applicable and appropriate Scrum Metrics to assess the Scrum Team's overall productivity and performance is one of the key essentials for the Scrum Team. The outcomes of their performance and collaborative efforts through these Metrics can certainly help them to improve their Scrum-based agile way of working and its associated processes. The Stakeholders can also get to see how the Scrum Team is performing by evaluating the Metrics. Such Metrics always allow all the Scrum Team members to measure, track, trace, enhance, and improve their overall performance to make the existing people, product, and process-specific entities better and safer.

As per the *Manifesto for Agile Software Development*, for the Scrum Teams, the working software product always needs to be their primary measure of progress. Also, they always need to deliver some customer/end-user value at the end of every Sprint. Based upon these primary expectations, the classification of Scrum Metrics for the Scrum Teams requires an anticipation for change and restructuring. The Scrum Team members hence always need to focus upon the Metrics, which are based on parameters such as quantification of time, effort, cost, delivered outcomes, and many more other aspects.

The Scrum Team members also need to focus on their overall planning, understanding, and execution/implementation of work items along with how much they can achieve during their ongoing Sprints. As shown in the following figure, a continuous assessment of various aspects such as value, productivity, predictability, stability, quality, collaboration, and competence, and so on, needs to be considered by the Scrum Teams while defining and establishing their required Scrum Metrics:

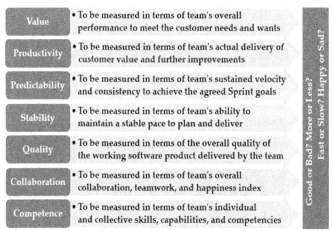

Figure 12.1: Scrum Metrics Considerations for Scrum Teams

Scrum Metrics need to ask the Scrum Teams to evaluate on whether they are creating and delivering the customer value incrementally, iteratively, quickly, early, and often or not. Having such a valid expectation from the Scrum Teams expects them to empower themselves having a constant commitment toward delivery of well-prioritized working software product increments. They also need to contemplate on feedback addressal. Metrics also need to ask the Scrum Teams to evaluate on whether they are creating and delivering the right things right or not. Scrum Teams hence need to focus on outcomes over outputs and to deliver more with less. Scrum Teams also need to evaluate on whether they are addressing the most crucial aspect of built-in quality, which helps them to minimize any kind of rework and to maximize their overall productivity and effectiveness.

As per the Scrum Guide, the Scrum Event Sprint always enables the overall predictability of incremental and iterative development and delivery for a Scrum Team. It asks them to have a process of continuous inspections and adaptations of their own progress, while accomplishing their agreed Product Goal and Sprint Goals. The Scrum Team hence needs to consider every Sprint as a short project. To forecast their overall progress during their ongoing Sprints, they can make use of various practices such as burndowns, burnups, velocity, and cumulative flows as Scrum Metrics. These Metrics are useful; however, they do not enhance/improve the overall significance and utilization of the process of Empiricism.

The Scrum Teams need to use their inspections to perform a forward-looking, consensus-based, and effective decision-making. Empiricism always helps the Scrum Team to reveal a genuine truth about how they are functioning by considering various people, product, and process specific aspects. Most of the time, the Stakeholders are not having a proper interpretation of realizing the tangible and actual value of the working software product (in terms of its work items getting developed and delivered during the Sprints) meeting the agreed Definition of Done and Acceptance Criteria. They want to see the Scrum Metrics in terms of some worthless statistics. It is important for the Scrum Teams, especially for the Scrum Master to educate and persuade the Stakeholders, so that Scrum Metrics can be used, but the focus always needs to be on aspects such as value, productivity, predictability, stability, quality, collaboration, competence, and many more useful aspects.

"It is not about proving anything to the world. It is all about proving your capabilities to yourself and stretching your own boundaries."

- Manoj Arora

The Scrum Teams always need to understand that the empirical testimony of their overall progress can only be uncovered through their capability of iterative development and delivery of high-quality working software product increments. The Scrum Metrics and their associated measurements getting defined and established by them always need to be aligned with their Sprint-based deliverables with an anticipation to achieve the agreed Sprint Goal. This is the reason; the customer value and associated quality compliance is a must and it needs to be evaluated as a primary measure for the increments getting delivered by them.

At the same time, the Scrum Teams also need to remember that the Scrum Guide does not recommend any specific Scrum Metrics that they need to use. It also does not suggest, advise, and endorse any specific practices and techniques for any Metrics. Scrum Teams hence need to come up with a proper understanding and evaluation on their own after a significant exploration of any of the Metrics, which they would like to make use of.

This approach hence can be considered as choices left open to them, where they might need some guidance, help, and support. The Scrum Master needs to facilitate them to the best of his/her knowledge, where he/she can provide them a proper overview, coaching, teaching, and mentoring to align their Scrum Metrics in line with the process of Empiricism. This is required for them to formulate an agreed process for how they can inspect and adapt using such Scrum Metrics and how they can enact on any scope for improvement.

"Failing to reach consensus and buy-in on metrics is the reason why so many Agile Programmes fail. As the Agile Author Scott M. Graffius put it: 'If you don't collect any metrics, you're flying blind. If you collect and focus on too many, they may be obstructing your field of view.'"
- Adrian Bridgwater

It is required for the Scrum Teams to choose their Scrum Metrics sensibly. Metrics should assess most of the aspects of their agile way of working considering people, product, and processes; however, they should not assess too many things causing any distractions to their focus. At the same time, the Scrum Teams should not select Metrics, only for the sake of having them and to make them feel good. They should properly introspect to achieve an actionable value out of any Metrics, which they would like to explore on their own and make use of.

"The most important metrics are: did we execute the way in which we said we would, and did we deliver the value to the business that we had promised?"
- Jamie S. Miller

Keeping in mind that the Scrum Team members are always going to help each other to reflect, collaborate, and improve their agile way of working, they always need to cross-check, inspect, adapt, and enact on whether they have performed the way with which they have already agreed and committed to perform or not.

With such an anticipated performance, they also need to cross-check on whether they are always delivering an optimized customer value or not. Scrum Teams always need to have some goals and objectives in their mind. By the virtue of such goals, they can expect a swift development and delivery with an increased efficiency, a viable and innovative collaboration, an enhanced quality of working software product, and their happy and satisfied customers. Along with these factors, considering one more important factor of Return on Investment (RoI), the Stakeholders also need to be engaged while formulating the Scrum Metrics, which can help the Scrum Teams to measure their way of working-specific processes and bring in the desired outcomes.

The following figure shows various steps involved under the process of formulation and continuous evaluation of Scrum Metrics to be followed by the Scrum Teams. The Scrum Team members need to discuss and determine their motivation for a change considering their goals, objectives, and previously mentioned considerations. They also need to convey their real need behind the Scrum Metrics, which they would like to explore on their own. A proper and valid consideration of all these entities makes the overall process of formulation and continuous evaluation of Scrum Metrics easy and straightforward.

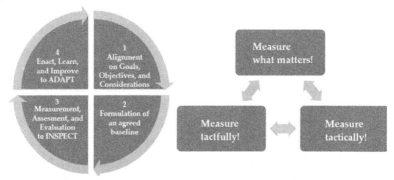

Figure 12.2: The process of formulation and continuous evaluation of Scrum Metrics

As a next step, they need to formulate an agreed baseline. It helps them to have a precise visibility of their positioning, using which they can assess a difference in between their earlier and current positioning. By analysing the speed to value and time to market (that is, the time required for them from their start until they deliver something valuable to their customers), by evaluating the amount of defect slippage (that is, the amount and severity of bugs/defects they have found after delivery), by understanding the amount of customer satisfaction, by setting up the key Scrum Metrics, and by applying them to latest Sprints can help them to define a baseline for a subjective comparison. Once a baseline is defined, they need to start with measurement, assessment, and evaluation of Scrum Metrics against the baseline.

"One accurate measurement is worth a thousand expert opinions."

- Grace Hopper

Scrum Teams need to perform tactical and tactful measurements and assessments along with continuous inspections, evaluations, and adaptations against their agreed Scrum Metrics. Such adaptations can help them to improve their selection of Metrics by considering their own value proposition, productivity, innovation, experimentation, competition, sustainability, performance, predictability, stability, collaboration, communication, engagement, alignment, competence, quality, understanding, and many other aspects.

Scrum Framework always expects that the Scrum Teams are embracing and welcoming any change occurring during/within the process of working software product development and delivery. It is hence required for the Scrum Teams to understand that the Metrics getting used by them to measure certain entities might cause some changes to their originally anticipated plans. By perfectly utilizing the Sprint Reviews, they need to get such changes reflected into their Product Backlog. While doing the same, they always need to consider and reflect on the critical parameters such as customer value and satisfaction, on-time development and delivery, product quality, and so on.

> *"Not everything that can be counted, counts.*
> *And not everything that counts can be counted."*
> *- Albert Einstein*

While addressing the expectations of Stakeholders, the Scrum Teams tend to feel dependent on the Scrum Metrics. These Metrics can differ at the different stages of their applicability and suitability; however, the most important thing for the Scrum Team members is always to have their lookout on whether they are doing better than their last introspection or not. To reflect on this, it is also crucial for them to perform regular introspections through continuous inspections and adaptations to continuously learn and improve. Continuous introspections also help them to enhance their overall Agility.

> *"Good decisions come from experience. Experience comes from making bad decisions."*
>
> *- Mark Twain*

By utilizing the unique characteristics of frameworks like Data Insight Belief Bet (DIBB) and Evidence Based Management (EBM), the Scrum Teams can analyse, assess, measure, manage, and enhance the customer value getting delivered by them. The DIBB framework is a decision-making framework used at Spotify. It asks the Scrum Teams to analyse the working software product's customer/end-user usage patterns and consequent data by evaluating the required insights in it. They also need to create some beliefs to bet on the subsequent assumptions, which can be provided as a feedback loop. The following figure shows the EBM framework developed and sustained by Ken Schwaber and Scrum.org. It asks the Scrum Teams to concentrate on improvement of customer value-driven outcomes and minimization of risks.

Figure 12.3: *Evidence-Based Management framework by Ken Schwaber and Scrum.org*

EBM framework asks the Scrum Teams to look at four Key Value Areas (KVAs), using which they can create some proper measures to have correct investments, smoother decision-making, and risk reduction for the purpose of an improved iterative and incremental development and delivery of working software product. Following is the four KVAs that need to contribute to the Scrum Team's ability to deliver an optimized customer value.

- **Current value**: It asks the Scrum Teams to measure the value which they have delivered to their customer or end-user as of today.

- **Unrealized value**: It asks the Scrum Teams to measure the value that could be realized by meeting all the potential needs of their customer or end-user.

- **Ability to innovate**: It asks the Scrum Teams to measure their ability to deliver a new capability, which might better serve their customer or end-user needs.

- **Time to market**: It asks the Scrum Teams to measure their ability to quickly deliver new capability, service, or product to their customer or end-user.

The Scrum Teams always need to look at their current/present customer/end-user delivered value to reflect on how much they are getting back against their investments, while establishing their agile way of working and its associated processes. They also need to look at their unrealized customer/end-user delivered value to be explored by them. By looking at their overall ability to speed up the value delivery and time to market, they also need to understand their own capabilities to determine and enact on the next steps required for them to improve upon.

By utilizing the benefits of their already established Scrum-based agile way of working and its constituents such as extreme programming practices, continuous integration/continuous delivery, and test-driven/behavior-driven development, they need to start analysing their current state. They need to begin with a continuous experiment loop, where they need to perform a process of hypothesis validation against the ideas to improve upon. It needs to be followed by an acceptable experimentation, measurement, evaluation, inspection, and adaptation. They need to do this until they reach their ultimate Strategic Goal through a series of intermediate Goals in between.

The most crucial aspect of having a proper understanding of the results of experimentation and corresponding measures to be taken always needs to be a part of the Scrum Team's ability to continuously inspect and adapt based on available information. The Assessment of the four KVAs under the EBM framework can always help them to evaluate their own processes, practices, capabilities, strengths, and weaknesses. It can also assist them to evaluate themselves on an evidence-based, cognizant decision-making, which always needs to seek for a continuous learning and continuous improvement. The EBM framework-based Key Value Measures (KVMs) can be considered as Metrics by the Scrum Teams. They can help the Scrum Teams to understand their current state, anticipated future state, and the considerations that might affect their capability to get better.

Considering the EBM framework's current value aspect, the following are the sample measurements that can be explored and evaluated by the Scrum Teams as Metrics:

- **Revenue per employee**: This Metric is a key competitive indicator that asks the Agile Organizations and their Scrum Teams to measure their current value in terms of a ratio, which can be given as their gross revenue per number of associates.

- **Product cost ratio**: This Metric asks the Scrum Teams to measure their total expenses and costs (including operational costs compared to revenue) being measured for the process of development and delivery of a working software product.

- **Employee satisfaction**: This Metric asks the Scrum Teams to make use of a sentiment analysis, using which they can determine their overall associate engagement, energy, enthusiasm, happiness, and satisfaction levels.

- **Customer satisfaction**: This Metric asks the Scrum Teams to make use of a sentiment analysis, using which they can determine their overall customer engagement, energy, enthusiasm, happiness, and satisfaction levels.

- **Customer usage index**: This Metric asks the Scrum Teams to measure their customer usage patterns and behaviors against the software product features. It can always help them to understand the usefulness of those features and functionalities considering the customer viewpoints. It can also help them to realize if the actual customer usage of the product is meeting the expectations or not.

Considering the EBM framework's unrealized value aspect, following are the sample measurements that can be explored and evaluated by the Scrum Teams as Metrics:

- **Market share**: This Metric asks the Scrum Teams to measure the overall relative percentage of the market (which is not controlled by the product) along with the potential market share (which the product might achieve if it really meets the customer/end-user needs).

- **Customer or user satisfaction gap**: This Metric asks the Scrum Teams to measure the difference between the overall anticipated experience versus the current experience of their customers.

- **Desired customer experience or satisfaction**: This Metric asks the Scrum Teams to indicate the overall anticipated experience of customers.

Considering the EBM framework's Time to Market aspect, following are the sample measurements that can be explored and evaluated by the Scrum Teams as Metrics:

- **Build and integration frequency**: This Metric asks the Scrum Teams to measure the total number of integrated and tested builds per time, where time can be hours or days or weeks, and so on, For a Scrum Team releasing their functionalities through a frequent/continuous deployment of builds, this Metric needs to be replaced with the Release specific Metrics explained further.

- **Release frequency**: This Metric asks the Scrum Teams to measure the total number of releases per time, where time can be hours or days or weeks, and so on. This Metric helps them to reflect on the time required for them to fulfil the customer needs with some new software product features and functionalities.

- **Release stabilization period**: This Metric asks the Scrum Teams to measure their time getting spent on correcting the product issues and problems. This time needs to be measured as a time in between the moment the developers confirm that the bug fix or problem correction is ready to release and the moment it gets released to the production environment, where the customers/end-users need to confirm if it is working fine. This Metric helps them to characterize the actual impact of their poor engineering practices, processes, and way of working.

- **Mean time to repair**: This Metric asks the Scrum Teams to measure the average amount of time it takes for them from when a bug/defect/an error is discovered and when it is fixed. This Metric helps them to expose their obvious knowledge and efficiency to fix their bugs/defects/errors.

- **Customer cycle time**: This Metric asks the Scrum Teams to measure the amount of time from the moment when their work starts on a customer release until the moment it gets released to the production environment, where the customers start to use the same. This Metric helps them to reflect on their evident ability to reach their customers.

- **Lead time**: This Metric asks the Scrum Teams to measure the amount of time from the moment when an idea is recommended as a feature (or a hypothesis is created) until a customer can get an actual benefit from it. This Metric acts as a contributing factor for customer satisfaction and can get changed based upon various types of customers and software products being used by them.

- **Lead time for changes**: This Metric asks the Scrum Teams to measure the amount of time getting spent by them from the moment they commit their code in their version control system until the moment it runs successfully in the production environment, where the customers need to start to make use of its underlying functionalities.

- **Deployment frequency**: This Metric asks the Scrum Teams to measure the number of times they have deployed and released a new version of their working software product to their customers.

- **Time to restore service**: This Metric asks the Scrum Teams to measure the amount of time between the start of a service outage in the production environment (where the customers/end-users are using every product functionality as a service) and the recovery, restoration point of full availability of the same service.

- **Time-to-learn**: This Metric asks the Scrum Teams to measure the total time required for them to sketch, build, deliver an idea or an enhancement to their customers and learn from their usage patterns, behaviors, and feedbacks.

- **Time to remove impediment**: This Metric asks the Scrum Teams to measure their average amount of time which they are spending from the moment when an impediment is raised until the moment when it is resolved. It acts as a supporting factor to Lead Time as well as Team's overall satisfaction level.

- **Time to pivot**: This Metric asks the Scrum Teams to measure their exact business agility, which represents the time passed between when the team members receive any feedback or any new information and when they enact on/respond back to the same.

Considering the EBM framework's Ability to Innovate aspect, following are the sample measurements that can be explored and evaluated by the Scrum Teams as Metrics:

- **Innovation rate**: This Metric asks the Scrum Teams to measure the percentage of effort or cost getting spent by them to develop and deliver any new product features and functionalities, which is separated by the total effort or cost. This helps them to understand their own capacity to address any new product capabilities by considering the customer needs and requirements.

- **Defect trends**: This Metric asks the Scrum Teams to measure the specific patterns in their bugs/defects since their last measurement, where a bug/defect is a product functionality, which is not working as expected and which diminishes the value proposition of the working software product for its customers/end-users.

- **On-product index**: This Metric asks the Scrum Teams to measure and assess the percentage of time getting spent by them, while working on the software product and the customer value associated with it.

- **Installed version index**: This Metric asks the Scrum Teams to measure the total number of versions of their software product that are being supported by them. This provides them a valuable insight about how much effort, time, and cost they are spending to support and maintain any of the available, older, existing versions of their software product.

- **Technical debt index**: This Metric asks the Scrum Teams to measure the amount of time and effort they are spending on any additional development, testing, and delivery-specific activities caused by any existing Technical Debt created by them only. It has an adverse impact on the iterative and incremental delivery of customer value, as it has a direct correlation with a preventable surge in wastes and risks being created by them.

- **Production incident count**: This Metric asks the Scrum Teams to measure the number of times the Developers were interrupted to fix any issue or problem (called as incidents getting reported by the customers) in an already installed and running software product or service. The number and frequency of incidents help them to signify the stability of the software product or service.

- **Active product (code) branches**: This Metric asks the Scrum Teams to measure the number of different versions of their software product or service. It provides them a perception about the possible impact of changes in those versions and the subsequent correlation to the overall complexity of work.

- **Time spent merging code between branches**: This Metric asks the Scrum Teams to measure the amount of time getting spent by them to apply the required changes across different available versions of their software product or service. It also provides them a perception about the overall possible impact of changes in those versions and subsequent correlation to the overall complexity of the work being performed by them.

- **Time spent context-switching**: This Metric asks the Scrum Teams to measure their time getting lost to the interruptions caused by meetings and calls, their time spent by them while switching between the tasks, and their time getting lost when they are interrupted by the people outside the team, where their help is required. This measurement provides them a simple and straightforward understanding of their time getting spent outside of their Sprint-based work.

- **Change failure rate**: This Metric asks the Scrum Teams to measure the percentage of software product changes already released by them, causing a degraded service and its required remediation such as hotfix, rollback, and patch, and so on.

Scrum Metrics help the Scrum Teams to keep their decision-making transparent and informed throughout the complete process of development and delivery of software product. Developers can make use of the valuable insights from these Metrics to boost their efficiency and to improve their product quality in the upcoming Sprints. Though this is the case, Metrics need not to be an utter priority for the Developers. Rather they should take a reference of following Metrics when it is required. At the same time, they always need to keep their primary focus on the actual development and delivery of customer value-driven needs, wants, desires, and preferences.

- **Formal Code Metrics**: These Metrics need to act as qualitative measurements, using which the Scrum Teams can evaluate on how much work was performed by them to define, measure, and assess some valuable aspects such as the total number of Lines of Code (LOC), Code Coverage, and Clean Code.

- **Developers Efficiency Metrics**: These Metrics ask the Developers to measure and evaluate their overall time spent on the development and delivery of specific tasks and activities, using which they can reflect on their efficiency.

- **Agile/Scrum Process Metrics**: These Metrics need to be effectively used by the Scrum Teams to measure the efficiency of their overall progress in terms of smaller parts of time under their ongoing Sprints.

- **Operational Metrics**: These Metrics help the Scrum Teams to verify the operative capability of their software product and its effective maintenance.

- **Engineering Metrics**: These Metrics help the Scrum Teams to evaluate their Code Quality in terms of their Code and Test Coverage, using which they can get to know about the overall quality of their software product along with the amount of Technical Debt present within its implementation.

- **Customer Satisfaction Metrics**: These Metrics help the Scrum Teams to get some valuable insights and understandings from the customer viewpoints, which can be measured using measurements such as Net Promoter Score (NPS), Customer Satisfaction (CSAT) Score, Customer Effort Score, and many more.

- **Team Satisfaction Metrics**: These Metrics help the Scrum Teams to get some valuable insights and understandings from the viewpoints of the Scrum Team members, which can be measured using measurements such as Team Happiness Index/Metric, Team's Skills Matrix, and many more.

Scrum Teams always need to establish and enhance several Key Performance Indicators (KPIs) and/or Objectives and Key Results (OKRs), using which they can regularly measure their performance against the agreed goals. The KPIs always need to refer to a set of quantifiable measurements used to measure the Scrum Team's overall performance and productivity, whereas the OKRs is a goal-setting framework to define and track the Scrum Team's Objectives and associated outcomes as Key Results. By associating a proper success definition against each KPI and/or OKR, the Scrum Team needs to monitor and realize their current state, which needs to be taken into consideration for an adaptation and evolvement of improvements with the help of lessons learned.

Following is some of the other important measurements, which can be thoroughly explored, evaluated, and applied by the Scrum Teams as Metrics:

- **Sprint Burndown**: The Scrum Teams always need to organize their iterative and incremental development and delivery of working software product functionalities within the time-boxed Sprints. They need to have a forecast on the amount of work which they can complete during the Sprints. The Sprint Burndown helps them to track, trace, and chase their completion of work throughout their active Sprints, where they need to evaluate their progress in terms of the time versus the amount of work left and to be completed by them. By always focusing on the objective of having all the forecasted work to be completed by the end of the ongoing Sprint, the Developers always need to keep an eye on the Sprint Burndown. By following this practice, they need to enact upon any issues, deviations, and delays. Using this Metric, the Scrum Teams can easily get to know about whether they are committing enough amount of work during their ongoing Sprints by avoiding both over allocation and under allocation of work. It helps the Scrum Teams to observe and identify if the work being worked upon by them has been perfectly broken down into granular pieces or not. By using the Sprint Burndown, the Scrum Teams get to know about a correlation between the overall Sprint progression and the remaining work items in an ongoing Sprint.

- **Release Burndown**: Release Burndown helps the Scrum Teams to track and chase their overall progress of development and delivery of working software product over a larger frame of work than the Sprint Burndown. Since the various types of releases such as major/minor/maintenance releases of a high-quality working software product can constitute of multiple Sprints, it is imperative for the Scrum Teams to reflect on any kind of scope creep by anticipating and addressing the changes under the Features to be developed by them. Also, to track their progress and performance toward the completion of releases, any scope creep causing additional work needs to be properly discussed and planned by the means of some proper trade-offs and negotiations between the Product Owner and the Developers. The Release Burndown keeps all the Scrum Team members aware of the details of all the work items to be worked upon by them as a part of their planned releases to release the software product to customers.

- **Velocity**: Velocity is one of the Metrics, which needs to be carefully used by the Scrum Teams. It asks them to measure the average amount of work they are completing during their every Sprint, which ideally needs to be measured using a relative estimate such as Story Points. Velocity is one of the useful Metrics for the Scrum Teams for the purpose of forecasting in their upcoming Sprints. It gives an ability to the Product Owner to foresee how swiftly the Developers can convert the Sprint Backlog into the working software product increments. It allows the Scrum Teams to track and measure their own forecasted and completed work over the period of several Sprints. As they progress ahead with a greater number of Sprints, they will be in a better positioning to predict their work completion more accurately. This can only be possible, if they are estimating their work items properly and they are following all the development, delivery, transparency, collaboration, and teamwork-specific best of the best practices to complete the committed work during their ongoing Sprints. Using this Metric, the Scrum Teams can get a unique opportunity to evaluate an overall impact of their performance on the people, product, and process-specific changes, where they might need to enhance and optimize the relationships within themselves and a full commitment under their way of working.

"Stable Velocity. Sustainable Pace."
- Mike Cottmeyer

A well-maintained and a stable velocity of a Scrum Team always acts as a sign of their continuously improving performance and productivity; however, it always needs to be stabilized after a certain number of Sprints to ensure that they have a stable velocity to achieve and sustain a consistence pace of work and delivery. On the other hand, a decrease in the average velocity of a Scrum Team always acts as a sign that some parts/entities within the Scrum Team's agile way of working and associated processes have become ineffective and inefficient. To avoid any adverse effects of such way of working in near future, such entities need to be investigated by the Scrum Teams.

Scrum Teams have their own unique velocity, which totally depends upon the factors such as complexity, uncertainty, risks, and dependencies associated with the work on which they are supposed to work on. The Stakeholders and the Product Owner need to understand the impact of these factors on the complex process of complex software product development and delivery. By assessing the level of effort and the expected outcome of the work (which also depends upon a Scrum Team's unique interpretation of relative estimates such as Story Points) being performed by the Scrum Teams, the Stakeholders need to resist their temptation of comparing the performance and productivity of various Scrum Teams based on their individual velocities.

By revisiting the Scrum Team's relative estimation process, any decent fluctuation in the velocity needs to be investigated by the Scrum Team members. In this process, they need to utilize their Sprint Retrospectives to focus on various aspects such as unanticipated challenges, which were not considered by them while estimating the work items. They need to find some better ways of breaking down the work items and discovering some of these challenges to push them beyond their capabilities and limits along with their faithfulness toward their already established agile way of working and its associated best practices to be further improved by them.

- **Control Charts**: The Scrum Teams need to make use of Control Charts to focus on their Cycle Time. The Scrum Teams with a quicker, shorter, and consistent Cycle Time are always likely to have higher productivity and predictability, while delivering the work items during their ongoing Sprints. By assessing the Cycle Time, the Scrum Teams try to become well-organized and adaptable, as the results of shifts for any alternatives getting applied to their way of working are immediately noticeable. Such varying alternatives and measures always allow them to make any further changes right away. By looking out at the trends in Control Charts, any fluctuations in Cycle

Time always need to be introspected by the Scrum Teams. Such fluctuations depend upon the Scrum Team's agreed Definition of Done and associated compatibility. Scrum Teams making use of Control Chart and measuring their Cycle Time need to make use of Sprint Retrospectives to inspect the gaps and to improve their estimation process.

- **Cumulative Flow Diagram**: This Metric can be used by the Scrum Teams to measure their overall amount of Work in Progress (WIP) at any state and at any given point of time in their ongoing Sprints. It helps them to recognize any of the hindrances that might lower down their anticipated speed and pace of their development and delivery specific way of working processes.

- **Unchecked Backlog Growth**: This Metric asks the Scrum Teams to evaluate on any unchecked growth of Product Backlog over time. It is mostly caused by lack of clean-up activities under their Product Backlog. Scrum Teams need to continuously monitor their Product Backlog Change Rate by observing the rate of work items being added, updated, removed, and reprioritized by the Product Owner and the Developers.

- **Product Backlog Change Rate**: It is the overall rate of the work items being added, updated, removed, and reprioritized by the Scrum Teams in their Product Backlog. If this rate is less, then the Scrum Teams (and especially the Product Owner) need to ensure that the software product specific functionalities through the applicable customer/end-user needs are getting captured properly. This needs to be done by an enablement of open feedback loops with their customers/end-users.

- **Percent Complete and Accurate**: This Metric asks the Scrum Teams to measure the total number of completed, fully functional, and acceptable work items. It helps them to make their delivery better and safer by measuring their rate of completion and the overall quality of working software product functionalities.

- **Flow Efficiency**: This Metric asks the Scrum Teams to measure the ratio of the time spent by them while working on a work item versus the time taken by them to complete the same. It helps them to regulate their WIP limits to minimize the delays.

- **Time Blocked per Story**: This Metric asks the Scrum Teams to measure the amount of time for which a work item was blocked during its development and/or delivery. It helps them to ascertain the overall cost of delay, so that they can collectively and proactively recommend some meaningful improvements.

- **Mean Time Between Failures**: This Metric asks the Scrum Teams to measure the average predicted elapsed time between the inherent software product system/service breakdowns and failures getting faced by their customers.

It helps them to improve their processes to overcome such failures in the future.

- **Mean Time to Recovery**: This Metric asks the Scrum Teams to measure the average time that their software product/service takes to recover from any failure getting faced by their customers. It helps them to improve their processes to minimize the recovery time in case of any failures in the future.

- **Blocker Clusters**: This Metric asks the Scrum Teams to measure the frequency and consolidation of impediments blocking completion of work items. It helps them to find out the causes behind such impediments further causing deviations and delays, so that they can collectively and proactively recommend some meaningful improvements.

- **Escaped Bugs/Defects**: This Metric asks the Scrum Teams to measure the total count of bugs/defects, which are being reported by the customers in the production environment. It helps them to find out the root causes behind such bugs/defects and to reflect on why they were not found prior to the release.

- **Escaped Bug/Defect Resolution Time**: This Metric asks the Scrum Teams to measure the amount of time required for them to resolve the escaped bugs/defects. It helps them to figure out its impact on the cost of resolution of bugs.

- **Release Success Rate**: This Metric asks them to measure the ratio of their customer accepted versus customer rejected software product releases.

    It helps them to assess and enhance their way of working processes by considering their overall collaboration, communication, engagement, and shared understanding with the customers/end-users.

- **Release Time**: This Metric asks the Scrum Teams to measure the amount of time required for them to release their working software product to the production environment, where the customers can start to make use of it. It asks them to evaluate and assess some better ways of making their working software product increments available for their customers, early and often.

- **Time Since Last Release**: This Metric asks the Scrum Teams to measure the amount of time they have released their software product to their customers/end-users since last time. It asks them to assimilate a real-time customer/end-user feedback for the purpose of any improvements and enhancements.

- **Cost Per Release**: This Metric asks the Scrum Teams to measure the total cost taken by them to complete their software product release to their customers. It asks them to have a proper consideration of all the financial factors to decide on when they should be releasing their software product.

- **Release NPS**: This Metric asks the Scrum Teams to measure the customer's or end-user's reactions against the working software product being used by them. It needs to be a quantitative feedback (to be measured using some numbers or ratings) along with a qualitative feedback (to be measured using some viewpoints and reviews). The team needs to collect and analyse these feedback measurements to agree on the next set of action items to be addressed by them. Action items help them to determine if they need to develop and deliver any new features aligned with the feedbacks received.

- **Release Adoption Rate**: This Metric asks the Scrum Teams to assess the total number of existing customers/end-users who have upgraded themselves to the latest version of the software product. It also asks them to assess the total number of new customers/end-users getting onboarded to make use of their software product. This way they can perform an overall assessment of the ROI on their software product development and delivery specific investments by validating their own assumptions.

- **Business Value Burnup**: This Metric asks the Scrum Teams to measure the amount of customer value provided by every work item completed by them within their ongoing Sprints by allowing their Stakeholders to operate on the expected ROI.

- **Risk Burndown**: This Metric asks the Scrum Teams to measure the amount of recognized and absolute risks over a period. It expects them to continuously self-manage and reduces any such risks occurring under their way of working.

- **Push/Pull**: This Metric asks the Scrum Teams to measure the ratio of work items completed versus work items added by them. Though it helps them to balance their work in upcoming Sprints, they should refer to velocity to understand their progress.

- **Product Forecast**: This Metric asks the Scrum Teams to forecast the upcoming trends in near future based upon their own past best-case and worst-case performance in terms of completion of work items during the Sprints.

- **Product NPS**: This Metric asks the Scrum Teams to evaluate and reflect on, whether their customers/end-users would like to refer, recommend their software product to others or not. Using this Metric, they can collect some simple and useful feedbacks to cross-check, if their software product meets their customer/end-user needs or not.

- **User Analytics**: This Metric asks the Scrum Teams to classify their customer/end-user usage patterns, while they are making use of the software product functionalities. It helps them to enact upon the usefulness of their overall development and delivery-specific activities by considering such evolving usage patterns.

- **Test Coverage**: This Metric asks the Scrum Teams to measure the percentage of codebase getting validated and verified by various automated tests. It helps them to improve their test coverage to maintain it at an agreed benchmarking.

- **Build Time**: This Metric asks the Scrum Teams to measure the total execution time it takes for them to run their automated builds and tests. It asks them to act against any sluggish automated builds, deployments, and test execution, which is causing any unnecessary deviations and delays.

- **Defect Density**: This Metric asks the Scrum Teams to measure the percentage of defects getting occurred under each module/component of their software product. Defect Density is usually determined across the software product's features, functionalities, and system architecture, where the Scrum Teams can categorize and work to improve the required quality.

- **Code Churn**: This Metric asks the Scrum Teams to measure the number of Lines of Code (LOC) changed by them to complete their work items. Using this Metric, they can reflect on an overall stability of their code constructs.

- **Code Ownership**: This Metric asks the Scrum Teams to measure the frequency at which they are introducing changes to their existing code base and committing those changes. It encourages the Developers to improve their collective code ownership.

- **Code Complexity**: This Metric asks the Scrum Teams to measure cyclomatic complexity of their existing code base using some tools. It helps them to do some research through which they can explore and apply some advanced engineering practices to follow and establish various aspects of clean code.

- **Coding Standards Adherence**: This Metric asks the Scrum Teams to assess on how they are aligned on their system architecture and engineering-specific best practices and standards. They need to continuously evaluate their current positioning against such best practices and standards, so that they can address the scope for improvement, if any.

- **Crash Rate**: This Metric asks the Scrum Teams to measure the frequency of problems, which caused their software product any failures/crashes. It allows them to perform the root cause analysis to reduce such failures/crashes in the future.

- **Failed Deployments**: This Metric asks the Scrum Teams to measure the number of times they faced issues related to deployments during every release of the software product in the production environment. They need to track and maintain a record of all such failed deployments and the reasons behind the failures under a checklist, using which they can cross-check before doing their next set of deployments and ensure that the deployments are issue free.

- **Committed PBIs/User Stories versus Completed PBIs/User Stories**: This Metric can be used by the Scrum Teams to measure their effectiveness and efficiency considering their knowledge, skill sets, and capabilities. By looking at the actual gaps and reasons behind the PBIs/User Stories committed by them and which they could not complete by the end of the Sprint, they need to perform a proper introspection. This prevents them from repeating similar kind of mistakes in their upcoming Sprints.

- **Unfinished Stories**: This Metric asks the Scrum Teams to reflect on how many PBIs/User Stories they were unable to complete at the end of the Sprint, especially because they were unable to meet the Definition of Done and/or the Acceptance Criteria. This Metric always asks them to check their adherence to the Definition of Done and the Acceptance Criteria, using which they can concentrate on getting things done during their every ongoing Sprint.

- **Technical Debt Evaluation and Management**: This Metric helps the Scrum Teams to assess their overall Technical Debt by considering the entire system architecture, code base, and other artifacts of working software product. This avoids the occurrence of any known Technical Debt, which might cause some issues at the time of delivery of product increments toward the end of every ongoing Sprint. It is hence required for the Scrum Teams to revisit all the areas of development and delivery to identify and enact on any existing Technical Debt.

- **Quality Delivered to Customer**: This Metric plays an important role to enable the Scrum Teams to evaluate the customer value-based outcomes being developed and delivered by them at the end of every Sprint. They need to utilize their Sprint Reviews to reflect on customer feedbacks and suggestions to ensure that they are always delivering the right software product and delivering the software product right.

- **Sprint Scope and Sprint Goal-related understanding of Developers**: Having a clear and proper idea of Sprint Scope and Sprint Goal Metrics is a subjective measure of the overall interaction between the Scrum Team and Stakeholders, using which the team needs to focus on their Sprint deliverables. It is required for their Sprint Scope and Sprint Goal to state the overall objective of their Sprints. The Scrum Master needs to guide them while creating such Scope and Goal.

- **Static Code Analysis**: Static Code Analysis asks the Scrum Teams to measure the quality of their code by performing a static analysis of code using some tools. This analysis needs to be a simple code analysis, where the tools need to automatically monitor the code to identify and report any Technical Debt, bugs, defects, improper code constructs, functional and non-functional design-specific and implementation-specific issues, code smells, and so on. Based upon the results received, the Developers need to enact and improve their code constructs accordingly.

- **Dynamic Code Analysis**: Dynamic Code Analysis asks the Scrum Teams to measure the quality of their code by performing a dynamic analysis of code using some tools, where the Developers need to run their code by running their software product and by evaluating any possible issues mainly based upon the end-user's perspective. Based upon the results received, the Developers need to enact and improve their code constructs accordingly.

- **Speed of Delivery**: This Metric asks the Scrum Teams to evaluate their speed of delivery/planned releases of working software product increments to their customers/end-users. By evaluating their own delivery/release frequency, they need to reflect on how often they are releasing their software product functionalities to the production environment for their customers/end-users. They also need to reflect on how long it takes and how easy it is for them to release those functionalities in the production environment. Based on such a variety of observations, they need to continuously enhance their processes to improve on.

- **Health of the current Sprint**: The Scrum Teams need to make use of this Metric to get a visual display of how they are performing in their current ongoing Sprint. By looking at the various measures through this Metric, they can check and enact upon scope for improvement, if any.

- **Defect Analysis**: Defect Analysis can help the Scrum Teams to understand about how many defects they have found during their development and delivery of working software product and after its release to their customers. They can also get to know about how many defects they have deferred to the next release, how many enhancements are getting suggested by their customers/end-users, and the percentage of automated test coverage. Developers need to introspect and act upon the build, user acceptance testing, and production-specific bugs by making use of automated testing and CI/CD implementations. By understanding the number of build-related defects, they need to gather insights about, whether they need to change any of their development and delivery-specific processes to find such defects at the earliest. They need to understand that any delay in their defect discovery can have its impact on the release expectations from the Stakeholders point of view. Developers also need to track the number of days they have taken for the PBI/User Story acceptance because of the defect discovery. They need to lower their overall time required to fix the defects.

- **Team Dependencies**: This Metric asks the Scrum Team to measure and assess the number and types of dependencies occurring within and outside the Scrum Team. Such dependencies always have a major impact on their Lead Time and Cycle Time. The measurement and assessment of such dependencies expect from the Scrum Teams that they are finding out the patterns of dependencies to ensure that they are resolving similar kind of dependencies in their upcoming Sprints.

- **Interruptions**: The Scrum Team members need to assess on how many times they need to face any interruptions to their work in progress during their ongoing Sprints. The rate of interruption depends upon many factors such as internal/external issues, customer/end-user proposed enhancements, maintenance/support specific work, and so on. By assessing such interruptions, the Scrum Team members can understand, where they are spending their effort and time outside of the Sprint Backlog-based work and the Product Owner can also make some better decisions accordingly.

- **Learning Log**: This Metric asks the Scrum Teams to measure all the lessons the Scrum Team members have learned so far, using which they can focus on the important aspect of experience-based/experience-led learning throughout their Sprints.

- **Whole Team Contribution**: This Metric asks the Scrum Teams to assess how many Scrum Team members are collectively contributing to the overall development and delivery process of completion of work items from their inception till their conception. It helps them to assess and improve their teamwork and collaboration aspect.

Apart from all the previously mentioned advanced Scrum Metrics, the Scrum Team members always need to evaluate their overall enthusiasm. The Scrum Master always needs to recognize the symptoms negatively impacting their enthusiasm and needs to evaluate on all the possible set of actions to prevent and/or settle such symptoms. The Scrum Master always needs to observe and sense the enthusiasm and engagement of Scrum Team members. To evaluate their individual and collective happiness index, the Scrum Team members need to reflect on their overall satisfaction, learning, strengths, weaknesses, opportunities, and risks. This helps them to create a thorough transparency by considering their happiness and satisfaction levels. By continuously improving through Sprint Retrospectives, they need to enhance their own ability to revisit and revise their own agile way of working and its associated approaches, processes, and practices. They always need to come up with some better alternatives to make their way of working more effective, engaging, and fun oriented.

It is important for the Scrum Team members to monitor, measure, evaluate, and assess their shared understanding, happiness, satisfaction, morale, productivity, self-organization, self-management, skill sets, capabilities, risks, dependencies, alternatives, continuous learning, experimentation, dynamics, culture, trust, transparency, priorities, interests, collaboration, communication, co-operation, co-ordination, enthusiasm, efficiency, effectiveness, success and failure rate of Sprint Goal achievement, time to market, cost of change, adherence to the Scrum values and rules, practices, processes, standards, and so on.

The Scrum Teams should also make use of some other applicable metrics, which can help them to analyse and represent their evaluation of psychological safety. In today's world of Volatility, Uncertainty, Complexity, and Ambiguity (VUCA), the psychological safety needs to act as a measure of a Scrum Team's overall ability to sustain and perform. The Scrum Team members need to analyse and represent their own evaluation of reliability, flexibility, and collaboration, using which they are supposed to perform and deliver the anticipated things on time along with a proper delegation and an even distribution of work among themselves.

By representing their mastery, autonomy, and purpose, the Scrum Team members always need to find a meaningful purpose to work on. While having a proper structure and clarity, they need to reflect on their own ability to define and to enact upon the evident roles and responsibilities to achieve their common, shared goals and objectives. They need to evaluate the potential impact of all the work they are doing, to ensure that it is effective for them to address a positive change in the complex software product development environment.

As shown in the following figure, the Scrum Teams can make use of the Agile Fluency Model (given at **https://www.agilefluency.org/**). It helps them to check their maturity based on their own capability development. As they adopt a Scrum-based agile way of working, a cultural shift needs to happen within the Scrum Team, where the team members need to focus on the customer value aspect by demonstrating the Focusing fluency. They also need to have a command on various advanced engineering practices by enhancing their skill sets and by demonstrating the Delivering fluency. When a shift of organizational culture asks them to utilize their capabilities to achieve the value-driven outcomes, they need to expect and deliver such outcomes by demonstrating the Optimizing fluency and by Strengthening themselves.

Figure 12.4: The Agile Fluency Model given at https://www.agilefluency.org/

Scrum Teams always need to understand that a smaller number of Metrics can help them to have simple measurements. The Scrum Teams also need to use the suitable Scrum Metrics to measure the value-driven outcomes. Metrics always need to be explored, selected, applied, and assessed by them, to measure the most applicable things which matter them the most.

Points to remember

- Making use of applicable and appropriate Scrum Metrics to assess the Scrum Team's productivity and performance is one of the key essentials for the Scrum Team. The outcomes of their performance and collaborative efforts through these Metrics can certainly help them to improve their Scrum-based agile way of working and its associated processes.

- Metrics allow all the Scrum Team members to measure, track, trace, enhance, and improve their overall performance to make their existing people, product, and process-specific entities better.

- A continuous assessment of various aspects such as value, productivity, predictability, stability, quality, collaboration, competence, and many more, need to be considered by the Scrum Teams while defining and establishing their required Scrum Metrics.

- The Scrum Teams always need to understand that the empirical testimony of their overall progress can only be uncovered through their capability of iterative development and delivery of high-quality working software product increments.

- The Scrum Teams need to remember that the Scrum Guide does not recommend any specific Scrum Metrics that they need to use.

- Scrum Teams need to come up with a proper understanding and evaluation after exploration of any of the Metrics, which they want to make use of. It is required for the Scrum Teams to choose their Scrum Metrics sensibly.

- While addressing the expectations of Stakeholders, the Scrum Teams tend to feel dependent on the Scrum Metrics. These Metrics can differ at the different stages of their applicability and suitability; however, the most important thing is always to have the Scrum Team's lookout on whether they are doing better than their last introspection or not. To reflect on this, it is also crucial for them to perform regular introspections through continuous inspections and adaptations to continuously learn and improve.

- By utilizing the unique characteristics of frameworks like Data Insight Belief Bet (DIBB) and Evidence Based Management (EBM), the Scrum Teams can analyse, assess, measure, manage, and enhance the customer value getting delivered by them. The DIBB framework asks the Scrum Teams to analyse the working software product's customer/end-user usage patterns and consequent data by evaluating the required insights in it. The EBM framework asks the Scrum Teams to concentrate on improvement of customer value-driven outcomes and minimization of risks.

- Scrum Metrics always help the Scrum Teams to keep their decision-making transparent and informed throughout the complete process of development and delivery of a high-quality working software product.

- Scrum Teams always need to establish and enhance several Key Performance Indicators (KPIs) and/or Objectives and Key Results (OKRs), using which they can regularly measure their performance against their agreed goals.

- The Scrum Team members need to evaluate their enthusiasm. The Scrum Master needs to recognize the symptoms negatively impacting it and needs to evaluate on all the possible set of actions to prevent and/or settle such symptoms. He/she needs to observe and sense the enthusiasm and engagement of the Scrum Team members.

- By evaluating their happiness index, the Scrum Team members need to reflect on their satisfaction, learning, strengths, weaknesses, opportunities, and risks. This helps them to create a thorough transparency by considering their own happiness and satisfaction levels.

- It is important for the Scrum Team members to monitor, measure, evaluate, and assess their shared understanding, happiness, satisfaction, morale, productivity, self-organization, self-management, skill sets, capabilities, risks, dependencies, alternatives, continuous learning, experimentation, dynamics, culture, trust, transparency, priorities, interests, collaboration, communication, co-operation, co-ordination, enthusiasm, efficiency, effectiveness, success and failure rate of Sprint Goal achievement, time to market, cost of change, adherence to the Scrum values and rules, practices, processes, standards, and so on.

- The Scrum Teams should also make use of some other applicable metrics, which can help them to analyse and represent their evaluation of psychological safety.

- The Scrum Team members need to analyse and represent their own evaluation of reliability, flexibility, and collaboration, using which they are supposed to perform and deliver the anticipated things on time along with a proper delegation and an even distribution of work among themselves.

- Scrum Teams always need to understand that a smaller number of Metrics can help them to have simple measurements. The Scrum Teams also need to use the suitable Scrum Metrics to measure the value-driven outcomes. Metrics always need to be explored, selected, applied, and assessed by them, to measure the most applicable things which matter them the most.

In the next chapter, readers will get to know about some of the advanced Scrum add-ons/techniques to help the Scrum Teams to scale up their Scrum-based agile way of working. They will also get to know about some evaluation techniques to reflect on the real needs and possible reasons for scaling their Scrum-based agile way of working, where they need to explore and apply various Scaling Scrum Frameworks-based approaches.

CHAPTER 13

Add-ons for Scaling Scrum

Introduction

In this chapter, readers will get to know about some of the advanced Scrum add-ons/techniques to help the Scrum Teams to scale up their Scrum-based agile way of working. They will also get to know about some of the important factors for a proper evaluation and assessment to reflect on the real needs and possible reasons for scaling their Scrum-based agile way of working, where they need to explore and apply various Scaling Scrum Frameworks-based approaches.

Objective

After studying this chapter, you should be able to:

- Understand various considerations for the Scrum Teams while exploring, applying, and establishing the Scaling Scrum Approach.

- Understand the concept of Scaling Scrum at various Organizational Levels.

- Understand the essential criteria while selecting a suitable Scaling Scrum Approach.

- Understand the considerations along with the main reasons/needs behind a required evaluation to be performed by the agile organizations to make use of a suitable Scaling Scrum Framework.

- Understand various Scaling Scrum Approaches.
- Recognize the variations and differences between various Scaling Scrum Approaches.

Steve 'The Program Manager' (in a discussion with Siva 'The Agile Coach'):

"I think, we should not restrict our agile transformation to these 4 Scrum Teams. We need to explore a mechanism to scale up and enhance our Scrum based agile way of working to have an appropriate structure, alignment, and governance in place. It should also help and support us to eliminate our functional, non-functional, cultural, technical, and operational issues. Hope I am making sense, Siva!"

Siva 'The Agile Coach' (smiling and replying):

"How is your 5-year-old doing with her new bicycle? Does it still have side wheels?"

Steve (replying immediately):

"Excuse me, but are you kidding? We are here to discuss on our agile transformation roadmap."

Siva (smiling and replying):

"Yes Steve, but answer my question first! Whether your daughter can ride her bicycle on her own?"

Steve:

"Huh! She is a beginner. So, no doubt, she still needs a support of side wheels."

Siva (replying immediately):

"Can't you simply remove those side wheels and ask her to ride on her own?"

Steve (replying with a worried tone):

"How is that possible, Siva? She has just started to learn cycling. I mean to say, in last week only!"

Siva:

"Yeah! So, when it comes to the way of working of our other Scrum Teams, they are also beginners and they need some time to improve. We can explore on a suitable Scaling Scrum Framework to cater your request; however, we need to keep some checkpoints on our agile transformation roadmap to evaluate rest of the Scrum Teams. Once it is done, we can surely decide on where exactly we need to go! Okay?"

Steve (smiling and replying):

"Okay, Siva! I think, such assessment will really help us to look at our next steps. We can also avoid any major accidents in future. I also want to know if we will need any side wheels there. Haha!"

A single Scrum Team working on the incremental and iterative development and delivery of a single software product and making use of a well-established of Scrum-based agile way of working should ideally have a single Product Backlog. The Scrum Teams need to utilize their planned Sprints to deliver a significant customer value through the PBIs/User Stories being selected by the Developers under their Sprint Backlog. The Product Backlog needs to specify an input to every Sprint. The Developers need to use the same input to deliver a fully functional and potentially shippable software product increment by the end of every Sprint.

If the scope of the working software product is much more than the capacity of an ideal size of a single Scrum Team (typically 10 or fewer team members) to work on, then it is required for them to scale up their Scrum-based agile way of working. In this case, the Product Owner also needs to utilize more than one Scrum Team, where the total number of Scrum Teams and their respective structures always need to be kept a bit flexible. This approach of scaling up the Scrum-based agile way of working for more than one Scrum Team can be called as Scaling Scrum. The primary reason for this approach is to develop and deliver the working software product features and functionalities faster, sooner, and better, which needs to be done by employing a greater number of Scrum Teams to work on a single Product Backlog.

> *"Values and principles scale, but practices are context sensitive. We all know it is hard to improve, but we know that we cannot buy our way to a better future."*
> *- Ken Schwaber*

As per the Scrum Guide, the ideal size of a Scrum Team is typically 10 or fewer team members. Still, they might have a need of more team members to work on a big software product. Their distinct knowledge, experience, skill sets, and capabilities need to be always utilized for one or more number of Sprints. While Scaling Scrum, all the core Scrum Values, Scrum Artifacts, Scrum Roles, Scrum Events, Scrum Components, and Scrum Rules need to be properly established, engaged, and utilized by all the Scrum Teams. It always helps them to strengthen their own inspection and adaptation-based agile way of working in both short as well as long term. It also creates a proper transparency, openness, risk regulation, and an encouragement for innovation, experimentation, collaboration, and co-ordination by boosting their overall productivity and performance to be more effective and efficient.

The Product Owner and the Stakeholders need to understand the fact that, multiple Scrum Teams need to work together on a single Product Backlog. As the Scrum Team members work together by showcasing their highest level of collaboration, their common, shared understanding gets increased through their continuous interactions. While Scaling Scrum, it is hence required for the Product Owner to thoroughly evaluate all the pros and cons of the team structure getting formed with multiple Scrum Teams in it. The Scaling Scrum approach-based way of working needs to operate based on those multiple Scrum Teams to accomplish a single Product Goal. They need to apply all the required techniques and processes to organize and to work on their Product and Sprint Backlogs, to resolve their dependencies, to integrate their work, and to deliver high-quality working software product increments.

While establishing an agreed Scaling Scrum approach, the Scrum Teams need to contribute with a joint effort/collaboration from all the sides. They need to be transparent toward the process of Empiricism. They need to emphasize on the measurement of customer value-based outcomes being generated by multiple Scrum Teams working on a single Product Backlog.

They need to continuously consider, evaluate, assess, and improve on various aspects such as the customer value getting delivered by them, the frequency of software product increment releases, the techniques and processes to be explored and applied by them to develop, integrate, and deliver their software product as per their anticipated release frequency, the measurement, evaluation, and assessment of development, integration, and delivery effort and practices of their software product releases, their Return on Investment (ROI), the overall costs and benefits against their ROI as per their anticipated release frequency, and the possible alternatives to improve their productivity, outcome-based customer value delivery, and time to market, to reduce their costs, and so on. The following figure shows various levels through which the agile organizations can scale up their Scrum-based agile way of working:

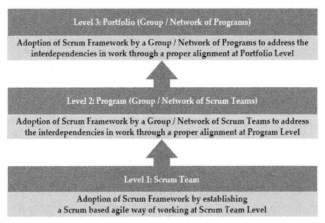

Figure 13.1: *Scaling Scrum at various organizational levels*

As the general process and its associated standards for the development and delivery of a high-quality software product is complex, it is always required for the agile organizations to continuously explore a suitable Scaling Scrum Approach, which needs to be applied beyond their Scrum-based agile way of working at three key levels. These three key levels are - Scrum Team level, Program, level and Portfolio level. While performing the explorations, they need to align their agile way of working by addressing any known inter-team dependencies and by also ensuring the outcome-based customer value with a cost-efficient and on time delivery.

The Scrum Framework always asks the Scrum Teams to focus on being compatible to change. It helps them to bring in a supreme agility at the Team level. The Scaling Scrum Frameworks-based approaches ask the Scrum Teams to enable and enrich their agility at scale. They help them to bring in agility at Program and Portfolio levels by establishing the required regulations, procedures, processes, and techniques to safeguard their agile way of working. Scaling needs to happen with a group/ network of multiple Scrum Teams under a Program and/or with a group/network of multiple Programs under a Portfolio of an organization.

While applying the Scaling Scrum approach at the three key levels, the agile organizations need to review and understand the overall level of maturity of their Scrum Teams. It makes them easy to reduce any of the possible risks for the selection of a proper Scaling Scrum approach with their unique organizational scale in place. They also need to emphasize on the following essential criteria, while selecting a suitable Scaling Scrum approach.

- There always needs to be a proper buy-in, support, and sponsorship from the executive leadership. Any Scaling Scrum approach from the Scrum Team level to the Portfolio/Organizational level requires a substantial cost, effort, and time. It also needs a well-balanced investment to be effective. Hence, the leadership and the key decision-makers always need to be evident about the anticipated outcomes.

- The Scrum Teams, Programs, and Portfolios need to be properly aligned, so that they can act and work under a self-organizing, self-managing, and cross-functional structure of agile way of working. They need to have a realistic common, shared vision and some clearly defined, measurable goals and objectives to collectively work on.

- They need to have a proper understanding and knowledge acquisition about agile values, principles, Scrum-based agile way of working, and its associated processes, while applying the Scaling Scrum approach. If there are any understanding gaps causing a poor implementation, they need to have a mechanism in place to bridge those gaps with an applicable and appropriate training, coaching, and mentoring from the Product Owners and/or Scrum Masters.

- Teams need to make use of effective Product Backlog Management techniques to ensure that they have all the customer/end-user requirements captured through the PBIs/User Stories under their Product Backlog. They need to make use of some of the effective Relative Estimation and Scrum Events-specific techniques to enrich their overall agile way of working. Teams also need to make use of the applicable advanced engineering practices, tools, and technologies to improve their technical agility.

- Teams always need to deliver the finest possible working software product increment at the end of every Sprint. They might also need to integrate with any of the applicable non-technical teams to ensure the overall functional stability and quality of their software product releases. It allows them to establish required working relationships within the organization. It also helps them to deliver their software product releases, as per the customer expectations by resolving cross-team dependencies, if any.

When there are multiple Scrum Teams working on a software product development effort at Program level, there are possibilities of disorganizations and inadequacies. With a greater number of Scrum Teams, greater number of issues might occur. The same problem might also occur at the Portfolio level due to a greater number of Programs within it. It is hence required for the agile organizations to explore and select a suitable Scaling Scrum Framework to have a proper alignment at almost every level of the organization. However, following are the main reasons/needs behind such evaluation to make use of a suitable Scaling Scrum Framework:

- To manage a Program with multiple Scrum Teams performing software product development and delivery. To support more than one Scrum Team under a Program/Portfolio. To handle the inter-team dependencies.

- To manage a Portfolio with multiple Programs performing software product development and delivery. To support more than one Program under a Portfolio, where one Program can have multiple Scrum Teams in it.

- To scale up a shared vision, strategy, and alignment from the Team level to the Program level and finally to the Portfolio/Organizational level.

- To deliver the Product Backlog features and functionality at a rapid and consistent pace by employing additional Scrum Teams within a Program.

- To co-ordinate and sync up the overall delivery of multiple Scrum Teams by properly integrating their working software product increments.

- To bring together multiple Scrum Teams under a Program/Portfolio, so that they can collectively collaborate and achieve their agreed, common purpose. To co-ordinate and synchronize their Scrum-based agile way of working.

- To provide a proper alignment between multiple Scrum Teams and their applicable Stakeholders, who are the supportive decision-makers of value optimization aspect.

- To provide a proper alignment between the multiple Product Owners for the purpose of an appropriate and fast decision-making to decide on what is next.

- To provide a proper visibility mechanism and to ensure a good transparency and commitment to the top-level management and leadership of the agile organization.

- To ease up the complexities and bottlenecks through effective interactions and sharing of best practices across multiple Scrum Teams under a Program/Portfolio.

- To increase the productivity of multiple Scrum Teams under a Program/Portfolio.

- To analyse and to meticulously evaluate all the pros, cons, and impact while scaling up the Scrum-based agile way of working at Program/Portfolio levels.

- To identify and to mitigate any issues, risks, and dependencies and to enhance the overall effectiveness and efficiency, while being transparent to multiple Scrum Teams.

- To utilize all the benefits of Scaling Scrum approach to become more agile.

The Scrum Framework is the most commonly and widely used agile framework, which can be scaled beyond a single Scrum Team; however, multiple Scrum Teams making use of a Scaling Scrum approach always need to be more apprehensive with what kind of software products are being developed and delivered by them. Scrum Teams should be also concerned about, how they can effectively and efficiently do the same. They need to reflect on when exactly they should apply the Scaling Scrum approach to multiple Scrum Teams.

As the Scrum Framework always asks the Scrum Teams to focus on customer value and outcomes-based delivery of high-quality working software products, they need to look at their individual structure and sizing to anticipate if there is a genuine need for them to scale. If they think that they need team members more than 10, then they must make a consensus-based decision to scale up their Scrum-based agile way of working beyond their Team. In this process, they need to form multiple Scrum Teams with 10 or fewer team members within those individual teams, instead of increasing team members within a single Scrum Team.

There is always a possibility that multiple Scrum Teams might cause some inter-team dependencies and gaps. Each Scrum Team may ask for additional co-ordination with the other Scrum Teams. It might impact the overall software product development and delivery by making it much more complex and complicated.

All the Scrum Teams need to co-ordinate and co-operate with each other to deliver the properly integrated software product increments. They should be always in line with the anticipations of the Product Owner, the Stakeholders, and their customers/end-users. Therefore, the Scrum Teams always need to have a considerable evaluation of various Scaling Scrum approaches, while establishing their Scaling Scrum approach-based agile way of working. If they perfectly scale it up, then it can surely result into a much better co-ordination and functioning across multiple Scrum Teams. The following figure shows various considerations for the Scrum Teams to scale up their Scrum-based agile way of working:

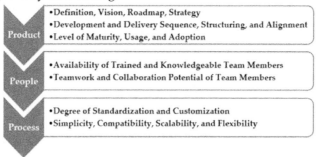

Figure 13.2: *Considerations for Scaling Scrum approach*

Any Scaling Scrum approach always expects multiple Scrum Teams to work together on a software product, where they need to replicate their Scrum-based agile way of working, only at a larger scale. By doing the same, the Scrum Teams can have a superior outlook toward the work being performed by them by having a presence of much better transparency. It offers more value and quality to their customers/end-users, to whom they are supposed to deliver their working software product increments.

While evaluating various approaches for Scaling Scrum, the Scrum Teams need to consider various aspects specific to their own software product, people, and processes. They need to consider and agree upon the definition, vision, roadmap, goals, and implementation strategy of the software product to be collectively implemented by them. They need to determine the boundaries for functional, non-functional, and technical areas of the software product. Even though Scaling Scrum has an involvement of multiple Scrum Teams, a proper common, shared understanding of required product specifics makes it possible for them to preserve and emphasize on a collective product ownership as a One Product Team. They need to identify all the possible interdependencies between the product features and functionalities to be implemented by them. They also need to consider their development and delivery sequence along with the level of maturity, usage, and adoption of the software product from the customer's/end-user's unique perspective.

"Great things are done by a series of small things that are brought together."

- Vincent Van Gogh

The overall collaboration and co-ordination within multiple Scrum Teams developing and delivering the working software product also needs to scale up. They need to maintain a single Product Backlog for their software product, which also needs to be fully visible and transparent to all the Scrum Teams. All the required Scrum Events (that is, Sprint, Sprint Planning, Daily Scrum, Sprint Review, and Sprint Retrospective) need to be conducted by them at the Team level, across all the Scrum

Teams. This approach helps everyone to be on the same page by avoiding and/or eliminating any understanding gaps. It helps them to have a formal agreement on what is being planned and how they can collaboratively work together to deliver the same. By enabling an evolving product vision, roadmap, and strategy, all the Scrum Teams need to inspect and adapt under their every Sprint. There needs to be a high availability of trained, skilled, and knowledgeable team members across Scrum Teams. They also need to have an extreme collaboration and teamwork potential.

The Scrum Teams need to have a proper understanding of their own expectations against the Scaling Scrum approach they would like to explore, assess, apply, and utilize. Even though there is no silver bullet, they need to explore and apply a degree of both standardization and customization for the required processes to be established and enhanced under their Scaling Scrum-based agile way of working. Any of the inter-team dependencies need to be properly categorized and visualized by the Scrum Team members, so that they can be accurately communicated, understood, worked upon, and resolved by them.

The inter-team dependencies within multiple Scrum Teams can be related to anything such as the software product development and delivery-specific sequence of activities, any gaps in the knowledge, skill sets, and capabilities of the Scrum Team members, any understanding gaps, any implementation gaps, and so on. The Scrum Teams need to consider all these factors, while selecting a Scaling Scrum approach. While evaluating options for the various Scaling Agile/Scaling Scrum Frameworks and to determine which is the best fit for them, they also need to look at their software product, if it has a single Product Backlog or not.

A single Product Backlog for one software product helps them to have a better alignment, giving them an overview of what they need to do next and uncovering the inter-team dependencies. They also need to decide on, if there can be a single person acting as a Product Owner having the responsibility to manage the Product Backlog. It helps the Scrum Teams to ensure that they have a proper familiarity and transparency with the product features. It also authorizes the effectiveness of Scrum Teams.

"All human beings have the capability of doing what they want, what they're attracted to."

- Jack Kirby

Scrum Teams need to evaluate and reflect on the overall knowledge, skill sets, and capabilities of Developers. When there are inter-team dependencies due to certain skills required to create fully functional and potentially releasable software product increments, they need to have an inter-team alignment. With such alignment, all the Developers need to improve on their skill sets. Scrum Teams also need to have a formal agreement to decide on when a product increment is okay to be confirmed as Done. This agreement needs to validate if the product increment is properly and fully functional, so that it can be deployed to the production environment for their customers/end-users. Inter-team dependencies can cause a significant delay in this process. Hence, a Scaling Scrum approach needs to be applied to take care of such delays. By considering the involvement of Stakeholders, the Scrum Teams need to ensure that they are reviewing their expectations. They need to utilize the characteristics of the Scaling Scrum approach to consider the feedbacks and suggestions of Stakeholders who influence the direction of the product roadmap. This approach helps them to scale up by having many additional roles, but it might slow down the overall decision-making process.

Scrum Teams also need to reflect on the way they would like to plan their Sprints by having some required trade-offs with their Stakeholders. As the features and functionalities of the software product need to be tracked in the PBIs/User Stories under a single Product Backlog, it is important for all the Scrum Teams to plan their work and to demonstrate their potentially releasable product increments, both collectively and competently. This helps them to improve their shared understanding, trust, and transparency. This approach also enables a collective ownership across multiple Scrum Teams, using which they can release their consolidated product increments on time and as per the customer anticipated value proposition. It not only enhances the overall process of their inspection and adaptation, but also helps them to become better at self-managing and self-organizing.

Forming individual Scrum Teams of small size can help the agile organizations to enable a better information and knowledge sharing. Restricting the number of specialized roles within the Scrum Teams can help them to be cross-functional, also reducing any unnecessary internal dependencies. Considering the inter-team dependencies, to maintain a consistent cadence of product increments delivery through two weeks of Sprint length can be a bit challenging thing for the Scrum Teams; however, they need to have a well-co-ordinated pace. Teams need to use the same Sprint lengths and investigate the ways to match each other to integrate their work toward the end of every Sprint. Having a common release definition, roadmap, and strategy across multiple Scrum Teams at scale can help them to have a structured alignment to deliver a series of product releases synchronized with their budgeting cycles.

"There's a big difference between making a simple product and making a product simple."

- Des Traynor

By considering the customer value and by keeping the batch size of the software product releases small and well-prioritized, it can help them to address the customer needs and feedbacks more rapidly. A proper synchronization of Scrum Rules, Scrum Artifacts, Scrum Events, Scrum Roles, and their associated responsibilities across multiple Scrum Teams can help them to perform handful trade-offs and negotiation with their Stakeholders.

The agile organizations struggling with the implementation of Scrum Framework at Team level might think that Scaling Scrum may help them to address their inter-team dependencies. However, they always need to understand that Scaling Scrum will work only if they have a proper implementation of Scrum Framework-based agile way of working at the Team level. Scaling Scrum can work for them only if they understand and apply the real benefits of scaling to become more agile. Scaling Scrum needs to act as an ability to enable and to drive agility at Scrum Team, Program, and Portfolio levels. It needs to be fully explored at the previously mentioned three key levels of an agile organization by applying various techniques, principles, processes, procedures, and practices.

The scaling Scrum approach always needs to act as a cultural transformation, where the people, product, and process specific aspects need to promise an improved collaboration. It also needs to enable the organization's complete capability to implement its strategy with a collection of decentralized and a consensus-based decision-making, faster time to market, superior transparency, better collaboration, and a proper positioning of value delivery.

While establishing a Scaling Scrum approach, the Scrum Teams should identify their current positioning. They need to explore and assess various Scaling Scrum Frameworks against it, so that they can select the most suitable one by marking the same as a baseline for them. However, before selecting and applying a Scaling Scrum Framework, they need to evaluate on if it can resolve their issues. Ideally, they should not scale up their Scrum-based agile way of working until their existing issues with Scrum implementation are not fixed. Many reasons to scale up the Scrum-based agile way of working can be eliminated if the Scrum Teams execute their agreed agile way of working through the properly established Scrum processes.

Though there is no 100% perfect way to have an implementation of a successful Scaling Scrum, there are various frameworks to address the basic needs of the Scaling Scrum approach. While exploring and applying any of these frameworks, the Scrum Teams can integrate some common practices, processes, and techniques. Even though it is not the case that they are completely implementing a Scaling Scrum approach-based agile way of working with the help of any of these frameworks, they can still adopt the underlying patterns. This can help them to continuously advance with the best practices and standards using any of these frameworks to scale up their agile way of working. The following figure shows various popular Scaling Agile/Scrum Frameworks-based approaches being used by agile organizations:

Figure 13.3: Various Scaling Agile/Scrum Frameworks-based approaches

The Scrum of Scrums is one of the most commonly and widely used approaches to scale up Scrum. This approach is created by Jeff Sutherland and it is getting used by many global agile organizations. It is one of the easiest solutions to scale up Scrum beyond the Scrum Team level. Multiple Scrum Teams can add one or more Scrum Events to their existing Scrum-based agile way of working to avoid any of the possible issues and risks with their proper collaboration, self-organization, self-management, cross-functionality, and transparency.

Scrum of Scrums approach always asks the individual representatives from multiple Scrum Teams to co-ordinate, so that the individual Scrum Teams can focus on their own work areas, resolve any inter-team dependencies, and integrate their work. It also allows multiple Scrum Teams to work on a single product, where they need to have a shared understanding and a structured alignment for effective collaboration. The representatives from each Scrum Team need to take a part in the Scrum of Scrums, which is a formal event to be conducted by them based upon their explicit needs. Generally, the Scrum Masters need to be Representatives in the Scrum of Scrums; however, the other Scrum Team members can also act as the same.

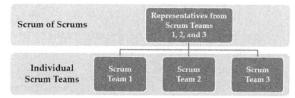

Figure 13.4: Scrum of Scrums

The Scrum of Scrums approach adds an additional Event to a normal Scrum-based agile way of working of Scrum Teams. It is known as the Scrum of Scrums Event only. Except this Event, the way of working with the standard Scrum Roles, Events, and Artifacts remains as it is. Multiple Scrum Teams need to focus on maximizing the product value and resolving the inter-team dependencies. Individual Scrum Teams need to implement small pieces of solutions to be integrated with the solutions from other Scrum Teams toward the end of every Sprint.

Scrum Teams always need to ensure that the representatives joining the Scrum of Scrums Event are asking, sharing, and discussing on the appropriate information by reducing any of possible communication gaps and by increasing the overall transparency within themselves. The Scrum of Scrums Event always needs to be emphasized as the unique opportunity for the Scrum Teams to inspect and adapt. For multiple Scrum Teams working on many features of a software product, a Scrum of Scrum of Scrums approach can be formulated, where the representatives from Scrum of Scrums can line up and get aligned with each other.

During the Scrum of Scrums Event, the Scrum Masters or any other representatives from the individual Scrum Teams need to take a special care to have a proper alignment between the multiple Scrum Teams being represented by them. They need to discuss on some better alternatives to improve their agile way of working through their collaborative interactions. The Product Owner role in Scrum of Scrums stays as it is. The Developers need to co-ordinate with their respective Scrum of Scrums representatives to notify the issues, dependencies, risks, and progress. This approach does not have any impact on the standard Scrum Artifacts.

All the standard Scrum Events also remain intact. The Scrum of Scrums Event always needs to act as an ultimate way to have a proper understanding between the Scrum Teams. It always needs to help them to deal with their inter-team dependencies by having a suitable integration of work. The outcomes from every Scrum of Scrums Event need to be evaluated to reflect on the completed work items and on the next steps for the Scrum Teams. The resolution of dependencies, impediments, issues, concerns, and risks also needs to be done by establishing a proper co-ordination between multiple Scrum Teams and their respective representatives.

Nexus is another Scaling Scrum Framework-based approach created by Ken Schwaber at Scrum.org. Nexus Framework shapes on a basic Scrum-based agile way of working only, but it adds, modifies, or substitutes some of the standard Scrum Roles, Scrum Artifacts, and Scrum Events. Even though the additional Roles, Artifacts, and Events create some additional complexity, Nexus remains aligned with the basic analogy of Scrum Framework. Ideally, it needs to be created as a Scaling Scum solutioning for approximately 3 to 9 Scrum Teams working on a single Product Backlog. Involvement of a greater number of Scrum Teams can result into some possible co-ordination and communication issues. As mentioned under the Nexus Guide (at **https://www.scrum.org/resources/nexus-guide**), there is one defined type of Nexus differing to any other Scaling Scrum Frameworks. The Nexus framework anticipates multiple Scrum Teams to work on the overall structuring, understanding, alignment, and integration-specific issues.

Scrum Teams need to formulate a Nexus Integration Team. They also need to have some events to be organized as a groundwork for the individual Scrum Events per Scrum Team. Nexus Sprint Planning needs to be conducted where the individual representatives of Scrum Teams need to discuss on the overall scope, dependencies, and expectations of software product features to be developed by them. They need to come up with an agreed Nexus Sprint Goal, which needs to be followed by the individual Sprint Planning events by considering the individual Sprint Goals of individual Scrum Teams. Individual Sprint Goals always need to be in line with the Nexus Sprint Goal. Nexus Daily Scrum needs to be used by the individual Scrum Teams to reflect on their current positioning, work alignments, and to discuss on their work integration-specific progress and issues prior to the Daily Scrums of individual Scrum Teams. Nexus Sprint Reviews need to substitute their individual Sprint Reviews. Nexus Retrospectives need to be utilized by them to converse on issues at the Nexus level prior to the next Nexus Sprint Planning and after the Nexus Sprint Reviews.

In a Nexus implementation, the Nexus Integration Team needs be an additional role. The Nexus Integration Team Members always need to ensure that the individual Scrum Teams within a Nexus recognize and implement some practices and tools required to identify any risks, issues, and dependencies and regularly integrate all their Artifacts to an agreed Definition of Done. The Nexus Integration Team Members also need to coach the individual Scrum Teams in a Nexus, so that they can learn and follow the practices and tools. Individual Scrum Teams in a Nexus need to collaborate and the Nexus Integration Team needs to supervise them while being solely accountable for the alignment and integration within them.

A Nexus implementation works with a single Product Backlog and a single Product Owner to be solely responsible for any decision-making. He/she needs to be a part of the Nexus Integration Team carrying the same responsibilities as of the Product Owners within individual Scrum Teams. The individual Scrum Teams need to start and end their individual Sprints at the same time. Sprints need to be of the same length. A Nexus implementation always asks the Developers to work exactly like that of a standard Scrum implementation.

The Developers of the individual Scrum Teams belonging to a Nexus implementation need to be self-managing, self-organizing, and cross-functional. The Scrum Master of the individual Scrum Teams belonging to a Nexus implementation also has the same role as of the Scrum Master within the standard Scrum Teams. There also needs to be a Scrum Master within the Nexus Integration Team who needs to ensure that the overall implementation of Scaling Scrum using the Nexus Framework is well understood and being endorsed by all the individual Scrum Teams within a Nexus. The Nexus implementation asks the Scrum Teams to split the Sprint Planning in two parts, where the first part is generally called as Nexus Sprint Planning. It needs to involve all the team members of all the Scrum Teams. The Nexus Sprint Goal needs to be defined by them, which needs to reflect a minimum collection of all the Sprint Goals of individual Scrum Teams. There also needs to be a Refinement, to be conducted as an additional Event within a Nexus framework-based Scaling Scrum implementation; however, it needs to be done based on the needs and demands of individual Scrum Teams within a Nexus implementation.

Scrum Teams within Nexus framework-based Scaling Scrum implementation need to work on their own Sprint Backlog like the standard Scrum implementation. The working software product increment needs to be integrated as a combination of individual product increments from individual Scrum Teams within a Nexus. It is required for the Scrum Teams to have it as an integrated working software product increment, which needs to be a separate Artifact. Nexus Sprint Backlog needs to be a composite of all the PBIs/User stories from the Sprint Backlogs of the individual Scrum Teams. The PBIs/User Stories always need to follow a proper Definition of Done like a standard Scrum Framework-based implementation.

The primary aim of a Nexus framework-based Scaling Scrum implementation with the multiple Scrum Teams in it is to sustain almost everything that a basic Scrum framework-based implementation demands. The overall structuring, understanding, collaboration, co-ordination, alignment, and integration needs to be covered by the Nexus Events, Artifacts, and Roles. The integration of all the work of the individual Scrum Teams within a Nexus always needs to be done within the Sprint and it always needs to be a crucial entity, which needs to be collaboratively addressed by the Nexus Integration Team.

The Scaled Agile Framework (SAFe) is another Scaling Scrum Framework-based approach. SAFe consists of a set of organization and workflow-specific patterns to implement the required agile practices and processes at an agile enterprise scale. It was originally constructed around various approaches such as agile software product development, lean product development, systems thinking, and so on. It encourages a proper structuring, alignment, collaboration, and an integrated delivery perspective across a significant number of Agile/Scrum Teams. The SAFe framework was created and introduced by Dean Leffingwell. It was originally called as Agile Enterprise Big Picture. As it is a top-down approach of Scaling Scrum, it places the actual purpose of Scrum Framework-based agile way of working under an intense pressure. It uses few additional concepts, practices, and processes because of an inclusion of some additional Roles, Artifacts, and Events within its implementation approach.

SAFe has four primary configurations. They are Essential SAFe, Large Solution SAFe, Portfolio SAFe, and Full SAFe. SAFe asks the software product development teams (called as Agile Teams) to work just like the standard Scrum Teams at the Team level; however, it is not mandatory for them to make use of Scrum Framework only. They can also work using XP, Kanban, and Scrumban Agile Frameworks. The Agile Teams using Scrum Framework need to work together to deliver the working software product every two weeks within Sprints. The Product Owner is solely responsible for managing the Product Backlog. The Sprint, Sprint Planning, Daily Scrum, Sprint Review, and Sprint Retrospective are equivalent to the standard Scrum-based agile way of working only. SAFe introduces various best practices for an incremental and iterative software product development and delivery. Teams need to deliver software products with built-in quality. They should have a proper Definition of Done at the Team level. It needs to be dominated by various aspects of built-in quality.

An Essential SAFe implementation asks multiple Agile Teams to work with a similar kind of way of working but with some scaled aspects at the Program level, where they need to work and deliver together. They need to create a Program Increment, which needs to be delivered after five consecutive Sprints. Each Sprint needs to be of two weeks. The Agile Teams and their Stakeholders are together called as an Agile Release Train (ART). They need to plan, develop, and deliver together, while always being in line with a common business/customer vision, goals, and objectives. The

Agile Release Train helps them to maintain a consistent pace for frequent delivery. By performing a proper planning of the software product features and functionalities, they always need to develop and release such features and functionalities by slightly decoupling them from their development-specific cadence.

The Product Managers need to determine the roadmap and strategy for an Agile Release Train. They also need to define a roadmap for the software product increments through a Program Backlog. It is a backlog having all the work items to be further taken up by the Agile Teams under their individual Team Backlogs. The Release Train Engineer needs to act as a Scrum Master at the Agile Release Train level. The Program Increment is a consolidated Product Increment, which needs to be collectively delivered by multiple Agile Teams under an ART. They need to have a Program Increment Planning meeting, where all the members of all the Agile Teams under an ART need to be present. They need to discuss on what needs to be taken up by them (to work on, within the scope of their Agile Release Train) from the Program Backlog. They also need to have a proper alignment and a common, shared understanding about their dependencies, risks, strategy, and planning.

Considering the number of Sprints under the next Program Increment Release and the overall capacity of Agile Teams, the members of all the Agile Teams need to map the features and high-level PBIs/User Stories on the Program Board. They also need to discuss and make all the inter-team dependencies visible on the Program Board. The Program Board hence always needs to showcase a complete visual summarization of all the features, their associated high-level PBIs/User Stories, and all the inter-team dependencies. While populating the Program Board, they always need to consider the scope of upcoming Program Increment release.

The Scrum Masters from the individual Agile/Scrum Teams and the Release Train Engineer at the Agile Release Train level need to have bi-weekly meetings to discuss and ensure that their agreed goals are within reach. They also need to discuss on any impediments, issues, and deviations. All the Agile Teams under the Agile Release Train need to be properly aligned to deliver the potentially shippable working software product increment through 4 Sprints of 2 weeks each. The 5th Sprint needs to be utilized for the purpose of innovation and planning, where they need to look at the experimentation and learning of new ideas and improvements. There needs to be a System Demo at the Program/ART level, where the Agile Teams need to demonstrate their fully functional Program Increment. Once it is done, there also needs to be a Program Increment Planning at the Program/ART level, where the Agile Teams need to reflect on the planning and maintenance-specific activities for the upcoming Program Increment by making use of an architectural runway. The architectural runway needs to have an overview of their existing code, components, and technical infrastructure based on which they need to implement the product features and functionalities in near future without too much redesigning as it might cause some unexpected delays.

A Large Solution SAFe implementation asks multiple Programs (containing multiple Agile Teams) to manage large solutions, which cannot be handled by a single Program, that is, by a single Agile Release Train. Such large solutions always need to be co-ordinated by a Solution Train. It needs to have a Solution Manager, a Solution Architect, and a Solution Train Engineer. They need to structure, align, and co-ordinate among multiple Agile Release Trains.

A Portfolio SAFe implementation asks the Portfolio Management to determine the overall path of multiple Solution Trains by assigning a proper budget. With this kind/level of implementation, the Product Managers need to expose a Backlog containing the required Epics (to act as parent level containers for all the required product features) to the individual Solution Trains. They can also make use of Kanban framework to limit the overall capacity of individual Solution Trains. A Full SAFe implementation signifies as the most inclusive configuration level. It helps to implement large integrated solutions at an enterprise scale, which requires hundreds of Associates/Agile Team members to develop and deliver them.

SAFe deviates a bit from Scrum in terms of certain key areas. It is not required for the Product Owners to own the Program Backlog. Instead, they need to own their respective Product Backlogs. They need to be populated from the Program Backlog. Generally, in case of a Full SAFe implementation, the Program Backlog needs to be owned by the Product Manager and it needs to be populated from the Portfolio or Large Solution level implementation. SAFe also works with the concept of Design Sprints, which is partially supported by Scrum. A Design Sprint is a time-constrained multi-phase process, which makes use of Design Thinking (which is a tactical process, using which the core design concepts in terms of User Experience can be developed) to reduce any risks, while introducing a new product feature to the Customers. SAFe makes use of hardening sprints, where the Agile Teams need to perform the testing, and documentation specific work, which is not practical for them in the ongoing Sprints; however, Scrum does not support such approach.

In any SAFe implementation, the prime accountability for the Product is not only with the Product Owners of individual Agile/Scrum Teams. It is also with someone at the Program/Portfolio level. There is a possibility where the Agile Release Trains may delay the process of timely inspection and adaptation by ignoring the expected value. To avoid this, a SAFe implementation always needs to put a restriction that all the Agile teams in the ART should work in a certain cadence. As SAFe has many additional Roles, Artifacts, and Events as compared to a standard Scrum implementation, the control of decision-making within a SAFe implementation always needs to be a distributed one. SAFe expects the Agile Teams to make use of all the best practices. SAFe also promotes a proper alignment of agile ways of working among multiple Agile Teams. It emphasizes to maintain a constant pace/cadence within multiple Agile Teams, so that their Sprints and overall agile way of working stays not only intact but also a bit flexible. The SAFe Scrum Masters need to facilitate all the Events for their own Agile/Scrum Teams. They need to co-ordinate with the other Agile/Scrum Teams within the ART.

SAFe tends to have more emphasis on reporting of metrics, where the Agile Teams need to have a good balance in between the metrics and the process of empiricism. If some of the Agile Teams under the Agile Release Train want to promote their Sprint-specific cadence, it might hamper the cadence of other Agile Teams. Hence, any such changes need to be properly discussed, evaluated, and agreed with all the Agile Teams upfront. The ART expects its Agile Teams to deliver as per the commitment given by them during their Program Increment Planning. The Agile Teams need to inspect and adapt considering the same commitment during every Sprint. Program Increment Planning and System Demo need to be the additional Events under a SAFe implementation. During the Daily Scrum, the Scrum Master needs to ensure that separate discussions are being conducted to tackle any issues being raised. SAFe needs to have an Iteration Review like Sprint Review. SAFe Team Retrospectives also need to be like Sprint Retrospectives; however, they need to be more authoritative. The Product Backlog Refinements within SAFe also need to be like standard Scrum only. In addition to the standard Events at the Agile/Scrum Team level, some additional Events also need to be conducted at the Program level.

As a Scaling Scrum approach, SAFe looks to be more suitable candidate for large enterprises having an anticipation of implementation of large solutions and product initiatives, where they always need to have a proper alignment considering their people, product, and process-specific entities. The organizations need to evaluate all the practices prescribed by SAFe by considering their own needs, wants, and suitability against its four configuration levels. Such evaluation might ask them to accept many additional entities, as a SAFe implementation always adds up many extra Roles, Artifacts, and Events to a standard Scrum-based agile way of working implementation. SAFe expects to have many entities and processes in place. Each entity has got its own significance; however, a proper evaluation of the required configuration level and a continuous improvement mindset can help and support the agile organizations to have a proper SAFe implementation in place.

Large-Scale Scrum (LeSS) is one more Scaling Scrum Framework-based approach obtained by Bas Vodde and Craig Larman. It allows an application of a standard Scrum-based agile way of working to a large-scale development and delivery of software products. LeSS implementation recommends less Rules, Roles, and Artifacts. This helps LeSS to stay truthful with an anticipation of Scaling Scrum to be kept as simple. LeSS shares some common patterns as of SAFe. It expects to have a standard Scrum implementation at the Team level, where multiple Scrum Teams need to share a common Product Backlog. They also need to undergo with a collaborative planning across multiple Scrum Teams, governing self-organization of multiple smaller Scrum Teams. It helps the Scrum Teams to stay in line with the Scrum Framework's intent and hence can be easily adopted by the Scrum Teams who are trying for small to medium-sized Scaling Scrum implementations.

A LeSS framework-based Scaling Scrum implementation has few differing reflections than a standard Scrum-based implementation. Sprints belonging to the individual Scrum Teams in a LeSS implementation need to have the same length. They also need to start and end at the same time for the individual Scrum Teams. All the individual Scrum Teams working on the Product Backlog need to be a part of the same Sprint. Sprint Planning needs to split into two parts, where the first part need not to be usually organized with all the team members of all the Scrum Teams.

Like Scrum of Scrums, every Scrum Team always needs to have one or more representatives participating in Planning, so that they can limit the number of participants. They need to set the Sprint Goal during the first part of the Planning. They also need to choose the PBIs/User Stories and define their agreed Sprint Goal. The Scrum Teams need to distribute those selected PBIs/User Stories within themselves. Individual Scrum Teams need to formulate their plans to finish those PBIs/User Stories and to achieve the Sprint Goal under the second part of the Planning. A LeSS implementation expects them to perform Planning exercises, while being collectively present. They need to have the required meaningful conversations to have a proper alignment between themselves.

A LeSS implementation always helps them to keep their Scrum-based agile way of working unharmed. There always needs to be a single Product Owner who needs to align with the Developers of individual Scrum Teams. They also need to collaborate for the purpose of inspection and adaptation, so that they can strive for continuous learning and improvement together. LeSS expects least number of changes to the standard Scrum Roles, Artifacts, and Events. Sprint Reviews and Retrospectives also need to remain intact, as they help Scrum Teams to boost their trust, openness, collaboration, inspection, adaptation, and transparency.

The role of a Product Owner in a LeSS implementation needs to be the same as that of in a standard Scrum implementation. A LeSS implementation works for a huge team size, typically for more than 8 Scrum Teams working on a single Product. In such an implementation, the Product Owner needs to be accountable for the Product Backlog. He/she needs to be supported by the Area Product Owners having respective Area Product Backlogs.

The role of Developers within a LeSS implementation is like the one in a standard Scrum implementation. The Developers always need to be self-managing, self-organizing, and cross-functional. The Scrum Master within a LeSS implementation also has the same role as of the Scrum Master in a standard Scrum implementation. The Daily Scrum within a LeSS implementation is also the same as that of in a standard Scrum implementation. A LeSS implementation recommends Scrum Teams to have a Team-level Product Backlog Refinement and a Multi-Team Product Backlog Refinement. The scope and schedule for Refinements need to be agreed upon by the Scrum Team members by always following all the standard recommendations provided by LeSS. Scrum Teams within a LeSS implementation always need to work on their own Sprint Backlog. They also need to integrate their potentially releasable working software product increments before the end of every Sprint. LeSS does not need any extra Artifacts on top of the standard Scrum Artifacts. It asks the Scrum Teams to follow a proper Definition of Done as described in a standard Scrum implementation.

LeSS always looks to be a straightforward Scaling Scrum approach. The individual Scrum Teams need to follow the process of Empiricism. They need to inculcate all the required values and behaviors to inspect and adapt, so that they can enhance their LeSS-based agile way of working. For a LeSS implementation, they need to follow all the best practices as per a standard Scrum implementation, to become better at self-management over time.

Disciplined Agile (DA) is one more Scaling Scrum approach. It is a learning-oriented and a process-based decision-making framework. It embraces an agile mindset of Agile Teams who need to scale up their Scrum based agile way of working beyond the Team level. By offering a strong and a consistent base, a Disciplined Agile implementation always allows enterprises to scale up their agile software product development and delivery specific approaches. It internally makes use of Scrum and Kanban frameworks to have a proper integration of agile way of working across various organizational areas such as HR, Finance, Governance, Portfolio Management, and so on. As compared to the other Scaling Scrum approaches, DA is believed to be much more adaptable and easier way to help the Agile Teams to scale up their Scrum-based agile way of working. While being a process-based decision-making framework, DA always needs to enable the proper ways to perform the agile transformation in agile organizations.

While making use of DA practices, it is hence required for the organizations to consider and continuously learn about various options. DA helps the organizations by providing some unique insights about what is happening around them and how can they improve their agile way of working beyond an Agile Team level. It refers to their real-time data points. By encompassing the entire software product development and delivery lifecycle, the DA approach is generally segmented into various areas such as Disciplined Agile Delivery (DAD), Disciplined DevOps, Disciplined Agile IT (DAIT), and Disciplined Agile Enterprise. The DAD approach given by Scott Ambler and Mark Lines is the core of DA approach, where the end-to-end software product development and delivery needs to be defined by considering the various phases to be planned by the Agile teams.

The Agile Teams need to perform initial planning and modelling. They also need to plan their budgeting for the purpose of continuous system design, development, testing, build, deployment, and monitoring during the entire software product development and delivery lifecycle. They also need to make use of various best practices provided by Disciplined DevOps and Agile IT (DAIT) to focus on the overall co-ordination across various teams of an organization. They need to model and manage their development and delivery cycle, product to service transitioning, operations, maintenance and support, data management, and few other essential entities by keeping them simple and effective.

The DA Enterprise implementation approach asks the agile organizations to foresee the market needs and technological advancements, so that they can plan their policies and strategies to have some better processes of software product development and delivery in place. The Disciplined Agile Delivery (DAD) needs to be explored by the Agile Teams as a hybrid approach. It needs to expand a standard Scrum-based agile way of working within multiple Agile Teams by combining the required best practices from various frameworks such as XP, Kanban, Lean, SAFe, and LeSS. A DAD implementation using Scrum framework always needs to be applied as a goal-driven Scaling Scrum approach to a greater number of Scrum Teams. It needs to be adopted by them through a right utilization of practices considering the present resources, so that the Scrum Teams can agree to decide on its suitable application and to improve their way of working.

The unique hybrid characteristics and features of a DA framework-based implementation can help multiple Agile Teams of an agile organization to evaluate, combine, and apply recognized techniques and processes belonging to the agile frameworks other than the Scrum framework. It also allows them to customize those techniques and processes, as per their exclusive needs. Such a hybrid implementation needs to be explored and applied by the agile organizations who are matured enough with a proper understanding and exposure of the agile mindset. It should not be used as an ideal framework by the organizations that are completely new to the understanding of agile mindset.

Scrum@Scale (S@S) is one more Scaling Scrum approach created by Dr. Jeff Sutherland. It is an extension of Scrum Framework. A Scrum@Scale-based implementation and its associated exploration needs to be adopted by the agile organizations that have already done a standard Scrum implementation with their Scrum Teams at the Team level and who want to spread it across the entire organization across many other Scrum Teams. It can help them to establish a common set of goals and objectives to scale up their Scrum-based agile way of working in a well-structured manner. The Scrum Masters and the Product Owners of the individual Scrum Teams need to make its use to co-ordinate with each other. Through a Meta Scrum approach, they need to scale up their Scrum-based agile way of working across the entire organization. Using the S@S approach, the agile organizations need to embrace an agile way of working to perform their work having multiple Scrum Teams at various levels. S@S needs to act as a framework using which multiple Scrum teams can address their complex problems and can deliver their software products with an optimized customer/end-user value.

As per the Scrum Guide recommendation, a standard Scrum implementation always needs to have 10 or fewer team members in a Scrum Team. However, the Scrum at

Scale (S@S) Guide (present at **https://www.scrumatscale.com/scrum-at-scale-guide-online/**) always expects agile organizations to scale up their Scrum-based agile way of working by experimenting with the Scrum Teams having a Linear Scalability and Sizing. Linear Scalability of agile organizations refers to their capability to retain a stable and proportional productivity rate, as they scale up their Scrum-based agile way of working across various levels of organization. This approach needs to refer to a similar kind of approach with a Scrum of Scrums implementation for an ideal number of Scrum Teams, while Scaling Scrum. S@S also has an anticipation that there should not be more than five team members within an individual Scrum Team while scaling up their Scrum-based agile way of working beyond Team level. While performing scaling across the entire organization, S@S approach needs to make use of a standard Scrum Framework implementation offering as its baseline.

Multiple Scrum Teams under a S@S implementation always need to understand and adhere to the concept of Minimum Viable Bureaucracy. This concept helps them to cut down the overall time required for them to perform decision-making at any level in the organization. S@S hence prefers to have smaller Scrum Teams, who can easily collaborate and co-ordinate with each other. The Scrum Teams can showcase their full engagement, co-operation, and teamwork in a significant way. It also requires the Scrum Teams to avoid working on the features having low or zero customer value.

The multiple Scrum Teams under a S@S implementation need to understand that a Hierarchy-based Bureaucracy restricts them from working and co-ordinating together. As it acts as a primary obstacle for the individual Scrum Teams to achieve a Linear Scalability and as it also slows down the process of decision-making, it decelerates the overall positive impact of the agile way of working on their software product development and delivery. The agile organizations hence need to keep such Bureaucracy at a bare minimum level and need to scale up their agile way of working beyond Team level by adopting S@S scaling approach as a transitioning/transforming phase.

A S@S implementation always needs to comprise of two key Cycles. They are the Scrum Master Cycle and the Product Owner Cycle. The Scrum Master Cycle needs to reflect on the how part and the Product Owner Cycle needs to reflect on the what part of a S@S implementation. These two Cycles need to be brought together, so that they can generate a high-potential scaling framework to help multiple Scrum Teams under a S@S implementation. Individual Scrum Teams always need to collaborate and co-ordinate with their collective efforts to achieve their common agreed goals and objectives. Like Scrum of Scrums approach, S@S also intends to associate multiple Scrum Teams under a S@S implementation to boost their software product's outcome-based customer value. The basic alignment between multiple Scrum Teams always needs to happen through a Scrum of Scrums and it might pass the probability of overlooking their cross-functional nature. They need to resolve their inter-team dependencies, so that a properly integrated working software product can be delivered.

The Product Owner Cycle within a S@S implementation needs to be used by multiple Scrum Teams to concentrate on an effective prioritization of customer value. It needs to have a structured planning, where the Product Owner needs to order the work items under their Product Backlog, as per the customer value proposition-based prioritization. The Product Backlog always needs to have all the work items prioritized and ordered, so that the Scrum Teams can work together to achieve their agreed goals and objectives. The Scrum Events and Artifacts for a S@S implementation remain the same as of a standard Scrum-based agile way of working implementation. S@S implementation approach also asks the Scrum Teams to establish their own Definition of Done, to ensure the completeness and stability of their working software product increments by the end of every Sprint.

The Agile organizations always need to remember that a S@S implementation approach can function properly only when there is always an effective and efficient Scaling of Scrum within multiple Scrum Teams. While implementing the Scaling Scrum under a S@S implementation, the Scrum Teams need to cover the entire organization starting from the bottom to the top by properly following the process of Empiricism. The unique aspects of inspection, adaptation, and transparency are always applicable for all the Scrum Teams under a S@S implementation.

The Scrum of Scrums Event within a S@S implementation needs to be organized by the Scrum Teams; however, it should not be limited as a formal Event. By restricting any of the possible adverse impacts on the overall process of Empiricism (to continuously inspect and adapt), the Scrum Teams under a S@S implementation always need to be much more proactive. While being proactive, they need not to wait for the Scrum of Scrums to resolve their inter-team dependencies. They should have required interactions to highlight, share, and resolve any issues, obstacles, dependencies, and impediments among themselves. They need to embrace the process of Empiricism and perform their desired work at the earliest. This way of working under a S@S implementation needs to encourage them to strive for a fundamental increase in trust, transparency, and teamwork. S@S approach hence needs to have the Scrum of Scrums Event to enhance a collaborative way of working style for multiple Scrum Teams working together in a complex software product development and delivery environment.

A S@S implementation asks the Scrum Masters and the Product Owners to be a part of the Scaling Scrum Team. The Scrum Masters need to be a part of the Scrum of Scrums and the Product Owners need to be a part of Meta Scrum. Similar Roles also need to be there for the higher-level Scrum Teams. A proper implementation and a continuous enhancement of S@S approach questions teams to re-create their structuring and alignment across various levels of organization. This approach anticipates that the teams need to be super ambitious. Smaller teams working together with a much better collaboration can make a big difference to get the expected outcomes out of the complete Scaling Scrum effort. Scrum Teams need to allow such scaling to happen more effectively and naturally. They always need to remember that some suitable enhancements within their own S@S implementation can be possibly done, only when they correlate their anticipated outcomes through a series of continuous inspections and adaptations.

Spotify Engineering Culture is one more Scaling Scrum approach being used at Spotify organization. It was not originally meant to be a Framework; however, a unique perspective to look at scaling agile way of working across multiple software development teams caused its inevitable emergence. Spotify Engineering Culture acts as a model. It is more of a self-sufficient people-driven framework for the purpose of scaling agile, which need not to be limited to Scrum Framework only. It emphasizes the prominence of organizational culture through a network of software product development teams. It needs to be utilized by multiple software product development teams to explore and share the best practices of software product development and delivery with each other. It always permits the software product development teams with a self-sufficiency and an autonomy to work together, while making use of Scrum or any other Agile Frameworks. The software product development teams need to work together as decoupled structures. The Spotify Engineering Culture based Scaling Scrum implementation approach needs to explore another unique perspective of Scrum Framework, where a well-organized structure of multiple software product development teams always needs to optimize the customer value getting delivered by them.

The Spotify Engineering Culture is also called as Spotify model. It can be applied as a Scaling Scrum approach to explore and apply the best possible practices by eliminating many disparities within any of the Nexus, SAFe, LeSS, and S@S approach-based Scaling Scrum implementations. It follows a different approach, where it is not mandatory that it should use Scrum framework only. The decision-making power for the selection of appropriate agile frameworks needs to be given to all the software product development teams within a Spotify implementation. They need to select the best possible and suitable approach as per their own needs. The Spotify Engineering Culture asks such teams to aim at a self-sufficiency and an autonomy along with a proper common, shared understanding and alignment. By promoting a strict combination of organizational structuring and restructuring, it also regulates the extensive need for alignment within the teams, by making them more autonomous.

Such autonomous software product development teams in a Spotify implementation are called as Squads. A Squad typically needs to have less than eight team members working together on a long-term mission. They need to have a complete end-to-end responsibility of the software product they are designing, developing, and delivering along with the support and maintenance-specific activities. Squads always need to be self-sufficient. They need to decide on what, when, and how aspects while implementing the software product. Such decision-making always needs to be in line with their vision, strategy, and goals. Being more self-sufficient and autonomous expects them to not only to perform a faster decision-making with less/limited Events to align with each other, but also to reduce their dependencies, risks, and unnecessary hand-offs. Squads need to be loosely coupled and tightly aligned. They need to focus on how to solve the problems. They need to choose the agile frameworks, tools, technologies, and processes, which are suitable for them. They need to follow a concept of cross-pollination, where if a Squad makes use a specific methodology that suits their needs, then other Squads also tend use the same, as it might act as a path of least struggle for them.

The overall system architecture of the software products to be developed and delivered by the Squads need to be divided into several distinct, small, and decoupled systems. With such system architecture, the Squads can have a complete end-to-end ownership of one or more systems. The Spotify Engineering Culture expects its autonomous Squads to establish a structure called as Tribe. The Tribe needs to consist of multiple Squads performing their work together and constructing a sustained system of a software product. In general, the alignment between various competencies-based individual Squad members need to happen through Chapters. Spotify always expects that the autonomous Squads are making their decisions by themselves by accepting a right sense of their positioning.

The autonomous Squads always need to have small, decoupled, and regular releases of software products being developed and delivered by them. The ultimate control of decision-making needs to remain with Squads only. They always need to be self-sufficient for the same purpose. The Spotify Engineering Culture also asks the autonomous Squads to fail fast, learn fast, and improve fast. The Squads always need to limit the overall effect of their agile way of working if certain things are not working as per their original expectations. In this case, they always need to minimize its overall harmful effect by limiting the impact area with a proper justification. While being outcome oriented, they always need to perform outcome-based customer value delivery instead of only fulfilling the planned commitments for the sake of the fulfilment of their original plans. The fully autonomous Squads always need to work as per the basic structure of Scrum Framework and the process of Empiricism. They need to keep their transparency, inspection, and adaptation at an optimum level.

A Spotify model-based Scaling Scrum implementation emphasizes the autonomous Squads to focus on the decoupled parts of a software product system instead of the entire software product. Therefore, the Squads always need to emphasize on innovation over predictability, while dealing with such small and decoupled parts of a software product system. Within a Spotify model-based/Spotify Engineering Culture-based Scaling Scrum implementation, it is extremely important for the autonomous Squads to discover an applicable and appropriate way to continually evaluate and assess if they are working on the most valuable, small, and decoupled parts of the working software product. For this purpose, there always needs to be a dedicated Product Owner for every small and decoupled system part, where a single autonomous Squad needs to be accountable and responsible. Squads need to have all the required skills sets and capabilities to develop, deliver, release, and sustain the integrated working software product system, where they need to integrate all the required small and decoupled parts of a big software product system. Squads rarely need to consider the work being performed by other Squads, as they are supposed to work on decoupled systems. With such a placement of Squads, their alignment is required to be kept at minimum.

As per the following table, it is crucial for the agile organizations to realize the variations and differences between various Scaling Agile/Scrum Frameworks-based approaches. They always need to have a proper evaluation before applying any of these approaches, while performing their own unique Scaling Scrum implementation with a proper intent.

Parameter	Scrum of Scrums	Nexus	Scaled Agile Framework (SAFe)	Large Scale Scrum (LeSS)	Disciplined Agile (DA)	Scrum @ Scale (S@S)	Spotify Engineering Culture
Approach	Simple Scaling Scrum Approach with multiple Scrum Teams	Scaled Software Product Development Initiatives	Complex Software Product Development with multiple Agile/Scrum Teams	Multiple Scrum Teams working together on a single Software Product	To help teams streamline their processes and achieve business agility	Multiple Scrum Teams working with highly customized processes in a complex environment	Cross-pollination of best practices within multiple Agile/Scrum Teams
Nature and Complexity	Prescriptive and Rigid	Prescriptive and Rigid	Prescriptive and Rigid	Prescriptive and Rigid	Goal Driven and Flexible	Prescriptive and Rigid	Optional and Flexible
Suitability	Small to Mid-sized Organizations	Small to Mid-sized Organizations	Mid to Large-sized Organizations	Mid to Large-sized Organizations	Mid to Large-sized Organizations	Mid to Large-sized Organizations	Small to Mid-sized Organizations
Ideal Team Size	5 to 10 Teams	3 to 9 Teams	50 to 120 team members	5 to 10 Teams	200 or more team members	5 Teams	30 Teams
Long Term Setup and Planning	Prescriptive, Specified, and Agreed	Prescriptive, Specified, and Agreed	Prescriptive, Specified, and Agreed	Prescriptive, Specified, and Agreed	Specified and agreed with Suggestions	Prescriptive, Specified, and Agreed	Optionally Specified and Agreed
Visibility and Transparency	Specified and Agreed	Specified and Agreed	Specified with Suggestions	Specified and Agreed	Specified with Suggestions	Specified and Agreed	Specified with Suggestions
Alignment	Required	Required	Required	Required	Recommended	Required	Least Required
Support	Available	Available	Available	Available	Available	Available	Limited
Deviation from Standard Scrum	Prescriptive, Specified, and Agreed	Prescriptive, Specified, and Agreed	Specified and agreed with Suggestions	Specified and Agreed	Specified and agreed with Suggestions	Prescriptive, Specified, and Agreed	Specified and agreed with Suggestions
Support for Multiple Teams	Provided	Provided	Provided with an agreement	Provided	Provided with an agreement	Provided	Provided
Scaled Team Naming	Scrum of Scrums	Nexus	Agile Release Trains	Areas	No formal naming as such	Scrum of Scrums	Tribes
Usage of various Agile Frameworks	Scaled version of Scrum	Scaled version of Scrum	Lean Agile principles, Scrum, Kanban, and XP	Scaled version of Scrum	Hybrid Agile approach with Kanban, Scrum, XP, Lean, SAFe, etc.	Scaled version of Scrum	Teams need to explore as per their own needs and suitability
Standard Scrum Events	Required	Required	Required	Required	Recommended	Required	Recommended
Distribution	High	Low	High	High	Medium	Medium	Medium
Management of Dependencies	Specified and Agreed	Specified and Agreed	Specified and Agreed	Specified with Suggestions	Specified with Suggestions	Specified and Agreed	Specified and Agreed
Adoption and Transparency	Simple	Simple	Complex	Average	Complex	Average	Average
On-Demand Release	Specified with Suggestions	Specified with Suggestions	Specified and Agreed	Specified and Agreed	Specified with Suggestions	Not distinctly Specified	Specified and Agreed
Support for DevOps CI/CD	Specified and Agreed	Specified and Agreed	Specified and Agreed	Specified and Agreed	Specified with Suggestions	Specified and Agreed	Specified and Agreed
Leadership Buy-in	Required	Required	Required	Required	Recommended	Required	Required

Table 13.1: *A quick comparison between Scrum of Scrums, Nexus, Scaled Agile Framework (SAFe), Large Scale Scrum (LeSS), Disciplined Agile (DA), Scrum @ Scale (S@S), and Spotify Engineering Culture Scaling Agile/Scrum Frameworks-based Approaches*

The agile organizations always need to understand and acknowledge the fact that there is no one-size-fits-all approach, while selecting and applying a specific Scaling Scrum Framework-based approach. It is hence required for them to consider numerous factors while selecting and applying the same. They need to have proper and required roles defined. Such roles and associated responsibilities can help them making their Scrum Teams more accountable and responsible. They also need to perform some required changes in their existing organizational structure, as recommended by the Scaling Scrum approach which they would like to go ahead with. They can also expect and get some additional support by removing their process-specific impediments and by enhancing their overall productivity at every organizational level.

"Customer centricity is a culture of putting the customer at the center of everything you do."

- Brian Solis

A proper structure of Scrum Teams with the properly defined roles can accelerate their Scaling Scrum Framework-based agile way of working. The agile organizations always need to be customer-centric, especially when it comes to their generic operating structure and agile way of working alignments. They need to establish Scrum Teams as a collection of associates representing various parts of organization to take a good care of customer centricity. Though a Scaling Scrum approach can constitute multiple Scrum Teams, individual teams need to work as a One Team to develop, integrate, and deliver the customer value-based outcomes.

Teams always need to perform their every action around the customer/end-user value which they are always supposed to bring in. For the same purpose, they need to have a look into the recommendations given by various Scaling Scrum Frameworks-based approaches. They need to modify/customize their traditional mindset, organizational structures, and their agile way of working approach by considering their people, products, and processes. By identifying the expected customer value to be provided out of the software product, they need to build the overall structuring of their Scrum Teams which needs to be around the customer value only.

"An all-in transition will almost certainly cost more than starting small. Because of the greater number of people learning a new way of working all at the same time, all-in transitions generally rely more heavily on outside Coaches, Scrum Masters, and Trainers. The slower pace of a start-small adoption allows the organization to build internal expertise and then use that to help the Scrum Teams that start later. Starting small also saves money because early mistakes affect only a subset of the organization."
- Mike Cohn

The agile organizations, their agile leadership, and agile teams exploring various Scaling Scrum Framework-based approaches always need to remember that, having any of the agile ways of working-specific processes just for the sake of calling them as agile does not make them agile. They also need to understand and practice all the agile values and principles along with the scrum values and rules of Scrum Framework at the Scrum Team level before scaling up their way of working across entire organization.

"It does not matter how slowly you go so long as you do not stop."

- Confucius

The agile organizations also need to understand that the selection, adoption, and application of any Scaling Scrum Framework-based approach takes a significant amount of time for them to change. It might also take a significant amount of time for them to achieve a good and an improved Scaling Scrum adoption. While getting themselves familiar with it, they need to go step by step and reach a certain level of maturity. They need to adopt many new processes by starting with one Scrum Team at a time, so that they can introspect about their level of maturity and their own continuous progress corresponding to it. They always need to manage their dependencies and risks. Regardless of what and how they are performing, they always need to perform with a fully determined effort to consider all the valuable feedbacks and better alternatives across all the teams and across all the levels of organization, so that they can observe, identify, and resolve any issues to achieve a faster time to market.

They need to recognize the dependencies and improve their way of working to resolve them actively. They need to look for better alternatives by structuring an entirely suitable alignment for any collaboration across various levels of organization. To have a proper mindset to make the Scaling Scrum successful (regardless of any Scaling Scrum Framework-based approach the agile organizations are selecting and applying), they must have an applicable and appropriate leadership buy-in. It needs to bring in the ultimate benefits considering various aspects of changes which they would like to see and measure in a long term. The leadership representatives also need to pursue the required knowledge through some formal trainings, while getting familiar with the new Scaled Scrum Framework-based agile way of working.

By utilizing the best practices from the concepts such as Systems Thinking, Design Thinking, DevOps, and Lean Agile Software Product Development, Delivery, and Ways of Working, the agile organizations need to encourage a healthy and a growth mindset-based culture across all the levels to support their own Scaling Scrum transformation. They need to understand that modifying their existing organizational culture is not a straightforward thing to do. It needs to take a significant amount of time. They need to continuously inspect, adapt, and enact to continuously improve their practices, processes, and culture to be agile.

They need to follow a basic understanding that the cultural shift needs to start by changing their thought process for their every action and its impact on the customer value optimization. They need to have an absolute consideration for the complete process of end-to-end software product development and delivery. They also need to eliminate any waste by following a Lean Agile Thinking. They always need to focus on a People First approach, where their decision-making always needs to be based on what is more suitable for the team members driving the transformation. Scaling Scrum needs to be an expanded version of Scrum to scale it up to the bigger teams. Scrum helps the teams to scale it up with required customizations. Teams need to deal with their inter-team dependencies to achieve their common goals, where they are not supposed to change the way they work as Scrum Teams, while being more Agile.

Points to remember

- The approach of scaling up the Scrum-based agile way of working for more than one Scrum Team can be generally called as Scaling Scrum. The primary reason for this approach is to develop and deliver the working software product features and functionalities faster, sooner, and better. This needs to be done by employing a greater number of Scrum Teams to work on a single Product Backlog.

- While scaling Scrum, it is required for the Product Owner to thoroughly evaluate all the pros and cons of the team structure getting formed with multiple Scrum Teams in it.

- While establishing a Scaling Scrum approach, the Scrum Teams need to contribute with a joint effort from all the sides.

- As the process of software product development is complex, the agile organizations need to continuously explore the Scaling Scrum Approach beyond their Scrum-based agile way of working at three key levels - Scrum Team, Program, and Portfolio.

- It is required for the agile organizations to explore, select, and introduce a suitable Scaling Scrum Framework to have a proper structuring and alignment at every level of organization. Scrum Framework is the most commonly and widely used agile framework, which can be scaled beyond a single Scrum Team; however, multiple Scrum Teams making use of a Scaling Scrum approach always need to be more apprehensive with what kind of software products are being developed and delivered by them.

- The Scrum Teams always need to have a considerable evaluation of various Scaling Scrum approaches, while establishing their Scaling Scrum approach-based agile way of working. A Scaling Scrum approach expects multiple Scrum Teams to work together on a software product, where they need to replicate their agile way of working, only at a larger scale.

- The overall collaboration and co-ordination of multiple Scrum Teams developing and delivering the working software product needs to scale up. The Scrum Teams need to have a proper understanding of their own expectations against the Scaling Scrum approach which they would like to explore, assess, apply, and utilize.

- The agile organizations struggling with the implementation of Scrum Framework at the Team level might think that Scaling Scrum may help them to address inter-team dependencies. They need to understand that Scaling Scrum will work only if they have a proper implementation of Scrum Framework at the Team level.

- Many reasons to scale up the Scrum-based agile way of working can be eliminated if the Scrum Teams perform their way of working through proper Scrum processes.

- Though there is no 100% perfect way to have a successful Scaling Scrum, there are various frameworks to address the basic needs of the Scaling Scrum approach. While exploring and applying any of these frameworks, the Scrum Teams can integrate some common practices, processes, and techniques.

- Scrum of Scrums is one of the most used approaches to scale up Scrum. This approach is created by Jeff Sutherland and it is getting used by many agile organizations.

- Nexus is a Scaling Scrum Framework-based approach created by Ken Schwaber from Scrum.org. Nexus shapes on a basic Scrum-based agile way of working, but it adds, modifies, or substitutes some of the Scrum Roles, Scrum Artifacts, and Scrum Events.

- Scaled Agile Framework (SAFe) is a Scaling Scrum Framework-based approach created by Dean Leffingwell. It consists of a set of organization and workflow-specific patterns to implement the required agile practices and processes at an agile enterprise scale. It is originally called as Agile Enterprise Big Picture.

- Large-Scale Scrum (LeSS) is a Scaling Scrum Framework-based approach obtained by Bas Vodde and Craig Larman. It allows an application of a standard Scrum-based agile way of working to a large-scale development and delivery of software products. LeSS implementation recommends less Rules, Roles, and Artifacts.

- Disciplined Agile (DA) is a Scaling Scrum approach. It a learning-oriented and a process-based decision-making framework. It embraces an agile mindset of Agile Teams who need to scale up their Scrum. The Disciplined Agile Delivery (DAD) approach given by Scott Ambler and Mark Lines is the core of DA approach, where the end-to-end software product development and delivery needs to be defined by considering the various phases to be planned by the Agile Teams.

- Scrum at Scale (S@S) is a Scaling Scrum approach created by Dr. Jeff Sutherland. It is an extension of Scrum Framework. It needs to be adopted by the agile organizations that have already done a standard Scrum implementation with their Scrum Teams and who want to spread it across the entire organization across many other teams.

- Spotify Engineering Culture/Spotify Model is a Scaling Scrum approach being used at Spotify organization. It was not originally meant to be a Framework; however, a unique perspective to look at scaling agile way of working across multiple software development teams caused its inevitable emergence.

- It is crucial for the agile organizations to realize the variations and differences between various Scaling Scrum Frameworks-based Approaches. They need to have a proper evaluation before they select, adopt, and apply them with a proper intent.

- The agile organizations always need to understand and acknowledge the fact that there is no one-size-fits-all approach, while selecting and applying a specific Scaling Scrum Framework-based approach. It is hence required for them to consider numerous factors while selecting and applying the same.

In the next chapter, readers will get to know about some of the additional advanced Scrum add-ons/techniques to help the Scrum Teams to establish and to further enhance their Scrum-based agile way of working.

CHAPTER 14
Additional Advanced Scrum Add-ons

Introduction

In this chapter, readers will get to know about some of the additional advanced Scrum add-ons/techniques to help the Scrum Teams to establish, enhance, and further improve their Scrum-based agile way of working. They will get to know about various considerations for Scrum-based agile way of working of Scrum Teams, using which they can establish and enhance their performance and productivity. They will also get an overview of some of the effective facilitation and gamification techniques for the Scrum Teams.

Objective

After studying this chapter, you should be able to:

- Understand some of the additional advanced Scrum add-ons/techniques to help the Scrum Teams to establish, enhance, and further improve their Scrum-based agile way of working.

- Understand the need of innovation and experimentation under the agile way of working of Scrum Teams.

- Understand various considerations for Scrum-based agile way of working of Scrum Teams.

- Understand various effective facilitation and gamification techniques for the Scrum Teams.

Alice 'The Scrum Master' (in a discussion with Tim 'The Product Owner'):

"Hey, Tim! Can we discuss on that Stakeholders related pending retrospective feedback? I think, you wanted to have a separate discussion with me for that one, right?"

Tim 'The Product Owner':

"Thank you so much Alice for bringing that topic up! I am not at all satisfied with the behavior of our Stakeholders. I always have a fear of rejection before facing them. You have already seen that no matter how we deliver during our Sprints, the Stakeholders are always annoying. You might have sensed that our Team's morale is getting down because of their such behavior. We need to do something about it."

Alice:

"I can understand, but let's not talk about Stakeholders for a moment. I want you to tell me something. What exactly you do when you face any health-related issue?"

Tim:

"So simple! I simply go to the Doctor and get a proper treatment done to get well soon."

Alice:

"Perfect! But the Doctor doesn't offer you the required treatment directly, right? You need to explain him or her about, what exactly the health issue is and what all symptoms you are having, right?"

Tim:

"Yeah! It helps the Doctor to understand what the reason behind the problem could be. Sometimes it is also required for me to share my medical history with the Doctor. They also ask me about if any allergic reactions or side effects of medicines I had in the past. I think, they also need to maintain their records with such information. They perform required check-ups and suggest further applicable treatments."

Alice:

"Can't we have similar kind of frequent consultations with our Stakeholders? Can't we treat each other like the way you have been treated by the Doctors? To have a successful working relationship with our Stakeholders, don't you think that we need to understand their expectations, needs, and pain points?"

Tim:

"Sure, why not? Hope is a good thing, maybe the best of things, and no good thing ever dies!"

A Scrum Framework-based agile way of working always helps the agile organizations in such a way that their Scrum Teams can reduce their time-to-market and can also improve the speed of value delivery, while being cost-effective. The Scrum Teams can deliver the most optimized customer value through iterative and incremental releases of their working software product increments. However, there is always a possibility that they might have misinterpreted and/or exploited the basic structure of Scrum Framework. It is hence important for the Scrum Teams to understand what Scrum is and what it is not.

A Scrum Framework-based agile way of working agreement always needs to emphasize on the evident customer/end-user requirements. It needs to be there even if such requirements are ever-changing throughout the process and progress of the development and delivery of a high-quality working software product to be done by the Scrum Teams. Customer/end-user requirements need to be clearly characterized and articulated as Features/PBIs/User Stories under the Product Backlog. Being a people and product-oriented framework, the Scrum framework always asks the Scrum Teams to have their PBIs/User Stories formulated with no stringent specifications and conditions. The PBIs/User Stories always need to offer an open discussion along with an agreement to keep them evolving over the time. The Scrum Teams hence need to understand the why, what, when, who, how, and few other important aspects around their overall functioning and while dealing with their Product Backlog.

"To say that companies or CIOs are reluctant to embrace agile is like saying they wouldn't take aspirin for a headache. And they're not only not taking the aspirin, but they're also banging their heads against the wall and wondering why it hurts."
- Jim Johnson

The key decision-makers of the agile organizations always need to understand that the overall formulation, structuring, and alignment of their self-managing, self-organizing, and cross-functional Scrum Teams needs to be done by embracing the agile mindset of the Scrum Team members. As the Scrum Framework emphasizes on people and interactions, it needs to be done more willingly than the capabilities of Scrum Team members. Their capabilities can be improved with a suitable knowledge sharing and continuous learning mindset. The Scrum Teams always need to remember that their software products are quantifiable and they have an applicable lifecycle. Scrum-based agile way of working hence anticipates that the Scrum Teams need to have a collective long-term as well as short-term strategic thought process.

Such thought process always needs to reveal some important insights and factors, where the Scrum Teams need to capture them under their agile way of working agreement. These insights and factors need to consider various aspects of their own agile way of working such as an involvement of Stakeholders, a proper utilization of every Sprint to deliver the customer value-based concrete outcomes through product increments, the agreed process of inspection and adaptation, an effective addressal of impediments causing deviations and delays, a proper communication, collaboration, co-ordination, and co-operation within and outside the Scrum Team, and a procedure to improve a product mindset.

During the Sprints, many unanticipated problems, uncertainties, dependencies, risks, and issues can arise. This might result into deviations and delays for a Scrum Team's Sprint-based delivery. Scrum Teams hence need to take an extra bit of care with the time management aspect. By recognizing the shared goals and objectives, the Developers need to enact on their activities, where they are supposed to invest their current time. They also need to enact on the activities and on the required things to be investigated by them at a later point of time.

When there are any anticipated understanding and/or implementation gaps within an already established Scrum-based way of working of Scrum Teams, it is most likely that their Sprints might have some unfinished work items remaining under the Sprint Backlog by the end of their Sprints. Most of the times, such incomplete work items get spilled over to the next upcoming Sprint causing unfulfillment of their agreed Sprint Goal. To bridge such gaps and to reduce the spill over of work items from current Sprint to the upcoming Sprint, various additional add-ons need to be rigorously explored and followed by the Scrum Teams.

Product Owners need to have a proper vision, understanding, and strategy along with a suitable formulation of objectives and Sprint Goals for the software product. They need to have a sole authority/mandate to determine and confirm on the ordering and prioritization of the Product Backlog. They should not simply pass on the requirements and features from the Customers and Stakeholders to Developers. The Scrum Master and the Developers always need to help the Product Owner to anticipate and to have a forward-looking plan. They need to collaboratively find all the possible goals and objectives along with any dependencies and risks for the upcoming Sprints in advance. This allows them to be more proactive and strategic instead of just creating and/or updating the work items in the Product Backlog.

Scrum Teams need to conduct the Product Discovery and Alignment Workshops, where all the Scrum Team members need to discuss on their reflections, opinions, thoughts, and concerns. They need to work with each other to create, update, and order all the required work items under their Product Backlog. The Scrum Teams need to make use of a suitable template to create their Sprint Goals. The Sprint Goal and the Sprint Backlog always needs to be visible to all the Scrum Team members, while working together in Sprints.

> *"Setting goals is the first step in turning the invisible into the visible."*
>
> *- Tony Robbins*

The Product Goal and the Sprint Goals formulated and agreed by the Scrum Teams always help them to enable their focus. Every Scrum Event needs to take a reference of the agreed Sprint Goal, using which the Scrum Teams need to evaluate on the ways to keep their focus on it. They also need to minimize the ultimate impact of not meeting the agreed Sprint Goal. They need to take care of refinement of work items to be worked upon by them in the upcoming Sprints, collectively and regularly. The Scrum Master needs to let them determine, when and how they want to do the same. There needs to be a proper collaboration in between the Product Owner and the Stakeholders for the same purpose. By utilizing the better possible alternatives, ideas, and insights, they need to collect appropriate feedbacks and work on them.

To encourage a true agile mindset with an enhanced self-management and self-organization, the Scrum Team members need to determine their own way of working by themselves. They need to understand the ultimate significance of all the components of Scrum Framework to be utilized under their way of working. Considering that there are many opportunities for every Scrum Team member to learn and grow, they need to work together and continuously improve. The Scrum Teams can explore some online work management tools. Such tools help them to bring in a good visibility of Scrum Artifacts. It offers them an ease of usage for a better tracking purpose. It also helps them to improve their overall quality of communication and transparency. All the Scrum Team members need to have an applicable and appropriate access and knowledge for such tooling in place, so that they can work collaboratively.

Innovation and Experimentation are must haves for the Scrum Teams. They always need to continuously innovate and experiment to find out what works best for them. They also need to experiment by considering various alternatives and solutions to enhance their existing way of working-specific practices and processes. The outcomes of such experimentation may vary based upon the structuring, alignment, capabilities, skills, understanding, rapport, and experience of the Scrum Team members. Nevertheless, it also asks them to explore their true potential and a true power of collective efforts.

> *"If we manage conflict constructively, we harness its energy for creativity and development."*
>
> *- Kenneth Kaye*

The Scrum Teams need to have constructive debates during their all the interactions. Such debates should not have any negative consequences/impacts on the overall team environment and on the rapport established in between the Scrum Team members. In case of conflicts, they need to decide together on how they can proceed ahead. By providing the Scrum Team members an ultimate opportunity to think, respond, and reflect on their opinions, some follow-up discussions need to be conducted, so that dialogues can happen.

It is important for the Scrum Master and the Product Owner to be energetic, sociable, and empathetic; however, they also need to be firm and proactive. They need to involve all the Stakeholders and the other required and intended parties to ensure that there is always a right consensus, while making their important decisions. They always need to give an enough freedom and openness to all the Scrum Team members, so that they can have enough dialogues with them by also making use of the concept of active listening.

The Product Owner needs to create an environment with a well-balanced emphasis to be given on product ownership, planning, commitment, delivery, and control. It is always required for the Product Owner to have constant interactions with the Stakeholders; however, the Stakeholders should also feel engaged with the Developers. It is not only the Product Owner, but the entire Scrum Team who needs to be constantly interacting with the Stakeholders, as and when needed. The Scrum Team members need to ensure that there is no bureaucracy present within their agile way of working, as it causes a less openness and engagement to enact upon the real expectations of Stakeholders.

> *"Creating the right sense of teamwork can be challenging. Scrum Masters can help by ensuring that the team embraces the concept of whole-team responsibility and whole-team commitment to deliver working software at the end of each sprint. Though the team might struggle at first to break long held habits of specialization and handoffs, increasing communication, decreasing the size of handoffs, and mixing the size of backlog items brought into a sprint will help individuals make the shift to working as a team."*
> *- Mike Cohn*

The Scrum Team members need to map their individual as well as collective skill sets and capabilities under the skills tracking quadrant/matrix. They need to reflect on their individual self-rated proficiency level (such as novice, advanced beginner, competent, proficient, expert, and so on) against their own skill sets and capabilities. By analysing the current positioning and distribution of their skill sets and by discussing its overall impact on their individual and collective productivity, they need to come up with some agreed action items to address any improvements. They need to have a formal agreement for themselves. They need to consider and decide on when, who, what, and how aspects (along with the required learning resources, strategies, approaches, timeline, and so on) to start improving at the earliest. This helps them to measure their improvement against the expected cross-functionality over time.

The Scrum Master needs to help and support the Product Owner by suggesting some valuable techniques and coaching, using which the Product Owner can have proper interactions and negotiations with the Stakeholders. This needs to be done to reduce any understanding gaps between the Scrum Teams and their Stakeholders. The Product Owner needs to become an advantage for the Scrum Team to clarify the customer/end-user and stakeholders' specific requirements. By considering the personas of stakeholders and customers/end-users, the Scrum Team needs to correlate them with the PBIs/User Stories in the Product Backlog. If there are any doubts and/or concerns for the Features, PBIs/User Stories to be worked upon by the Developers, they need to get them clarified with the Product Owner at the earliest.

"Strive for continuous improvement, instead of perfection."

- Kim Collins

During the Sprint Retrospectives, Scrum Team members need to reflect on how they can improve their ability to get themselves familiarised with the current need of time. They always need do the needful for the most valuable things to be done by them. They need to discuss and describe the better approaches, alternatives, and improvements to streamline their agile way of working. It is important for them to understand that identification and sharing of potential improvements in their way of working is important; however, enacting on those improvements is more important. By prioritizing the most important things first, they need to agree and address those improvements one by one. Sprint Reviews and Retrospectives always need to be persistent activities, where they need to inspect and adapt their agile way of working and decide on what needs to be changed and what needs to be kept as it is.

Developers need to automate the tasks/activities which are required to be done manually and frequently. This helps them to improve the completion of tasks/activities with a greater speed. Limiting their own work in progress and applying restrictions on the amount of new work to be started (with any existing work which is already in progress) can improve their cross-functional collaboration. They need to make use of Daily Scrum to request and offer required help from and to each other, so that they can complete their existing work in progress as soon as possible. By pairing up and supporting each other, they can share the required knowledge. It can help them to improve their capabilities. By making use of a collaborative approach like Specification by Example, they need to collaborate with their Customers and Stakeholders. By making use of such emerging practice, they can work together to build their working software product based on the end-user behavior-specific realistic examples and use cases.

"The value of experimentation is not the trying. It's the trying again after it fails."

- Simon Sinek

By experimenting and applying some of the suitable microstructures belonging to the concept of Liberating Structures, the Scrum Master and the Product Owner always need to ensure a complete involvement of all the Scrum Team members during their every interaction. They can make use of Liberating Structures such as Min Specs and Ecocycle Planning to maintain their Product Backlog. They can use a Liberating Structure like 9 Whys during their Sprint Planning. It helps them to decide the ultimate intent of their upcoming Sprint. The Scrum Master needs to ask some powerful questions to help the Developers and the Product Owner by considering the why aspect of their decision-making.

They can also use a Liberating Structure like What, So What, Now What during their Sprint Reviews and Retrospectives. It helps them to reflect on their own annotations and concerns. They need to interpret them and come up with some action items to work upon. By making use of the Liberating Structures such as TRIZ, 1-2-4-ALL, Impromptu Networking, Wise Crowds, Troika Consulting, and 25/10 Crowd Sourcing, they can quickly recognize the high customer value features to perform the required ideation, innovation, and implementation. By mixing up various Liberating Structures and using some advanced techniques such as Empathy Maps, Design the Box, Magic Estimation, and so on, the Scrum Master needs to facilitate all the Scrum Events, by making them extremely collaborative and interactive.

The Sprint Review needs to be used by the Scrum Team members as a perfect occasion to collect some feedbacks about their working software product. The Stakeholders need to be engaged and to be made aware about the overall progress of the Scrum Team. By making use of Liberating Structures such as Agree/Certainty Matrix, 1-2-4-ALL, Impromptu Networking, and What, So What, Now What, the Stakeholders can inspect the product increments and can recommend and share their valuable recommendations and feedbacks to improve upon. The Scrum Master needs to adjust and alter the format of the Sprint Review based on its context. The aim of Sprint Reviews for Scrum Teams always needs to be to find the best possible way to collect feedbacks from the Stakeholders.

The Scrum Teams need to be 100% truthful about any work which is incomplete during the Sprints. During the Sprint Reviews, by reviewing the incomplete PBIs/User Stories, they can share the details about issues and impediments faced by them, so that the Stakeholders can understand the genuine reasons behind such issues and impediments. Sprint Retrospectives always need to be also utilized by them to reflect on such issues and impediments, so that they can avoid similar issues with some better proactive alternatives from next time onwards.

"Capacity to learn is a gift; Ability to learn is a skill; Willingness to learn is a choice."

- Brian Herbert

The Scrum Teams need to search, evaluate, apply, and assess various techniques to improve their agile way of working. By determining which techniques work best for them, they need to drive a transitional effort by moving away from the plan-based advancements and by encouraging the process of Empiricism. Application of such techniques can help them to enable transparency, inspection, and adaptation, to coach everyone in the agile organization to have a proper collaboration within and outside of their Scrum Teams, to handle the process of self-management, self-organization, and cross-functionality, to inculcate an open-minded ideation, innovation, and experimentation culture, to encourage a team environment for the Scrum Teams, where they can continuously learn and improve by giving their best.

"A good Scrum Master will push for permission to remove impediments to team productivity. A great Scrum Master will be prepared to ask for forgiveness."
- Geoff Watts

The Scrum Master always needs to be proactive, courageous, mindful, and resourceful while removing any impediments. To encourage the Scrum Team members to become more self-managing and self-organizing, he/she needs to ask them some open-ended powerful questions without giving them direct inputs to resolve their impediments. This encourages the Scrum Team members to think and enact on their impediments. The Scrum Teams need to focus on their real impediments. To confirm on whether their every problem is a genuine impediment or not, they need to understand if the problem getting faced by them is blocking their progress or not. The Scrum Master needs to deal with many problematic encounters by influencing the culture of continuous experimentation, learning, and improvement.

This influence needs to be there in such a way that, their own collective accomplishments as a one Scrum Team always need to be given more emphasis over the accomplishments of individual Scrum Team members. Using some agile contracts and a formal agile way of working agreement, the Scrum Master needs to support a stable, reliable, and well-balanced Scrum Team composition, where the Scrum Team's general agile mindset, their behaviors, collective ownership, and teamwork always needs to be taken into the consideration. The Scrum Master hence needs to act as a Change Agent. Using the servant leadership style, the Scrum Master always needs to lead by influence. He/she needs to embrace and facilitate the process of change management within and outside of the Scrum Teams.

It is important for the Stakeholders and the key decision-makers from top-level management to understand, help, and to support the Scrum Masters within an agile organization to drive the process of change management, so that they can give their best to lead the high-performing Scrum Teams as Servant Leaders. Such Scrum Teams can collaboratively deliver the customer value optimized outcomes. To visualize a clear-cut distinction between the blockers and resolvable impediments, the Scrum Teams need to make use of an Impediment Board. They also need to make sure that they are using such Board to visualize the real impediments (and not just every impediment/problem/issue/), which they are unable to resolve by themselves.

The Scrum Board always needs to be maintained by the entire Scrum Team and not just by the Scrum Master. It can be also referred at the time of Daily Scrum; however, the Developers of a Scrum Team should not wait till the Daily Scrum to highlight, share, and discuss on such impediments. The Developers always need to consider the impact of impediments on the achievement of their agreed Sprint Goal. They also need to seek some help from the other Developers, if required. Not every impediment is an impediment. The Scrum Master always needs to focus and enact on the resolution and removal of the real blockers and impediments, which the Developers cannot resolve by themselves within an ongoing Sprint.

"As an Agile coach, you don't need to have all the answers;
it takes time and a few experiments to hit on the right approach."
- Rachel Davies and Liz Sedley

To establish and to continuously improve the practices and processes of a Scrum-based agile way of working within a Scrum Team or at various levels of an agile organization, the Scrum Master always needs to act as an Agile Coach. It is the responsibility of the Scrum Master to teach, coach, and mentor the Scrum Teams to enable an agile mindset within them. He/she also needs to collaborate with the Product Owner. Many times, the impediments might be related to the knowledge and/or understanding and/or implementation gaps present within the Scrum Teams. It is hence required for the Scrum Master, the Product Owner, and the Developers to have a rock-solid understanding-based rapport in place to fill-in such gaps.

"A block affects only a single task, whereas an impediment acts like a parachute, slowing
down overall progress. Quite often, the Developers can fix blocks by themselves,
whereas impediments need to be fixed by the Scrum Master."
- Ilan Goldstein

The Scrum Master and the Product Owner need to be able recognize the real impediments. They need to help each other to arrive at a consensus-based decision-making. By asking some open-ended powerful questions, they always need to reflect on their rational assumptions about the proposition, optimization, and prioritization of customer value, alignment of work items, and identification and proactive resolution of dependencies and risks. Using a Liberating Structure like Min Spec, the Product Owner can strategize the Product Backlog ordering and prioritization by having interactions and negotiations with the Developers.

It certainly makes a difference for the Scrum Teams to have their Scrum Events and other required impromptu meetings as workshops, where they can promote their conversations by having an extreme engagement of all the participants. Instead of having their events and meetings as monotonous, uninteresting, and energy-draining, they can make use of Liberating Structures to have them fun-oriented. By starting with a clear objective and through a series of facilitation formats, they need to help each other to keep their energy levels up and to create an atmosphere with a shared understanding. Allowing the participants to have a proper engagement and making use of a diverge-converge kind of interaction pattern can help them to have both separated and collective sharing of valuable insights. All the events and meetings need to consider a summarized reflection of their numerous observations, thoughts, insights, suggestions, learnings, improvement measures, and the required action items.

*"Self-discipline is about taking charge of your mind and
directing it to act in the best interest of yourself."*

- Gaur Gopal Das

The self-disciplined Scrum Teams need to have their focus on the achievement of an agreed Sprint Goal by maintaining a consistent pace and a stable velocity. Any meetings causing unnecessary deviations to this bare minimum expectation need to be strictly restricted. There should be a least context switching for the Developers. The Developers always need to have a collaborative strategy to develop and deliver the work items selected by them under their Sprint Backlog. Any ad-hoc meetings standing out of the reach of such strategy should not be there at all. The Scrum Events should be utilized in such a way that any need for additional meetings not defined as per the basic structure of Scrum Framework should be minimized. By following time-boxes allocated for the Scrum Events being participated by them, they should not lose their focus. By eliminating any wastage of time and effort, they need to get the most out of all the Scrum events by giving a proper importance to clear objectives.

The Product Backlog Refinements need to be used by them to refine their work items by performing the mapping, ordering, sizing, slicing, prioritization, and by capturing the required clarifications. The Sprint Planning needs to be used by them to set and agree on the Sprint Goal. They also need to identify and select the work required to achieve the same. Daily Scrum needs to be used by them to create a daily plan to work together toward the achievement of Sprint Goal. They also need to reflect on their overall progress toward the achievement of Sprint Goal. The Sprint Review needs to be used by them to collect the valuable feedbacks from their Stakeholders. They also need to collectively decide on what are the action items for them to improve on, based on the feedbacks received. The Sprint Retrospective needs to be used by them to inspect various entities from the latest completed Sprint. They need to recognize the required actionable improvements to work upon later. All the standard Scrum Events need to be conducted to achieve their basic purpose. This approach can also help them to avoid/reduce the need for any additional meetings outside of the Scrum Events, where they need to minimize and bridge any gaps, both collectively and proactively.

The Scrum Teams always need to have a proper thought process, a clear strategy, and a formal understanding to align themselves on various considerations of their Scrum-based agile way of working. As shown in *Figure 14.1*, they need to focus on some of the important factors, while defining their own agile way of working. This needs to be done by them by considering a unique significance of all these factors, both individually as well as collectively.

Figure 14.1: *Considerations for Scrum-based agile way of working of Scrum Teams*

The agile way of working agreement of a Scrum Team needs to be formed by considering the software product's vision. Such vision needs to be a clear and concise declaration of the anticipated future state of working software product after its development and delivery. The product vision always needs to provide a path for the working software product to control and accomplish its eventual purpose, goals, and objectives.

"Control leads to compliance; autonomy leads to engagement."

- Daniel H. Pink

There needs to be a shared understanding of such purpose, goals, and objectives across all the Scrum Team members. They should tend to get better at their capabilities, so that they can work on such a shared understanding and convert the same into reality. They should always have an involvement to increase their autonomy and to keep themselves integrated with their work. By tracking their own positioning against the levels of integration, autonomy, and an integrated autonomy, they need to reflect on areas of improvement and actionable steps. An agile mindset-based way of working and its associated practices need to be mirrored under their way of working agreement, using which they need to enhance their overall agility.

By making use of Roman Pichler's Product Vision Board, the Scrum Teams can capture their product vision. The entire Scrum Team along with their Stakeholders always need to understand that the overall process of software product development and delivery is extremely volatile and unpredictable. Therefore, they always need to work together by finding out some simple and better alternatives. They need to plan and re-plan their required activities and actions to achieve their vision accordingly.

"As a rule of thumb, for every user who tells you about a problem,
there will be between 10 and 100 other users who experienced the same problem
and didn't think to get in touch."
- Paul Butcher

Keeping the nature of PBIs/User Stories a bit flexible can help the Scrum Teams to capture all the required functional, non-functional, and technical aspects of customer requirements under them. While creating the PBIs/User Stories, the Scrum Teams always need to give their highest attention to the actual expectations and perspectives of their customers/end-users.

The Product Owner needs to understand that an accurate estimation of work items is almost impossible. Even though the Scrum Teams can make use of relative estimates, they still cannot guarantee that they are estimating work items by covering all the possible, ideal scenarios, complexity, risks, dependencies, external factors, potential issues, and various other insights, which might influence their original estimates. The most common and important concern the Product Owners always has is, whether the Developers will be able to complete all the work items under their potentially releasable working software product increment by the end of every Sprint or not. The Scrum Teams need to understand and remember the fact that the most important reason behind the estimation of work items is to enable some predictability and forecasting against the anticipated delivery of software product increments. It needs to be up to the Scrum Teams to decide and agree on what kind of estimation they need to use.

"Experience seems to most of us to lead to conclusions, but empiricism has sworn never to draw them."

- George Santayana

As per the Scrum Guide, the Scrum Framework is based on the empirical process control theory or Empiricism, which always needs to assert that the knowledge comes from experience and from making the decisions based on what is known to the Scrum Teams. By following the same analogy, Scrum Teams need to adopt predicting the number of work items to be taken under a Sprint based on historical data of relative estimates. By using the concept of No Estimates through techniques such as Drip Funding and Probabilistic Forecasting, they can focus on lessons learned from the past Sprints. This approach helps them to reduce their overall efforts of estimation and planning, so that they can truly focus upon their development and delivery-specific activities. No Estimation need not to be about not estimating. Rather it needs to be about reducing and/or eliminating the waste in their overall process of estimation.

The Scrum Teams also need to reflect on their work activities such as build, release, and documentation, and so on, to be performed by them once the working software product increment is marked as Done. They need to consider the amount of effort required to promote their changes across agreed environments, which are already worked upon and completed by them. This needs to be done by them until they make their changes available to their Customers/End-Users under their Customer-specific production environment.

It is one of the fundamental responsibilities of the Scrum Master to help, support, and coach the Scrum Team to continuously enhance their agreed Definition of Done. It helps the team to minimize the amount of work left and to be performed by them once the software product increment is marked as Done. They can utilize such saved time and effort to explore and learn the suitable advanced engineering practices. Such practices can act as key enablers for their Technical Agility. They need to be utilized by them in such a way that they can release their working software product increments in a much faster and easier manner, without losing the quality, stability, and few other functional and non-functional aspects of the software product.

"If you define the problem correctly, you almost have the solution."
- Steve Jobs

It is vital for the Scrum Teams to simplify their roles, responsibilities, objectives, alignments, expectations, understanding, and associated processes under their agile way of working. They need to confirm on their decision-making process. It needs to optimize their understanding and associations, so that they can define their concerns and problems accurately and discuss further to have some appropriate solutions in place. Even though the Developers need not commit to the Sprint Backlog, they still need to commit to many other entities such as the core values and components of the Scrum Framework, an accomplishment of their agreed Product Goal and Sprint Goals, a continuous, incremental, and iterative development and delivery of high-quality working software product increments, an extreme level of collaboration, communication, co-ordination, co-operation, and teamwork to achieve their agreed Product Goal and Sprint Goals, and frequent inspections and adaptations, and so on.

"Exploration is really the essence of the human spirit."

- Frank Borman

The Scrum Team members always need to help themselves to have a strong grip on an evolving landscape of the Product Backlog and the Sprint Backlog. They always need to apply required changes to the work items taken by them under their Sprint Backlog, as they start to explore them and get to know about any new findings. To remain on the same page, they always need to collaborate with the Product Owner, as and when they think that it is required for them. Any changes being performed by them under their Sprint Backlog always need to be in line with the basic purpose of accomplishment of their agreed Sprint Goal to develop and deliver a fully functional, high-quality potentially releasable working software product Done increment.

As per one of the important agile principles, it is mandatory for the Product Owner to bring in the simplicity as the art of maximizing the amount of work not done by the Developers. This also needs to be essential, where the Product Owner always needs to remember that the Scrum Team needs to deliver the anticipated customer value-based outcomes instead of just developing and delivering the software product features/functionalities faster. The Scrum Teams always need to let go of their old habits, which are not adding any value to their agile way of working. They should adopt new habits by supporting and facilitating the required change to bring in more focus, discipline, perseverance, and commitment.

The Scrum Teams establishing and enhancing their Scrum-based agile way of working for the first time struggle a lot. When their top-level management asks them to follow a traditional waterfall model-based Software Development Life Cycle (SDLC) with a command-and-control approach, the Scrum Master needs to step up. The Scrum Master needs to have proper discussions with the management to educate them and to let them know about the basics of Scrum Framework, its values, and components along with the agile values and principles. The Management also needs to understand the same instead of just following a traditional SDLC. The Scrum Team needs to adopt an iterative and incremental software product development and delivery through a proper usage of advanced engineering practices and an agile mindset. This always helps them to improve their overall teamwork and performance.

> *"Scrum aims to harness the power of self-organizing, autonomous, engaged teams*
> *who take responsibility for delivery and collaborate directly with their customers."*
> *- Geoff Watts*

By making use of a technique like Dependency Spider, the Scrum Team needs to be always aware about their frequently occurring dependencies, both within and outside of the Scrum Team. When they need anything from any other teams (not necessarily that the other teams are also following Scrum) or directly from their customers / end-users, they need to follow the simplest and fastest routes based upon the lessons learned in the past. They need to record such routes under a Dependency Spider. They need to measure the average amount of waiting time for all such dependencies. It needs to be reviewed by them at the time of Sprint Reviews and Sprint Retrospectives, so that they can apply some better alternatives-based routes.

> *"Dependency harms culture. People thrive the more they can be self-reliant."*
> *- Wesley J. Smith*

The Scrum Team members need to determine a process to cut down any adverse impacts of their commonly occurring dependencies on their ability to develop and deliver working software product increments. While resolving and removing their inter-team dependencies, they need a proper help and support from the Product Owner and the Stakeholders to make their way of working environment open as well as transparent. The Dependency Spider needs to be used by them to visualize and to enact upon any bottlenecks, which are blocking them and their way of working to become more efficient, useful, and progressive.

It is required for the Scrum Team members and their Stakeholders to consider each other as Partners. The Developers need to realize the distinctive viewpoints getting shared through the valuable feedbacks and recommendations given by the Stakeholders through the Product Owner. At the same time, the Stakeholders also need to have a suitable consideration along with a strong admiration for the Developers. Mutual respect and understanding with a proper collaboration and co-operation-based agile way of working agreement can help them to set some basic expectations and to keep such expectations balanced and addressed.

It is important for the Scrum Master to shield and protect the Developers when the Product Owner and the Stakeholders are overly demanding. There is always a possibility that they are asking for too much, too early, too frequently, and too violently. This causes a break down, where the Developers tend to take shortcuts. Such behavior and actions of Developers might result into quality issues introducing a Technical Debt. Hence, such behavior and actions always need to be avoided and stopped by them. The Scrum Master needs to protect them and have a properly structured way of working agreement to prevent any Technical Debt.

The Scrum Teams always need to be aware of protecting themselves from a feeling of self-satisfaction, fixed mindset, and a sense of limited learning and growth. The Scrum Master needs to educate them about such feelings and perceptions, which need to be avoided by the Scrum Team members, both individually and collectively. They always need to seek for constant learning and continuous improvement.

The Scrum Teams need to remember that to become high-performing and hyper-productive teams, they always need to restrict themselves from having a fixed mindset-oriented thinking that they have nothing left to explore, learn, and improve on. They should always encourage themselves to explore and try out new things by nurturing an experimentation-based mindset. Such experimentation might not always get into successful outcomes; however, they can surely get to know about various possible alternatives and options, out of which the ones which work best for them, can be selected by them to improve their way of working.

The Scrum Master needs to keep in mind that he/she always needs to assist and guide rest of the Scrum Team members to perform extremely well and not to make themselves just to look well. A successful Scrum Master is one who coaches, teaches, and mentors his/her Scrum Team who is performing well, both extremely and constantly. At the same time, it is also required for the Scrum Master to do less, both noticeably and deliberately, so that the rest of the Scrum Team members can become more self-managing and self-organizing. Even if the Scrum Teams get matured over a period, they still tend to think that they need to have a Scrum Master to continuously teach, coach, mentor, help, guide, and support them. However, in a long run, all the Scrum Team members always need to understand that they need to be more self-managing and self-organizing on their own, so that they themselves can act as a Scrum Master, Servant Leader, and a Change Agent to teach, coach, mentor, help, guide, and support themselves. This approach always helps all of them to learn, follow, apply, and conquer the skills required to become Servant Leaders and Change Agents.

It is not required for the Scrum Master to solve every problem of the Developers. Rather the Scrum Master always needs to build and nurture their true potential and capability, so that they can work on their own problems and try to resolve them on their own. The Scrum Master always needs to remember that the Developers are collectively and collaboratively smarter and knowledgeable. This is true because the overall agility, especially technical agility of Developers is always going to be continuously improving over the period. It is hence necessary for the Scrum Master to inculcate a proper agile mindset within them to achieve the shared vision, purpose, goals, and objectives. The Scrum Master needs to allow them to establish and enhance such a team dynamics and culture, where they need to be motivated to give their best. They also need to be open, curious, empathetic, courageous, and self-sufficient.

It is always essential for the Scrum Masters and the Product Owners to not to commit to the Stakeholders without checking and consulting with the Developers, especially when they are unsure about various technical aspects involved/required in the process of software product development and delivery. They should not have a false sense of authoritative power on the behalf of the Developers to agree with any new functionalities, enhancements, and any change requests, irrespective of the kind and size they have. The entire Scrum Team needs to have the required discussions during their Product Backlog Refinements, Sprint Planning, and Daily Scrum before they commit anything to their Stakeholders.

Many times, the process of decision-making involving some of the required interactions with the Stakeholders and the corresponding acknowledgement to the Stakeholders always needs to be a considered under the interactions between the Product Owner and the rest of the Scrum Team members. Such interactions always need to happen in advance. With such process in place, it is always required for the Scrum Team members to have a proper consensus within themselves first. It is imperative for the Scrum Master and the Product Owner to be present at the centre of all such required discussions, dialogues, interactions, and conversations with rest of the Scrum Team members. On the other hand, sometimes, it is also imperative for them to support the rest of the Scrum Team members during such conversations. Enhancing the overall flow, visibility, and focus of communication and sharing the required valuable information through every interaction always needs to be given a topmost priority by all the Scrum Team members across all the Scrum Events.

"Failure is simply the opportunity to begin again, this time more intelligently."
- Henry Ford

Even if there are any failed Sprints and there is a limited development and delivery of anticipated customer value-based outcomes through such Sprints, the Scrum Teams should not look at them as failures. The Scrum Master needs to help the Scrum Team members to inspect and adapt, so that their own critical thinking can help them to acknowledge such Sprints that fall short of anticipations with their truthful efforts than failures. It is also required for the Scrum Master and the Product Owner to appreciate and applaud the Scrum Team members in case of their good work and collaboration, both individually and collectively.

There always needs to be a sense of appreciation within the Scrum Team. An appreciation always needs to be done by the Scrum Team members, both genuinely and suitably. Avoiding any false compliments and at the same time letting the Scrum Team members know when they do good work can always boost their morale. This also helps to keep them motivated.

"You improvise. You adapt. You overcome."
- Clint Eastwood

If the Scrum Team experiences mistakes during their Sprints, they need to understand the impact and consequences of such mistakes, so that they can learn from those mistakes. The Sprint Retrospectives can be utilized to reflect on such mistakes, where they can include and discuss with whoever was involved in and affected by mistakes. It is a must have for them to disengage themselves from any of the negative sentiments and the behavior of blaming, pinpointing someone around such mistakes. By reflecting on the patterns, they have observed and the real cause behind such patterns, they need to learn through such mistakes, so that they can make certain to avoid the occurrence of similar mistakes thereafter.

While performing blameless post-mortems, the Scrum Master needs to encourage the Scrum Team members to perform a reverse engineering process. This can be done by creating a timeline of events, actions, and patterns, and by identifying gaps, missing elements, and root causes within their overall agile way of working flow, agreement, and associated processes. The Scrum Team members need to discuss and brainstorm with their thoughts, observations, opinions, interpretations, and conclusions, so that they can get a better sense of all the mistakes happened in the past. Based on the facts and data points, they need to come up with some proactive measures to be followed by them in the future, using which they can try to minimize or to protect themselves from performing similar mistakes in the future.

"Agile leaders lead teams; non-agile ones manage tasks."
- Jim Highsmith

Instead of being tasks/activities focused, the Scrum Team members always need to be value/outcome focused. Instead of individual efforts, the Scrum Teams always need to thrive for collective efforts. They need to perform their actions to deliver the anticipated customer value-based outcomes. Their conversations and efforts always need to be focused on the agreed Sprint Goal to complete the Features, PBIs/ User Stories. They need to make them fully functional and potentially releasable, instead of just completing them partially with the completion of few tasks/activities belonging to the PBIs/User Stories. They need to highlight any dependencies/ issues if they are struggling. By remaining silent and by performing active listening, the Scrum Master needs to let the Developers to figure out their own solutions for their own problems. Though it is a bit difficult thing for Developers, they still need to learn to not to be dependent on the Scrum Master to solve their every problem. It is okay for the Scrum Master to offer them suggestions, but the Developers need to solve the problems on their own through a coaching process. In this process, the Scrum Master always needs to ask them some powerful questions to trigger their strengths without giving them any solutions directly.

Many times, the Scrum Master struggles when he/she needs to perform the role of coach/agile coach. While being a coach/an agile coach, it is required for the Scrum Master that he/she needs to guide, help, and support the Scrum Team members toward self-organization. A continuous experimentation culture by limiting the fear of failure needs to be embraced by them, which also needs to give them a self-confidence to try out experiments on their own. Sometimes, while the entire Scrum Team is in the middle of a Daily Scrum, the Scrum Master can clarify his/her expectations out of the ongoing Daily Scrum and purposefully get out of it. Such behavior of a Scrum Master needs to expect that the rest of the Scrum Team members are inculcating the highest level of autonomy and self-organization, using which they can have their interactions through a proper engagement within themselves. In this case, they also need to maximize their self-awareness and self-management.

The Scrum Team members always need to get rid out of a feeling that they always need the Scrum Master to lead/drive all their conversations/interactions during Daily Scrum. Even though a sudden exit of a Scrum Master from Daily Scrum can make them a bit awkward, still this way of serving the Scrum Team to boost their self-sufficiency can help them to follow a proper flow of their interactions. It also helps them to become more focused and to have a much-improved commitment along with a real sense of collective ownership, accountability, and responsibility.

It is also required for the Scrum Master to help and support the Scrum Teams (typically those who are new to the Scrum Framework-based agile way of working) during their interactions-based dialogues. While being a part of a new Scrum Team, the Scrum Team members might feel uncomfortable, unconnected, and awkward with each other as the process of rapport building takes time. Such discomfort might result into less/limited interactions, causing an unavoidable silence during their interactions. In this scenario, the Scrum Master needs to make use of effective facilitation skills and ask some powerful and open-ended questions. To minimize their discomfort, he/she needs to allow them to think and speak. He/she needs to act as an effective mediator for the rest of the Scrum Team members and as a coach to improve their working environment by making them comfortable through their interactive dialogues.

Instead of blindly following a standardized, bookish knowledge of Agile Mindset and Scrum Framework, the Scrum Teams always need to explore their own agile way of working by themselves. They need to understand that being agile is always more important than doing agile as per the standardized, bookish knowledge. They need to live the Agile Mindset by following the Agile Values and Principles, Scrum Values, and Empiricism, both thoroughly and rigorously. It helps them to build and nurture the highest level of agility within them.

All the Scrum Team members always need to devote their valuable efforts and energy to utilize the ultimate power of active listening, holistic thinking, sensemaking, brainstorming, and performing all their activities. They need to inspire themselves by triggering their self-motivation to work hard as well as smart. They need to own their successes as well as failures by encouraging a collective ownership of everything they are doing.

There always needs to be a proper trust established within the Scrum Team members. It needs to act as a foundation for all the Scrum Values, using which they can build their rapport and healthy, sustainable relationships. The trust always needs to be established through an extensive collaboration and co-operation among themselves. They always need to accept their mistakes and take both corrective as well as preventive actions, so that they can minimize any risks and harmful impacts of such mistakes on their deliverables.

All the Scrum Team members always need to challenge themselves to see through various perspectives, so that they can come up with some better alternatives to improve their Scrum-based agile way of working. There always needs to be a comprehensive coherence, compliance, and dynamism within their agile way of working. By making use of some team-building activities, the Scrum Teams can improve their team dynamics and culture. They can anticipate a significant increase in their trust levels along with a constructive criticism and meaningful socialization of Scrum Team members. Some team-building activities through gamification can help them to foster their overall positioning, alignment, understanding, and collaboration. They always need to explore and try out various activities such as effective team building techniques/exercises. The gamification-based teamwork activities/exercises through some icebreaker games and some strategic team-building activities always need to act as energizers for them.

By making use of the Kudo Cards, the Scrum Team members can make use of any possible opportunities to share their appreciations and to complement each other. This can act as a great source of motivation and encouragement for all the Scrum Team members to reflect on the moments when they have contributed to enhance their own capability to help, share, learn, and grow together. This approach also acts as an enabler for them to get out of their comfort zone. They can make use of such Cards at the time of Sprint Retrospectives and Sprint Reviews to appreciate all the good teamwork being done by them. They can also make use of the concept of Appreciative Inquiry which is a model to accelerate a proper engagement of their Stakeholders for the purpose of a self-determined change.

By making use of a technique like Lean Coffee during their informal conversations on various topics, the Scrum Team members can become empowered by increasing their engagement through some fun-based interactions. By sharing the copies of relevant books to have the group reading activities, by sharing and reading the relevant blog posts, articles, and by listening to the relevant podcasts, they can share and confirm their understanding through their individual perspectives. This helps them to reflect on their personal takeaways and share some insightful intuitions through such exclusive collaborative activities. Creating a culture of continuous learning within the Scrum Teams always requires them to spend their priceless time, efforts, determination, trust, transparency, focus, courage, openness, commitment, and integrity. There might be some software development teams in an organization who are supposed to execute their way of working through a command-and-control style of leadership and within a fixed scope, time, and cost manner. This makes them to have their way of working as traditional waterfall model-based (and not Scrum-based) way of working.

With such a way of working, the Scrum Framework-specific practices might be partially integrated. This is nothing but a doing agile mindset and not a being agile mindset. This way of working has many adverse impacts on the overall trust and transparency within the software development. It becomes difficult for the team members to achieve Scrum Values and Empiricism without a proper presence of trust and transparency. Trust and transparency always need to provide them a strong feeling of psychological safety, effectiveness, and a true sense of continuous improvement to be more productive and successful.

The Developers of a Scrum Team always need to deliver the fully functional and completely done working software product increments by the end of the Sprints. Any partially done work needs to be avoided, as it causes confusion for the Product Owner to identify the current positioning of deliverables. The Developers should not exaggerate their effort and goals while delivering their Sprint-based commitments. They need to maintain a stable velocity which always need to help the Product Owner to be better at predictability. All the completed work needs to be kept transparent to everyone. The Product Owner should not ask the Developers to have a continuous rise in their velocity during their every Sprint. Such expectation is totally wrong and can result into over commitment by the Developers. It might also cause highly manipulated relative estimates in place.

There should not be a command and control driven micro-management within the Scrum Teams, as it reduces the overall trust along with the important aspects of self-management and self-organization within the Scrum Teams. The Scrum Master and the Product Owner should always make use of a leading with influence-based strategic, decisive, and tactical leadership style, while collaborating with the Developers to make the best use of all their strengths. The Product Owner should not commit to the work instead of a proper consent of the Developers during the

Sprint Planning. Instead of having fixed deadlines and obligatory commitments, there should be goals and objectives to ask the Developers to explore their full potential and to contribute by showcasing their best potential. The Product Owner and the Scrum Master should not decide the how part of development and delivery of the working software product being implemented by the Developers. The Product Owner and the Scrum Master should always allow the Developers to decide the same. There always needs to be a transparency, simplicity, and clarity for the product vision, goals, objectives, purpose, and strategy, so that the Scrum Team members can feel a genuine association with all these important aspects of the software product being developed by them.

The globally distributed Scrum Teams might have some cultural differences. Such Scrum Teams not communicating through face-to-face conversations might get into some confusions, misinterpretations, and chaos. It is hence always required for them to make use of some suitable online tools to encourage themselves to have face-to-face conversations. By making use of techniques such as Trust Canvas and Trust Assessment Exercise, they need to reflect on their opinions about overall trust, rapport, and bonding within the Scrum Team. They need to identify and enact upon any factors that are causing a deficiency of openness, transparency, and trust within themselves.

By having a common, shared understanding about trust (as a baseline for all the core values of Scrum Framework), the Scrum Team members always need to share their thoughts to discuss on various factors to be explored by them to enhance their way of working in a long term. They need to have an appropriate alignment for bridging any gaps, which are impacting their agile way of working by applying techniques such as Information Radiators, Schneider Model, SCARF Model, Management 3.0 Delegation Poker Exercise, and so on.

> *"Everyone in a complex adaptive system has a slightly different interpretation.*
> *The more interpretations we gather, the easier it becomes to gain a sense of the whole."*
> *- Margaret Wheatley*

The Scrum Framework always expects the Scrum Teams to work on a proper resolution of the Complex Adaptive Problems belonging to the Complex Adaptive Systems under a Complex Environment. These problems are the ones that might change their direction and distinction, while the Scrum Team is working on them and before they solve them by implementing the anticipated solutions. They are undeniably difficult to understand and must be always taken into the consideration through a highest level of focus and collaboration among the Scrum Team members. While making use of the empirical process control theory through inspection, adaptation, and transparency, the Scrum Team members always need to work on such problems by the means of productive and collaborative development and delivery of high-quality working software products with the highest possible, optimised customer value.

It is hence required for the Scrum Team members to understand that the Complex Adaptive Problems and their corresponding solutions need to evolve Sprint by Sprint. The Scrum Team members need to perform a continuous inspection of their Sprint Backlog through their every product increment. It needs to lead them to a continuous adaptation of their Product Backlog, which effectively needs to obtain the scope of any complex problem in their hands.

> *"Efforts and courage are not enough without purpose and direction."*
>
> *- John F. Kennedy*

By following the process of Empiricism, the Scrum Teams need to start with their incremental and iterative software product development. They need to frequently check on if they are progressing ahead in the right direction, as per their agreed vision, purpose, goals, and objectives or not. If there are any deviations causing any delays, they need to make sure that they are resolving such deviations in a much better, simpler, safer, and faster way.

They need to remember that the Scrum Framework will not solve such deviations and issues. Rather it will help them to make them visible and transparent through their continuous inspections. Instead of resolving those issues directly, the Scrum Framework always acts as a mirror and asks the Scrum Teams to investigate the real reasons behind such issues. This helps the Scrum Teams to reflect on their current positioning and on where exactly they would like to see themselves thereafter, by exploring and applying various possible alternatives through the concept of Empiricism.

Points to remember

- A Scrum Framework-based agile way of working agreement needs to emphasize on the evident customer/end-user requirements. It needs to be there even if such requirements are ever-changing throughout the process and progress of software product development and delivery to be done by the Scrum Teams.

- The key decision-makers of agile organizations always need to understand that the overall formulation and structuring of their self-managing, self-organizing, and cross-functional Scrum Teams needs to be done by embracing the agile mindset of Scrum Team members.

- By recognizing the shared goals and objectives, the Developers need to enact on their activities, where they are supposed to invest their current time.

- The Developers also need to enact on all the activities and on the required things to be investigated by them at a later point of time.

- To encourage a true agile mindset with an enhanced self-management and self-organization, the Scrum Team members need to determine their own way of working by themselves. They need to understand the significance of all the components of Scrum Framework to be utilized under their agile way of working.

- It is important for the Scrum Master and the Product Owner to be energetic, sociable, and empathetic; however, they also need to be firm and proactive. They need to involve all the Stakeholders and the other required and intended parties to ensure that there is always a right consensus, while making their important decisions.

- The Scrum Team members need to map their individual as well as collective skill sets and capabilities under the skills tracking quadrant/matrix. They need to reflect on their individual self-rated proficiency level (such as novice, advanced beginner, competent, proficient, expert, and so on) against their own skill sets and capabilities.

- By always experimenting and applying some of the suitable microstructures belonging to the concept of Liberating Structures, the Scrum Master and the Product Owner always need to ensure that there is a complete involvement of all the Scrum Team members during their every interaction.

- The Scrum Teams need to search, evaluate, apply, and assess various techniques to improve their own agile way of working. By determining which techniques work best for them, they need to drive a transitional effort by moving away from the plan-based advancements and by encouraging the process of Empiricism.

- The Scrum Master always needs to be more proactive, courageous, mindful, and resourceful while removing any of the genuine impediments. To encourage the Scrum Team members to become more self-managing, the Scrum Master always needs to ask them some open-ended powerful questions without giving them any direct inputs to resolve their impediments.

- It is important for the Stakeholders and the key decision-makers from the top-level management of organizations to help and support the Scrum Masters to drive the overall process of change management, so that they can give their best to form the high-performing Scrum Teams, who can collaboratively deliver the customer value optimized outcomes. The Scrum Masters always need to focus and enact on the resolution and removal of the real blockers and impediments which could not be done by the Developers.

- The Scrum Teams, especially the Developers always need to have their focus on the achievement of an agreed Sprint Goal by maintaining a consistent pace and a stable velocity. They need to have a proper agenda and strategy to align themselves on various considerations of their Scrum-based agile way of working.

- The Scrum Teams always need to reflect on their work activities such as build, release, and documentation, and so on, to be performed by them once the working software product increment is marked as Done.

- It is vital for the Scrum Teams to simplify their roles, responsibilities, objectives, alignments, expectations, understanding, and associated processes under their agile way of working. They need to confirm on their decision-making process. It needs to optimize their understanding and associations, so that they can define their concerns and problems more accurately and discuss to have some appropriate solutions in place.

- It is required for the Scrum Team members and their Stakeholders to consider each other as Partners. Developers need to realize the distinctive viewpoints getting shared through the valuable feedbacks given by the Stakeholders. At the same time, the Stakeholders also need to have a suitable consideration along with a strong admiration for the Developers.

- It is not required for the Scrum Master to solve every problem of the Developers. Rather the Scrum Master always need to build and nurture their true potential and capability, so that they can work on their own problems and try to resolve them on their own.

- Even if there are failed Sprints and there is a limited development and delivery of anticipated customer value-based outcomes through such Sprints, the Scrum Teams should not look at them as failures. The Scrum Master needs to help the Scrum Team members to inspect and adapt, so that their critical thinking can help them to acknowledge such Sprints that fall short of anticipations with their truthful efforts than failures.

- If the Scrum Team experiences mistakes during their Sprints, they need to understand the impact and consequences, so that they can learn from those mistakes. By reflecting on the patterns, they have observed and the real cause behind such patterns, they need to learn through such mistakes, so that they can make certain to avoid the occurrence of similar mistakes thereafter.

- Instead of blindly following a standardized, bookish knowledge of Agile Mindset and Scrum Framework, the Scrum Teams need to explore their own agile way of working by themselves. They need to understand that being agile is more important than doing agile.

- There always needs to be a proper trust established within the Scrum Team members. It needs to act as a foundation for all the Scrum Values, using which they can build their rapport and healthy, sustainable relationships. They always need to explore and try out various activities such as effective team building techniques/exercises. The gamification-based teamwork activities/exercises through some icebreaker games and some strategic team-building activities always need to act as energizers for them.

- The Developers of a Scrum Team always need to deliver the fully functional and completely done working software product increments by the end of the Sprints. Any partially done work needs to be avoided, as it causes confusion for the Product Owner to identify the current positioning of deliverables.

- There should not be a command and control driven micro-management within the Scrum Teams, as it reduces the overall trust along with the important aspects of self-management and self-organization within the Scrum Teams. The Scrum Master and the Product Owner should always make use of a leading with influence-based strategic, decisive, and tactical leadership style, while collaborating with the Developers to make the best use of all their strengths.

- The globally distributed Scrum Teams might have some cultural differences. Such teams not communicating through the required face-to-face conversations might get into confusions, misinterpretations, and chaos. It is hence always required for them to make use of suitable online tools to encourage themselves to have face-to-face conversations.

- The Scrum Framework always expects the Scrum Teams to work on a proper resolution of the Complex Adaptive Problems belonging to the Complex Adaptive Systems under a Complex Environment. These problems are the ones that might change their direction and distinction, while the Scrum Team members are working on them and before they solve such problems by implementing the anticipated solutions. It is hence required for the Scrum Teams to understand and accept the fact that the Complex Adaptive Problems and their corresponding solutions need to evolve Sprint by Sprint.

- By following the process of Empiricism, the Scrum Teams need to start with their incremental and iterative software product development. They need to frequently check on if they are progressing ahead in the right direction, as per their agreed vision, purpose, goals, and objectives or not. They need to remember that the Scrum Framework will not solve such deviations and issues. Rather it will help them to make them visible and transparent through their continuous inspections.

In the next chapter, readers will get a quick reflection of the latest updated version of Scrum Guide, that is, Scrum Guide 2020. They will get to know about the changes got introduced in it along with how the Scrum Teams can have a right leverage out of it.

CHAPTER 15

A Quick Reflection on Scrum Guide 2020

Introduction

In this chapter, readers will get a quick reflection of the latest updated version of Scrum Guide, that is, Scrum Guide 2020. They will get to know about the changes got introduced in it. They will also get to know about, how they can take the right leverage out of this latest updated version, so that they can correlate those changes with the exploration of some more additional advanced Scrum add-ons/techniques to get their eventual benefits.

Objective

After studying this chapter, you should be able to:

- Understand the important considerations of the Scrum Framework for the changes done in the latest updated version of Scrum Guide, that is, Scrum Guide 2020.

- Understand the actual changes done in the Scrum Guide 2020.

- Understand what has not changed in the Scrum Guide 2020.

Many Agile and Scrum Practitioners were waiting for the release of the latest updated version of the Scrum Guide, that is, Scrum Guide 2020. It was recently released by Jeff Sutherland and Ken Schwaber (the co-creators of Scrum) in November 2020 as a much leaner version of Scrum Guide. The first version of the Scrum Guide was released in 2010, where the primary rationale behind its creation was to make people aware about the Scrum Framework. There were continuous updates in it, which kept it continuously evolving over the period. There are small and useful changes got introduced in its structure and contents so far. Few contents were removed, which were not required in terms of their value/usage point of view, whereas some were substituted by some better approaches to be followed by the Scrum Teams to establish and enhance their Scrum-based agile way of working. All these changes were done based on the following important considerations of the Scrum Framework.

- The Product Owner always needs to understand, convey, and elaborate the customer value proposition through the product vision, roadmap, and strategy to the rest of the Scrum Team members. While being a Value Optimizer, this always needs to be done by him/her for the purpose of continuous incremental and iterative development and delivery of the working software product increments.

- The Scrum Master always needs to build and nurture a proper Agile mindset-based working environment and a Scrum-based agile way of working for his/her Scrum Team, while being a Servant Leader and a Change Agent.

- The Scrum Team, especially the Developers always need to convert their own selection of work items into a potentially shippable high-quality working software product increment during their every Sprint. This always needs to be done by them by thoroughly considering and properly understanding the customer value proposition. They also need to inspect their agile way of working along with the Sprint-based outcomes, so that they can fine-tune and enact on it by taking the required actionable steps and by considering any scope for the continuous improvement.

The Scrum Practitioners should understand that even if the Scrum Guide is updated and few things are also removed from it, it still acts as a bible explaining the basic structure and components of the Scrum Framework. The changes happening under the Scrum Guide are simply giving the impression that the Scrum Framework needs to be explored by the Scrum Teams, where they need to evaluate and assess on the best possible usage of such changes.

"Courage and confidence are what decision making is all about."

- Mike Krzyzewski

While establishing and enhancing the agreed Scrum-based agile way of working, there still needs to be an open and flexible way of decision-making, where the Scrum Teams can decide an ultimate utilization of the Scrum Framework. The Scrum Roles,

Events, Artifacts, and Rules always need to be rigid and unchangeable. It is possible for the Scrum Teams to establish a Scrum-based agile way of working in parts, but the outcome will not be a true Scrum.

A proper Scrum-based agile way of working can be established through a proper application of Scrum framework, only if it is present in its true form. Such a complete (and not partial) establishment and a continuous enhancement of Scrum-based agile way of working can serve well for the Scrum Teams, where they always need to apply the suitable practices, processes, methodologies, techniques, and add-ons. It can also help them to recognize their patterns and behaviors, which also has a significant impact on their culture, dynamism, and self-actualization of responsibilities and accountabilities of Roles.

"Shifting customer needs are common in today's marketplace. Businesses must be adaptive and responsive to change while delivering an exceptional customer experience to be competitive. Traditional development and delivery frameworks such as waterfall are often ineffective. In contrast, Scrum is a value-driven agile approach which incorporates adjustments based on regular and repeated customer and stakeholder feedback. And Scrum's built-in rapid response to change leads to substantial benefits such as fast time-to-market, higher satisfaction, and continuous improvement, which supports innovation and drives competitive advantage."
- Scott M. Graffius

The Scrum Teams always need to have their complete focus and commitment for the outcome-based customer value delivery of high-quality software products by following an empirical agile way of working. This always helps them to accomplish their shared goals and objectives contained by the complex environment of ever-changing market conditions and technological advancements. It is hence required for the Scrum Teams to understand the basic concepts of Scrum Framework from the Scrum Guide. Once it is done, then they can apply some suitable advanced Scrum add-ons/techniques on top of those concepts.

"Change is inevitable. Growth is optional."

- John Maxwell

The latest updated version of the Scrum Guide has few changes in it, where it deeply elaborates its purpose now. The definition of Scrum framework looks to be extended. It also has an inception of Lean Thinking along with the properly emphasized Scrum Values. As the advantages of the Scrum Framework are already known to the entire agile software product development community, they are now removed from the Scrum Guide. The Scrum Guide now says that the Scrum Teams need to be self-managing over self-organizing. There is also a naming convention change in it for the Scrum Role - Dev Team. This role is now supposed to be called as Developers. The overall ownership, accountability, and responsibility of all the three Scrum Roles is now also emphasized; however, the overall prominence of time-boxing of

Scrum Events is given a limited importance. Sprint Planning has got three aspects now. They are why, what, and how. The why aspect has been newly introduced. By permitting the Scrum Teams to improve their Sprint Backlogs for upcoming Sprints, it also anticipates from them that they have the best possible utilization of their Sprint Retrospectives now.

The three primary questions to be answered by the Developers during the Daily Scrum, as per the previous versions of Scrum Guide are now removed from the Scrum Guide. During the Daily Scrum, the Developers can follow any appropriate format they want to follow by keeping their focus toward achievement of Sprint Goal. They need to plan for required action items to complete the work in hand, which helps them to be better at self-management. Scrum Guide also recommends a more focussed commitment of the Scrum Teams now. Product Goal is an additional commitment added to the Product Backlog along with the Product Definition. The Scrum Team, especially the Developers need to confirm to the agreed Definition of Done to be associated with every potentially releasable working software product increment.

"The secret of change is to focus all of your energy,
not on fighting the old, but on building the new."
- Socrates

The latest updated version of the Scrum Guide, that is, Scrum Guide 2020 has a lesser amount of prescriptiveness. While comparing to this version of Scrum Guide, the earlier versions of Scrum Guide looked to be extra prescriptive. However, by eliminating few things and by moderating the overall prescriptiveness of language getting used under the latest updated version, the Scrum Guide now focuses on getting the Scrum Framework back to the normal. It also signifies the Scrum Framework as an agile framework to be nominally and sufficiently understood by the Scrum Teams.

As compared to the previous versions, the Scrum Guide 2020 looks to have reduced sections, especially when it comes to the Scrum Team's overall agreement regarding Sprint termination. It has now eliminated the need and mention of the three primary questions to be answered by the Developers during the Daily Scrum. It also helps the Scrum Team members to ease out on the elaboration of the important characteristics of their PBIs/User Stories and around the Sprint Retrospective expectations from the Sprint Backlog's point of view.

"If two or three agree on a common purpose, nothing is impossible."
- Jim Rohn

The Scrum Guide 2020 has an expectation from the Scrum Team to be and to act as a one team, who always needs to be focused on the delivery of their own high-quality working software product increments. As per the previous versions of Scrum Guide, there were three Scrum Roles-the Product Owner, the Scrum Master, and the Development Team. With the presence of these three roles under the Scrum-based agile way of working of Scrum Teams, there used to be a notion of having a separate team within the Scrum Team. It might have led to a conflicting and adversely impacting behavior in between the Product Owner and the Developers. The Scrum Guide 2020 asks them to address such behavior and expects that they need to be and to act as a one team to concentrate and to work upon a common purpose. This needs to be true even if there are different levels of responsibility, accountability, and ownership for the Product Owner, the Scrum Master, and the Developers.

The Scrum Guide 2020 has got an inception of a Product Goal. It needs to act as an additional commitment to be added by the Scrum Teams to their Product Backlog. The Scrum Teams need to have a proper commitment, focus, and transparency to achieve the customer value-based outcomes to be developed and delivered at the end of every Sprint. It can help their working software product to come nearer to its overall Product Goal. The earlier versions of Scrum Guide introduced the concepts such as Sprint Goal and Definition of Done just for the sake of defining them. There was no formal distinctiveness for them and hence they were supposed to be tied up with the Scrum Artifacts such as Sprint Backlog and Product Increment, respectively.

The Product Goal needs to define and elaborate the context of the Product Backlog. It needs to have a reflection of the future state of working software product as an anticipated aim for the Scrum Teams. It also needs to be measurable. The Scrum Teams need to strive for it and accomplish the same by taking the small steps. As the Product Goal is a constituent of the Product Backlog and it needs to illustrate the customer value of the work to be performed by the Scrum Teams, its value optimization and accountability always need to stay with the Product Owner only. It needs to advance with the contents of the Product Backlog, as per the customer value proposition.

The Product Goal always needs to be kept simple, brief, and transparent to go hand in hand with the Product Backlog, while leading its advancement. The Scrum Teams can correlate the concept of Product Goal (specific to the Product Backlog) to the concept of Sprint Goal (specific to the Sprint Backlog). During the Sprint Review, they need to make use of the Sprint Goal as well as the Product Goal to review their working software product increments. This helps them to not only to reflect on their overall progress toward the Product Goal, but also to incorporate things to be improved upon along with an effective decision-making for the Sprint Planning of next Sprint.

Along with the concept of Product Goal, the Scrum Guide 2020 also asks the Scrum Teams to have the three Scrum Artifacts to be associated with formal commitments. The Scrum Team needs to follow these commitments. The Product Goal needs to be a formal commitment for the Product Backlog. The Sprint Goal needs to be a formal commitment for the Sprint Backlog. The Definition of Done needs to be formal commitment for the Product Increment. These three commitments always need to help the Scrum Teams to have more transparency to support the measurement of overall positioning of all three Scrum Artifacts.

By signifying a proper fundamental description of the primary expectations and features of every Scrum Artifact, the commitments always need to boost up the ultimate power of Empiricism and all the core Scrum Values under the agile way of working of a Scrum Team. The commitments always need to be followed by all the Scrum Team members, as they are mandatory. However, their overall emphasis and visibility can diverge based upon the Product placement and the overall structure of a Scrum Team. If a Scrum Team tries to bypass the mandatory commitments, they might end up with a Scrum Malfunctioning.

The commitments need to be the constituents of Scrum Artifacts. There needs to be a suitable correlation between the Scrum Artifacts and their associated Commitments. Like the Product Owner has an accountability for the Product Goal, the Scrum Team also needs to have an accountability for the Sprint Goal and Definition of Done. Along with what and how aspects, the Scrum Guide 2020 introduces the why aspect for the Sprint Planning Event. The why aspect also needs to be correlated with the Sprint Goal.

As the Scrum Guide 2020 asks the Scrum Teams to become more self-managing instead of just being self-organizing, they should have a right sense of collective ownership. While being a self-managing team, they should give more importance to who needs to do the work, what work needs to be done, and how it needs to be done. The Scrum Guide 2020 expects that the Scrum Team is not having any separate team of Developers (which was used to be called as a Development Team as per the earlier versions of Scrum Guide) within its structure. Rather they should promote one Product and one Scrum Team analogy, to be fully focused on one common, shared Purpose and Goal.

"Accountability breeds response-ability."

- Stephen Covey

To remain truthful and honest toward the same expectation, all the three Scrum Roles should always give a proper stress on their accountabilities and responsibilities, both individually and collectively. The Scrum Guide 2020 does not expect from the Scrum Teams to have their Sprint Retrospective action items-based commitments to be taken as a part of the Sprint Backlog of upcoming Sprint. However, the prioritization and addressal of those commitments always needs to be addressed by them as soon as possible.

As per the Scrum Guide 2020, it is not required for the Scrum Teams to keep their 10% capacity for the purpose of Product Backlog Refinements. Also, to achieve the basic purpose of all the Scrum Events, it is required for them to explore and apply all the best possible alternatives and techniques. The key elements of the PBIs/User

Stories in the Product Backlog such as their description, ordering, and size are not mandatory for the Scrum Teams. However, they always need to inspect and adapt by observing and measuring their progress as well as their productivity to achieve their agreed Sprint Goals and Product Goal.

"A slight shift in perspective changes everything."
- Jimmie Butler

As per the Scrum Guide 2020, it is required for the Scrum Teams to have their transitioning from being self-organizing to self-managing. Being a self-managing team, they need to decide among themselves on who does what, when, and how. Scrum Teams always need to make their own choices when it comes to anything specific to their work and way of working. This makes them more empowered to take their own consensus-based decisions and by realizing an ease of way of working. It always asks them to be more agile, so that they can solve the complex problems in complex environment and can deliver customer value-based outcomes.

Within a well-established Scrum-based agile way of working of a Scrum Team, the Product Owner always needs to be a value optimizer to optimize the customer/ end-user value aspect. The Scrum Master always needs to be a coach to increase the overall efficiency and effectiveness of the Scrum Team's agile way of working and its associated processes. The Developers always need to develop and deliver high-quality working software product increments. These three Scrum Roles need to perform all the software product development and delivery-specific activities together. This needs to be done by them by performing and managing all the required work during the Sprints. In this case, it is required for them to be self-governing, where they need to keep a hold on their own governance.

"Agility is the ability to adapt and respond to change.
Agile organizations view change as an opportunity, not a threat."
- Jim Highsmith

As per Ken Schwaber (one of the co-creators of Scrum Framework), the significance of allowing the Scrum Teams to have their formation, structuring, and alignment to be done by themselves can make them more self-empowered. By applying the various practices from Management 3.0 collection of practices, such self-empowered Scrum Teams can self-manage their agile way of working. Using such practices, they can become high performing as well as hyper-productive through a proper support and delegation to be provided by the agile leadership of agile organizations. Even though the Scrum Guide 2020 expects that the Scrum Teams need to be self-managing over self-organizing, it still supports the concept of self-organization. Also, the Lean Thinking add-on in Scrum Guide 2020 expects that the Scrum Teams need to act, drive, organize, and smooth out their activities, so that they can produce more customer value-based outcomes by eliminating any waste.

By simply comparing the Scrum Guide 2020 with its earlier versions, the Scrum Teams need to understand the impact of changes got introduced in it to their existing Scrum-based agile way of working. Even though the latest updated version of Scrum Guide has got only few changes introduced in it, there are contents from the earlier versions, which are kept as it is. No major changes have been applied to the core components and values of Scrum Framework.

"If you want to be successful, be consistent."

- Don Draper

It is hence required for the Scrum Teams to understand that they are not supposed to change the core structure of their already established Scrum-based agile way of working. They should not skip and ignore the core components and rules of Scrum Framework. Rather, they should take the changes to explore their way of working and its associated processes, so that they can apply the benefits through the required changes. The Scrum Framework still anticipates an early, often, iterative, and incremental software development and delivery-based way of working. It still asks the Scrum Teams to follow the concept of Empiricism through a proper, continuous inspection, adaptation, and transparency.

Even though the Scrum Guide is updated, the Scrum Team members still need to truly live and rigorously follow all the five core values of the Scrum Framework, namely, Commitment, Focus, Openness, Respect, and Courage. They still need to accept and follow all the rules of Scrum Framework. The Definition of Done and the Acceptance Criteria still needs to be used by them to confirm the complete transparency and the genuine fulfilment of their working software product increments at the end of every Sprint.

"On one side of accountability is courage, on the other is freedom."

- Jean Hamilton-Fford

The accountabilities of all three Scrum Roles are still intact. The Product Owner still needs to have an accountability when it comes to the aspect of customer value optimization through the software product being developed and delivered by the Scrum Team. The Scrum Master still needs to have an accountability to guarantee that the Scrum Team has a proper and a thorough establishment and continuous enhancement of Scrum-based agile way of working. The Developers still need to be self-organizing and cross-functional to develop and to deliver the customer value optimized high-quality working software product increments.

The Scrum Artifacts are still intact. There still needs to be a single Product Backlog for a single Product. The Product Backlog still needs to be a single reference of the customer value optimized work items to be worked upon by the Scrum Team. It still needs to be well-ordered, well-prioritized, and continuously evolving, so that the working software product gets improved over time. The Sprint Backlog still needs to be associated with an agreed Sprint Goal. It still needs to be a collection of work items such as the PBIs/User Stories to be selected at the time of Sprint Planning and to be worked upon by the Developers during their next Sprint. With more and more exploration and learning to be performed by the Developers, it needs to evolve during the ongoing Sprint to which it belongs to. The Product Increment still needs to be an anticipated customer value-based outcome of every Sprint. It still needs to be developed and delivered by the Scrum Teams at the end of every Sprint.

The Scrum Events are still intact. They still need to be utilized by the Scrum Teams to get the real benefits of Empiricism. The Sprint still needs to be at the crux of Scrum-based agile way of working of the Scrum Teams, where the Product Owner still has a right to terminate it. The Sprint Planning still needs to be an Event for the whole Scrum Team, where the Scrum Team still needs to collaborate and formulate an agreed Sprint Goal. By deriving the prioritized work items from the Product Backlog, the Developers still need to select them under the Sprint Backlog. They also need to have a plan to develop and deliver them. The Daily Scrum still needs to be an Event, where the Scrum Teams need to inspect their progress toward agreed Sprint Goal and adapt the Sprint Backlog. The Sprint Review still needs to be an Event, where the Scrum Team needs to collaborate with Stakeholders, so that they can inspect achievements of the latest Sprint and decide on what needs to be done in the upcoming Sprints. The Sprint Retrospective still needs to be an Event, where the Scrum Team needs to inspect things that happened during the latest Sprint considering various aspects of their agile way of working.

> *"It was the Scrum Master's job to guide the team toward continuous improvement-*
> *to ask with regularity, "How can we do what we do better?" Ideally, at the end of each*
> *iteration, each Sprint, the team would look closely at itself-at its interactions, practices, and*
> *processes-and ask two questions: "What can we change about how we work?"*
> *and "What is our biggest sticking point?" If those questions are answered forthrightly,*
> *a team can go faster than anyone ever imagined."*
> *- Jeff Sutherland*

Even though there are changes done by Jeff Sutherland and Ken Schwaber (the co-creators of Scrum) in the Scrum Guide 2020, the Scrum Framework is still intact. They have applied these changes based upon the experiences and feedbacks they have received from the global community of Scrum Practitioners. As the Scrum framework is still intact, the Scrum Teams and their anticipated Scrum-based agile way of working along with the properly anticipated and associated continuous improvements in it also remains intact.

A collective, collaborative, and convincing Scrum-based agile way of working still needs to be established by the Scrum Teams. They still need to build, apply, and nurture their collective effort and wisdom with a right sense of collective ownership and intelligence to continuously enhance their already established Scrum-based agile way of working. Scrum still looks like an incomplete framework, where the agile organizations and their Scrum Teams still need to explore and employ various advanced Scrum add-ons, techniques, practices, processes, procedures, alternatives, learnings, and options based upon their own contexts, needs, and suitability. During such exploration, they always need to follow all the values and principles of Agile Manifesto and all the core values and rules of the Scrum Framework along with the concept of Empiricism, both constantly and rigorously. The Scrum Guide 2020 hence needs to be properly studied, understood, applied, and utilized by the Scrum Teams to have the Scrum Framework to be used as a nominally sufficient framework. At the same time, they need to remember that they always need to be fully committed to deliver an optimized customer value and to learn and to apply the better options for it. This mindset helps them to be more agile.

> *"Scrum is a general-purpose framework applicable in complex situations,*
> *where more is unknown about the parameters than is known.*
> *The rules of empiricism and self-organizing make it work within short iterations that*
> *control the risk and increase chances of finding answers and creating value.*
> *The few roles, artifacts and events are fixed, so the Scrum team can focus on unravelling*
> *complexity. REMEMBER: Scrum is simple. Stop worrying about polishing it up,*
> *so it is perfect because it never will be. Anyway, there are far too many complex,*
> *chaotic situations in our world that you are skilled to help others address.*
> *We do not need to waste our time staring at our belly-buttons.*
> *Scrum On!"*
> *- Ken Schwaber*

Points to remember

- Many Agile and Scrum Practitioners were waiting for the release of the latest updated version of Scrum Guide, that is, Scrum Guide 2020. It was recently released by Jeff Sutherland and Ken Schwaber (the co-creators of Scrum) in November 2020 as a much leaner version of Scrum Guide. It is essential for the Scrum Practitioners to understand that even if the Scrum Guide is updated and few things are also removed from it, it still acts as a bible explaining the basic structure and components of the Scrum Framework.

- The latest updated version of Scrum Guide has few changes in it, where it deeply elaborates its purpose now. The definition of Scrum framework looks to be extended. The latest updated version of Scrum Guide, that is, Scrum Guide 2020 has a lesser amount of prescriptiveness. The Scrum Guide 2020 has an expectation from a Scrum Team to be and to act as a one team, who always needs to be focused on the delivery of their high-quality working software product.

- The Scrum Guide 2020 has got an inception of Product Goal. It needs to act as an additional commitment to be added by the Scrum Teams to their Product Backlog. The Scrum Guide 2020 asks the Scrum Teams to have the three

Scrum Artifacts to be associated with formal commitments.

- As the Scrum Guide 2020 asks the Scrum Teams to become more self-managing instead of just being self-organizing, they should have a right sense of collective ownership. As per the Scrum Guide 2020, it is also required for the Scrum Teams to have their transitioning from being self-organizing to self-managing.

- Within a well-established Scrum-based agile way of working of a Scrum Team, the Product Owner always needs to be a value optimizer. The Scrum Master always needs to be a coach to increase the overall efficiency and effectiveness of the Scrum Team's agile way of working and its associated processes. The Developers always need to develop and deliver the high-quality working software product increments.

- By comparing the Scrum Guide 2020 with its earlier versions, the Scrum Teams need to understand the impact of changes got introduced in the Scrum Guide 2020 to their existing Scrum-based agile way of working. It is required for the Scrum Teams to understand that they are not supposed to change the core structure of their already established Scrum-based agile way of working. They should not skip and ignore the core components and rules of Scrum Framework. Rather, they should take the changes to explore their way of working and its associated processes, so that they can apply the benefits through the required changes.

- Even though there are changes done by Jeff Sutherland and Ken Schwaber (the co-creators of Scrum) in the Scrum Guide 2020, the Scrum Framework is still intact. The Scrum Guide 2020 needs to be properly studied, understood, applied, and utilized by the Scrum Teams to have the Scrum Framework to be used as a nominally sufficient framework.

References

Books

Stages of group development - Bruce Tuckman, Mary Ann Jensen

A theory of constraints approach incorporating a Kanban pull system on a project in Microsoft's IT department - David J. Anderson

Kanban: Successful Evolutionary Change for Your Technology Business - David J. Anderson

The Principles of Product Development Flow - Donald Reinertsen

Scrumban - Essays on Kanban Systems for Lean Software Development - Corey Ladas

Extreme Programming Explained - Kent Beck

DSDM: Dynamic Systems Development Method: The Method in Practice - Jennifer Stapleton

The Story Behind Feature-Driven Development - Jeff De Luca, Kevin Aguanno

Crystal Clear: A Human-Powered Methodology for Small Teams: A Human-Powered Methodology for Small Teams - Alistair Cockburn

Lean-Agile Software Development: Achieving Enterprise Agility: Achieving Enterprise Agility - Alan Shalloway, Guy Beaver, James R. Trott

Scrum Insights for Practitioners: The Scrum Guide Companion - Hiren Doshi

Scrum Mastery: From Good to Great Servant Leadership - Geoff Watts

Scrum: A Pocket Guide - Gunther Verheyen

Agile Product Management with Scrum - Roman Pichler

The Great ScrumMaster - Sochova Zuzana

Scaling Lean & Agile Development Thinking and Organizational Tools for Large-Scale Scrum - Craig Larman, Bas Vodde

Practices for Scaling Lean & Agile Development: Large, Multisite, and Offshore Product Development with Large-Scale Scrum - Craig Larman, Bas Vodde

Peopleware: Productive Projects and Teams - Tom DeMarco, Timothy Lister

Scrum: The Art of Doing Twice the Work in Half the Time - Jeff Sutherland

FIRO; a Three-dimensional Theory of Interpersonal Behaviour - Will Schutz

Effective Public Relations - Scott Cutlip, Allen Center

Servant Leadership - Robert K. Greenleaf

Mastering Professional Scrum: A Practitioners Guide to Overcoming Challenges and Maximizing the Benefits of Agility - Stephanie Ockerman, Simon Reindl

Zombie Scrum Survival Guide - Christiaan Verwijs, Johannes Schartau, Barry Overeem

The Surprising Power of Liberating Structures: Simple Rules to Unleash A Culture of Innovation - Keith McCandless, Henri Lipmanowicz

Agile Contracts: Creating and Managing Successful Projects with Scrum - Andreas Opelt, Boris Gloger, Wolfgang Pfarl, Ralf Mittermayr

Essential Scrum: A Practical Guide to the Most Popular Agile Process - Kenneth S. Rubin

Growing Agile: A Coach's Guide to Mastering Backlogs - Samantha Laing, Karen Greaves

Agile Estimating and Planning - Mike Cohn

Dynamics of Software Development - Jim McCarthy

The Pragmatic Programmer: From Journeyman to Master - Andrew Hunt, Dave Thomas

Clean Code - Robert Cecil Martin

Web

Manifesto for Agile Software Development - **https://agilemanifesto.org/**

14th Annual State of Agile Report - **https://stateofagile.com/**

Organizational Agility - Aaron De Smet from 'McKinsey & Company' - **https://www.mckinsey.com/business-functions/organization/our-insights/the-keys-to-organizational-agility/**

Scrum Guide - Ken Schwaber & Jeff Sutherland, the originators of Scrum - **https://www.scrumguides.org/scrum-guide.html**

https://kanbanguides.org/

http://www.extremeprogramming.org/

https://ronjeffries.com/xprog/what-is-extreme-programming/

The State of Scrum Report - **https://www.scrumalliance.org/learn-about-scrum/state-of-scrum/**

https://en.wikipedia.org/wiki/Scrum_(software_development)

https://hbr.org/1986/01/the-new-new-product-development-game/

https://www.scrumalliance.org/

https://resources.scrumalliance.org/

https://www.scruminc.com/

https://www.scruminc.com/scrum-blog/

https://www.scrum.org/

https://www.scrum.org/resources/blog/

https://www.greenleaf.org/products-page/the-servant-as-leader/

https://www.lyssaadkins.com/new-blog/2013/1/14/high-performance-tree/

https://www.romanpichler.com/blog/

https://www.mountaingoatsoftware.com/blog

https://www.scrum.org/resources/8-stances-scrum-master/

https://www.scruminc.com/swarming-instantly-boost-scrum-team-productivity/

http://www.payton-consulting.com/agile-team-working-agreements-guide/

https://www.scruminc.com/backlog-refinement-vision-value/

https://www.jpattonassociates.com/wpcontent/uploads/2015/03/story_essentials_quickref.pdf

https://www.jpattonassociates.com/wp-content/uploads/2015/03/story_mapping.pdf

https://www.jpattonassociates.com/wp-content/uploads/2015/01/how_you_slice_it.pdf

http://wiki.c2.com/?XpSimplicityRules

https://en.wikipedia.org/wiki/Reinforcement_learning

https://ammeon.com/the-8-wastes-snake/

https://agilestrides.com/blog/40-ideas-to-spice-up-your-retrospective/

https://www.scrum.org/resources/evidence-based-management-guide

http://www.theagilefactor.com/

https://martinfowler.com/articles/agileFluency.html

https://www.agilefluency.org/

https://sites.google.com/a/scrumplop.org/published-patterns/product-organization-pattern-language/scrum-of-scrums

https://www.scrum.org/resources/online-nexus-guide

https://www.scaledagileframework.com/blog/

https://less.works/blog/index.html

https://www.pmi.org/disciplined-agile/resources

https://scrumatscale.scruminc.com/scrum-at-scale-guide-online/

https://engineering.atspotify.com/tag/engineering-culture/

https://management30.com/

https://agileforgrowth.com/scrum-master-books/

https://scrumglossary.org/

Index

Printed in Great Britain
by Amazon

18696008R20221